CATARACT CANYON

CATARACT CANYON

A Human and Environmental History of the Rivers in Canyonlands

Robert H. Webb

Jayne Belnap

John S. Weisheit

The University of Utah Press

Salt Lake City

The Defiance House Man colophon is a registered trademark of
The University of Utah Press. It is based upon a four-foot-tall
Ancient Puebloan pictograph (late PIII) near Glen Canyon, Utah.

08 07 06 05 04
5 4 3 2 1

LIBRARY OF CONGRESS CATALOGING-IN-PUBLICATION DATA

Webb, Robert H.
  Cataract Canyon : a human and environmental history of the rivers in
Canyonlands / Robert H. Webb, Jayne Belnap, John S. Weisheit.
      p. cm.
Includes index.
  ISBN 0-87480-781-6 (hardcover : alk. paper)—ISBN 0-87480-782-4
(pbk. : alk. paper)
  1. Cataract Canyon Wilderness (Utah)—History. 2. Natural
history—Utah—Cataract Canyon Wilderness. 3. Cataract Canyon
Wilderness (Utah)—Environmental conditions. I. Belnap, Jayne, 1952–
II. Weisheit, John S., 1954– III. Title.
  F832.C37W43 2004
  979.2'52—dc22
                              2003023050

This book is dedicated to Retsik Belnap,
   who loved the canyon country more than would seem possible;

Susette Weisheit, Toni Yocum, and Steve Anderson
   for putting up with all of us;

and, last but not least, to the river rangers of Canyonlands National Park,
   who make work there safe and enjoyable.

CONTENTS

TABLES

ILLUSTRATIONS

PREFACE

We decided to write this book for several reasons. In the course of our careers in Canyon Country and Cataract Canyon, we heard a lot of mythology and lore about the canyon. As river runners, geologists, botanists, and historians, we found a lot of the published information on this region to be incomplete and, in some cases, confusing. Some accounts are more introspective than informative.[1] We also knew a lot of information on the human and natural history that would be of interest to those who enjoy it, and determined a way to translate and collate the information in a useful manner. We matched 329 historical photographs of the Green and Colorado rivers, and the repeat photography helped us answer some questions directly as well as raise interesting hypotheses about the nature of Cataract Canyon.

This book describes wildlands in eastern Utah that require a rugged spirit to visit and a desert soul to appreciate. Edward Abbey described the perfect attitude to visiting anywhere, but particularly the Canyonlands region, when he wrote:

> Do not jump into your automobile [or boat] next June and rush out to the Canyon country hoping to see some of that which I have attempted to evoke in these pages. In the first place, you can't see *anything* from a car [or boat]; you've got to get out of the goddamned contraption and walk, better yet crawl, on hands and knees, over the sandstone and through the thornbush and cactus. When traces of blood begin to mark your trail, you'll see something, maybe. Probably not. In the second place, most of what I write about in this book is already gone or going under fast. This is not a travel guide but an elegy. A memorial. You're holding a tombstone in your hands.[2]

We endorse Abbey's sentiments. Have fun and please consider your part in conserving this fragile environment.

Notes on Units and Nomenclature

Several notes are needed on our use of units and names. As scientists, we are accustomed to using metric units. In this book, however, we use English units and selected metric ones that are most familiar to lay readers. River miles were established by the 1921 U.S. Geological Survey expedition, a topic that will be discussed in Chapter 2. Precipitation is given in inches instead of millimeters, which may be more familiar to some readers of natural history. River discharges are given in cubic feet per second (ft^3/s); this unit is also abbreviated as *cfs* or *second-feet* in older publications.

We discuss our use of geographic names in Chapter 1, but we emphasize that other names may exist that should rightfully take priority over ours—if only we knew those names. Scientific names are somewhat more problematic. Botanical names are constantly changing; one of our favorite examples is "winterfat," a shrub species common in the region, which has a Latin name that in our experience has been changed from *Eurotia lanata* to *Ceratoides lanata* to its current incarnation of *Krascheninnikovia lanata*. We had to accept many Latin names without comment, although we attempted to use *A Utah Flora*[3] as our guide to both common and Latin names. Any deviations are silent but well intentioned.

Notes on the Illustrations

In Chapters 6, 8, and 10, we use digital orthophotographs instead of maps to depict the location of places of interest in Cataract Canyon. These orthophotographs were created from aerial photography that was produced in the early 1990s and have been rectified to eliminate distortion. As the scale on these orthophotographs indicates, they are equivalent to maps, only they use images instead of contours. In Chapter 11, we use a digital hillshade model developed from a 30-meter, digital elevation model. The original data for this model was developed from the 1:24,000 scale topographic maps produced by the U.S. Geological Survey. Finally, the longitudinal profile data given in Figures 3-4 and 12-1 come from handwritten notes from the Eugene C. LaRue collection at the Huntington Library, San Marino, California. The published profile only has drops in five-foot increments, while the original data was collected at 0.1-foot accuracy.

Notes on the Photographs

For historical data on the photographs, we thank the following institutions: U.S. Geological Survey Photographic Library at Denver, the Dan O'Laurie Canyon Country Museum at Moab, the Cline Library at Northern Arizona University, the Marriott Library at the University of Utah, the Marston and the E.C. LaRue collections at the Huntington Library, the Utah State Historical Society, the National Archives, and the New York Public Library. Any photographs not credited to these sources are part of the Desert Laboratory Photographic Collection at the U.S. Geological Survey in Tucson, Arizona. Gary Bolton, Steve Tharnstrom, Dominic Oldershaw, Ted Melis, Steve Young, and Robert Webb matched most of the photographs shown in this book. These photographs, as well as others analyzed as part of this study, are stored in the Desert Laboratory Photograph Collection. Each photograph has an accompanying "stake number," which provides the reference information to this collection.

Acknowledgments

The authors are extremely grateful to Canyonlands National Park and its marvelous staff for allowing us to work effectively in the park. We particularly thank Jim Braggs, Steve Swanke, and Charlie Schelz for providing us with permits and access to the river corridor. At various times, we have had the good fortune to travel with river rangers Dave Walton, Steve Swanke, Mark Yeston, Jim Braggs, and Steve Young.

Young, in particular, contributed heavily to the ideas and content of this book.

Numerous people have helped us during our research trips in Cataract Canyon. These include Steve Anderson, Jim Bennett, Gary Bolton, Diane Boyer, Cassie Fenton, Peter Griffiths, Mia Hansen, Tillie Klearman, Connie Mc-Cabe, Alex McCord, Ted Melis, Dominic Oldershaw, Sue Phillips, Dave Pratt, Matt Salzer, Charlie Schelz, Jack Schmidt, Steve Tharnstrom, Rich Valdez, Sam Walton, Susette Weisheit, Tom Wise, Toni Yocum, and Steve Young. Conversations with Jack Schmidt, in particular, greatly influenced this work. Michael Collier relayed his amazing story of winter boating in Cataract Canyon. Peter Griffiths aided in digitizing longitudinal profiles and drainage-basin perimeters, as well as helping analyze stratigraphy and debris-flow deposits. Charlie Schelz and Sonya Daw provided the species checklists for Canyonlands National Park that are the basis for two of the appendices. Bego Gerhart gave generously of research books and river lore.

We also thank the following individuals for information and review of individual chapters: Brad Dimock, Al Holland, Rosalyn Jirge, Jim Knipmeyer, Jim Mead, Richard Quartaroli, George Simmons, Roy Webb, Dave Wegner, Steve Young, and the members of Clio, a river history email server. We greatly appreciate Diane Boyer's editorial comments and preparation of the photographs in this book. Tillie Klearman, Beth Coker Roy, Rachel Schmidt, and Ellen Wohl reviewed the entire manuscript. We also thank the National Park Service, Navtec, and Tag-A-Long Expeditions of Moab for logistical support.

Robert Webb
Jayne Belnap
John Weisheit

Notes

1. Craig Childs, *Stone Desert, A Naturalist's Exploration of Canyonlands National Park* (Englewood, Colorado: Westcliffe Publishers, 2001), 201 p.

2. Edward Abbey, *Desert Solitaire* (New York: Ballantine Books, 1968), vii.

3. *A Utah Flora* ed. S.L. Welsh, N.D. Atwood, S. Goodrich, L.C. Higgins (Provo, Utah: Brigham Young University, Second Edition, 1993).

1

GEOGRAPHY AND PREHISTORY

The Plethora of Names and the First Inhabitants of Canyon Country

No language is adequate to convey a just idea of the strange and impressive scenery.
– John Macomb, 1859[1]

Cataract Canyon lies within Canyonlands National Park, which is in the Canyonlands Section, one of six subdivisions of a greater physiographic province called the Colorado Plateau.[2] Informally, we refer to this region as *Canyonlands* when conveying information specific to the National Park or immediate area, or *Canyon Country*, in reference to the broader province.[3] Three large rivers dominate the landscape: the Colorado, the Green, and the San Juan. We are concerned here with the first two of these rivers, and we are interested primarily in the perspective of the country one gets from river travel.

THE CONFUSION OF NAMES

What we call places and how those names came to be can be interesting and confusing, and this is certainly true of Canyon Country. Names, and some politically driven name changes, mark the physiography of this region. The confluence of the Green and Colorado rivers is simply called *the Confluence*, although it once was named the Junction. Upstream from the Confluence, the Colorado River was originally named the Grand. During the debates over who ultimately controlled the Colorado River's water, the fine citizenry of Colorado decided they didn't like the fact that this watercourse, which drains much of its state, wasn't known as its namesake until well downstream in Utah. In 1921, they convinced Congress and the state of Utah to change the river's name.[4] This left many vestigial place names in the region, including Grand Lake, Grand Junction, Grand Mesa, Grand Valley, Grand County, Grandview Point, and Grand Bench. Being sentimentalists, we occasionally lapse

and refer to the Colorado River as the Grand, particularly with respect to the river's history before 1921.

Downstream from Green River and Moab, Utah, and extending to the Arizona–Utah border, the Colorado and Green rivers flow through a series of canyons that carve the country into places that are difficult to reach without a boat. These canyons were originally named (sometimes more than once) by John Wesley Powell, who led the first expeditions down the rivers in 1869.[5] The Green River in the Canyonlands region flows through what are called *Labyrinth* and *Stillwater* Canyons, although the section where the former ends and the latter begins once was called *Tower Park*.[6] Powell named Cataract Canyon, and he called the short, straight reach between Mille Crag Bend and the mouth of the Dirty Devil *Narrow Canyon*. The original Powell names of "Mound" and "Monument" Canyons[7] were converted to *Glen Canyon* in Powell's account of his expeditions, published in 1875. Powell's expedition didn't go down the Colorado River above the Confluence, so others named those canyons.

On the Colorado River side, our book is concerned with the reach from the mouth of the Dolores River to the Confluence. We decided to take a geographical approach to this narrative, and present the geology, history and ecology as one encounters it when traveling downstream. Our trip begins at the Dewey Bridge, which crosses the Colorado just below the Dolores where the river enters a canyon mostly confined within the bounds of Wingate Sandstone. Extending downstream to Moab, this canyon is called *Professor Valley*, although others have separate names for the diverse short reaches in this section. Moabites refer to

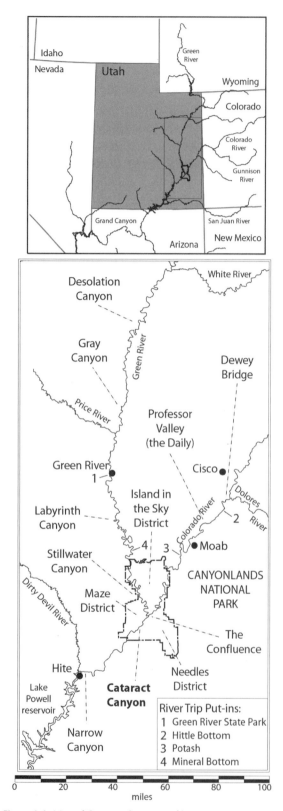

Figure 1-1. Map of Cataract Canyon and its access canyons

this stretch of river as *the Daily* because many run it privately or commercially day after day after day.

The town of Moab lies in the Spanish Valley, which was named for its trade route connection to Santa Fe. The river flows in the open here for a short distance, only to enter another canyon in a dramatic fashion at a place locals call *the Portal*. Historically, the canyon from the Portal to the Confluence had no name. To fill that void, geologist Don Baars informally called the reach between Moab and the Confluence *Meander Canyon*.[8] We use Baars's name, hoping to cast it in stone. Sixty miles downstream from the Portal, the Colorado meets the Green at the Confluence and then enters the towering yet crumbling walls of Cataract Canyon. We end our trip at Lake Powell, where the waters behind Glen Canyon Dam have silenced the voices of the free-flowing river. Even this name is confusing, since by definition a lake is a naturally formed body of water and a reservoir is impounded by a human-created dam. Because of this, we frequently refer to Lake Powell as *the reservoir* despite the fact that some might find this offensive.

The Canyonlands region has innumerable other names attached to its landscape features, as humankind has the propensity for naming everything from little hills to major rivers. Few people completely agree on all of these names. In this book, we will use the names found on topographic maps, which usually are affirmed by the Board of Geographic Names. One notable exception is Lee's Ferry, which was named for John D. Lee and deserves the possessive apostrophe. Other names we have learned from our long presence in the Canyonlands region or from association with others who have been in the region longer than we have. Still other names we just made up because of that human propensity mentioned earlier.

Measuring the distances of the rivers in this book presents a similar issue. We use river miles as assigned by the U.S. Geological Survey in 1921 and repeated in popular river guides.[9] The Colorado River Compact of 1922 divided the Colorado River basin at Lee's Ferry, Arizona, into the upper and lower basins. River miles are assigned accordingly in an upstream and downstream direction, which explains how the mileage at the Confluence of the Green and Colorado rivers is mile 216.6. However, because of the significance of the Confluence, river miles were again reset, which means that the distances upstream on the Colorado River change from mile 216.6 to mile 0.0 when one passes the mouth of the Green. Locations are given in this book as river mile-side, and by convention the side (*e.g.*, river left) is determined by looking downstream.

The rivers divide Canyonlands National Park into three areas. The Maze District, which includes the phenomenal rock art of Horseshoe (Barrier) Canyon, lies to the west of the Green River and to the north and west of the Confluence. The Needles District lies southeast of the Colorado River. The Island-in-the-Sky District is in the V-shaped section of land between the Green and Colorado rivers upstream from the Confluence. In this book, we will take short excursions into these three units, as well as into other lands adjacent to the rivers.

At one time, Cataract Canyon had between forty-seven and fifty-two rapids, depending on whom you want to believe.[10] The original names for these rapids were numbers, although some were renamed later for a variety of reasons as discussed in this book. Construction of Glen Canyon Dam (completed in 1963) inundated about half of them beneath its reservoir. Lake Powell, once euphemistically called "the Jewel of the Colorado,"[11] is both beloved and hated for reasons discussed in Chapter 9. Most of this book is concerned with the remaining seventeen free-flowing river miles in Cataract Canyon, but we also discuss Professor Valley and Meander, Stillwater, and Labyrinth canyons. All told, this represents 120 miles of the Green River, 112 miles of free-flowing Colorado River, and about thirty-two miles of the reservoir.[12]

LAND OWNERSHIP AND MANAGEMENT

Government Land Management

Most of the Colorado Plateau is part of the public domain administered by various federal agencies for the general welfare of the American people. Some agencies have regulatory authority over things that live in these landscapes, including the Bureau of Reclamation (dams and water) and the U.S. Fish and Wildlife Service (wildlife and endangered species). Others have regulatory authority over the land base, including the National Park Service, the Bureau of Land Management, and the USDA Forest Service.

The National Park Service has a major presence in the Canyonlands region. This region contains three national parks (Canyonlands, Arches, and Capitol Reef), four national monuments (Colorado, Rainbow Bridge, Natural Bridges, and Hovenweep), and one national recreation area (Glen Canyon). Although the mission of the Park Service is to preserve and protect their lands, they are also mandated to provide recreational access, which often is in conflict with preservation and protection.

The Bureau of Land Management (BLM) manages millions of acres of the Canyonlands region, and their lands typically surround the national park units. Traditionally, their emphasis has been on consumptive uses such as mining, grazing, and development. Particularly in recent decades, recreation has become a dominant use of BLM lands. The BLM-managed Grand Staircase—Escalante National Monument—was established in 1996, giving BLM a different land-use agenda of protecting the resources for at least part of the Canyon Country. The only other federal agency that manages land in the region is the Forest Service. The five national forests of the Canyonlands—Uncompaghre, San Juan, Manti-La Sal, Fishlake, and Dixie—are managed mostly for consumptive uses and outdoor recreation.

These agencies are often at odds with each other, as well as with the wishes of disparate segments of the American public. At the same time, the American people put conflicting and unrealistic demands upon these management agencies, forcing them to take contradictory management actions. Irrespective of what departments of the federal government to which they are assigned to, all these agencies have the mandate to manage their lands in a sustainable fashion to maintain the land's potential for future generations. However, given our conflicting goals as a society for this region, how could these agencies fully succeed? The actions of these agencies affect Cataract Canyon profoundly. Therein lies one of the major quandaries in writing a book about the natural history of a place: decades from now, the physical features we describe in Cataract Canyon may no longer be as we say, and certain species may no longer be present.

There are many sovereign Indian Nations on the Colorado Plateau that are governed by tribal councils with federal assistance provided by the Bureau of Indian Affairs. The tribes managing lands wholly or partially on the Colorado Plateau include the Ute, Paiute, Navajo, Apache, Hopi, and Zuni tribes. The latter two tribes consider themselves as descendants of peoples who once built large cities on the Colorado Plateau. These people were collectively referred to in older literature as the *Anasazi*, which originally meant "Ancient Ones" but came to be known as "Ancient Enemy." This nomenclature became offensive to the Hopi, who now call them the *Hisatsinom*,[13] and the archaeological literature now refers to them as the *Ancestral Puebloans*. Although modern tribes do not have lands close to the specific region discussed in this book, many of these tribal groups used the Canyonlands region historically and want to have a voice in its management. They seldom get it.

Lands administered by the State of Utah are also spread in a checkerboard across the region. At the time of statehood, two out of every thirty-six square miles were given to Utah to provide economic assistance to the state and its school systems. Through the years since statehood, land purchases and exchanges have changed the checkerboard pattern somewhat and relatively large, contiguous units of state-administered lands are present in the Canyonlands region. Some of these are state parks, including Dead Horse Point, Goblin Valley, Valley of the Gods, Newspaper Rock, and Anasazi State Parks. Scattered about are school-trust lands that are administered for maximum income, and these lands generally sustain high levels of consumptive uses such as grazing and mining. Where school-trust lands meet federal park lands, the politics of states rights versus the mandates of federal agencies can create huge friction, often to the detriment of the environment.

Finally, large tracts of lands along the Green River and Colorado River upstream from the Confluence are privately owned. "Anything goes" is the policy on most of these lands, including uses such as grazing, mining, subdivision, movie-making, recreation, and industry. Some major holdings—notably the site used by the Atlas Corporation to mill uranium ore near Moab—are potentially major threats to Cataract Canyon owing to the possibility of pollution. Some owners of private lands manage their lands in a way that does not pose such threats. A notable example is The Nature Conservancy, which owns the Matheson Wetlands at Moab sloughs and upstream property in Professor Valley.

Tourism and Development

The Colorado Plateau is replete with national parks, which serve as the magnet for tourists to the region. President Herbert Hoover established Arches National Monument in 1929 to preserve its unique namesakes. The tourism industry in Moab exploded following the monument's creation, despite the fact that visitation during its early years was hampered by the poor transportation choices to the region. The most famous park ranger from Arches National Monument was Edward Abbey, whose seminal work chronicles his experiences there.[14] Arches became a national park in 1971 and is probably the most visited tourist attraction in the vicinity of Moab.

In the last two decades of the twentieth century, developments associated with tourism sprang up along the banks of the Colorado River upstream and downstream from Moab. Several river companies provide jet-boat service to extract canoeists paddling the flatwater stretches of the Green River above the Confluence, while other river companies run daily trips down the whitewater of the Colorado River in Professor Valley. Additional developments include dude ranches and high-priced cottages catering to travelers who want to experience the scenic landscape.

Development is great for the local economy but can be at odds with an environmental ethic that many Moabites strive for in their hometown. Moab, with its full-time population of 6,000 residents, can sustain 100,000 visitors per month. Highway 191 through Moab is now lined with hotels and fast-food establishments, catering to the mountain bikers, river runners, and tourists. If the commercial excess of Moab appalled Harold Leich in 1933 (see Chapter 2), he would be apoplectic now. On the other hand, the growth in tourism has intensified the desire of long-term residents and visitors alike to preserve the natural environments of Canyon Country so that they continue to attract these tourists. It remains to be seen how Moab and environs will respond and how Cataract Canyon will be affected.

Canyonlands National Park

The term *Canyonlands* refers to the region at large, and is also now synonymous with Canyonlands National Park, established by an act of Congress in 1964.[15] The free-flowing reaches of Cataract Canyon were included within Canyonlands National Park and are protected under the National Park Service's Organic Act of 1916. At its highest water levels, Lake Powell reservoir just reaches to the base of Big Drop 3; to the delight of whitewater boaters, recent drops in the reservoir level have exposed more rapids below the Big Drops. The inundated Cataract Canyon is part of Glen Canyon National Recreation Area, which was established in 1972 and is administrated by the National Park Service. At the time of this writing, the reach from Rapid 27 to near Hite is filled with sediment. Hite Marina, the takeout point for Cataract Canyon river trips, is not expected to last beyond 2010. The differences between the water-dominated parts of both units are striking: Canyonlands is managed for whitewater recreation under relatively pristine conditions, and Lake Powell reservoir is managed primarily for high-speed motorized recreation. The two uses often collide in the inundated reach of Cataract Canyon.

The establishment of Canyonlands National Park was not the first attempt to preserve this unique landscape. In 1935, then Secretary of the Interior Harold Ickes recommended the establishment of Escalante National Monument to President Franklin D. Roosevelt.[16] They would have used the Antiquities Act to establish the park and protect the unique archaeological resources of this region, most of which are now under the surface of Lake Powell.[17] This park would have been huge—7,000 square miles—and if this park had been established you would have entered it at the Portal and left it at Lee's Ferry, if you were traveling by boat. It was not to be. As would be the case when the Grand Staircase was established in 1996, rural Utahns were opposed to Escalante National Monument. The demand for hydroelectric power, mining concerns related to the emerging nuclear industry, the activities of ranchers, and ultimately the national attention given to World War II killed Escalante National Monument.

PREHISTORIC PEOPLES

The human history on the Colorado Plateau starts with aboriginal cultures. Though Canyonlands National Park has many archaeological sites to visit and enjoy, Cataract Canyon is exceptional in that there is only sparse evidence of Pre-Ccolumbian cultures.[18] This fact should not really surprise us, for the walls of Cataract Canyon are mostly fractured rock that is rapidly falling or sliding into the Colorado River; hence, the unstable slopes and frequent debris flows have made preservation of artifacts a hit-or-miss proposition. Even if prehistoric cultures used Cataract Canyon, the probability is high that evidence of their use is buried. Moreover, the alkaline soils developed from a limestone-dominated terrain support plants that would not attract a hunter-gatherer culture, let alone an agrarian culture such as the one that thrived downstream in now-inundated Glen Canyon.[19]

What is known of aboriginal cultures mostly centers on the approaches to Cataract Canyon and the uplands that surround it. Archaeological sites are clustered in side canyons with permanent water, indicating the dependence on agriculture for most of the cultures.[20] The earliest evidence of agricultural dependence is associated with the first humans to arrive in North America. Paleoindians, exemplified by the Clovis Culture, visited Canyon Country between 12,000 and 9,500 years ago.[21] Projectile points characteristic of several Paleoindian cultures were excavated from the Squaw Butte area in the Needles District, south of Cataract Canyon. Beyond the scant artifacts, little is known of how these people lived in Canyon Country.

The Archaic Culture is poorly known but archaeologists have documented that this culture inhabited the region from about 2000 B.C. to A.D. 500.[22] These peoples were mostly hunters and gatherers who did not build permanent structures. They did, however, leave spectacular artwork on canyon walls behind them. Because of the significance of this artwork, the Horseshoe Canyon area was added to Canyonlands National Park in 1971 despite the fact that it is not connected with the remainder of the park.

The last five centuries of Archaic Culture overlap with the Ancestral Puebloans. This diverse group of peoples begins with the Basketmaker Culture, which began around A.D. 1, followed by the Pueblo peoples. In addition, the Fremont Culture, considered a separate group, inhabited the region from about A.D. 700 to 1200, which, like the Archaic Culture left behind rock art but few structures. Most of the structural remains are attributed to the Ancestral Puebloans in the three phases of Pueblo I-III cultures, which span the period of A.D. 900-1300. These peoples were mostly farmers who preferred uplands to the lowland environments adjacent to rivers.[23] They were at their northern extent in Canyonlands; most of their population centers in southeastern Utah were along the San Juan River.[24]

Both the Fremont and Ancestral Puebloan peoples abandoned Canyon Country between about A.D. 1300 and 1400. Speculation abounds as to why they left, but theories include the related concepts of extended drought, possible catastrophic disease, flood damage to irrigation systems, internal strife, and pressures from other peoples from adjacent regions.[25] We probably will never know the exact reason(s) for the exodus, but the remains of their civilization provide a rich heritage that the National Park Service and Bureau of Land Management are attempting to preserve. Canyon Country wasn't left without human occupants for long: the Utes, and later the Navajos, roamed through the region and like the others before them they did not leave significant structures.

Cultural artifacts, structures, and other evidence appear throughout the corridors of the Green and Colorado rivers. Activity was concentrated in a number of sites, particularly Jasper and Horse canyons on the Green River side (miles 9.5 and 14.5, respectively) and Salt and Indian creeks on the Colorado River side (mile 3.5 and 16.5, respectively). The most commonly visited Ancestral Puebloan structures on the Green River include the tower at Fort Bottom (mile 40), the granaries at Turk's Head (mile 21.0) and Jasper Canyon. The sites on the Colorado River, which are less impressive, are opposite Lathrop Canyon (mile 23.5), at mile 20.1, and at Indian Creek.

The presence of Native American artifacts presents a major conservation problem because people are attracted to—and pick up—whatever pieces remain. In one experiment near Moab, the "artifact theft rate" from two deliberately created piles was 0.7 artifacts per day at a heavily used site.[26] At this rate, even large lithic scatters or sherd piles would be quickly depleted. To avoid closure or more stringent management of sites with archaeological resources, river runners are reminded of half of the old cliche: take only photographs.

THE ONSET OF RECORDED HISTORY

Canyonlands may have been devoid of permanent residents when a mysterious man named Denis Julien visited the region in 1836. Although Utes were known to travel through Spanish Valley, and Navajos lived in and near Glen Canyon, the early explorers of Cataract saw no people or evidence of settlement. Traveling by boat, these explorers first inscribed their history in rock, then waxed poetic about the stark landscapes, and finally photographed the scenery to share their impressions of Cataract Canyon with the rest of civilization. We will discuss their experiences in detail in Chapter 2.

Notes

1. John Macomb and J.S. Newberry, *Report of the Exploring Expedition from Santa Fe, New Mexico, to the Junction of the Grand and Green Rivers of the Great Colorado of the West, in 1859, with Geological Report* (Washington, D.C.: Government Printing Office, 1876).

2. C.B. Hunt, *Cenozoic History of the Colorado Plateau*

THE EARLIEST AGRICULTURE IN CANYONLANDS

Eric Brunnemann

Utah's prehistoric agriculturists understood farming in a desert. The fast-moving Colorado River, confined within narrow, rocky canyons, flushes out sediments and leaves insufficient soil for agriculture in most places. To succeed as a prehistoric farmer, the recipe includes not only accessible moisture but also well-watered, arable land, preferably in an ecotone that offers as much floral, faunal, and geological diversity as possible. The Colorado River corridor in Canyon Country does not offer such resources.

Instead, the region's arid landscape lies in a rain shadow between the Rocky and Sierra Nevada mountain ranges. Only a small amount of moisture ever reaches the ground as precipitation. Thus, ephemeral canyons and benches surrounding the river have poorly developed soils, which are low in organic matter, with only *eolian* (windblown), *colluvial* (mass-wasting), and *alluvial* (river-transported) parent materials. Any attempt to utilize river water in these mostly alkaline soils would prove unproductive.

The earliest appearance of maize (corn) on the Colorado Plateau was about 200 B.C. Relying on agriculture precipitated these early farmers to shift gradually to semi-permanent residential camps located near crops. A larger portion of their diet consisted of wild plants and marginally tended plants associated with farming. With unpredictable weather and variable crop production from year to year, land strategies based upon storage, exchange, and one's use of landscapes (particularly at ecotones, such as the edge between forest and shrub lands) must have been part of the aboriginal equation of settlement. In this landscape, settlement patterns include numerous smaller logistical sites—such as field houses near crops—and limited or specialized activity sites—such as procurement of appropriate rock types for weapon production and areas where food was processed. This strategy implies the use of larger areas based upon settlement patterns that were not completely sedentary.

South of the Colorado River in the Needles District of Canyonlands National Park is the Salt Creek Archeological District. The district contains riparian threads of land within the desert landscape because of perennial drainage from the Abajo Mountains that flows gradually from an elevation of about 8,000 feet to its rendezvous with the Colorado River at 4,000 feet, across an area of about thirty miles. Winding and dissipating through canyons and pockets, these drainage areas are blanketed by alluvium as much as sixty feet deep. Such tributaries offered aboriginal farmers the correct formula for the potential for accessible, well-watered, arable lands and a complete ecosystem sufficient for farming.

The Colorado River is a powerful force with deep canyons and abundant water. It is obvious from the archeological record that prehistoric peoples knew about and visited the river; but like the surrounding desert, it is the inaccessibility of this water to arable land that precluded its use by Utah's earliest agriculturists. As John Wesley Powell said in 1869, just prior to entering the Colorado River at the Confluence:

> The landscape everywhere, away from the river, is of rock—cliffs of rock, tables of rock, plateaus of rock, terraces of rock, crags of rock—ten thousand strangely carved forms; rocks everywhere, and no vegetation, no soil, no sand. In long, gentle curves the river winds about these rocks.[27] This observation explains perhaps better than any other why Native Americans mostly avoided Cataract Canyon.

(Washington, D.C.: U.S. Geological Survey Professional Paper 279, 1956), 3.

3. C.G. Crampton, *Standing Up Country: The Canyon Lands of Utah and Arizona* (New York: Alfred Knopf, 1965), 4.

4. R.A. Firmage, *A History of Grand County* (Salt Lake City: Utah State Historical Society, 1996), 247.

5. John Wesley Powell, *The Exploration of the Colorado River and Its Tributaries* (New York: Dover Publications, 1961), 117–267.

6. Ibid., 204. We thank Brad Dimock for reminding us of this name.

7. F.S. Dellenbaugh, *A Canyon Voyage: The Narrative of the Second Powell Expedition* (New York: Putnam, 1908), 137.

8. Don Baars, *A River Runner's Guide to Cataract Canyon and Approaches* (Evergreen, Colorado: Cañon Publishers, 1987), 33.

9. U.S. Geological Survey, *Plan and Profile of Colorado River, Lees Ferry, Arizona, to the Mouth of Green River, Utah; San Juan River, Mouth to Chinle Creek, Utah; and Certain Tributaries* (Washington, D.C.: U.S. Government Printing Office, U.S. Geological Survey, 1922 [1955 printing]), 22 sheets (A–V).

An example river guide is Bill Belknap, Buzz Belknap, and L.B. Evans, Belknap's *Revised Waterproof Canyonlands River Guide* (Evergreen, Colorado: Westwater Books, 1996).

10. The various explorers of the Colorado River counted different numbers of rapids in Cataract Canyon (see Chapter

11). Presumably they were all running the same river. More realistically, the number of rapids changes with water level and recent debris-flow activity.

11. U.S. Bureau of Reclamation, *Lake Powell: Jewel of the Colorado* (Washington, D.C.: Bureau of Reclamation, Government Printing Office, 1965).

12. Belknap et al., *Belknap's Revised Waterproof Canyonlands River Guide*, 79.

13. This spelling comes from the official web site of the Hopi Nation: The term illustrates a problem with transliteration, since another spelling by a Hopi writer is Hitsotsinom; see Leigh Kuwanwisiwma, "Hopit Navotiat, Hopi Knowledge of History," in *Prehistoric Culture Change on the Colorado Plateau, Ten Thousand Years on Black Mesa,* ed. Shirley Powell and F.E. Smiley (Tucson: University of Arizona Press, 2002), 162.

14. Edward Abbey, *Desert Solitaire: A Season in the Wilderness* (New York: Ballantine Books, 1968).

15. Maxine Newell, "Modern History of Canyonlands," *Naturalist* 21 (1970): 40–47.

16. E.R. Richardson, "Federal Park Policy in Utah: The Escalante National Monument Controversy of 1935–1940," *Utah Historical Quarterly* 33 (1965): 109–133.

17. J.D. Jennings, *Glen Canyon: An Archaeological Summary* (Salt Lake City: University of Utah Press, 1998); P.R. Geib, *Glen Canyon Revisited* (Salt Lake City: University of Utah Press, Anthropological Papers Number 119, 1996).

18. Few archaeological sites are known from Cataract Canyon. Petroglyphs are preserved downstream from Lower Red Lake Canyon, and a lithic scatter is known from sand dunes near Rapid 4. Robert Brewster Stanton reported finding arrowheads of unknown origin at a point in lower Cataract Canyon (now under Lake Powell) that was only accessible by boat.

19. J.D. Jennings, *Glen Canyon: A Summary* (Salt Lake City: University of Utah Press, Anthropological Paper 81, 1966).

20. J.D. Jennings, "Aborigines of Canyonlands," *Naturalist* 21 (1970): 12–13.

21. J.D. Jennings, *Prehistory of Utah and the Eastern Great Basin* (Salt Lake City: University of Utah Press, 1978); B.L. Tipps, *Holocene Archeology Near Squaw Butte, Canyonlands National Park, Utah* (Denver, Colorado: National Park Service, Selections from the Division of Cultural Resources No. 7, 1995), 46–50.

22. A summary of the general progressions of prehistoric peoples in Utah appears in J.D. Jennings, "Early Man in Utah," *Utah Historical Quarterly* 28 (1960): 3–27.

23. R.H. Lister, "Salvage Archaeology Today and the Glen Canyon Project," in *The American West: An Appraisal*, ed. R.G. Ferris (Santa Fe: Museum of New Mexico Press, 1963), 219–225.

24. M.D. Varien, W.D. Lipe, M.A. Adler, I.M. Thompson, and B.A. Bradley, "Southwestern Colorado and Southeastern Utah Settlement Patterns: A.D. 1100 to 1300," in *The Prehistoric Pueblo World*, A.D. *1150–1350* ed. M.A. Adler (Tucson: University of Arizona Press, 1996), 86–113.

25. J.S. Dean and G.S. Funkhouser, "Dendroclimatic Reconstructions for the Southern Colorado Plateau," in *Climate Change in the Four Corners and Adjacent Regions: Implications for Environmental Restoration and Land-Use Planning*, ed. W.J. Waugh (Grand Junction, Colorado: U.S. Department of Energy, Workshop Proceedings CONF-9409325, 1995), 85–104; R.C. Euler, G.J. Gumerman, T.N.V. Karlstrom, J.S. Dean, and R.H. Hevly, "The Colorado Plateaus: Cultural Dynamics and Paleoenvironment," *Science* 205 (1979): 1089–1101.

26. N.J. Coulam, "Collector Pile Experiment at Moab or Courthouse Wash Rock Art Panel, Arches National Park, Utah" (Moab, Utah: Canyonlands National Park, unpublished manuscript, 1992).

27. Powell, *Exploration of the Colorado River*, 206.

2

"WE DECIDE TO NAME THIS CATARACT CANYON"[1]

A Brief River Running History of Canyonlands

I catch a six-pound "whitefish" or Colorado salmon [Colorado pikeminnow, now an endangered species]. The flesh of this fish has a peculiar characteristic in that if fried soon after being caught the muscular contractions cause the pieces to wriggle about in the skillet in a manner astonishing to anyone not accustomed to it, so much so that the Adam's apple of one member of the party tried to turn a somersault when he was offered a helping.

– Julius Stone, 1909[2]

The human history of Cataract Canyon begins with a story of general avoidance by prehistoric cultures (as discussed in Chapter 1). The first European explorers continued to pay scant attention to it; the Franciscan friars Domínguez and Escalante circled the region in 1776, not daring to cross its deep canyons.[3] In 1836, rock inscriptions dimly reveal the exploration of a French-speaking fur trader. Exploration by an American scientist in 1869 revealed details of the scene. Between 1869 and the establishment of Canyonlands National Park in 1964, the canyon was occasionally visited by geologists, civil engineers, miners, trappers, cattlemen, outlaws, adventure travelers, dam builders, environmentalists, and even Hollywood filmmakers. The common denominator for most visits to Cataract Canyon was boat travel, as it is today. Approximately 7,000 visitors now enjoy the whitewater adventure of Cataract Canyon every year. A chronology of the history of Cataract Canyon and the surrounding regions appears in Table 2-1.

THE EXPLORERS

The Fur Traders

Trappers first came to the Colorado Plateau in 1821 in search of fur-bearing animals, particularly beaver. Mexico had achieved independence from Spain,[4] and the search had expanded into our region after these animals became scarce under trapping pressure in the Mississippi-Missouri watershed. The demand for fur came predominantly from the garment industry, which exported most of the supply to Europe. Trapping began on the Green River then spread to the San Juan, followed by the Dolores, and finally the main stems of the Grand and Colorado rivers.[5]

Besides the French-speaking trappers (see following section), English-speaking trappers used these rivers as well. Alexander MacKenzie of the Hudson Bay Company trapped the upper Green in the 1820-1821 season. General William Ashley and a consortium of trappers traveled down the Green River and left an 1825 inscription in Red Canyon upstream from Lodore Canyon.[6] The group had a boating accident at a place later called Ashley Falls, now submerged under the reservoir behind Flaming Gorge Dam. Jedediah S. Smith retired from Ashley's company in 1826 and with two others made a now-legendary journey from Bear Lake in northern Utah to California. Their route took them down the Price River and across the headwaters of the Fremont River to the west of Canyonlands.[7] Smith later joined the Rocky Mountain Fur Trading Company and etched an inscription in 1844 not far from the mouth of the Dolores River.

TABLE 2-1. Chronology of Human Experience in the Cataract Canyon Region

12,250 B.C. to 7800 B.C.	Various Paleoindian cultures inhabit the region to unknown extent.
7800 B.C. to A.D. 500	Archaic Desert culture leaves evidence of occupation.
A.D. 500 to A.D. 1300	Fremont and Ancestral Puebloan cultures leave extensive structures, artwork, and agricultural fields in region.
A.D. 1300 to present	Ute, Paiute, Navajo, Hopi cultures roam through the region.
1540	Spaniards under Francisco Vázquez de Coronado enter the Colorado Plateau.
1680	The Pueblo Revolt results in Spaniards leaving their northern frontiers.
1692	The Spaniards regain control of the Pueblos.
1765	Spanish merchant Juan Maria Antonio Rivera explores west-central Colorado.
1775	Spanish traders Pedro Mora, Gregorio Sandoval and Andrés Muñiz explore west-central Colorado.
1776	Spanish Franciscan priests Francisco Atanasio Domínguez and Silvestre Vélez de Escalante encircle the Colorado Plateau and discover the Green River.
1806	Zebulon Pike is arrested by the Spaniards for spying during a U.S. Army expedition into the Rocky Mountain region.
1821	Spanish territories become the possession of an independent Mexico.
1824	Fur traders enter the Canyonlands region.
1828	Trader Antoine Robidoux builds a fort near confluence of the Uncompahgre and Gunnison Rivers.
1830	George Yount and William Wolfskill's trapping party cross the Colorado River below the mouth of the Dolores River and the Green River at the present-day town of Green River.
1836	Trapper Denis Julien explores the rivers of the area that will become Canyonlands National Park.
1846	The Mexican-American War begins.
1847	Members of the Church of Jesus Christ of Latter-day Saints (Mormons) settle in Utah territory.
1848	Mexican-American War ends and Utah territory becomes the possession of the United States. Orville Pratt leads settlers on Old Spanish Trail through Spanish Valley (Moab) and crosses 1,800 feet above the Portal.
1853	E.F. Beale crosses the Green River near present-day Green River, Utah. John W. Gunnison, of the U. S. Army Corps of Topographical Engineers, surveys the 38th parallel for a railroad route and crosses the Green River near where Beale crossed. John C. Fremont crosses the Green River near the mouth of the San Rafael River.
1854	William Huntington enters Spanish Valley on an expedition for the Mormon Church.
1855	Elk Mountain Mission temporarily settles in Spanish Valley.
1859	The U. S. Army Corps of Topographical Engineers searches overland for the Confluence.
1862	The largest historical flood occurs on Colorado River (~400,000 ft³/s in Arizona).
1869	John Wesley Powell's first river expedition travels from Green River, Wyoming, to the mouth of the Virgin River, Nevada.
1871	John Wesley Powell's second river expedition occurs in three phases, from Green River, Wyoming, to Kanab Creek, Arizona (final phase in 1872).
1872	Almon H. Thompson surveys southern Utah overland for Powell; discovers the Escalante River, the last-named river in the continental United States; climbs the Henry Mountains; and floats through Glen Canyon a second time.
1874	Crispen Taylor brings the first significant herd of cattle to Spanish Valley.
1875	Ferdinand V. Hayden supervises survey of the Uncompahgre Plateau and the La Sal and Abajo Mountains. Powell supervises survey of the Henry Mountains by Grove Karl Gilbert.
1877	William Granstaff ("Negro Bill") settles in Spanish Valley area.
1879	A U.S. Post Office is established in the town of Moab.
1881	The Moab ferry becomes operational. A Post Office is established in Grand Junction.
1882	The Ute Tribe is confined to reservations. The Denver and Rio Grande Railroad enters Grand Junction from the south. Ferry service is established in Grand Junction. The first irrigation projects near the Colorado River are established at Grand Junction/Grand Valley.
1883	Cass Hite prospects in upper Glen Canyon. Denver and Rio Grande Railroad is completed through Emery County, Utah.
1884	U.S. Weather Service begins gaging the Colorado River at Fruita, Colorado, and records a record flow of 125,000 ft³/s on July 4; flow in Cataract Canyon is estimated at 225,000 ft³/s.
1885	The Roan Toll Road connects Glenwood Springs to Grand Junction. Funds are approved to build Grand Junction's first bridge over the Colorado River.
1887	A U.S. Post Office is established at Westwater, Utah.
1888	Elmer Kane is the first boatman to traverse Westwater Canyon.

1889	Frank Kendrick surveys Colorado River from Grand Junction to the Confluence for the Denver Colorado Canyon Pacific Rail Road. Robert Brewster Stanton surveys the Colorado River from the Confluence to Hite. Stanton launches his second expedition from Hite to complete his survey through Grand Canyon.
1890	Emery County is divided and Grand County is established with Moab as the county seat. The Denver and Rio Grande Railroad enters Grand Junction, standard rails replace narrow gauge rails, and a new route is built through Ruby Canyon.
1891	The Best Expedition, headed by James Best of the Colorado, Grand Cañon Mining and Improvement Company, runs Cataract and destroys a boat in Rapid 15. First oil well in Utah is drilled near Elgin.
1892	George M. Wright and Friend G. Faatz run Cataract Canyon separately and meet up later in Glen Canyon. Battlement Mesa Forest Reserve near Grand Junction is established.
1893	Steamer *Major Powell* makes the round trip from the San Rafael River to Cataract Canyon at Spanish Bottom.
1894	Nathaniel Galloway makes a solo run of Cataract Canyon.
1896	Utah achieves statehood. George Flavell and Ramon Montéz and Nathaniel Galloway and William Richmond separately run Cataract Canyon. A ferry is established at Dewey, Utah.
1897	Drs. Babcock and Miller run Westwater Canyon. Galloway again runs Cataract Canyon.
1898	A U.S. Post Office is established at Dewey.
1900	The Kings Toll Road (Highway 128) is completed. An oil shale boom occurs at Parachute Creek, Colorado, leading to increased exploration in the region.
1901	The maiden voyage of the steamship *Undine* occurs; Frank Summeril proposes a resort at Spanish Bottom.
1904	The maiden voyage of the gasoline-powered *Wilmont* occurs. Nathaniel and Parley Galloway and Louis M. Chaffin and Alonzo G. Turner separately run Cataract Canyon.
1905	The maiden voyage of the gasoline-powered *City of Moab* occurs.
1906	La Sal Forest Preserve is established near Moab.
1907	Charles Russell, Bert Loper, and Edwin Monett run Cataract Canyon. A.G. Turner runs Cataract Canyon. The maiden voyages of the steamer *Black Eagle* and the gasoline-powered *Paddy Ross* occur. Tom Wimmer provides gasoline-powered boat services until 1924 with such boats as the *Marguerite*.
1909	The Stone expedition runs Cataract Canyon. Henry E. Blake conducts the maiden voyage of the *Ida B.*
1910	J. H. Hummel runs Cataract Canyon.
1911	Ellsworth and Emery Kolb run Cataract Canyon. Charles Smith runs Cataract Canyon. Colorado National Monument is established near Grand Junction.
1912	Moab's first bridge crosses the Colorado River. Charles Smith and Nathaniel Galloway run Cataract Canyon together.
1914	The Tadje-Russell expedition runs Cataract Canyon. The U.S. Reclamation Service drills at the Confluence to test for damsite suitability.
1915	Near Palisade, Colorado, work is completed on a highline diversion dam, the first significant dam upstream of Cataract Canyon.
1916	Ellsworth Kolb and Bert Loper run Westwater Canyon. The Dewey Bridge is completed across the Colorado River.
1917	Second largest twentieth-century flood passes through Cataract Canyon (145,000 ft³/s).
1921	Largest twentieth-century flood passes through Cataract Canyon (147,000 ft³/s). A USGS expedition surveys Cataract Canyon for potential damsites. The Grand River is renamed the Colorado River.
1922	Colorado River Compact allocates Colorado River water to the seven western states.
1924	John and Parley Galloway run Cataract Canyon.
1925	The Shafer brothers discover oil and gas in Meander Canyon. Moab Garage Company begins a boat-transport service that by 1927 would haul 3,500 tons of freight annually.
1927	The Clyde Eddy and Pathé-Bray expeditions separately run Cataract Canyon.
1928	Boulder Canyon Act authorizes construction of Hoover Dam. Glen and Bessie Hyde run Cataract Canyon, making Bessie the first known woman river runner.
1929	Arches National Monument is established.
1933	The Frazier-Hatch expedition runs Cataract Canyon. Harold Leich boats and hikes the Colorado River from Grand Lake, Colorado, to Hite.
1935	The Escalante National Monument is proposed along Green and Colorado rivers from Moab to Arizona border.
1937	Haldane "Buzz" Holmstrom makes a solo run of the Green and Colorado rivers.

TABLE 2-1. Chronology of Human Experience in the Cataract Canyon Region (continued)

1938	Amos Burg runs first inflatable boat through Cataract Canyon. Holmstrom becomes first to run every rapid from Green River, Wyoming, to lower Grand Canyon. Norman Nevills runs first commercial river trip in Cataract Canyon. Bernard DeColmont and Antoine DeSeyne are the first to kayak Cataract Canyon. Russell Frazier up-runs the Colorado River from Hite to Dark Canyon.
1941	Testing is performed at the Dewey Bridge Damsite.
1943	Bert Loper runs Cataract Canyon.
1944	The United States signs a treaty with Mexico for 1.5 million acre-feet of Colorado River water. Loper again runs Cataract Canyon.
1945	W. Herwig runs scow with freight through Cataract Canyon.
1947	Harry Aleson and Georgie White Clark make first run of Cataract Canyon in WW II surplus-neoprene, inflatable rafts. Don Harris and Jack Brennan run Cataract Canyon.
1948	Otis Marston becomes the first known person to run Dolores River.
1949	John Ford directs "Wagon Master" for Hollywood in Professor Valley. Kenneth Ross runs Cataract Canyon.
1952	Charlie Steen discovers uraninite near Big Indian Valley, starting a mining boom.
1953	Don Harris runs the first power boat through Cataract Canyon.
1954	Leslie Jones canoes Cataract Canyon from Moab to Hite in thirty-six hours.
1955	Ed Hudson runs the first power boat run through Westwater Canyon.
1956	Congress authorizes the Colorado River Storage Act.
1957	Construction of Glen Canyon Dam begins. Georgie White Clark runs thirty-three-foot, G-rig pontoon and Fred Eiseman runs fifteen-foot triple rig through Cataract Canyon in high water. The Canyon Country River Marathon, a boat race, begins.
1958	The Friendship Cruise from Green River, Utah, to Moab begins as an annual Memorial Day weekend event.
1959	Dead Horse Point State Park is established. National Park Service begins to study the concept of Canyonlands National Park.
1962	Dam construction begins on the Gunnison River.
1963	The Denver, Rio Grande and Western Railroad spur road is completed to Potash. Glen Canyon begins storing Colorado River water. The inventory and salvage of Glen Canyon's human history is completed. Flaming Gorge Dam regulates the Green River.
1964	Glen Canyon Dam begins generating electricity. Canyonlands National Park is established.
1965	William Somerville up-runs Cataract Canyon in a jet boat.
1971	Arches is converted from a national monument to a national park. More land is added to Canyonlands National Park, including the detached Horseshoe Canyon unit.
1980	The reservoir reaches full pool elevation of 3,700 ft.
1981	The Department of Energy identifies sites immediately east of Needles District as among alternatives for a nuclear waste repository; the plan was dropped in 1986.
1982	Glen Canyon Environmental Studies begins to study the effects of Glen Canyon Dam operations on Grand Canyon.
1983	Flows through Cataract Canyon peak at 104,000 ft^3/s, causing brief river closures. The spillway at Glen Canyon Dam fails and the emergency high-pool elevation is raised to 3,707.4 ft (normal pool elevation is 3,700 ft). Grazing privileges expire in Canyonlands National Park. The reservoir backs up to the base of Big Drop 3.
1984	Flows through Cataract Canyon peak at 115,300 ft^3/s.
1989	The Secretary of the Interior orders an Environmental Impact Statement on the operations of Glen Canyon Dam and its effects on Grand Canyon (record of decision in 1996).
1990	After near extirpation by trappers in the late nineteenth and early twentieth centuries, river otters make their reappearance in the Colorado River above Glen Canyon Dam.
1992	A long period of drought from 1989-1991 brings the reservoir to its lowest pool elevation (3,611 ft) since the reservoir filled in 1980. Lower Cataract Canyon becomes a river through perched silt banks for thirty miles. Congress passes the Grand Canyon Protection Act.
1993	Cataract Canyon peaks at 70,600 ft^3/s. Colorado Plateau River Guides is established.
1995	Cataract Canyon peaks at 80,700 ft^3/s.
1996	Glen Canyon Dam releases the first deliberate flood from a dam to improve downstream habitat (45,000 ft^3/s) with no effect on Cataract Canyon.
1999	The pool elevation of the reservoir rises again, drowning out Rapid 27 in Cataract Canyon.
2000	Drought decreases inflow to the reservoir and its level drops, re-exposing Rapid 27.
2002	Lowest spring peak for the Colorado River in recorded history peaks at 9,550 ft^3/s. Islands of sediment appear on the reservoir below the mouth of the Dirty Devil River and above Hite Marina.

William Wolfskill was the first American we know of who crossed the Green River at what later became Green River, Utah. In 1830, Wolfskill let a trapping party of eleven men from Taos to Los Angeles, crossing Utah on the Spanish Trail.[8] George Manly attempted a Green River trip in 1849 and got as far as the Uinta Basin above Desolation Canyon; Manly and his men then went immediately overland to California through Death Valley. As the fur trade dwindled, the hunt for gold became the primary reason for visiting Canyon Country.

Many of the river runners discussed in this chapter reported sightings of beaver and, on occasion, otters in their diaries. A few of them made a living at fur-trapping, justifying their trips on the rivers. Because of the depletion of beaver, open trapping eventually became illegal in Utah but remained legal in Arizona; consequently, some trappers started their river trips in Utah, trapping as they went, and sold their furs in Arizona. Because such enterprise was illegal, the participants did not wish to gather attention about their activities and consequently did not leave a record of their exploits. Therefore, we may never really know just how many, or who, actually ran the canyons of the Colorado River.

Denis Julien — 1836

Denis Julien is best known to history as a mysterious explorer with a penchant for carving his name on rocks in Canyon Country.[9] He was a very real person: a husband, father, fur-trapper, soldier, and possibly the first American of European descent to enter into the bowels of Cataract Canyon, a full 33 years before John Wesley Powell's famous expedition down the Green and Colorado rivers. Julien's activities were little known during this period because Utah was under Mexican control and did not become part of the Union until ratification of the Treaty of Guadalupe Hildago ended the Mexican-American War of 1846–1848. In 1836, when Julien chiseled his inscription near Cove Canyon in lower Cataract Canyon, he likely possessed a trapping permit from the Mexican government. Many documents related to Julien have survived, thanks to various religious and government

archives. They include the baptismal records of Julien's children, archived by the French authorities prior to the Louisiana Purchase of 1803, and Julien's militia record, archived by the government of the United States during the War of 1812.

Julien was a French-speaking frontiersman who was possibly born in St. Louis in the early 1770s. At that time, St. Louis was an outpost under the dominion of the Spanish monarchy and later, in 1783, under the French monarchy. As a young man, Julien worked as a trapper-trader in the trans-Mississippi River watershed, married an Indian woman, and fathered three children. After the acquisition of these territories by the United States, Julien volunteered under territorial Governor/General William Clark (of Lewis and Clark fame) in a militia of the Louisiana Territory.

By 1826, Julien had attached himself to a trading company operated by Francois Robidoux. The Robidoux Company held Mexican permits to work in the Colorado River watershed. Trading posts were established at two places: the confluence of the Uncompaghre and Gunnison rivers in west-central Colorado, and in the White Rocks area of the Uinta River in north-central Utah, where Julien inscribed his name on a rock in 1831. This fur-trading company operated in the watershed until 1844, when Ute raids successfully ended the enterprises of the Robidoux Company. In addition, the fur-trapping business was decreasing owing to over-trapping of beaver in the region. Julien's last known inscription was carved in what is now Arches National Park in 1844.

There is much speculation about Julien's mode of transportation. Most historians think that Julien operated a rigid row boat on the Green and Colorado rivers because of what is depicted on the inscription sites at Hell Roaring Canyon on the Green River (see Chapter 5) and the site near Cove Canyon in Cataract Canyon. At the Hell Roaring site, Julien etched an image of a boat in the rock,[10] and the Cove Canyon site was not accessible by foot in either low or high water stages before being submerged beneath Lake Powell. Grove Karl Gilbert, a geologist working for the Powell Survey (1875–1878), first discovered a Julien inscription in 1875 while conducting research in the areas adjacent to the present-day Capitol Reef

National Park;[11] this inscription has not been relocated.

In Canyonlands, two of Julien's inscriptions are on the Green River and two are on the Colorado River in Cataract Canyon. The search for other Julien inscriptions continues, as does the debate about their authenticity. John Colton Sumner, head boatman of the 1869 expedition led by John Wesley Powell, tried to discount Julien's presence in Canyonlands. In a letter dated some years after the expedition, Sumner wrote: "The D. Julien 1836 marks on the rocks were probably made by Andy Hall [another expedition member], as he was always up to some prank."[12] Obviously many nineteenth-century explorers were unwilling to accept the notion that someone had preceded Powell into an area that was considered by his peers to be a largely unknown region.

The Search for Railroad Routes

Three notable explorers passed north of Canyonlands in search of the route for the first intercontinental railroad. Senator Thomas Hart Benton of Missouri wanted to promote a route from St. Louis to California that passed through the Rocky Mountains.[13] To promote his route, he proposed that E.F. Beale travel the route for publicity reasons; Beale crossed the Green River on July 25, 1853.[14] Benton wanted his son-in-law, John C. Frémont, to lead the official exploration, but instead that task fell to Lt. John W. Gunnison. Gunnison's expedition used the same guide that Beale had used (Antoine Leroux) and crossed the Green at the same site on September 23. Gunnison was killed later that year near Delta, and his legacy in the region is assured with the naming of Gunnison Butte at the end of Gray Canyon on the Green River. Frémont, who later became the first Republican candidate for the presidency, began his rise to national fame as an explorer. At the end of his final and most arduous exploration, Frémont crossed the Green River near the mouth of the San Rafael River late in 1853.[15] Frémont spent a miserable and deadly winter in the mountains of Utah,[16] and his explorations were commemorated with the naming of geographic features (*e.g.*, the Fremont River) and plants (*e.g.*, cottonwood, *Populus frémontii*).

John Macomb — 1859

The 1858 map of the Utah Territory produced by the U.S. Army Corps of Topographical Engineers has the words "Region Unexplored Scientifically" pasted over what is now southeastern Utah. In July 1859, a group of scientists and soldiers left Santa Fe, New Mexico, under the auspices of the U.S. Army Corps of Topographical Engineers. Captain John N. Macomb led the exploration party into the area we now call the Needles District of Canyonlands National Park. Macomb's expedition tried to establish the exact latitude and longitude of the confluence of the Grand and Green rivers. The rugged and dissected terrain prevented their even smaller reconnaissance team from actually viewing the Confluence, but they saw enough topography to produce a crude map that was published in 1860.[17]

Macomb's personnel included Dr. John Strong Newberry, a physician and naturalist who would later become a charter member of the National Academy of Sciences. In the course of the Macomb Expedition, Newberry coined the name we use today to describe this physiographic province: the Colorado Plateau. He was also the first to describe the Abajo Mountains, which were formed by intrusion of igneous rock between sedimentary strata. This unique type of landform subsequently was termed a *laccolith* by Grove Karl Gilbert in his studies of the nearby Henry Mountains.[18] Macomb's exploits aren't remembered in the region's names, but Newberry's name was used for some plants (*e.g.*, Newberry Twinpod, *Physaria newberryi*).

The First Powell Expedition — 1869

John Wesley Powell was a science instructor from Illinois who saw the need for scientific exploration of the West. He was particularly interested in the course of the Colorado River, still uncharted in the late 1860s, and the geology of its canyons. When his crew rowed downstream on the Green River from the newly established transcontinental railroad crossing in Green River, Wyoming, Powell entered into the much respected realm of American exploration inhabited by the likes of Meriwether Lewis, William Clark, Benjamin Bonneville, Stephen Long, and John C. Frémont.

Powell's developing career as an instructor at a private college was interrupted by the Civil War. Powell enlisted in the Union Army as a private; although he was honorably discharged as a Brevet Lieutenant Colonel, he was affectionately called "Major" until his death in 1902.[19] As a leader of men, Powell is one of the most controversial figures in western history, being either revered[20] or vilified.[21] Jack Sumner, crew member for the first expedition, summed up the dichotomy:

> [Powell] was a man of many traits, good, bad, and indifferent. He was vastly over-estimated as a man... As a scholar and scientist he was worthy of all praise.[22]

Part of the controversy deals with the somewhat fictionalized account of his first exploration down the Colorado River, an account that is still in print and is widely read today.[23] Although his leadership of explorers is open to question, Powell stands in the first rank of nineteenth-century Americans as a scientist and reformer.[24]

Most of the individuals Powell chose for his first river expedition were rugged frontiersmen: George Bradley, William Dunn, Andy Hall, Billy Hawkins, Oramel Howland, Seneca Howland, Walter Powell, Frank Goodman, and Sumner. Much of what we know to be true from this expedition comes from the diaries or later accounts of these men. For Powell, the stalwart qualities of these men were both a blessing and a liability. They had the fortitude necessary to complete a rigorous trip, but they were also fiercely independent and had little use for Powell's military forbearance.[25]

Powell made many preparations for what was to be a lengthy expedition:

> We take with us rations deemed sufficient to last ten months; for we expect, when winter comes on and the river is filled with ice, to lie over at some point until spring arrives; so we take abundant supplies of clothing. We have also a large quantity of ammunition and two or three dozen traps. For the purpose of building cabins, repairing boats, and meeting other exigencies, we are supplied with axes, hammers, saws, augers, and other tools, and a quantity of nails and screws. For scientific work, we have two sextants, four chronometers, a number of barometers, thermometers, compasses, and other instruments.[26]

The trip was funded privately and the scientific instruments were provided on loan from the Smithsonian Institution. Unfortunately, the Powell Expedition lost a boat, precious equipment, and food upstream on the Green River in Lodore Canyon. With low provisions, Powell could not carry out his plans to make winter quarters in Canyon Country, which would have allowed time for detailed investigations of the uncharted land. Instead, the trip became a test of endurance. For Powell and his brother Walter, the expedition ended three months later at the mouth of the Virgin River in Nevada. Frank Goodman left the expedition soon after the boat wreck in Lodore Canyon, and the Howland brothers and Dunn left the expedition in western Grand Canyon and hiked to their murders (see below). Four of the crew continued downstream: Bradley and Hawkins apparently left the river at Yuma; and Sumner and Hall went all the way to the Gulf of California, then rowed and sailed back upstream to Yuma.[27]

Powell was intrigued with the geology of Cataract Canyon beginning at the Confluence, which he reached by boat on July 16, 1869. He recognized the geographical significance of this place and set about establishing it accurately on his map. According to Bradley's journal,[28] the group camped at the Confluence for five nights, more than any other place during an expedition that lasted a total of ninety-nine days. They climbed from the bottom of Cataract Canyon to the east rim (Needles District) and to the west rim (Maze District) through routes that are essentially slots in the cliffs. The access canyons on the right side of the Green River about one mile upstream of the Confluence and on the left side of the Colorado River about a half mile downstream from the Confluence are each now informally called "Powell Canyon." After repeated astronomical observations from the cliffs, they moved downstream on July 21.

The men ran Rapid 1, which they referred to as a "very bad rapid."[29] Becoming more cautious, they portaged three rapids, probably Rapids 2, 4, and 5. In either Rapid 6 or 7, Powell's boat, the *Emma Dean* (named for Powell's wife), flipped and the oars were lost. The party hewed replacements out of the abundant driftwood found in the pool below Rapid 7.[30] At Tilted Park, Powell was sufficiently intrigued with the prominent bedrock slumps (called Toreva blocks; see Chapter 3) that he ordered a layover camp that was probably on river left.

Powell found the geology of Cataract Canyon perplexing. Because he was the first scientist to observe the features of this canyon, he had much to say about them in his book.[31] He waxed eloquently on the erosional features of what is now called the Cedar Mesa Sandstone in the Doll House. Further downstream, he mused on the features that are preserved in the twisted walls of the canyon. As Bradley recorded in his diary:

> Made a short run today, only 1-1/2 miles for Major wanted to determine what has so disarranged the strata here. . . . The strata all along here dips both ways from the river which Major says is caused by sliding down of part of the [canyon walls].[32]

What Powell observed are the effects of what we now attribute to deformed sub-surface layers of salt, potash, and gypsum in the Paradox formation.

The expedition reached the head of Mile Long Rapid and began the arduous task of portaging. Four portages were made in a half-mile, but the group ran the next five rapids. On the evening of July 23, they may have camped on the large beach above Big Drop 1 on the left bank. The Big Drops were all portaged on July 24, and as a result they only traversed three-quarters of a mile that day. These two days of portaging would prove to be the most arduous of their entire trip through the canyons of the Colorado River, including Grand Canyon, and the toil wore on the men. Their mood in the middle of Cataract Canyon became surly.

What began with the boating accident in Lodore Canyon flared into quarreling in the Big Drops of Cataract Canyon.[33] According to Billy Hawkins:

> Now our trouble begins, and plenty of bad rapids in the river. . . . At noon, while we were making a portage and letting the boats over a bad place, the ropes happened to catch Bill Dunn under the arms and came near drowning him, but he managed to catch the ropes and come out. While we were eating our dinner, Sumner said that Dunn came near being drowned and the Major's brother made the remark that it would have been of little loss. The Major spoke up and said that Dunn would have to pay thirty dollars for a watch [this watch was in Dunn's pocket when he was dragged into the river] belonging to him that had been soaked with water and ruined, and that if he did not he would have to leave the party.[34]

According to Sumner, tempers flared into a display of firearms.[35] At the heart of this matter was the disintegrating mental health of Walter Powell that began during his time in a Confederate prison. The incident in the Big Drops further diminished the control Powell had on the rest of the expedition and eventually led to the departure of the Howlands and Dunn at Separation Rapid in western Grand Canyon. Powell pronounced them cowards; more likely, the trio was probably fed up with Powell and sought a relatively easy exit. These three subsequently died, supposedly at the hands of Shivwit Paiutes. However, some historians believe the three men were mistaken for government spies and executed by the same group of Mormons who had been implicated in the 1857 Mountain Meadows massacre.[36]

Powell and his men took seven days to pass the forty-seven rapids in the forty-nine miles of river through Cataract Canyon. Powell's first expedition proved that passage through the canyons of the Colorado River was feasible, although difficult. He described the geology briefly and made notes on the flora and fauna, but the speed of the trip and the loss of data in some incidents resulted in many incomplete observations. Powell decided another river trip would be necessary for the completion of his work.

The Second Powell Expedition — 1871

Powell reentered Cataract Canyon in September 1871 with a completely new crew. Powell's experiences with the frontiersmen of the first trip proved to be an invaluable lesson. Beginning with the second expedition, Powell managed his subordinates in a way that would directly benefit him during his overland surveys in the 1870s and while he served as the second Director of the U.S. Geological Survey from 1880 to 1896. Now that this territory was charted and better understood, it was time to explore these wonders with a crew that had scientific backgrounds. As acknowledgment of the publicity the first trip generated, this time Powell received a $10,000 appropriation from Congress.

Science was the primary focus of the second expedition and the crew displayed quite a different spectrum of personalities from the first trip. This time, Powell chose many of his friends and relatives to accompany him. The members of the second expedition were E.O. Beaman, Francis M. Bishop, Frederick S. Dellenbaugh, Andrew Hatten, John K. Hillers, Stephen Vandiver Jones, Clement Powell, John F. Steward, and Almon Harris Thompson.[37] These men were collectively less hardened to the rigors of the outdoors, but their temperaments were better suited to Powell's overbearing personality. They understood and appreciated his scientific intentions. Some, particularly Dellenbaugh, came to worship him.

This expedition was also more productive, as far as the information they gathered, spending 154 days between Green River, Wyoming, and Lee's Ferry, Arizona (compared to seventy-two days on the first expedition). Eleven of those days were spent in Cataract Canyon, resulting in the first map of the canyon produced by cartographer Bishop. A most valuable person accompanied this trip: Powell recruited E.O. Beaman, a professional photographer from New York, to be the expedition's photographer. Beaman brought along several large format cameras to expose wet-plate negatives of the geologic and topographic features of the Green and Colorado rivers. The wet-plate process involved applying a thin coat of collodion (a mixture of bromides and iodides of cadmium, potassium, and ammonium) onto a plate of clear glass. The exposure was made while the collodion was still wet and developed by immersion into a solution of alcohol, iron sulfate, and acetic acid. The plate was then dipped into an acidic solution of silver nitrate. Printing of the negative awaited return to a printing laboratory where the negative was exposed onto light-sensitive papers.[38]

The explorers began their slow trip through Cataract Canyon by once again climbing to the rims above the Confluence on both sides. One of Beaman's assistants was former teamster Jack Hillers, who eventually took over the photographic responsibilities for the Powell Survey and later became the official photographer of the U.S. Geological Survey. Beaman needed an assistant: imagine the toil involved in lugging nearly a hundred pounds of heavy box cameras and glass plates to the rims above the Green and Colorado rivers! Despite the hard work, Hillers—or Jolly Jack as he was known to the crew—was impressed with the scenery of what is now called the Doll House. He wrote in his diary:

> All hands excepting Bish and Jones started up to see the parks. After an hour's climb we reached the top then and walked two miles to the parks. Such a sight I shall never forget. I counted five parks enclosed by pinnacles formed by erosion. They looked to me like monuments in a cemetery. Everything looked somber and deathlike. Nothing disturbed the scene except the sighing of the wind or the falling of a chip of rock. The water collects in a large basin in the center of each park and from thence into a gulch into the river.

The expedition eventually halted at Lee's Ferry, and the crew spent the 1871-72 winter at Kanab, Utah. During the following summer, they resumed the trip through Grand Canyon and exited at Kanab Creek, 137 miles from its end. Powell cited a variety of reasons for the early end to the second expedition, from the rising flood waters to the potential for hostile Paiutes in western Grand Canyon. Powell became famous as a result of his expeditions, and eventually he settled into a bureaucratic life in Washington, D.C. His scientific publications, well regarded at the time, led to the directorship of the U.S. Geological Survey as well as the Bureau of Ethnology. His work added landmarks to the crude maps of the region, forever eliminating the phrase "Region Unexplored Scientifically." After the second Powell Expedition, Cataract Canyon remained unvisited by river runners for nineteen years, at which time another landscape photographer came to work.

EXPLORATION FOR EXPLOITATION

The Brown-Stanton Expedition — 1889

Transportation through the newly explored Four Corners region was essential to the national mandate for economic development of the West. Railroads were, at the time, the most efficient means for transporting freight, and the possibility of a railroad through Cataract Canyon inspired the third expedition. This exploration was largely funded by Colorado banker Frank Mason Brown, who founded the Denver, Colorado Cañon, and Pacific Rail Road. He hired two civil engineers, Frank Kendrick and Robert Brewster Stanton, to design the railroad grade. Stanton was an up-and-coming engineer, having previously earned a reputation by designing the railroad loop to the Georgetown Mining District of Colorado.

Brown got the idea for the railroad from an Arizona prospector named S. S. Harper. The railroad was to follow the natural grade of the Colorado River from Grand Junction, Colorado, to Yuma, Arizona. The railroad would have passed through Westwater, Meander, Cataract, Glen, and Grand Canyons, as well as the numerous canyons of the lower Colorado River now inundated by various reservoirs such as Lake Mead. Trains would deliver coal and ore to markets in California, supplies to miners and ranchers in the remote areas of Arizona and Utah, and promote scenic tourism. Had oil not been discovered in southern California and had the 1891 depression not occurred, this railroad probably would have been built despite the large construction costs that massive bridge-making and tunneling would have required.[39]

There were two separate parties comprising the railroad survey. The first, led by Kendrick, surveyed the Colorado River from Grand Junction to the Confluence and returned via the Green River to the town of Green River, Utah. The second survey, conducted by Stanton, set out to design the railroad grade along the Colorado River from the Confluence down through Cataract Canyon. Kendrick and his party left Grand Junction after a promotional ceremony orchestrated by Brown on March 28, 1889. Kendrick, his main assistant Thomas P. Rigney, and Frank Knox, George Cost, and Charles Brock used an open dory-like boat for hauling camp gear. A steel chain-linked tape was used to measure distances, and a transit and rod to measure elevations down to the Confluence. They transported their boat by wagon around the fierce whitewater of Westwater Canyon and surveyed the canyon on foot. They reached the head of Cataract Canyon on May 4, where they inscribed a station number on a large red rock on the Maze side of the Confluence. They then rowed and towed the open dory upstream to Green River in twelve days. In order to avoid starvation, they sought provisions from the Wheeler brothers at their ranch across from the confluence of the San Rafael and Green rivers. At the town of Green River, they turned their boat over to Brown and Stanton.

Stanton had attempted to discuss river navigation with Powell. Powell, however, had developed a proprietary attitude about the Colorado River[40] and refused to discuss its nature with Stanton. Rebuffed, Stanton turned to Powell's book for information. As a result of his experiences, Stanton was the first to question the accuracy of Powell's accounts.

Brown and Stanton had fourteen men and six boats. In addition to the leaders, the men included William H. Bush, Edward Coe, George W. Gibson, Peter M. Hansbrough, G. Edward Howard, James N. Hughes, John Hislop, Franklin A. Nims, Charles W. Potter, Ethan A. Reynolds, Henry C. Richards, Thomas P. Rigney, George A. Sutherland, and Edward W. Terry. This crew was a mixture of Brown's friends who viewed the trip as a vacation, Stanton's crew of professional surveyors, and two of Stanton's family servants—Gibson and Richards—as cooks.

Photography was an integral part on this expedition as well. Nims was a professional photographer who had worked with pioneering western photographer William Henry Jackson in Denver. Not wanting to be burdened with heavy glass plates, Nims used a new paper-stripping film, developed by Eastman Kodak, that was, essentially, butcher paper with emulsion applied to one side. To make prints, the paper was oiled until translucent. This film proved to be reliable but unstable unless the emulsion was floated from the paper onto stable backing. Nims picked camera stations that showed the proposed railroad bed and usually took two negatives per station: one upstream and one downstream. In addition, Nims photographed some things for the sake of history and art. Among other things, he photographed a stringer of Colorado pikeminnow that the crew caught near the Confluence.

The boats were of thin cedar, clinker-built (nailed), and designed more for the hunter-sportsman than for the rigors of whitewater. Brown's idea was to portage the light craft as much as possible, thereby avoiding the heavy work Powell's men had endured. Unfortunately, Brown provided no personal flotation devices for himself or for his men. The boats were so flimsy that they needed immediate repair once they were unloaded from the train cars at the Green River Railroad Station. In addition to the five cedar boats, for the kitchen boat Brown used Kendrick's dory, named the *Brown Betty* after a Dutch oven-baked breakfast treat made with flour, spices, and apples.

The cedar boats came with five zinc-plated, water-resistant compartments that were originally thumb-screwed to the floors. The large amount of provisions packed into the boats left little room for personnel, so they tethered the zinc-plated (galvanized) boxes with ropes and towed them behind the *Brown Betty*. This boat was rowed by Gibson and Richards, who became the first African Americans to participate in a river trip down the Green and Colorado rivers.

On May 25, Brown and his party launched their boats into the annual snow melt that had swollen the Green River and proceeded quickly to the Confluence. The survey crew located the survey mark at Kendrick's inscription near the Confluence and began work down the left side of the Colorado River. Based on the photos from this trip, we estimate flows for Cataract Canyon at about 45,000 ft³/s, much higher than what Powell experienced and making the Brown-

Stanton Expedition hazardous due to the big waves and strong eddies. Accordingly, they were plagued with boating incidents immediately upon entry into Cataract Canyon.

The first mishap occurred above the very first rapid. Although the survey crew was working on river left, making that side a logical place to camp, Brown inexplicably ordered the boatmen to ferry across to river right for the evening camp. The most likely reason for this decision was to facilitate a safer portage of Rapid 1 the following day. While Gibson and Richards were rowing the *Brown Betty* from the left to right banks, the current caught the cumbersome boxes in tow and began to drag the entire contraption into the rapid. To stop this uncontrolled entry Gibson and Richards cut the tow rope and made it to safety. The boxes that carried important camp gear and food bobbed down the river; some boxes were subsequently retrieved in eddies downstream. Because of this incident, Rapid 1 is affectionately known today as "Brown Betty."[41]

While lining Rapids 4 and 5, one boat capsized and the strong current submerged and pinned it to a rock. Miraculously, the boat sustained minimal damage and the crew got it afloat again, but more gear was lost. At a nearby camera station, Nims's camera blew over and was smashed; fortunately he had brought two extras. The next day while lining Rapid 6 (Stanton records it as Rapid 10), the *Brown Betty* was pinned against a large rock and was lost, despite a diligent rescue attempt that saved a few camp necessities. Thus, Rapid 6 claimed boats from the 1ˢᵗ and 3ʳᵈ expeditions through Cataract Canyon.

At what must have been a very uncomfortable camp in the vicinity of Rapid 6, Stanton records that the men were becoming demoralized:

> Talked to several of the men and find a good deal of dissatisfaction among them as to the way Mr. Brown is managing the expedition and the way Hughes and Reynolds (guests of Brown) try to boss the handling of the boats. I will have a talk with all the men at breakfast tomorrow.[42]

While camping downstream at Tilted Park, Stanton determined that they had lost about two thirds of their food. Despite the hardships of the trip, work was never far from his mind. He notes in his diary that the open area where Y and Cross Canyons converge could serve as a place for side tracks for the trains.

In the section now known as Mile Long Rapid, another boat was abandoned after her floor boards were ripped from the main frame. A couple of rapids later, another boat's bow was caved in but was repaired from the wood parts of the abandoned boat left upstream. Even though the group retrieved some of the zinc-plated boxes as they progressed downstream, they were quickly running out of provisions. The combined work of surveying and portaging made downstream progress slow, requiring a change of plans.

Brown decided to split the group in two, one to continue surveying and one to seek more provisions at the mining camps downstream in Glen Canyon. Below the Big Drops, the Brown-led group rowed ahead of the survey team to secure necessary supplies at Dandy Crossing (Hite), with the idea of rowing back upstream to meet the survey team in progress. This turned out to be unnecessary, as Brown's party met the survey team not far upstream from Dandy Crossing. Just before the groups reunited, Stanton discovered the mysterious D. Julien inscription near Cove Canyon.[43]

Things then went from bad to worse: Brown decided to split his expedition again. In his haste to attend an upcoming meeting with investors to encourage continuing interest in his railroad project, Brown left the surveyors with Bush in charge to continue the instrumental survey through Glen Canyon and took Stanton, Nims, and the rest of the expedition downstream to Lee's Ferry. After a visit to Kanab, Utah, where they resupplied their provisions, they rowed downstream on July 9 for a quick photographic reconnaissance of Marble and Grand Canyons. The next day, eleven miles downstream of Lee's Ferry, Brown was thrown from his boat and drowned in a strong eddy current. His decision to save money by not providing lifejackets cost him his life. Fourteen miles later, Richards and Hansbrough drowned when their boat ran into an overhanging wall and capsized. A dejected Stanton wisely abandoned the expedition at South Canyon.

Despite the difficulties he encountered, Stanton firmly believed that the railroad was feasible and he took Brown's place as the president of the Denver, Colorado Cañon and Pacific Rail Road. Stanton returned to the head of Glen Canyon in November 1889 and completed the survey and the second passage through Grand Canyon. No additional lives were lost, although a boat was destroyed and seven men deserted or left the expedition. Although his railroad was never built, Stanton returned to Glen Canyon in an attempt to extract placer gold from its terraces and river beds.[44] His career on the Colorado Plateau, in many respects unsuccessful and tragi-comic, ended in 1902. Like a few of his predecessors on the river—especially Frederick Dellenbaugh—Stanton was so enamored with the river that he became one of its first historians. He became a champion of truth over hype concerning the Colorado River, and in so doing became Powell's nemesis. He died in 1922 without publishing his mammoth, thousand-page history; luckily, others have mined it for its nuggets of river lore.[45]

The Green Grand & Colorado River Navigation Company — 1890–1891

Unimaginable as it seems, steamboats briefly plied the Green and Colorado rivers to deliver supplies to ranchers and miners and to guide tourists to the picturesque canyons. The idea of steamboat traffic began in 1890 with B. S. Ross of Rawlins, Wyoming.[46] Ross and his companion rowed a small boat from the town of Green River, Utah, to the first rapid of Cataract Canyon and back, determined to prove that motorized watercraft could navigate the river. He convinced some prominent investors to form the Green Grand & Colorado River Navigation Company, with plans to build a hotel at Spanish Bottom for guests transported there by the steamboat.[47]

In 1891, the company purchased a steam launch from a Chicago company, shipped her to Green River, Utah, and named her the *Major Powell*. The thirty-five-foot long, eight-foot wide boat was powered by two steam engines that each turned a propeller (or screw) and drafted eighteen inches of water without a load. The steam was supplied by an upright boiler fired by kerosene. On the trial run in August 1891, the screws were damaged by the shallow, cobble-lined river. After modifications were made to shield the propellers, the company made its maiden voyage in April 1892. However, the *Major Powell* was vastly underpowered for river navigation, and the craft barely made it back up the Green River near the mouth of the San Rafael River. The boat was abandoned there for the dual reasons of the increased gradient of the river upstream and the presence of a wagon road to Green River. The turn-around point is not precisely known, but the crew made it at least as far as Fort Bottom (mile 40, or eighty miles downstream from Green River).[48]

The Best Expedition — 1891

The 1889 Brown-Stanton Expedition was a poorly-planned trip run by inexperienced men. In contrast, the next expedition to pass through Cataract Canyon was much better prepared and run by outdoorsmen, some with experience gained from the Brown-Stanton expedition. The former head boatman from Stanton's second expedition, Harry McDonald, spread the word to speculators about the ore deposits he saw below the mouth of the Little Colorado River (in Grand Canyon). As a result of McDonald's influence, James D. Best, a successful real estate broker from Denver, founded and became the president of the Colorado Grand Cañon, Mining and Improvement Company in 1891.[49] Best and McDonald chose the most experienced boatmen from Stanton's second crew, including William H. Edwards, John Hislop, and Elmer Kane. John McCormick was the expedition's photographer; the final two members were John Jacobs and Luther Jewell.

Best obtained $10,000 from investors to fund the expedition. McDonald, who had assisted in designing a better whitewater boat for Stanton's second expedition, further improved upon that boat design. The camp outfits and the personal needs of the crew were first-rate and included amenities such as rubber-coated canvas bags, cork lifejackets, and practical river clothing to protect them from the harsh environment. They launched in two boats from Green River,

Utah, on July 15, 1891, in low water.[50] Cataract Canyon in low water is a maze of rocky rapids that require precise entry and maneuvering. McCormick's photographs show that this expedition decided to run rapids, not walk around them. One photograph shows an expedition member standing as his boat passed through the waves of Rapid 9 (see Chapter 8). They obviously intended to have fun on their trip.

As well-prepared and experienced as it was, the expedition met trouble at Rapid 15 in Mile Long Rapid. The steersman of boat No. 1 lost momentum in an eddy fence above the rapid, a place choked with large rocks. The boat slammed sideways into a mid-stream boulder and became hopelessly pinned, spilling the crew members into the river. Edwards described the incident rather dramatically: "I cried out in great excitement 'Look at Kane! The back of his head is all torn off!'"[51] In fact, what he really saw was the red bandana that covered Kane's head. He and Jewell bobbed downstream in their lifejackets, eddied out, and walked back up. McDonald clambered from the boat to the top of the rock and later pulled Best up after he floated free from the cockpit of the pinned boat.

They were in an ideal position to start the procedure of rescuing the boat. However, the extraction of the boat would prove insurmountable. They built a wooden A-frame on the rock to which they attached ropes for moving people and supplies to and from shore. Attempts to pull the boat free with the ropes failed. Plan B was more dramatic: they would blow the rock into pieces by impact-drilling a hole and packing it with explosives. Hislop hiked to Dandy Crossing to acquire the necessary powder, but by the time he got back the rope to the boat had worn to the breaking point, making access to the rock impossible. Moreover, rising water from a summer storm had submerged the pinned boat, and at last they gave it up for lost.[52]

The expedition had wasted eight days on the aborted rescue. While waiting, members of the crew chiseled inscriptions into the boulders on river right (see Chapter 10). Leaving Rapid 15, the Best Expedition had eight men and one boat. The crew alternately walked the shorelines in rapids and rode on the boat deck in calm water. The expedition ran all but one of the rapids in Cataract Canyon, including Big Drops 2 and 3 and Dark Canyon Rapid, without additional incident; they apparently portaged their boat around Big Drop 1. At Dandy Crossing, they acquired a new skiff and continued down river to Lee's Ferry, where they left the river and traveled overland with stock animals to investigate ore deposits in eastern Grand Canyon, their original destination. Thereafter, the company dissolved without ever conducting a single mining operation.

F.G. Faatz and G.M. Wright — 1892

We would probably know nothing about the river trips of Friend Grant Faatz and George M. Wright if they hadn't left inscriptions on various rock faces along the river.[53] These men prospected and mined the placer gold deposits that were common between the town of Green River and the mouth of the San Rafael River, and in Glen Canyon. It is reasonable that Faatz and Wright would prefer a water route over the rough overland trails to reach these potential mining areas. Their launch points are unknown; they probably left from the town of Green River, although they could have launched from Grand Junction to work placer deposits along the Colorado River from Grand Junction south to about the northern boundary of the current Canyonlands National Park. These placer deposits may have inspired many prospectors to navigate Cataract Canyon to get to the Glen Canyon area, but their names and activities are not recorded in river history.

Faatz and Wright jointly left inscriptions at two places in 1892. According to the dates of these inscriptions, they launched at different times but eventually traveled together in the lower reaches of Glen Canyon. The sites where both men inscribed their names are at Rapid 15 in Cataract Canyon and Colorado River mile 10.4 above Lee's Ferry, in Glen Canyon. At Rapid 15, the Faatz inscription is dated August 27, 1892, and the Wright inscription is dated September 16, 1892. Wright also left an inscription dated October 11, 1892, at Sheep Canyon, which was the last rapid in Cataract Canyon (now submerged).

The inscriptions in lower Glen Canyon have both names inscribed on the panel and are dated November 16, 1892.

William Hiram Edwards — 1893

William H. Edwards was born in Belleview, New York, on December 6, 1866, and was one of the more interesting river runners on the Colorado.[54] His many achievements include pioneering river trips through Cataract and Grand canyons; mining placer deposits on the San Juan and Green rivers; and the discovery of at least four D. Julien inscriptions in Labyrinth, Stillwater, and Cataract Canyons while engaged in various river trips from 1891 to 1893.[55] His river-running experience began in 1889 with Stanton's second expedition and continued with the Best Expedition in 1891.

After the Best Expedition, Edwards spent some time in San Juan Canyon downstream from Bluff, Utah, during the placer boom of 1892, which turned out to be a bust. He later moved near the town of Green River and lived there until about 1897. Because of his river experience, he became the captain of the first mechanized craft to enter Cataract Canyon: the previously-abandoned steam-powered *Major Powell*. Edwards was not involved with the trial voyage of the *Major Powell* on the Green River in 1891, nor the voyage in 1892 when the vessel was abandoned near the mouth of the San Rafael River. Edwards took a skiff down river during the late winter of 1892–1893 to assess the damage to the steamer. He determined that it could be repaired and went to Denver to buy the necessary materials and to negotiate a leasing arrangement with the owners.

Edwards and two companions repaired the *Major Powell*, converting the boiler to burn wood rather than kerosene. The three men then ran the steamer downstream to Spanish Bottom in Cataract Canyon. There, on river right, they painted the following inscription:

1st STEAMER; MAJOR POWELL; March 24, 1893;
W. H. EDWARDS; H. F. HOWARD;
G. M. GRAHAM.

They turned around and steamed back up to the mouth of the San Rafael River. Edwards, like his predecessors, was unable to return the boat to the town of Green River because of the increased river gradient above the San Rafael River and a riffle called "The Auger."

Edwards took the *Major Powell* downstream again in April with Lute Johnson, an adventure travel writer for the *Denver Post*,[56] along with H. F. Howard, Louis N. McClane, and T. H. McDonald. At the conclusion of this trip Edwards again left the steamer at the Wheeler Ranch near the mouth of the San Rafael River.

In 1894, while Edwards was working a placer deposit nine miles downstream from Green River, he saw the *Major Powell* for the last time. Four men brought the steamer up to the opposite side of the placer deposit, removed the engines and boiler, and took them to Green River for use in a wrecking plant venture. The hull was abandoned and probably floated downstream in one of the Green River's periodic floods. By 1896, Edwards and river companion John Hislop were two of twenty men involved in this placer mining operation. It became a fully mechanized, dry-dredging operation on river left. The dredge (or amalgamator) was powered by steam-driven electrical generators and could process a yard of gravel per minute. The dredging operation ended in late 1896, whereupon Edwards sold the dredge and transported it to Idaho. He died in the mid-1940s.[57]

RIVER RUNNING FOR FUN AND PROFIT

Nathaniel Galloway — 1894 and the 1909 Stone Expedition

Nathaniel Galloway is one of the more famous river runners of this region, largely because he developed rowing techniques that are still used to this day. He ran the rapids of Cataract Canyon six times, more than anybody else could claim until the 1960s. He summed up his career in an 1898 newspaper interview at his home town in Vernal, Utah:

It is a well known fact among my acquaintances that I have made several such trips through the cañons of the Green River and the Colorado as far as Lee's Ferry, Arizona, but it has never been my desire to gain fame or notoriety of any descriptions whatever in such proceedings. These trips have been made only to gain what little profits I might in following such pursuits as I do (trapping and prospecting).[58]

Galloway's six Cataract Canyon trips included a solo run in 1894; a trip with William C. Richmond in January 1897; a solo run later in 1897; a trip with son Parley Galloway in 1904; a trip as head boatman for Julius F. Stone in 1909; and a trip in 1912 with Charles Smith, another placer miner of Glen Canyon. On the 1912 trip, Galloway trapped ninety-five beavers along the Green River and through Cataract Canyon.[59]

Galloway's rowing technique was different from the style of the Powell, Stanton, and Best expeditions, and most of those who followed him would emulate it. Before the Galloway improvisation, boats usually required three boatmen: two oarsmen in the fore and aft positions pulled on their oars with their backs to the downstream, providing maximum speed, while a third boatman used one longer oar mounted to a stern pin to steer. Because Galloway was a solo boater, he needed something that would work for one person and thus developed the "stern first" technique. The oarsman faced downstream by running rapids stern-first and pulled on his oars to slow the boat down. By facing downstream, the solo oarsman could see the obstacles ahead and steer by applying *ferry angles*. A typical ferry angle is made by turning the boat no more than 45° to the direction of the current. This is a natural propulsion system that, for example, ferry boats once used to move across rivers on a suspended cable; the energy comes from the river's current deflecting off of the angled boat. Norm Nevills, a pioneering outfitter on the Colorado River, described the technique succinctly: "Face your danger."[60]

Unfortunately, Galloway's diaries and photo albums were destroyed in a house fire. Most of the details of his river-running history come from his children, most notably John and Parley; other stories come from contemporaries such as Bert Loper, David Rust, Ellsworth Kolb, and Julius Stone. Inscriptions corroborate some of Galloway's history: twenty-one miles above Lee's Ferry in Glen Canyon there is an inscription site known as Galloway Cave. Three inscriptions (1894 and two dates in 1897) by Galloway were in this cave, which is now under the reservoir.[61] He used the cave as a shelter camp; on one occasion, he almost drowned there when flood waters in the night nearly trapped him inside.

The highlight of Galloway's river-running career occurred after a chance meeting in 1899 with industrialist Julius Stone. Stone visited Glen Canyon to inspect his investment in a placer gold wet-dredging operation called the Hoskaninni Mining Company, managed by Robert Brewster Stanton. Galloway worked as a laborer for this mining operation and during this time guided Stone on trips through Glen Canyon and into the Henry Mountains.[62] Stone was enamored with the Canyonlands region and planned a river trip to retrace Powell's 1869 route. He planned to row his own boat and invited a friend and a relative to participate; what Stone needed was a boat builder and a river guide to see it come to fruition. The obvious choice for both needs was his new friend "Than" Galloway. Stone chose his brother-in-law, Raymond C. Cogswell, to be the trip photographer; Stone would grow to despise him over the course of the trip.[63] Cogswell's photographs were used to illustrate Stone's book[64]—as well as the book presently in your hands.

On September 12, 1909, Stone, Galloway, Cogswell, Seymour Dubendorff, and Charles Sharp launched from Green River, Wyoming, in four boats. Each person had his own boat except Cogswell, who rode with Galloway through most of the canyons. After many adventures upstream, they reached the town of Green River, Utah, on October 9. Continuing downstream, they passed through Labyrinth and Stillwater canyons in three days, quickly arriving at the Confluence where they found a flock of snow geese. One of these was unlucky enough to feel a blast from Stone's shotgun and was soon afterward subjected to the heat from Galloway's fire. That evening they camped on the left side above Rapid 1 of Cataract Canyon and ate well.

Cogswell was an opportunistic photographer and used his time wisely, knowing that Stone was an impatient sort. Cogswell frequently had to snap his photos from a moving boat. At Bowknot Bend on the Green River, Stone let him hike over the meander's neck with his camera, where he took a photograph—as Beaman and other photographers that followed him would do—that simultaneously shows the Green River on the upstream and downstream sides of the bend. At Rapid 1, while the others were busy preparing their boats for the whitewater ahead, Cogswell hiked and photographed. He also kept an informative journal, which provides counterpoint to Stone's repeated criticism of Cogswell in his diary.[65]

The water was low and the boatmen, except Galloway, were mostly unseasoned. Stone had occasional bouts of pleurisy during the trip, which might explain some of his grumpy attitude towards Cogswell. They lined many of the rapids and portaged Rapid 5. Moving slowly and cautiously through the canyon, they found a wrecked boat and a man's coat near Rapid 6. Despite this ominous sign, they ran eight rapids and camped at the head of Lake Cataract, a term we now use to designate the slack-water section above Range Canyon. They ran the less difficult rapids and lined and portaged the more difficult ones—including a "hard portage" at Dark Canyon Rapid—before exiting the canyon on October 21.

All in all, their traverse through Cataract Canyon was rather routine except for one incident at Rapid 18. Cogswell described it in his diary:

> While running the last rapid . . . Duby, whose boat was too heavily loaded, struck a rock and [capsized]. Luckily he had on his jacket and swam out safely, the jacket keeping him up and also away from the rocks. . . . The boat was picked up by Mr. G.[66]

During the incident, the boat hatches opened, cameras were soaked, a shutter was jammed, and some of Cogswell's film—he mentions six images specifically—were destroyed, explaining the gap in his photographic coverage of Cataract Canyon. Although he had two other cameras, he could do nothing about recovering these lost images.[67]

The group made their way downstream through Grand Canyon and quit the river at Needles, California. Stone lived to be eighty-nine and felt the accolades of a younger generation of river runners, but Dubendorff succumbed to Rocky Mountain spotted fever in 1910[68] and Galloway died prematurely in 1913.[69] Despite Stone's low opinion of him, Raymond Cogswell made a huge contribution to history and science by photographing about two thousand scenes in the canyons of the Green and Colorado rivers. He became an electrical and mining engineer and spent most of the rest of his life in Ohio; he later considered photography to be merely a hobby. When he died on July 2, 1964, he was one month shy of his ninety-second birthday, and no mention was made in his obituary about his brief career as a photographer of the Colorado River.[70]

Flavell and Montéz — 1896

George Flavell is peerless among river runners on the Colorado River. Seemingly on a lark, he chose to retrace Powell's 1869 route in one boat with an inexperienced passenger named Ramon Montéz. Flavell was a boatswain, a confident boatman, and a competent outdoorsman. When he launched on August 27, 1896, Flavell operated the first solo boat to run all the canyons of the Colorado River drainage.[71] Montéz helped with linings and portages but appeared to do little else than provide company and hang on for dear life as Flavell pounded through rapid after rapid.

Flavell and Montéz entered Cataract Canyon on September 30. They found two men identified only as Mr. Summers and Mr. Gieger in the act of flushing a deer out of brush near Spanish Bottom. The two men watched as Rapid 1 got Flavell and Montéz wet but left them upright. Like the Best Expedition, Flavell was fearless and promptly ran eight rapids in succession. Rapid 15 filled half the boat with water but they missed the big rocks, faring much better than Best and his crew. Flavell's most notable characteristic was his tremendous sense of humor and his exuberance. After running some particularly rough rapids in Grand Canyon, he wrote in his journal: "There is only one stone we must not hit, that we must miss at all hazard—our tombstone!" In Cataract Canyon, they ran all but one rapid, which they lined but didn't iden-

tify.[72] While running rapids, Flavell would shout "Whoops! Aha!" to show his extreme enthusiasm for whitewater action.[73] Their trip ended in at Yuma, whereupon Montéz is lost to history. Flavell died in 1900 or 1901, apparently of typhoid fever.[74]

More Steamboats — 1901–1909

William Hiram Edwards's failure with the underpowered *Major Powell* foreshadowed subsequent steamboat traffic events on the rivers of Canyonlands. The next steamboat, the *Undine*, was launched in 1901 to accommodate the anticipated freight and tourist trade from the town of Green River downstream to the Confluence and upstream on the Colorado River to Cisco, Utah, which is forty-seven miles upstream from Moab. Its owner, Frank H. Summeril, wanted to build a hunting lodge at Valentine Bottom on the Green River and a health resort at Spanish Bottom. Being a sternwheeler, the *Undine* should have had a navigational edge over the propeller-driven boats, but the water was too low on the maiden voyage from Green River to Moab in November 1901; the *Undine* repeatedly hit sandbars. After a stay above Rapid 1, the forty-six to fifty-foot boat ascended the Colorado River to Moab in just three days.[75]

Whereas Summeril was more attracted to the concept of tourism, the freight traffic between Moab and the railroad at Green River fueled the enthusiasm of locals. Despite this enthusiasm, no one really trusted the sternwheeler's long-term prospects. Besides, a railroad connection could be made by wagon, going alongside the Colorado River to Cisco and using the ferry at Dewey, which was operational by 1896. The rapids in Professor Valley offered severe obstacles to upstream traffic, and Summeril engaged in vain attempts to blast rocks from the rapids.[76] His upstream endeavor proved fatal to the *Undine* in 1902 when she capsized in a riffle above Big Bend, about seven miles upstream from Moab.

Despite this failure, more bouts of wishful thinking followed. After all, the *Undine* did make one round trip between Green River and Moab, proving that regular traffic was a possibility. In 1904, the Green & Grand River and Moab Navigation Company built the *City of Moab*, a propeller-driven, fifty-foot boat powered by two marine twenty-five-horsepower gasoline engines. The launch on May 1, 1905, took an ominous turn when the boat was temporarily trapped against a piling of the railroad bridge at Green River.[77] Up-running on the spring floodwaters, the *City of Moab* could not surmount the riffle at The Slide, one mile above the Confluence on the Colorado River. The return back up the Green River was an exercise in extraction from sandbars, complete with broken propellers and long waits in mid-stream. Like the *Major Powell*, the boat was abandoned short of the town of Green River. The company did not quit. They rebuilt the *City of Moab,* installed steam engines, and re-named her the *Cliff Dweller*. Again, the attempt to reach Moab failed. The boat was shipped to the Great Salt Lake and became a tour boat.

Still, the enthusiasm for steamers did not waver. The next boat was the *Black Eagle*, smaller but driven by a propeller instead of the better-suited paddle-wheel. On its maiden voyage in 1907, the boat's boiler blew up at Valentine's Bottom. This effectively ended the attempts at large-scale tourist traffic using steamers in the Canyonlands region. However, river traffic for local freighting was just beginning. The *Black Eagle*'s pilot was Harry T. Yokey of Elgin, Utah, the small town across the river from the town of Green River. His insight into the natural world was quite profound and very colorful:[78]

> I have finally got around to replying to your two epistles of late date; so pull down yer vest; wipe off yer chinn & on following begin. Yes, we had a steamboat blow-up or blow-out some years back on lower River Green. I was builder, owner, commander, and pilot of craft (*Black Eagle*—of Elgin), J. A. Ross, fireman; E. J. Cook, engineer; when I did not have time to monkey with the engine & a cap, us four & no more. Fortunately, or unfortunately, we had a water tube boiler & flood of mud for water. A couple of tubes got plugged with mud; naturally blowed themselfs killing the fire. Thus we had no power other than arm-strong rowboat. Plenty of wild meat and scenery for desert [*sic*]. Naturally no rush about getting out. However, if it had been a flue-type boiler, we would be overdue to

this day; just another mysterious disappearance on high seas of time or destiny in vast port of missing men. However, later we were picked up by a boat bound for San Rafael. There I secured a team and wagon, thus landing my surviving men in their home ports of Elgin and Green River.

Yokey was also very attentive to the geologists for whom he later provided boat services at the Confluence while they were investigating a dam site in 1914. When asked the question: "Did you note evidences of river cutting down through solid rock to its present location?" Yokey responded:

> This is the biggest hunk of geological bologna on Earth. Some years back I was employed by U.S.R.S. to transport MEN, GRUB & TOOLS down into the canyon of Lower Green to search for Bedrock for proposed power dam site in many cases. The workers discovered the bed of river was on a vast mass of slide rock (like you seen on both sides of river in Cataract Canyon & many other places along the waterway across the desert). I have infested the Earth for over 80 years. Been awake most of the time, too. Noting what has been done & its affect on will be done. I am the man on the ground, seas and Rivers. Thus know what I am talking about. I have seen enough to know, old Mother Earth has had other fixed axis of rotation; other than she now has & two great unbalancing factors now accumulating & have been for some millions of years. It's absolutely necessary for Earth to Delouse & ReNew itself. New continents, new Islands, Seas, Rivers, & Sea. After a period of erratic unbalanced rotation, during which no part of Earth's surface has enough regular exposure to Sun to prevent freezing, yea Bo; be tougher than old Billy Bedamned, damn few survivors.
>
> Signed: Yours as she looks—Captain H. T. Yokey

Steam power was losing favor as a means of propulsion on the turbulent rivers. In 1904, Edwin T. Wolverton, whose family had a long history on the Green River in Canyonlands, built the *Wilmont*, a gasoline-powered, stern-wheel launch that was to supply a mine twenty-five miles downstream from Green River. Initially this boat was underpowered, but a renovation made her successful and encouraged more watercraft experimentation. This resulted in the *Paddy Ross,* built by Milton Oppenheimer; the *Utah,* built by Henry E. Blake; and the *Marguerite,* built by Thomas Wimmer; the Moab Garage Company, and a few other entrepreneurs. The freighting and passenger business thrived, especially those servicing the petroleum industry, until the Depression slowed the economies of the river communities.[79]

Bert Loper and Charles Russell — 1907 and 1914

Bert Loper is known as the "Grand Old Man of the Colorado River" after his long and illustrious river-running career.[80] In his folksy style, he described his feelings about the rivers that dominated his life:

> There have, without doubt, been better boatmen than I who have traversed that mighty Canyon, but there have never been any that have given the time to the study of it than I have, for as I said, I seem to be part of it, for I have lived in it, on it, with it, and in an instance or two, under it. I have after a day's work laid on the bank and listened to it—I have listened to the grinding of Mush Ice—I have listened to it when it hardly made enough sound to hear at all. Then there would come a time when there would be a gentle murmur, which told me that it had begun to awake. Then from that there would come a swish as though it were becoming peeved at something. Then from that there would be boils, swirls, eddies, and whirls, and then I knew that the river had started house cleaning.[81]

Loper began teaching himself about rivers and boats in 1893 while placer mining on the San Juan River, a career that was briefly interrupted by his military service in the Spanish American War. In 1899, while hard rock mining in Telluride, Colorado, he developed a friendship with mining engineer Charles Silver Russell.[82] Russell, who had progressive dementia resulting from a head injury, nevertheless was a courageous individual who made big river plans upon hearing Loper's tales. Russell's reasons for exploring the canyons of the Colorado were diverse: prospecting, adventure, publicity, and photography.

As mining migrants, Russell and Loper met Edwin Monett in Goldfield, Nevada. In September 1907, the three men started downstream in three boats from Green River, Utah, with cameras and prospecting tools. The sixteen-foot-long manufactured boats from Michigan were made of galvanized steel with fore and aft water-resistant compartments.[83] Monett flipped once in Cataract Canyon and again in Narrow Canyon, and Loper's camera shutter rusted shut from frequent dousing.[84] They ran every rapid though, making them the first documented river runners to successfully navigate Cataract Canyon.

In a move that some have considered an act of cowardice,[85] Loper stayed behind at Red Canyon (near Hite) waiting for a repaired shutter via mail. Russell and Monett leisurely prospected their way through Glen Canyon to Lee's Ferry, where the three had planned to rendezvous before entering Marble and Grand canyons. Loper's shutter arrived after a long delay of over two months, and he rowed on down to Lee's Ferry to discover that his companions had left without him. As Russell and Monett had a two-week head start, Loper knew that it was impossible to catch up, so he rowed and dragged his boat 180 miles upstream to Red Canyon. It took a month, through the mush ice of January, to reach his home. Loper had missed his first chance to see Grand Canyon from the river, and his loyalty to Russell was then questioned.[86]

Russell and Monett made it through the Grand Canyon but with few pictures of any quality,[87] little publicity, and no profit. After viewing the Kolb brothers' movie (see next section), Russell decided he could do a better job and convinced Loper to make another try. As Russell had the uncanny knack for saving money and Loper did not, it was Russell's trip financing that probably swayed Loper to go. In June 1914, Loper and Russell again launched steel boats from Green River.[88] Loper complained about Russell's unwillingness to help with camp chores, not understanding that Russell was reluctant to work hard for a trip that he had financed. Loper was very surprised and concerned about the extremely high water they observed in Cataract Canyon.[89] To counter their wild speed through the rapids, they decided to drag steel chains to slow their momentum. Unlike Loper, Russell avoided the mainstream, and while struggling for control in a violent eddy above Tilted Park his boat slammed into a rock. The force of the blow punctured the steel skin and the steel chain, coiled on the deck, fell into the river and snagged on the rocks below, carrying the boat to the bottom.[90]

They decided to abandon the trip and cached the remaining boat, with the idea of continuing downstream after securing a replacement boat for Russell. They walked upstream to Spanish Bottom, through the Land of Standing Rocks, and on to the Hite area where Loper had horses pastured. A fight between the two broke out in the course of this hike due to resentments, stress, and Russell's dementia. Wrote a reflective Loper:

I have spoken of the change in Russell, as we were coming down the river and I might have been about 75 yards in advance. I thought I heard someone talking so I eased down on my rowing and it was Russell and while I could not hear all that he said I could tell by what I did understand and by the tone of his voice that he was fighting someone. So in the P.M. I again heard him going over the same talk that he made in the forenoon and this time I could hear most of the words he used and the next day it was the same both in the morning and again in the evening. So in the course of time I memorized the entire talk and while my name was not mentioned I was positive that it was I whom he was fighting and our first night in Cataract we made camp on the left bank of the river and the campfire was between us and in the night I was awakened and Russell was sitting up in bed and going at it again and when one takes into consideration that we were 120 miles from a human being it was just a little creepy but the worst was still to come.[91]

They staggered into Hite with Loper periodically coaxing Russell back to reality.[92] The trip ended the friendship between these two men: to Russell, Loper was a cheapskate; to Loper, Russell was an imbecile. Loper decided to work for the U.S. Reclamation Service at the Confluence where investigations for a dam were underway. Russell decided to get another boat and new companions. The boat was the *Ross*

Wheeler, a metal boat built by Loper and commissioned by Russell.[93] Loper didn't want Russell to have the *Ross Wheeler*, so he entrusted the boat to a friend. Russell convinced this man that the *Ross Wheeler* was Russell's, which was true since Loper had not yet repaid Russell for the boat. With his new crew—Bill Reeder and August Tadje—Russell headed downstream to retrieve the boat cached in Cataract Canyon. At the Confluence, Loper recognized Russell in the *Ross Wheeler* and a fist fight ensued. Bystanders intervened, and Russell continued downstream with the boat.

The rest of the story is one of the most colorful Colorado River tales ever told around a campfire's glow. Before it was over, three more steel boats sank, Tadje and Reeder (and subsequent replacements Goddard Quist and Jake Jeffs) deserted, and Russell finally gave up 108 miles below Lee's Ferry where the *Ross Wheeler* lies at rest to this very day. In 1925, Russell died in a Phoenix asylum. In 1949, Loper suffered a fatal heart attack in Marble Canyon at the oars of his homemade wooden boat. That boat, too, lies at rest forty-one miles below Lee's Ferry, at the mouth of what is now called Bert's Canyon.

The Kolb Brothers — 1911

Ellsworth and Emery Kolb moved from Pennsylvania to the south rim of the Grand Canyon in 1902. They stumbled into the photography business and prospered on the tourist dollar. Not completely satisfied, they decided to make an adventure movie of a river trip that traced the route of the first Powell Expedition. What began as an enterprising gimmick resulted in one of the longest-running movies of all time as well as a pictorial book about the journey that is still in print.[94] In the process, they became the first photographers to match purposefully someone else's picture—the theme of this book. They launched in September 1911 without any prior whitewater experience, having only their courage and purpose to motivate them. They arrived at Needles, California, in January 1912, and Ellsworth would finish the journey to the Gulf of California on the crest of a flood in 1913.

The brothers left Green River, Wyoming, in two boats of Galloway design[95] with Powell's (1875) and Dellenbaugh's (1908) books as river guides.[96] The Kolbs never said or wrote that they matched Beaman's photographs from the second Powell Expedition, yet the evidence is undeniable.[97] For example, they climbed to the same perch at the Gates of Lodore and at Bowknot Bend. In the Maze District of Canyonlands, they climbed to the rim on October 25th and matched several of Beaman's photographs.

The next day they started running the rapids of Cataract Canyon. The water was low and they carefully looked at Rapid 5. Ellsworth ran it as Emery filmed.[98] They saw fresh footprints at the heads of rapids and expected to see a man and a dog at every turn in the river. After scouting Rapids 6 and 7, they were shocked to turn and see one of their boats, the *Edith*, running the river without them. The boat fortunately lodged in an eddy downstream. Now the Kolbs were having the adventures that they had hoped for.

After running Rapid 12, they finally saw the man they knew was ahead of them. A cleanly-shaven Charles "One-eyed" Smith greeted the brothers in a suit and tie—perhaps he smelled them coming. Smith was a trapper and prospector; the dog tracks were from wild coyotes he had trapped using fish heads.[99] Smith's boat was also of Galloway design but was old and waterlogged, forcing Smith to line it past every rapid. Although Smith declined the Kolbs's invitation to join them, he did pose for a photograph. Smith leisurely made his way through Cataract Canyon in 1911, but apparently he did not survive a 1913 attempt as his boat's wreckage was later discovered on an island in Glen Canyon.[100]

The Kolbs ran Mile Long Rapid, increasing their confidence for what they would face downstream in Grand Canyon. After careful inspection, they ran the first two Big Drops and camped on the right above Big Drop 3. To make their mark on the canyon, they climbed the talus slope a short distance above their camp and brushed their names on the cliff face using some paint left by the Stone Expedition. The river water had made Emery ill, so they stayed two days at this camp. Impressed with the dangerous whitewater

surrounding them, they photographed the boulders in both Big Drop 2 and 3. On Monday, October 30, Ellsworth ran Big Drop 3 while Emery photographed.

The Kolbs capped their Cataract Canyon experience a day later by running Dark Canyon Rapid, which had waves "more like breakers of the ocean."[101] This run gave them a lifetime of thrills and ended four days of running rapids without incident other than the ghost run of Rapid 7. Two miles upstream from Hite, they met Alonzo G. Turner, who had run Cataract Canyon solo in 1907 and painted his name in black on the right wall at Rapid 12. The Kolbs's experiences indicate that by the early twentieth century the rivers were starting to swell with adventurers and others trying to make a living. There were few other "firsts" to be achieved.

There is one notable postscript: Ellsworth Kolb became famous after his book was published in 1914. He later befriended Julius Stone and Bert Loper, with whom he would explore the Gunnison and Colorado rivers on different trips, taking more photographs and making more motion pictures.[102]

FROM DAM BUILDING
TO COMMERCIAL RIVER RUNNING

The U.S. Geological Survey — 1914 and 1921

Over a quarter of the United States is desert, and much of that area is within the Colorado River drainage. Those who would harness its waters for irrigation, power, and flood control looked throughout its canyons for dam sites. In 1914, the U.S. Reclamation Service focused on a site just below the Confluence. Accompanied by a U.S. Geological Survey hydraulic engineer named Eugene C. LaRue, the Reclamation Service built a drill rig on a wood platform near the mouth of the San Rafael River and floated it downstream to a point one-half mile below the Confluence. They drilled holes 100–125-feet deep only to find what was believed to be talus rolled into the river from the local cliffs; the engineers estimated they still had another seventy-five feet to bedrock. This deep alluvial fill eliminated the Confluence dam site from further consideration. While working on the fourth drill hole, flotsam arrived from a summer storm upstream, snagging the platform and its anchoring cables; it eventually failed and listed from the pressure of the current against the tangled mass.

LaRue was a brilliant engineer, a tenacious advocate for dams, a pioneer in panoramic photography, and an arrogant man who rubbed his fellow river runners the wrong way. Like other river runners before him, bouts of poor health—in LaRue's case, stomach ulcers—made him intolerant and grumpy. Raymond C. Moore, the geologist on the 1923 expedition through Grand Canyon, described LaRue as "sort of an ass."[103] LaRue designed a dam system for the Green and Colorado rivers that would have eliminated nearly every inch of free-flowing water, but his system would also have minimized evaporation in the desert climate.[104] LaRue may have taken more photographs—mostly in a panoramic format—of the Green and Colorado rivers than anyone besides Raymond Cogswell, and he illustrated his reports liberally with them. He was forced to resign from the U.S. Geological Survey in 1927 for his zealous advocacy of the Lee's Ferry dam site over the Black Canyon site which was downstream of Grand Canyon.[105]

Reports of high, vertical walls in Cataract Canyon invited further inspection by dam builders. Funded jointly by the federal government and Southern California Edison Power Company, the U.S. Geological Survey launched an expedition in early September 1921 to investigate the potential for dam sites, particularly in the canyons above the Dirty Devil River. The trip leader was William Chenoweth, a topographic engineer; Sidney Paige was the geologist and LaRue the hydraulic engineer.[106] Ellsworth Kolb headed the boating crew which also included Leigh Lint, who later became a notable boatman in his own right. Emery Kolb dubiously attached himself to the trip as a guest photographer and rowed the *Edith*, the boat he used during the 1911 trip with his elder brother. The Kolbs, Paige, and LaRue all carried cameras, which would make this trip the most photographed in the history of Cataract Canyon.

They reached the Confluence on September 15, 1921 and began their survey to produce an accurate map and longitudinal profile of the river. The dis-

charge was less than 10,000 ft³/s, and many rocks were exposed in the rapids. Ellsworth and Emery ran the boats through the rapids, sometimes fully loaded and sometimes empty. They moved through the canyon quickly, reaching the Dark Canyon dam site on September 27. Ellsworth ran the *L.A.* into a sieve of rocks in Dark Canyon Rapid, requiring a rescue that took the better part of two days. Paige's film was damaged in the wreck, but LaRue had his packaged in watertight jars.[107]

Fortunately for the river environment, nothing came of the effort to build dams in Cataract Canyon. LaRue proposed dam sites near Dark Canyon and near Mille Crag Bend. Paige realized that the underlying substrate—the salt-filled Paradox Formation—was less than satisfactory for dam safety. Chenoweth's surveying yielded reservoir capacities, but his most notable achievement was a longitudinal-profile map of the Colorado River, which today still remains the only reasonably accurate profile.[108] Another lasting contribution from the 1921 U.S. Geological Survey Expedition was the naming of Cataract's topographic features and the systematic numbering of its low water rapids, a system that persists to this day.

Harold Leich — 1933

Completely inexperienced men were now making their way into Cataract Canyon, seeking not fortune but adventure. Foremost among these was Harold Leich, who in 1933 had a near-death experience while having the thrill of his lifetime. Leich was a young, mobile easterner who was inspired by Clyde Eddy's adventures (see below). Construction of Boulder (later Hoover) Dam focused the nation's attention on what was perceived as the wild, out-of-control Colorado River. Unlike most would-be river runners, Leich wasn't interested in running the Green River. He was one of the first to challenge the Colorado River from its headwaters to the Gulf of California.[109]

Leich bought a folding rubber kayak and shipped it to Grand Lake, Colorado. After testing the *Rob Roy* on the natural lake, he plunged into the wild Colorado River and made it through notorious Gore Canyon. Without too much fanfare, he ran the lesser rapids and riffles down to Grand Junction. Here he built a cataract boat named the *Dirty Devil* using lumber purchased from the local store; he thought the boat had "a coffin-like appearance." Unfortunately his boat would not reach the mouth of the river it was named for, and Leich would not reach his ultimate destination: the Colorado River delta.

Westwater Canyon, downstream from Grand Junction, had first been run by Elmer Kane (boatman for the Stanton and Best expeditions) and two companions in 1888, next by Drs. Babcock and Miller (dentists from Glenwood Springs) in 1897, and then by Bert Loper and Ellsworth Kolb in 1916. Leich became the fourth, running rapids that he described as far worse than those upstream. He ran all the rapids in one day, specifically noting what are now known as Funnel Falls and Skull rapids. His confidence growing, he rowed to Moab where he repaired and painted the *Dirty Devil*. On August 24, he pushed off and headed down Meander Canyon toward the Confluence, complaining in his journal about the "garish billboards and hot dog stands." Three days later, he camped at Rapid 1.

Leich had the 1921 map and river profile of Cataract Canyon to guide him, but still the Canyon eventually got the best of Leich. The water was low, he hit rocks, and because he thought he couldn't portage or efficiently line his 400-pound boat by himself, he ran everything. He was thrown out of the boat in one rapid (probably in Mile Long Rapid), and a large recirculating hole held his boat for a time before breaking free. He ran Big Drop 2, hitting more rocks, ran the left chute at Big Drop 3, and in the spirit of fun and adventure he also took time for photographs.

His boating career ended in a rapid just below Big Drop 3. Night was falling, but Leich wanted to go a little further before camping. While his attention was focused downstream deciding what his route would be, the *Dirty Devil* crashed into a rock and pirouetted onto a second. Pinned in the strong current, Leich broke his oars trying to pry his boat from the river's grasp. In less than a half hour, he lost his boat and all his food but saved his rubberized packsack that contained much needed survival items like matches and a revolver. He swam for shore but was swept into the rapid and into a hole that pulled him down and snatched his sack from his grip. Saved by his life-jacket, but exhausted from the swim, he pulled himself into an eddy on the right to find his floating pack.

His hiking career began immediately upon reaching shore. After contemplating his choices, he decided to head downstream for Hite and safety. Some of his food and outfit was floating downstream in eddies; he retrieved as much as he could. Partly hiking and swimming when cliffs limited overland travel, he reached Clearwater Canyon and found what he thought were fresh footprints, remains of a campfire, and damaged movie film. This gave him hope that someone was ahead that could help him. However, with further investigation, he noted a thin coat of rust on one of the milk cans, dashing his hopes of rescue. At Dark Canyon Rapid, water filled the canyon wall to wall, and he had to swim the lower half of the rapid—where water flowed under an overhanging cliff—to get downstream. He also had to swim much of the length of Narrow Canyon to avoid the sheer cliffs rising from the water.

Leich finally staggered into Hite three and a half days after his boat sank, only to find no one there. Exhausted, lame, and nearly out of food, he realized his next move was a forty-five-mile hike to Hanksville. He fired his revolver at everything that moved but could not augment his meager rations. He hiked back upstream to North Wash and prepared for a dry overland hike. Luckily, twenty miles from the river, he met three prospectors in the middle of the night who fed him and bolstered his flagging spirits.

The prospectors were heading down the Colorado, in the opposite direction from civilization. Leich stubbornly walked on, as he described it, "to Hanksville or Hell." Out of water at sunset, he met a truck driver named Ekker, who gave him drinking water and the news that he was only nine miles from town. He reached Hanksville before midnight. Harold Leich's body was a mass of blisters, bruises, and sore muscles, but he was alive. He had wrecked his boat and hiked out of the unforgiving Cataract Canyon. In doing so, he had two things in common with the legendary Bert Loper: both had navigated Westwater Canyon and both had walked out of Cataract Canyon after a boat wreck.

OTHER NOTABLE RIVER RUNNERS

Clyde Eddy had a brief river-running career notable for its ineptitude and grandiosity. In 1927 he discarded the sum of all prior river-running knowledge and decided to run on high water with equipment and techniques similar to Powell's and thus conquer "The World's Most Dangerous River."[110] Eddy based this claim for the Colorado on what he perceived to be a gruesome history of boat-related fatalities in Cataract and Marble canyons. For his crew, he sought a dozen "pink-wristed collegiates" that he would need to portage his boats. He had his three boats built to Powell's design and named them after the first explorer of the Colorado Plateau, the *Coronado*; the first Colorado River explorer, the *Powell*; and the first published Colorado River historian, the *Dellenbaugh*. Eddy, twelve men, one brown-eyed dog, and a fuzzy bear cub survived this high-water run through Cataract Canyon largely by avoiding all of its rapids: those "pink-wristed collegiates" carried or lined the boats around them.[111] They continued on through Grand Canyon on falling water, exiting the river at Needles.

The U.S. Geological Survey expeditions in the Colorado River drainage trained a guild of river boatmen who were occasionally paid to guide others through the canyons. In October 1927, Hollywood's Pathé-Bray Company decided to make an adventure epic centered on the dangers of river running.[112] They hired Eugene C. LaRue, newly retired from the Geological Survey, to be the trip leader. They had six boats built in the Galloway style and painted white to show up better on film against the muddy water. They spent a cold November lining and running the rapids through Cataract Canyon with little incident other than generating some contrived publicity about being lost in the canyons.

Another notable river trip involved a honeymoon. Bessie Hyde became the first woman to traverse Cataract Canyon in 1928 with her newly wedded husband, Glen. The couple launched their fateful trip from Green River, Utah, on October 20 after constructing a wooden scow. A scow is a box-like craft maneuvered with long and heavy, counter-balanced, oar-like sweeps that are mounted to the bow and stern; the boatman stands mid-ship angling the boat down the current and around obstacles. The couple was last seen alive at Hermit Rapid in the Grand Canyon. After an airplane search, the scow was found snagged in an eddy in western Grand Canyon with no explanation for the disappearance of the couple. To this day, the mystery surrounding the case of the missing honeymoon couple is a popular and outstanding river tale.[113]

Harold Leich knew he was following a group of river runners through Cataract Canyon. Little did he know that he was following a light-hearted group of gritty Utahns who were to become staples in the evolving trade of river tourism. Bus Hatch and other members of his extended family and friends had been messing around in boats for many years on the Green River above their home in Vernal, Utah. They decided it was time to tackle the rest of the Green and the Colorado. With financing provided by Dr. Russell Frazier, a physician from the mining town of Bingham, Utah, they launched from Ouray, Utah, on July 24, 1933.[114] For the Hatch family, this was the beginning of their river outfitting business. This business became firmly established by 1953 during the Sierra Club's campaign to prevent two proposed dams in Dinosaur National Monument from ever leaving the proposal stage.

The year 1938 proved pivotal to river running on the Colorado River. Norman D. Nevills, from Mexican Hat, Utah, began his commercial river-running career by taking two women botanists from the University of Michigan from Green River, Utah, to Hoover Dam.[115] Dr. Elzada Clover and her graduate student, Lois Jotter, wanted to conduct a botanical survey of the Colorado Plateau. Clover and Jotter became the second and third women to pass through Cataract Canyon, following Bessie Hyde. The publicity from this trip basically announced to the world that river-running was now safe enough for women, a concept now laughable, considering the diversity found within the river running community today.

Nevills returned to Cataract Canyon in 1940 and 1945.[116]

Don Harris began his long and illustrious river career on Nevills's 1938 trip, but found the style of the imperious Nevills disagreeable. Nevills overdramatized the river's dangers to boost his passenger's confidence in his ability and judgment. Because of the high water, Nevills mostly made his passengers hike around the more difficult rapids. After arriving at Lee's Ferry, Harris informed Nevills that he would not continue with him through the Grand Canyon. Harris continued his whitewater career with others, eventually forming his own company. In 1939, Harris and Bert Loper tackled their first Grand Canyon trip; Loper finally fulfilled his life-long dream at age seventy. Said Loper, ". . . it would be hard to conceive a more delightful trip anywhere . . ."[117]

Haldane "Buzz" Holmstrom achieved what Harold Leich first attempted: a solo trip through the canyons of the Colorado River. Holmstrom built a wooden boat of a design superior to any that had floated the Colorado River previously and passed solo through Cataract Canyon in the fall of 1937.[118] Holmstrom wisely portaged his four-hundred-pound boat around Big Drop 3, avoiding Leich's arduous hiking adventure out of the canyon. Holmstrom returned the following year with his wooden boat and Amos Burg, who rowed the first inflatable boat through Cataract Canyon, lining the more formidable rapids.[119] On this 1938 trip, Holmstrom ran every rapid from Wyoming to Lake Mead reservoir, another first. Holmstrom was the second person to run all the rapids of Cataract Canyon, but he was the first to do so in a solo boat and without incident, a remarkable feat.

A group of three kayakers from France tackled the Green and Colorado rivers in the fall of 1938.[120] Geneviève de Colmont became the first woman to operate a boat under her own power through Cataract Canyon, as well as the fourth woman to make the trip. Trips for the whitewater challenge or pure pleasure had replaced the trips made solely for exploration or exploitative motives.

The commercial tourist river industry along the Colorado River system received its start in the 1850s with the advent of steamboats operating where Arizona, Nevada, and California share boundaries with the river, and in Mexico. Boats for hire, though few at first, appeared in the upper basin by the 1890s. Nathaniel Galloway, in 1909, was the first person to receive compensation (from Julius Stone) for a chartered adventure vacation. David Dexter Rust, who ran Glen Canyon in 1917, was probably the first to derive a fare for outfitter services similar to those available today. Nevills brought commercial whitewater trips to the attention of the American elite via the national press, and later Georgie Clark made river running accessible to the masses via national television.

In 1945, Clark began her river career swimming long reaches of the Colorado River. In the fall of 1947, Clark ran Cataract Canyon with Harry Aleson in a small war-surplus neoprene boat that was twelve-feet long and originally designed for military reconnaissance, demolition, and invasion.[121] Clark quickly realized that her marketing future lay in utilizing boats made from massive neoprene bridge pontoons. These inflatable pontoons were originally designed to be tied together from shore to shore, topped with a rigid decking, and thus serve as a temporary floating bridge during a national emergency or military conflict. She powered such a pontoon with a small outboard motor by 1953, and by 1955 she was lashing three pontoons side-by-side to engage the biggest standing waves she could find. In 1957, she ran the spring flood of 90,000 ft³/s through Cataract Canyon with her "big rig," completing the once-unthinkable high-water trip with a *yahoo!* attitude. She promoted her "share the expense" trips by traveling around the country showing her homemade movies to attentive crowds, and even appeared as a guest on various television shows. As a result, Georgie Clark opened the river to the general public who also longed to experience the world's most exciting river.

In the 1950s, most people who wished to run the rivers needed a river guide—other than a book such as Powell's account. To fill that void, a daring canoeist from central Utah—Leslie Jones—made the first river guide, a scroll map with historical notes and the longitudinal profile from the 1921 U.S. Geological Survey Expedition.[122] Jones preferred to travel alone in his

Figure 2-1. Upstream from Trin Alcove (Green River mile 91.2) August 18, 1968. Two pioneers of repeat photography on the Green and Colorado rivers, Gene Shoemaker (left) and Hal Stephens, are at work just upstream from Trin Alcove. Stephens is poised behind the medium-format camera they used to record the rivers in the summer of 1968. (Stephens DO1-3, Stake 3905)

decked canoe with outriggers for stability. He earned the nickname "Buckethead" Jones because he installed a movie camera in a paint bucket that he wore on his head and activated with a bulb he pressed between his teeth. During the many years after Jones made his map, other river guides to Cataract Canyon were published and Jones's map has been largely forgotten.[123]

By the 1960s, river running was routine. Trips with a scientific mission were also common, but one in particular is notable with respect to our repeat photography. In 1968, Eugene Shoemaker and Hal Stephens of the U.S. Geological Society launched a trip at Green River, Wyoming, to commemorate the 1869 Powell Expedition. Their goal was to match as many photographs as possible that had been taken by E. O. Beaman during the second Powell Expedition.[124] Beaman's photos were matched again for this book during the 1990s.

In 1964, as the waters were rising behind the newly completed Glen Canyon Dam and just before the establishment of Canyonlands National Park, William

Somerville from Denver up-ran the rapids of Cataract Canyon in a jet boat. These days, up-runs are not permitted in Cataract Canyon because of the danger of collisions with downstream traffic. Jet boats are now used daily in the warm-weather season for touring and shuttling canoeists back to Moab from the Confluence.

"THE GRAVEYARD OF THE COLORADO"

In 1933, when Harold Leich pulled himself from the river downstream of Narrow Canyon, at least 105 people had traveled through Cataract Canyon (Table 2-2). This number is probably lower than the actual numbers because an unknown number of prospectors who left no record of their journeys also passed downstream en route to the placer deposits of Glen Canyon. We have no way of knowing how many of these prospectors perished on their journeys, but a mythology developed concerning rampant death among those who dared traverse the Colorado River, particularly in Cataract Canyon. This myth was begun by none other than John Wesley Powell, who used it as a means of personal aggrandizement.[125] Powell wanted to accentuate his own feats by claiming that others who followed had perished. The image of Cataract Canyon as "the graveyard of the Colorado" was perpetuated by the people of Green River, Utah,[126] who also thought "The Auger" on the Green River, a minor riffle, was extremely dangerous.

How dangerous is the Colorado River, particularly in Canyonlands National Park? Since the Park's creation in 1964, fourteen people have died in Cataract Canyon;[127] before that, only twelve deaths have been claimed but not fully verified.[128] In the decade of 1990 through 2000, seven people died in Cataract Canyon, and four of these were in the high water of 1993. During the same period, only two deaths resulted from boating accidents in the dam-regulated Colorado River through Grand Canyon.[129] Most injuries and fatalities in recent years have been caused by excessive drinking combined with poor judgment; nothing illustrates this more than the numerous "wrong turns" (right versus left) at the Confluence during the Friendship Cruises (see Chapter 6).

TABLE 2-2. The first 105 known river runners through Cataract Canyon, 1836–1933.

No.	Name	Year	Expedition
1	Denis Julien	1836	Solo
2	George Bradley	1869	Powell
3	William Dunn	1869	Powell
4	Andy Hall	1869	Powell
5	Billy Hawkins	1869	Powell
6	Oramel Howland	1869	Powell
7	Seneca Howland	1869	Powell
8	John Wesley Powell	1869	Powell
9	Walter Powell	1869	Powell
10	John Colton Sumner	1869	Powell
11	E.O. Beaman	1871	Powell
12	Francis Marian Bishop	1871	Powell
13	Frederick S. Dellenbaugh	1871	Powell
14	Andrew Hatten	1871	Powell
15	John K. Hillers	1871	Powell
16	Stephen Vandiver Jones	1871	Powell
17	Clement Powell	1871	Powell
18	John F. Steward	1871	Powell
19	Almon Harris Thompson	1871	Powell
20	Frank Mason Brown	1889	DCC&PRR
21	William H. Bush	1889	DCC&PRR
22	Edward Coe	1889	DCC&PRR
23	George W. Gibson	1889	DCC&PRR
24	Peter M. Hansbrough	1889	DCC&PRR
25	G.E. Howard	1889	DCC&PRR
26	J.N. Hughes	1889	DCC&PRR
27	John Hislop	1889	DCC&PRR
28	Franklin Asa Nims	1889	DCC&PRR
29	C.W. Potter	1889	DCC&PRR
30	Ethan A. Reynolds	1889	DCC&PRR
31	Henry C. Richards	1889	DCC&PRR
32	Thomas P. Rigney	1889	DCC&PRR
33	Robert Brewster Stanton	1889	DCC&PRR
34	George A. Sutherland	1889	DCC&PRR
35	E.W. Terry	1889	DCC&PRR
36	James D. Best (DCCMIC)	1891	Best
37	William Hiram Edwards	1891	Best
38	Elmer Kane	1891	Best
39	John Jacobs	1891	Best
40	Luther Jewell	1891	Best
41	Harry McDonald	1891	Best
42	James A. McCormick	1891	Best
44	Friend G. Faatz	1892	Solo
43	George M. Wright	1892	Solo
44	Nathaniel Galloway	1894	Solo
45	George Flavell	1896	Flavell
46	Ramon Montéz	1896	Flavell
47	William Richmond	1896	Richmond-Galloway
48	Parley Galloway	1904	Solo
49	Louis M. Chaffin	1905	Solo
50	Alonzo G. Turner	1905?	Solo
51	Albert Loper	1907	Russell-Monett
52	Edwin Monett	1907	Russell-Monett

Table 2-2. The first 105 known river runners through Cataract Canyon, 1836-1933.

No.	Name	Year	Expedition
53	Charles Silver Russell	1907	Russell-Monett
54	Raymond C. Cogswell	1909	Stone
55	Seymour Silvester Dubendorff	1909	Stone
56	Charles C. Sharpe	1909	Stone
57	Julius F. Stone	1909	Stone
58	J.H. Hummel	1910	Solo
59	Ellsworth Kolb	1911	Kolb
60	Emery Kolb	1911	Kolb
61	Charles Smith	1911	Solo
62	August Tadje	1914	Tadje-Russell
63	William R. Chenoweth	1921	USGS
64	John Clogston	1921	USGS
65	Eugene C. LaRue	1921	USGS
66	Leigh Lint	1921	USGS
67	Sidney Paige	1921	USGS
68	Henry Rauch	1921	USGS
69	Frank Stoudt	1921	USGS
70	Harry Tasker	1921	USGS
71	Frank "Bunny" Barnes	1921	Solo
72	W. Gordon Adger	1927	Eddy
73	Robert Bartl	1927	Eddy
74	Frank Blackwell (Bradley)	1927	Eddy
75	Vincent F. Callaway	1927	Eddy
76	Vincent F. Carey	1927	Eddy
77	Clyde Eddy	1927	Eddy
78	Frederick L. Felton	1927	Eddy
79	Edward L. Holt	1927	Eddy
80	John H. Marshall	1927	Eddy
81	The hobo McGregory	1927	Eddy
82	O.E. Seager	1927	Eddy
83	Robert H. Weatherhead	1927	Eddy
84	Devergne Barber	1927	Pathé-Bray
85	Owen Clark	1927	Pathé-Bray
86	Dean Dailey	1927	Pathé-Bray
87	Frank B. Dodge	1927	Pathé-Bray
88	Pat Gannon	1927	Pathé-Bray
89	Vernon T. Herrick	1927	Pathé-Bray
90	Glen Kerschner	1927	Pathé-Bray
91	Constantine Rodin	1927	Pathé-Bray
92	Nick Samoff	1927	Pathé-Bray
93	Leigh Smith	1927	Pathé-Bray
94	John Shubert	1927	Pathé-Bray
95	Valentine Woodbury	1927	Pathé-Bray
96	Bessie Hyde	1928	Hyde
97	Glen Hyde	1928	Hyde
98	Bill Fahrni	1933	Hatch-Frazier
99	Russell Frazier	1933	Hatch-Frazier
100	Alton Hatch	1933	Hatch-Frazier
101	Robert Rafael Hatch	1933	Hatch-Frazier
102	Tom Hatch	1933	Hatch-Frazier
103	Frank Swain	1933	Hatch-Frazier
104	Royce Mowry	1933	Hatch-Frazier
105	Harold Leich	1933	Leich

Many deaths occur away from the river. Although three members of the Brown-Stanton Expedition perished in Grand Canyon in 1889, the first known fatality in Cataract Canyon occurred in 1908,[130] by which time fifty-three river runners are known to have passed through its supposedly treacherous waters. The presence of wrecked boats in the canyon, particularly between 1909 and 1913, perpetuated Powell's myth, however, leading to several reports of death by supposition instead of body retrieval. Harold Leich's experience, in particular, indicates that a boat wreck doesn't necessarily mean death in Canyonlands. Despite the recent spate of fatal boating accidents, historically Cataract Canyon has been safer than Grand Canyon.[131]

More so than most other whitewater reaches on the Colorado Plateau, Cataract Canyon challenges boaters because of its highly variable rapids. At low water, rock gardens abound; at flood stage, frightful waves come from every direction. Despite these challenges, early explorers and the pioneers of commercial river running laid the groundwork for today's whitewater industry, encouraging near-constant visitation during most months of the year. That access also has provided knowledge of the secrets and treasures of Cataract Canyon: its geology and biology.

REPEAT PHOTOGRAPHY IN CANYON COUNTRY

The history of Canyon Country is also a history of landscape photography in the western United States. John C. Frémont pioneered photography on the Colorado Plateau during his 1853-1854 expedition, although the daguerreotypes exposed by Frederick von Eggloffstein were mostly destroyed in a fire at the Frémont residence.[132] Major Powell and his contemporaries pioneered the use of the camera as a tool for scientific documentation in 1871. In 1911, the Kolb brothers began the long-standing practice of repeat photography in the region, although their motive was profit, not science. Stephens and Shoemaker were the first of many to match photographs for scientific interpretation of landscape change. As many have shown, matching photos, especially the really old ones, allows examination of changes in vegetation and the environment that have occurred through time at a given location.[133] In and near our study area, repeat photography has been used for both art and science.[134]

Repeat photography is not for the faint of heart: finding the exact spot and replicating the exact height from which a photograph has been taken can take hours, days, or even years unless a prominent landmark just happens to appear in the original. We have matched 329 photos above, within, and below Cataract Canyon. We selected thirty-seven sets of repeat photographs for these for this book, choosing those that we felt best represented facets of the river channel, rapids, beaches, vegetation, and hillslopes discussed in the text. The changes, and lack thereof, will be discussed throughout this book.

Notes

1. John Wesley Powell, *The Exploration of the Colorado River and Its Tributaries* (New York: Dover Publications, 1961), 216.

2. Julius Stone, *Canyon Country, The Romance of a Drop of Water and A Grain of Sand* (New York: G.P. Putnam's Sons, 1932), 72.

3. *The Domínguez-Escalante Journal: Their Expedition Through Colorado, Utah, Arizona, and New Mexico in 1776*, ed. T.J. Warner, trans. Fray Angelico Chavez (Salt Lake City: University of Utah Press, 1995).

4. James Knipmeyer, "The Old Trappers' Trail through Eastern Utah," *Canyon Legacy* 9 (1991): 10.

5. An overview of the early trappers is given in R.G. Cleland, *This Reckless Breed of Men, the Trappers and Fur Traders of the Southwest* (New York: Alfred A. Knopf, 1952).

6. Roy Webb, *If We Had a Boat: Green River Explorers, Adventurers and Runners* (Salt Lake City: University of Utah Press, 1986), 21.

7. J.D. Smith, *The Southwest Expedition of Jedediah S. Smith, His Personal Account of the Journey to California, 1826–1827*, ed. G.R. Brooks (Lincoln: University of Nebraska Press, 1977).

8. Cleland, *This Reckless Breed of Men*, opp. 180, 258–260.

9. James Knipmeyer, "The Denis Julien Inscriptions," *Utah Historical Quarterly* 64 (1996): 52–69. Also see Doug Carithers, "Serendipity: The Denis Julien Inscriptions of Cataract Canyon," *Canyon Legacy* 32 (1998): 24–26. Robert Brewster Stanton discovered the Cove Canyon

inscription in 1889, the Best Expedition (with several Brown-Stanton crew members) discovered the Hell Roaring Canyon inscription in 1891, and William H. Edwards (veteran of both Brown-Stanton and Best expeditions) likely discovered the others.

10. Both Denis Julien inscriptions in Cataract Canyon—at Hell Roaring and Cove canyons—apparently were discovered by members of the Best Expedition in 1891. John McCormick, the expedition's photographer, left a tantalizing note in his diary: "We learned that members of a former Expedition [Brown-Stanton] had found another inscription by the same man in Marble Canyon, just below Lees Ferry, Arizona." J.A. McCormick, *Colorado Grand Cañon Mining and Improvement Company Expedition of 1891* (Golden, Colorado: Colorado School of Mines, unpublished manuscript, 1891).

11. C.B. Hunt, *Geology of the Henry Mountains, Utah, As Recorded in the Notebooks of G. K. Gilbert 1875–76* (Boulder, Colorado: Geological Society of America Memoir 167, 1988), 27.

12. Letter, John C. Sumner to Frederick S. Dellenbaugh, February 15, 1904; Marston Collection, Huntington Library, San Marino, California. See John Weisheit, "John C. Sumner," *The Confluence* 3 (1996): 9.

13. C.G. Crampton, *Standing Up Country, the Canyon Lands of Utah and Arizona* (New York: Alfred A. Knopf, 1965), 56.

14. R.A. Firmage, *A History of Grand County* (Salt Lake City: Utah State Historical Society, 1996), 69.

15. A closer examination of diaries have led some historians to conclude that Frémont crossed the Green River near the mouth of the San Rafael River; see J.H. Knipmeyer, *Butch Cassidy Was Here, Historic Inscriptions of the Colorado Plateau* (Salt Lake City: University of Utah Press, 2002), 23.

16. Andrew Rolle, *John Charles Frémont, Character as Destiny* (Norman: University of Oklahoma Press, 1991).

17. F.A. Barnes, *Hiking the Historic Route of the 1958 Macomb Expedition* (Moab, Utah: Canyon Country Publications, 1989).

18. G.K. Gilbert, *Report on the Geology of the Henry Mountains* (Washington, D.C.: U.S. Government Printing Office, U.S. Geographical and Geological Survey of the Rocky Mountain Region, 1880).

19. W.C. Darrah, *Powell of the Colorado* (Princeton, New Jersey: Princeton University Press, 1951).

20. F.S. Dellenbaugh, *A Canyon Voyage: The Narrative of the Second Powell Expedition* (New York: Putnam, 1908); Darrah, *Powell of the Colorado*; Wallace Stegner, *Beyond the Hundredth Meridian, John Wesley Powell and the Second Opening of the West* (Boston: Houghton Mifflin Company, 1953); Donald Worster, *A River Running West, the Life of John Wesley Powell* (New York: Oxford University Press, 2001). Note the discussion by Martin J. Anderson of Dellenbaugh's devotion to Powell in R.B. Stanton, *Colorado River Controversies* (Boulder City, Nevada: Westwater Books, 1987), 253–259.

21. Stanton, *Colorado River Controversies*, 214–232.

22. *Ibid.*, 212.

23. John Wesley Powell, *The Exploration of the Colorado River of the West* (Washington, D.C.: U.S. Government Printing Office, 1875); the first questioning of Powell's account was Stanton, *Colorado River Controversies*, 97–137. Also compare the diary entries from the 1869 trip with Powell's account in John Cooley, *The Great Unknown* (Flagstaff, Arizona: Northland Publishing, 1988).

24. Worster, *A River Flowing West*, 569–572.

25. References to Powell's military forbearance and his boatmen's irreverence towards him in 1869 are scattered throughout the chronologically ordered diary entries given in Cooley, *The Great Unknown*. Also see Billy Hawkins and Jack Sumner's accounts in Stanton, *Colorado River Controversies*, 138–213.

26. Cooley, *The Great Unknown*, 30.

27. There is confusion concerning these four's activities after parting with the main body of the first Powell expedition. Darrah, *Powell of the Colorado*, 144, states that Sumner and Bradley left the river at Fort Yuma (as it was then known). Sumner's own accounts (in Stanton, *Colorado River Controversies*, 210–211; Don Lago, "Jack Sumner Looks Back," *Boatman's Quarterly Review* 15 (2002): 40–41), the only one written in first person, is accepted here.

28. *Ibid.*, 107.

29. *Ibid.*, 116.

30. John Weisheit, "Where the Hell Am I," *The Confluence* 2 (1995): 13–15.

31. Powell, *Exploration of the Colorado River*.

32. Bradley diary entry for July 22, 1869. See Cooley, *The Great Unknown*, 117. See also W.C. Darrah, "Geology Notes of John Wesley Powell," *Utah Historical Quarterly* 19 (1947): 134–139.

33. *Ibid.*, 127–130. Also see Stanton, *Colorado River Controversies*, 200–201. Some river guides believe this incident occurred at Rapid 24 and call that rapid "Powell's Pocket Watch."

34. Cooley, *The Great Unknown*, 127–130.

35. Stanton, *Colorado River Controversies*, 201–202.

36. W.P. Larsen, "'The Letter,' or Were the Powell Men Really Killed by Indians?" *Canyon Legacy* 17 (1993): 12–19. For information on the Mountain Meadows massacre, see Juanita Brooks, *John Doyle Lee: Zealot—Pioneer Builder—Scapegoat* (Glendale, California: Arthur H. Clark, 1962).

37. As with the first expedition, they kept diaries that tell us the details of the second expedition, which Powell never discussed in print. Dellenbaugh, *A Canyon Voyage*, might be considered the "official history" of this expedition.

38. H.G. Stephens and E.M. Shoemaker, *In the Footsteps of John Wesley Powell: An Album of Comparative Photographs of the Green and Colorado Rivers, 1871–72 and 1968* (Boulder, Colorado: Johnson Books, 1987).

39. R.B. Stanton, *Down the Colorado*, ed. D.L. Smith (Lincoln: University of Nebraska Press, 1965), 126.

40. P.T. Reilly, "How Deadly Is Big Red?" *Utah Historical Quarterly* 37 (1969): 244–260.

41. Brown Betty Rapid was named by river historian Otis Reed Marston; see Western River Guides Association newsletter, Aleson Collection, Utah Historical Society, Salt Lake City.

42. D.L. Smith and C.G. Crampton, *The Colorado River Survey: Robert B. Stanton and the Denver, Colorado Canyon and Pacific Railroad* (Salt Lake City, Utah: Howe Brothers, 1987).

43. Stanton, *Down the Colorado*, 67.

44. P.T. Reilly, *Lee's Ferry: From Mormon Crossing to National Park*, ed. by R.H. Webb (Logan: Utah State University Press, 1999), 156–186, 226–233.

45. Stanton's narrative account is published in Stanton, *Down the Colorado*; his research on James White and the Powell Expedition is published in Stanton, *Colorado River Controversies*; and his diary is published as Smith and Crampton, *The Colorado River Survey*.

46. R.E. Lingenfelter, *Steamboats on the Colorado River* (Tucson: University of Arizona Press, 1978), 109.

47. James Knipmeyer, "The *Major Powell* Inscriptions," *The Confluence* 4 (1997): 8–10.

48. Grand Junction, Colorado, *The Colorado Sun*, July 3, 1892, "Steam Boating in Colorado; The Grand Cañon Entered by a Steamer; A Regular Line Inaugurated; The Story of the Event."

49. Robert Sorgenfrei, "'A Fortune Awaits Enterprise Here:' The Best Mining Expedition to the Grand Canyon in 1891," *Journal of the Southwest* 40 (1998): 437–462.

50. Although Sorgenfrei, "The Best Mining Expedition," 448, asserts that runoff was high, McCormick's photographs indicate the discharge was a little less than 10,000 ft³/s, which constitutes low water in Cataract Canyon.

51. W.H. Edwards, "Diary of the Best Expedition–1891," entry for September 21, 1891, New York Public Library, New York City.

52. Sorgenfrei, "The Best Mining Expedition," 454.

53. James Knipmeyer, "The F.G. Faatz Inscriptions," *The Confluence* 6 (1999): 20–21; James Knipmeyer, "The G.M. Wright Inscriptions," *The Confluence* 7 (2000): 19–20.

54. W.H. Edwards, "Testimony: River Bed Case: The Steamer *Major Powell*," ed. John Weisheit, *The Confluence* 4 (1997): 10–11.

55. Letter, William Hiram Edwards to Robert Brewster Stanton, February 22, 1907. Stanton Collection, New York Public Library.

56. Anonymous (probably Lute Johnson), "De Julien, An Unknown Explorer," *Outing Magazine* 46 (1905): 601–605. Marston Collection, Huntington Library, San Marino, California.

57. Edwards left several written and oral records of his adventures, including his testimony during the River Bed Case in 1929 (Edwards, "Testimony," 10–11) and an interview with Harry Aleson in March 1942 (Harry Aleson Collection, Utah Historical Society, Salt Lake City, Utah).

58. Nathaniel Galloway interview, *The Vernal (Utah) Express*, 1898. Also see John Weisheit, "Nathaniel Galloway and William Richmond: The Voyage of the *Emma Dean* and the *Maid of the Cañon*, 1896/1897," *The Confluence* 4 (1997): 16–18.

59. Marston Collection, box 72, folder 26, Huntington Library, San Marino, California.

60. Norman Nevills Collection, Marriott Library, University of Utah, Salt Lake City.

61. Weisheit, "Nathaniel Galloway and William Richmond," 16–18.

62. Roy Webb, *If We Had a Boat, Green River Explorers, Adventurers, and Runners* (Salt Lake City: University of Utah Press, 1986), 88.

63. David Lavender, *River Runners of the Grand Canyon* (Grand Canyon, Arizona: Grand Canyon Natural History Association, 1985), 40.

64. J.F. Stone, *Canyon Country* (New York: G.P. Putnam, 1932).

65. *Ibid.*, 71, 73.

66. R.A. Cogswell, unpublished diary, entry for October 18, 1909, courtesy of the Marston Collection, the Huntington Library, San Marino, California.

67. Stone, *Canyon Country*, 73–74. The dates in Cogswell's diary, as well as some of the incidents, do not agree with those in Stone's account. Cogswell's diary, written on the spot, is probably more accurate than Stone's book, which was published twenty-three years after the fact.

68. Lavender, *River Runners of the Grand Canyon*, 42.

69. Nathaniel Galloway died on December 22, 1913, from a brain tumor. His son, Parley Galloway, became a noted river runner and was the head boatman for the Clyde Eddy trip in 1927.

70. Folder 18, Box 34, Marston Collection, Huntington Library, San Marino, California. The authors thank Rosalyn Jirge for her diligent research on Cogswell.

71. G.F. Flavell, *The Log of the Panthon, An Account of an 1896 River Voyage from Green River, Wyoming to Yuma, Arizona Through the Grand Canyon*, ed. N.B. Carmony and D.E. Brown (Boulder, Colorado: Pruett Publishing, 1987), 40–44.

72. *Ibid.*, 44. We speculate that Flavell lined Big Drop 3.

73. *Ibid.*, 42.

74. *Ibid.*, 14.

75. Lingenfelter, *Steamboats on the Colorado*, 112.

76. *Ibid.*, 112.

77. *Ibid.*, 113.

78. H.T. Yokey's quotations are from correspondence with river runner Bill Davis, who helped river historian "Dock" Marston locate inscription sites; Marston Collection, Huntington Library, San Marino, California.

79. *Ibid.*, 118.

80. Loper earned his name posthumously, because his companions painted "Grand Old Man of the Colorado" on his boat after they found it; see Pearl Baker, *Trail on the Water* (Boulder, Colorado: Pruett Publishing, 1970).

81. Bert Loper, "Thoughts That Come to Me in the Still of the Night (Of the Men That Have Traveled with Me on My Many Trips)," ed. John Weisheit, transcr. Rosalyn Jirge, *The Confluence* 3 (1996): 11–13.

82. Baker, *Trail on the Water*, 31–32.

83. Manuscript by Bert Loper, "An Incomplete Trip," box 121, file 3, Marston Collection, Huntington Library, San Marino, California.

84. Lavender, *River Runners*, 44–45.

85. *Ibid.*, 45.

86. Baker, *Trail on the Water*, 49.

87. See David Allen, "A Daring Voyage Down the Grand Canyon," *Boatman's Quarterly Review* 14 (2001): 4–9.

88. Most records reveal that the trip launched in July, but Loper mentions the flow of the river was 85,000 ft³/s. Comparing U.S. Geological Survey records reveals that a date in June is more likely. Loper, "Thoughts That Come to Me," 11–15.

89. Discharges in June 1914 ranged from 55,000 to 118,000. ft³/s, which would make the water level for Loper and Russell's trip the highest ever attempted until 1957. However, there is uncertainty in the dates for the trip, including a note from Russell's brother that claimed the trip was in July 1914, not June; Folder 23, Box 121, Marston Collection, Huntington Library, San Marino, California.

90. Lavender, *River Runners,* 51.

91. Loper, "Thoughts That Come to Me," 11–15.

92. Baker, *Trail on the Water*, 80–82.

93. Ross Wheeler was a friend of Bert Loper in Green River who would later serve as a deputy sheriff to the community. He would eventually die in a house fire, which may have been set to cover up his murder.

94. E.L. Kolb, *Through the Grand Canyon from Wyoming to Mexico* (New York: MacMillan Company, 1914).

95 Webb, *If We Had a Boat*, 92.

96. Kolb, *Through the Grand Canyon*, 7, 135.

97. Many of these photographs look identical to Beaman's photographs, mostly because the Kolb brothers attempted to match Beaman's. The Kolbs's real purpose is better revealed in the "Copyright by Kolb Bros." label that appears below each one that Ellsworth published. Emery Kolb, in particular, attempted through much of his early photographic career to be *the* photographer of the Colorado River, leading to conflicts with the leaders of some of his later river trips. Beaman's photographs became public domain after they were transferred to the U.S. Geological Survey in the 1880s. Kolb, *Through the Grand Canyon*, plate opposite 132.

98. Kolb, *Through the Grand Canyon*, 130.

99. *Ibid.*, 133.

100. *Ibid.*, 342.

101. *Ibid.*, 148.

102. Loper, "Thoughts That Come to Me," 13.

103. R.C. Moore, interview with Otis Marston, 1948; Marston Collection, Huntington Library, San Marino, California.

104. E.C. LaRue, *Water Power and Flood Control on the Colorado River Below Green River, Utah* (Washington, D.C.: U.S. Geological Survey Water-Supply Paper 556, 1925), 176.

105. W.B. Langbein, "L'Affaire LaRue," *Water Resources Division Bulletin*, WRD Historical Note 1 (1975): 6–14.

106. R.E. Westwood, *Rough-water Man: Elwyn Blake's Colorado River Expeditions* (Reno: University of Nevada Press, 1992), 51–61.

107. *Ibid.*, 59.

108. U.S. Geological Survey, *Plan and Profile of Colorado River, Lees Ferry, Arizona to the Mouth of Green River, Utah; San Juan River, Mouth to Chinle Creek, Utah; and Certain Tributaries* (Washington, D.C.: U.S. Government Printing Office, 1922 [1955 printing]), 22 sheets (A–V).

109. Harold Leich, *Rapids and Riffles*, 1933, unpublished diary, Marston Collection, Huntington Library, San Marino, California.

110. Clyde Eddy, *Down the World's Most Dangerous River* (New York: Frederick A. Stokes Company, 1929).

111. Lavender, *River Runners*, 66–70.

112. *Ibid.*, 71–72.

113. Brad Dimock, *Sunk Without a Sound: The Tragic Colorado River Honeymoon of Glen and Bessie Hyde* (Flagstaff, Arizona: Fretwater Press, 2000).

114. Roy Webb, *Riverman, the Story of Bus Hatch* (Rock Springs, Wyoming: Labyrinth Publishing, 1989), 34–37.

115. P.T. Reilly, "Norman Nevills: Whitewater Man of the West," *Utah Historical Quarterly* 55 (1987): 181–200; William Cook, *The Wen, the Botany, and the Mexican Hat* (Orangevale, California: Callisto Books, 1987), 34–50; Nancy Nelson, *Any Time, Any Place, Any River: The Nevills of Mexican Hat* (Flagstaff, Arizona: Red Lake Books, 1991), 8.

116. Cook, *The Wen, the Botany, and the Mexican Hat*, 142.

117. Loper, "Thoughts That Come to Me," 11–15.

118. Vince Welch, Cort Conley, and Brad Dimock, *The Doing of the Thing* (Flagstaff, Arizona: Fretwater Press, 1998).

119. Lavender, *River Runners*, 94.

120. B. de Colmont, B., A. de Seynes, and G. de Colmont, "Voyage on the Green River and the Colorado River," *Paris L'Illustration*, 1939, No. 5017; Webb, *If We Had a Boat*, 116–118.

121. R.E. Westwood, *Woman of the River, Georgie White Clark, Whitewater Pioneer* (Logan: Utah State University Press, 1997), 25, 27, 80–81.

122. L.A. Jones, *Scroll Map of Cataract Canyon* (Bountiful, Utah: privately published, 1962); L.A. Jones, *Scroll Map of Rivers from Moab to Green River Utah* (Bountiful, Utah: privately published, 1961).

123. The most popular river guides are J.K. Rigby, W.K. Hamblin, R. Matheny, and S.L. Welch, *Guidebook to the Colorado River, Part 3: Moab to Hite, Utah through Canyonlands National Park* (Provo, Utah: Brigham Young University Geology Studies, v. 18, Part 2, 1971), 91; F.E. Mutschler, *River Runners' Guide to Canyonlands National Park and Vicinity, with Emphasis on Geologic Features* (Denver, Colorado: Powell Society, 1977), 99; Don Baars, *A River Runner's Guide to Cataract Canyon and Approaches* (Evergreen, Colorado: Cañon Publishers, 1987), 80; Bill Belknap, Buzz Belknap, and L.B. Evans, *Belknap's Revised Waterproof Canyonlands River Guide* (Evergreen, Colorado: Westwater Books, 1996), 79. Only the Belknap guide covers the full geographic scope of this book.

124. Stephens and Shoemaker, *In the Footsteps*.

125. Reilly, "How Deadly Is Big Red?," 249.

126. Eddy, *Down the World's Most Dangerous River*, 5.

127. National Park Service records; see *www.nps.gov/cany/river/reports.htm*.

128. Reilly, "How Deadly Is Big Red?," 259.

129. T.M. Myers, C.C. Becker, and L.E. Stevens, *Fateful Journey: Injury and Death on Colorado River Trips in Grand Canyon* (Flagstaff, Arizona: Red Lake Books, 1999), 124–125.

130. Reilly, "How Deadly Is Big Red?," 251.

131. *Ibid.*, 259, claims twenty boating fatalities in Marble and Grand canyons compared with twelve in Cataract Canyon. Between 1964 and 2000, sixteen fatalities occurred in Grand Canyon in the same period that seventeen perished in Cataract Canyon; see Myers *et al.*, *Fateful Journey*, 124–125.

132. Rolle, *John Charles Frémont*, 153, 158, credits von Eggloffstein as the photographer. Robert Taft, *Photography and the American Scene, A Social History, 1839–1889* (New York: MacMillan Company, 1938), 262–266, incorrectly credits S.N. Carvalho as the expedition's daguerreotypist and notes that famed Civil War photographer Matthew Brady copied them to plates, which were later destroyed by fire.

133. Many scientific studies have used repeat photography to document changes; see G.F. Rogers, H.E. Malde, and R.M. Turner, *Bibliography of Repeat Photography for Evaluating Landscape Change* (Salt Lake City: University of Utah Press, 1984). For information on repeat photography, readers should see J.R. Hastings and R.M. Turner, *The Changing Mile* (Tucson: University of Arizona Press, 1965); G.F. Rogers, *Then & Now, A Photographic History of Vegetation Change in the Central Great Basin Desert* (Salt Lake City: University of Utah Press, 1982); Mark Klett, Ellen Manchester, JoAnn Verburg, Gordon Bushaw, and Rick Dingus, *Second View: The Rephotographic Survey Project* (Albuquerque: University of New Mexico Press, 1984); R.H. Webb, *Grand Canyon, A Century of Change* (Tucson: University of Arizona Press, 1996); K.D. Klement, R.K. Heitschmidt, and C.E. Kay, *Eighty Years of Vegetation and Landscape Changes in the Northern Great Plains: A Photographic Record* (Miles City, Montana: U.S. Department of Agriculture, Agricultural Research Service, Conservation Research Report No. 45, 2001).

134. Repeat photography of San Juan County is shown in E.C. Hindley, J.E. Bowns, E.R. Scherick, P. Curtis, and J. Forrest, *A Photographic History of Vegetation and Stream Channel Changes in San Juan County, Utah* (Logan: Utah State University Extension Service, unnumbered monograph, 2000). One beautiful book that illustrates repeat photography as art is Tom Till, *Utah, Then and Now* (Englewood, Colorado: Westcliffe Publishers, 2000), 168. In addition to Stephens and Shoemaker, *In the Footsteps*, repeat photographs of the Colorado River include one in T.J. Noel and John Fielder, *Colorado, 1870–2000, Revisited, The History Behind the Images* (Englewood, Colorado: Westcliffe Publishers, 2001), 308–309; their photograph shows channel narrowing similar to what we document further downstream in the flatwater reaches.

3

THE TWISTED ROCKS AND THE RIVER

Geology and Hydrology of Cataract Canyon

Climbed naked rocks in front of bend. In every direction...naked rocks prevail. Buttes are seen scattered on the landscape, now rounded into cones, now buttressed and columned, now carved out with alcoves and sunken recesses and pockets. All varying from orange to dark brown, often stained black.

– John Wesley Powell, September 8, 1871

The Canyonlands region can be regarded as geology and geomorphology with ecology holding on for dear life. The seemingly barren landscape owes its existence to the arid climate, which allows little weathering and even less soil formation. What weathering occurs generally results from the winter freeze-thaw cycles, and much of the loosened material is washed away in summer runoff. The salts and clays of the rocks, many of which are of marine origin, contribute to the false impression of a wasteland. Because what lies beneath the surface creates an inherently unstable landscape, the cliffs in Cataract Canyon are tilted and appear to be falling into the river. Slopes are mantled with broken rocks, and little channels lead to the heads of rapids. The Colorado River has attempted to move the rocks that the canyon walls have thrown in its path, but the presence of well-vegetated rubble piles along the channel indicates that it has been a long time since the river directly eroded the bedrock in its channel.

NAKED, BROKEN ROCKS

Most of the rocks exposed in Cataract Canyon and the approaches to the Canyon are from the Mesozoic and Paleozoic eras, about 300 to 130 million years ago. Whole books and long scientific papers have been written on the colorful bedrock of Canyon Country. Here, we briefly summarize the bedrock geology and the forces that have acted upon it over its long history. For more information on the spectacular geology of

the Canyonlands region, readers are directed to the many popular and scientific books written on the geology of the Colorado Plateau and Utah.[1] A generalized stratigraphic section with the river miles where the rocks may be seen is given in Table 3-1; Figure 3-1 shows the stratigraphy at Big Drop 3, the deepest part of the noninundated Cataract Canyon. What follows are generalized descriptions of the strata, emphasizing their influence on the course of the Colorado River.

PALEOZOIC ERA

The Hermosa Group

The lowermost rocks in Canyonlands National Park that comprise the Hermosa Group are barely exposed

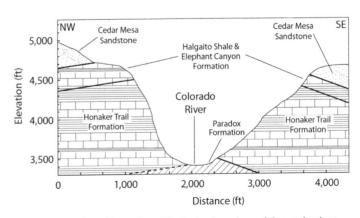

Figure 3-1. Stratigraphic section of the bedrock geology of Canyonlands at Big Drop 3 in Cataract Canyon.

along the Colorado River, and only at a few isolated points. The Pennsylvanian Paradox Formation outcrops as bedrock only at Big Drop 3, on the left side; at Gypsum Canyon; and at other small and isolated outcrops. Because the Paradox Formation contains salt lenses, it exerts a large influence on the structural geology of Canyonlands and leaves other evidence of its subsurface presence. *Anhydrite diapirs*, also known as salt domes, are shaped like upside-down teardrops, rising through bedrock from the Paradox Formation (Figure 3-2). They are present at Moab, the mouth of Lower Red Lake Canyon, Cross Canyon, Rapid 12, and in Gypsum Canyon, providing conspicuous reminders of this formation and its importance to the geology of the Canyonlands region. The effect of salt deformation will be discussed later in this chapter and in Chapter 8.

Most of the rocks at river level in Cataract Canyon, and for many miles of the approaches, are of the Pennsylvanian Honaker Trail Formation. This formation, named for a miner's twisting trail to the San Juan River, consists of limestones alternating with relatively thin, grey beds of marine sandstones, mudstones, and shales. The Honaker Trail Formation is 1,000 feet thick in the region, but only the upper layers are exposed through much of Cataract Canyon. The entire thickness of the formation, although compressed and stretched to about 800 feet thickness, is exposed above the anhydrite diapir at Lower Red Lake Canyon.[2] The thickness was reduced owing to the stretching forces applied to the rocks by the rising diapir.

The Cutler Group

The red rocks of Canyonlands have long intrigued casual visitor and geologist alike. Depositional characteristics of the Cutler Group are a very complicated story, to say the least, with individual layers interfingering with others and thicknesses ranging from nothing to massive to altogether absent in other nearby localities. Many of these rocks were deposited in the Permian Period (245 to 290 million years ago) when sea-level fluctuations resulted in alternating marine and terrestrial deposition on what is now the Colorado Plateau. These rocks have names such as the

TABLE 3-1. Stratigraphy of the River Corridors in Canyonlands[1,2]

End time (Ma)	Time period	Epoch	Group	Formation
0	QUATERNARY	Holocene		Generally unnamed
0.01		Pleistocene		Generally unnamed
2	TERTIARY			
66	MESOZOIC	Cretaceous		Mancos Shale
96				Dakota Sandstone
100				Cedar Mountain Form
144	MESOZOIC	Jurassic	San Rafael Grp.	Morrison Formation
165				Summerville Formation
167				Curtis Formation
170				Entrada Sandstone
175				Carmel Formation
190		Triassic	Glen Canyon Group	Navajo Sandstone
195				Kayenta Formation
200	MESOZOIC			Wingate Sandstone
208				Chinle Formation (6 members)
239		Permian		Moenkopi Formation (4 members)
265	PALEOZOIC		Cutler Group	Undivided
265	PALEOZOIC			White Rim Sandstone
270				Organ Rock Formation
275				Cedar Mesa Sandstone
275				Elephant Canyon Form. [facies change to] Halgaito Shale
290	PALEOZOIC	Pennsylvanian	Hermosa Group	Honaker Trail Formation
300				Paradox Formation (of 4 substages, only Ismay is exposed)

Where seen on rivers	Significance
Throughout Canyonlands	River terraces, bottomlands, debris fans, talus cones.
Green River: Between Green River and about Bowknot Bend. Colorado River: Professor Valley, Spanish Valley, upper reaches of Meander Canyon, Mille Crag Bend and downstream to Hite	River cobble terraces containing extralocal quartzites and intrusive igneous rocks, high soil surfaces.
	Not present in significant amounts in Canyonlands; exposed to north.
Green River: mile 120, 115	Not present in significant amounts in Canyonlands; exposed to north, northeast, and southeast.
Green River: mile 119	Not present in significant amounts in Canyonlands; exposed to north, east, and south.
Green River: mile 119, mile 111	Not present in significant amounts in Canyonlands; exposed to the west.
Green River: mile 118.5–105	In higher elevation areas of Canyonlands.
Green River: mile 105–103.5	The Anvil, prominent landmark on the Green River, forms in the Summerville Formation.
Green River: mile 103.5–101.5	
Green River: mile 101.5–96.5. Colorado River: between mouth of Dolores River and Dewey Bridge and visible from river in Professor Valley	Most of the arches formed in the Canyonlands are in Entrada Sandstone, but most of these are not near the Green and Colorado Rivers.
Green River: mile 96.5–95. Colorado River: none	Forms benches and often tops Navajo Sandstone cliffs.
Visible through most of the approaches to Cataract Canyon. At river level — Green River: mile 95–88 and particularly Trin Alcove, mile 90; Colorado River: cliffs in Professor Valley, Meander Canyon	Forms the most recognizable features associated with the Colorado Plateau but is not significant to most of the corridors of the Green and Colorado Rivers.
Green River: mile 88–85 Colorado River: several locations between Dewey Bridge and Potash	Forms prominent benches between Navajo and Wingate sandstones.
Visible through most of the approaches to Cataract Canyon. At river level — Green River: mile 85–79 Colorado River: Professor Valley and mile 77 to 64, Hite	Forms massive cliffs along the Green and Colorado Rivers.
Visible through most of the approaches to Cataract Canyon. At river level — Green River: mile 79–52, particularly well exposed around Bowknot Bend. Colorado River: Professor Valley (particularly Big Bend area) and base of initial cliffs in Meander Canyon	Largest source of uranium in Canyonlands. Non-lacustrine members of the Chinle Formation, particularly the Owl Rock Member, are capable of producing debris flows when present in cliffs. Many important bottomlands occur where Chinle Formation is at river level.
Visible through most of the approaches to Cataract Canyon. At river level — Green River: mile 52–37, visible along river to about mile 20. Colorado River: mile 50–47.5, Meander Canyon	Bottomlands are common when Moenkopi Formation is at river level. Several members of the Moenkopi Formation produce debris flows when present in cliffs. Base of Buttes of the Cross are Moenkopi Formation.
Colorado River: river level at Fisher Towers in Professor Valley, upper sections of Meander Canyon near Potash	Insufficient thicknesses of shales and mudstones to produce debris flows or significant talus cones.
Green River: mile 37–32 at river level, but visible for many more miles Colorado River: Starts on river right near Shafer Canyon (mile 34.9), never on river left	Forms extensive benches along the Green River; White Rim Cliffs serve as the dividing topographic unit between Labyrinth and Stillwater Canyons.
Green River: mile 32–19. Colorado River: not at river level but can be seen in distance beneath White Rim Sandstone	Appears at the bases of many buttes and monuments, particularly in Monument Valley to the south. Does not produce debris flows because it's never high on cliffs.
Green River: gradually appears beginning at mile 32. Colorado River: gradually appears around mile 15 in Meander Canyon and visible in cliffs down to Hite. Some is visible at Dead Horse Point. Forms Narrow Canyon.	Forms massive cliffs along the Green and Colorado Rivers. Some of the largest blocks in the rapids of Cataract Canyon are Cedar Mesa Sandstone. Few bottomlands form when Cedar Mesa Sandstone is at river level.
Green River: Elephant Canyon only, mile 16.5–7. Colorado River: Elephant Canyon, mile 47.5 to mile 212.5 in Cataract Canyon; Halgaito Shale, in cliffs from mile 212.5 to mile 183 in Cataract Canyon	Elephant Canyon Formation is controversial; position is considered "lower Cutler Group" in the vicinity of Moab. Halgaito Shale is the major debris-flow producer in Canyonlands.
Green River: near the Confluence, mile 7–0. Colorado River: at Potash (Shafer Dome), and beginning above the Loop (mile 12) it appears through Cataract Canyon to about the start of Mille Crag Bend	Forms prominent cliffs in Cataract Canyon. Locally, mudstones produce small debris flows. Large blocks form the core of rapids in Cataract Canyon. Bottomlands generally absent (except Spanish Bottom) when Honaker Trail Formation is at river level.
Colorado River: exposed at Big Drop 3 (mile 202) and Gypsum Canyon (mile 197)	Forms slip surfaces for large rotational slumps (e.g., Tilted Park); produces anhydrite diapirs throughout Canyonlands; causative factor for unloading rotational features and grabens along Colorado River and in Needles District.

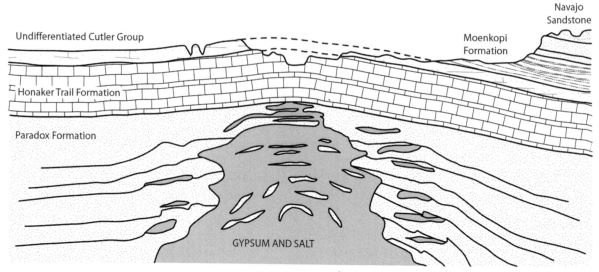

Figure 3-2. Schematic diagram of an anhydrite diapir in Canyonlands National Park (modified from Prommel and Crum, 1927).

Halgaito Shale, the Elephant Canyon Formation, the Cedar Mesa Sandstone, the Organ Rock Formation, the Undifferentiated Cutler, and the White Rim Sandstone. The White Rim Sandstone caps the Cutler Group in Canyonlands National Park (except in the Needles District), forming a conspicuous layer that is visible through much of the northern part of the park and along the river approaches to Cataract Canyon; the White Rim reappears near Hite. Near Moab, these formations are completely absent, except for the Undifferentiated Cutler. Petrified wood in the Elephant Canyon Formation is a reminder of the terrestrial depositional environment of most of these sediments and can be visited at river mile 36.8 on the Colorado River above the Confluence (Meander Canyon).

Of these rocks, the Halgaito Shale is an important factor in the shape and nature of Cataract Canyon because of its contributions to debris flows. As will be discussed at the end of this chapter, the occurrence of debris flows is one of the primary reasons for the rapids of the Colorado River. This relatively thin and nondescript unit once was mapped as the Hermit Shale, another important debris-flow producer in Grand Canyon.[3] The Halgaito Shale is thought to have been deposited in slow-moving rivers, possibly on a coastal plain. As a result, it is rich in single-layer clays dominated by the minerals illite and kaolinite. For reasons that are not clearly understood, these minerals, when mixed in a slurry with larger particles, create debris flows that flow long distances in bedrock canyons on the Colorado Plateau. In contrast, most of the marine shales, discussed in the following sections, do not produce significant debris flows.

MESOZOIC ERA

Moenkopi and Chinle Formations

The Moenkopi Formation, deposited during the early Triassic Period (208 to 245 million years ago), is one of the most conspicuous formations on the Colorado Plateau, particularly on the approaches to Cataract Canyon. It forms parts of some of the most spectacular landmarks in Canyonlands, including the top of the Fisher Towers in Professor Valley and the base of the Buttes of the Cross in Tower Park (Stillwater Canyon). Unlike the Moenkopi Formation the Chinle Formation is relatively unobtrusive as a landmark because it usually is covered with talus cones and boulders, but is quite important economically and historically: most of the uranium extracted from Canyonlands came from the Moss Back Member of the Chinle. At most localities, the Chinle Formation forms slopes and benches either between or at the bases of cliffs.

Glen Canyon Group

During the Jurassic Period (144 to 208 million years ago), the Glen Canyon Group—the Wingate Sandstone, Kayenta Formation, and Navajo Sandstone—was deposited throughout what is now the Canyonlands region. This group more than any other defines the scenery of the Colorado Plateau; whole national parks, such as Capitol Reef and Zion, were established because of these spectacularly beautiful formations. Both the Wingate and Navajo sandstones are *lithified* dunes (turned to stone) from great sand seas that covered the Jurassic landscape. At this time, the climate is thought to have been arid. The Kayenta Formation, which separates the two sandstones, represents a period of more temperate climate when through-flowing streams and rivers crossed the region, leaving the evidence of small channels and floodplain deposits in the stratigraphic record. More than most other groups, this terrestrial depositional sequence reminds us of the swings in climate that the region has undergone through geologic time.

The Middle and Late Jurassic

Well after deposition of the Navajo Sandstone ceased, a small and shallow inland sea formed during the middle Jurassic Period. Several prominent formations are associated with this sea, but in our region the only important one is the Carmel Formation, a nondescript group of sandstones, siltstones, shales, and limestones seen on the Green River near the mouth of the San Rafael River. After recession of this shallow sea, the return of arid conditions and *eolian activity* resulted in deposition of windblown sand, which eventually lithified into the Entrada Sandstone. This sandstone is known mostly because of its propensity to form arches upon weathering, and is the featured strata of Arches National Park.

In the Canyonlands region, the Morrison Formation dominates the late Jurassic Period. The Morrison Formation is notable for two reasons: dinosaur remains and uranium. Dinosaurs inhabited the margins of a large freshwater lake and the floodplains of its catchment rivers during this period. The lowermost unit of the Morrison—the Salt Wash Member—consists of inter-bedded sandstones and shales and contains significant amounts of uranium. These sandstones and shales originally were deposited in a freshwater lake and therefore are considered to be *lacustrine* in origin. Because of its dual features, the Morrison Formation is considered to be one of the most studied geologic formations on Earth.[4]

The Cretaceous Period

Of the numerous formations deposited in eastern Utah during the Cretaceous Period (66 to 144 million years ago), the Mancos Shale is one of the most important to the visual landscape of the Canyon Country, although only on its northern margin. This incredibly thick shale was deposited over millions of years in what has been termed "a stagnant ocean."[5] The Mancos Shale forms the broad, seemingly featureless landscapes along Interstate-70 between Cisco and Green River. These badlands support a healthy population of antelope, eagles, hawks, and prairie dogs. This formation also forms the base of the Book Cliffs.

CENOZOIC ERA

Tertiary Period

Events in the Tertiary Period (2 to 65 million years ago) shaped the landscape of Canyon Country. Despite the huge changes that occurred during this period, few Tertiary-aged sedimentary deposits are present in Canyonlands, although these deposits are abundant to the north and west. With respect to Cataract Canyon, the most important of these deposits are associated with Lake Uinta, an ancestral lake that filled most of the area north of the Canyonlands region in the Tertiary. Desolation Canyon on the Green River is incised into the Green River and Wasatch formations, which are related *depositional facies* of Lake Uinta. Depositional facies represent sediments that are related in time and event, but have different particle sizes. For example, coarse-grained *deltaic* sediments are deposited where a river enters a lake, whereas shales that are rich in clays might be deposited at the same time in the deep water of the same lake. Further north, the ancestral Green River deposited the Duchesne Formation, providing the first clues as to the age of the modern Green River.

Quaternary Period

Quaternary-aged sediments (the last two million years) are abundant in the Canyonlands region. The most common Quaternary deposits are *eolian landforms* (sand dunes), *alluvium* (river deposits), *colluvium* (accumulations of fallen particles), and *talus* (rockfalls). The least common but most interesting Quaternary deposits are Pleistocene river cobbles, which typically are found in terraces at various heights above the rivers and only upstream from the Confluence. These terraces usually were deposited in the late Pleistocene (about 100,000 to 11,000 years ago) during glacial climates, and they represent deposition by much higher flows than what occur in today's rivers. Pleistocene gravel terraces are common along both the Green and Colorado rivers beginning about fifty miles upstream from the Confluence, but they are not present in Cataract Canyon for reasons to be explained later. These gravels contained placer gold and were magnets for early explorers (see Chapter 2). Till deposited by mountain glaciers in the La Sal Mountains grade into these river terraces southeast of Moab.[6]

Deposits of Holocene age (last 11,000 years) are particularly abundant in the Canyonlands and along the Colorado River in Cataract Canyon. Sandbars along the rivers and sand dunes in the uplands are mostly of Holocene age. Talus cones, the depositional expression of rockfalls, are abundant along the Green and Colorado rivers. *Debris fans* are the net accumulation of poorly sorted particles at tributary mouths in Cataract Canyon; *debris bars* are accumulations of material eroded or *reworked* (selective removal of particles) from debris fans during Colorado River flows. Debris fans and bars along the rapids in Cataract Canyon are all of Holocene age.

THE FORCES ON THE ROCKS

As any geologist would tell you, most of the sedimentary strata of Canyonlands were originally deposited in flat-lying or subhorizontal layers. The most obvious exceptions are the lithified eolian dunes, where deposition sometimes occurred at the angle of repose; even these strata are, overall, relatively flat-lying. Long after deposition, forces within the Earth—and sometimes under smaller areas of the Earth—bent, twisted, or broke the horizontal strata into the sometimes tortured-appearing landscape of the region. Water and wind completed the sculpting process, rendering a sometimes sensuous, sometimes cruel-looking scene.

While some forces on the rocks were generated from large-scale crustal forces, other forces came from the intimate characteristics of the rocks themselves. The large-scale forces include major mountain-building events, or *orogenies*. The most well known of these is the Laramide Orogeny, and another is the continental-scale crustal extension that formed the Great Basin to the west of the Colorado Plateau. The small-scale forces include anhydrite diapirs arising from the Paradox Formation, which underlies all of Canyonlands, and the forces exerted by vertically standing cliffs on underlying shale beds.

The Orogenies Begin

Orogenies in their simplest form can be considered "mountain-building events," but the phrase "geologic upheavals" or another phrase or terms connoting drastic convulsions in the Earth's surface may be more appropriate.[7] Two major orogenies that shaped the geologic structure of central Utah began in the Cretaceous Period. The Sevier Orogeny, the first of the two, mostly affected Utah to the west of the present-day Wasatch Front. The Laramide Orogeny, which began during the late Mesozoic and ended in the early Tertiary (84 to 66 million years ago), shaped most of the landscape in the western United States. In particular, the Rocky Mountains, the headwaters of the modern Colorado River, rose during the Laramide Orogeny.[8]

The most important result of this uplift was the

creation of the Uinta Mountains to the north of Canyonlands. The monoclines, anticlines, and folds—including the Uncompahgre, the San Rafael Swell, the Circle Cliffs, and the Raplee Anticline —that surround Canyonlands formed during the Laramide.[9] A *monocline* forms where past stresses have bent the strata into an S-form cross section, and the strata rise from one elevation to another. An *anticline* is a local rise or mound in a sedimentary deposit; anticlines trap oil and gas and are of economic importance in Canyon Country (see Chapter 5). Because of regional uplift during the Laramide, eastern Utah remained above sea level, eliminating marine deposition but not the formation of extensive inland lakes. Most of the bending and cracking of Paleozoic and Mesozoic strata in Canyonlands appear to be related to the Laramide Orogeny. Because few deposits of Tertiary age remain in Canyonlands, the timing of various convulsions remains elusive.

Tertiary Trauma

The Tertiary was a period of uplift, faulting, erosion, and igneous intrusion. Between 31 and 23 million years ago, the *laccoliths* of the Henry, La Sal, and Abajo mountains formed, adding the last major mountains to Canyon Country.[10] Laccoliths are mountains pushed up by subsurface injections of molten rock between layers of sedimentary rocks. Some major structures, such as the Moab fault at the Portal on the downstream side of Spanish Valley, are of Tertiary age.[11] This fault has about 2,600 feet of displacement north of the Colorado River.

Because of the uplifts and contortions in the bedrock, drainage networks were disrupted or even reversed in direction. Large lakes formed north of Canyonlands in what is now known as the Uinta Basin. Several formations—particularly the Green River Formation—are evidence of the extent and longevity of these lakes. At least near the end of this period of lacustrine deposition, the major source of water was from the north,[12] suggesting that the Green River drainage in Wyoming may have been in existence for as long as 30 to 40 million years. Before that time, the upper Green River is thought to have been a

tributary of the Platte River, which drains to the Mississippi and the Gulf of Mexico.[13] The Colorado River developed on the rising Rocky Mountains and flowed into the Uinta Basin, probably on a course more northerly than is found today.[14]

Major stretching of the Earth's crust to the west of the Colorado Plateau ultimately would affect the landscape of the Canyonlands region. Beginning about 15 million years ago, the Basin and Range Province began to form. Fault offsets resulted in blocks called *grabens* falling between the faulted mountains (rising blocks are also known as *horsts*) and lowering the overall base level. The highlands that previously blocked drainage to the west were fractured, allowing flow towards the Pacific Ocean via the Gulf of California. At the same time that the bottom was dropping out to the west, eastern Utah was rising somewhere between 7,000 and 10,000 feet.[15] This differential shift in elevations set up the gradients that were required to shift drainages from flowing northeastward or toward the Rio Grande to drainages flowing toward the arid regions of what is now California and Arizona.

Quaternary Deformations

Numerous faults of Quaternary age cross parts of the Canyonlands region. Many of these faults, such as those in Salt Valley in Arches National Park, are related to deformation caused by the underlying salt of the Paradox Formation.[16] In particular, the grabens of the Needles District, Canyonlands National Park, are linked both to the underlying salt and the proximity to the southern cliffs of Cataract Canyon.[17] Many of the grabens have continued to move, historically, disrupting the channels of tributaries to the Colorado River.[18]

The central Colorado Plateau typically is thought of as earthquake free, although seismic surveys reveal consistent points of low-level seismic activity.[19] Most of the recent seismic activity appears centered near human-influenced areas (*e.g.*, the Potash mine) and along the Colorado River upstream from the Confluence. Surprisingly, the graben area generates relatively few earthquakes, at least recently. Although the potential for large earthquakes in the Canyonlands region is real, none have been recorded.

MAJOR POWELL AND THE AGE OF CATARACT CANYON

The nineteenth-century scientist-explorers who were confronted with the bent and broken landscape contributed to our understanding of the science of geology. In particular, John Wesley Powell tried to explain the landscape using either relatively new geological concepts or his own observations. He saw the monoclines and anticlines and knew that they affected the river systems. In Powell's geological notes on Cataract Canyon, which were not entirely included in his report of 1875, he observed:

> The river here seems to cut through an irregular anticlinal axis [now called the Meander Anticline].[20]

While he was able to recognize the primary structural units, such as the Meander Anticline, Powell struggled to explain why the rivers in the region seemingly went through the tops of mountains and through high structural deformations instead of around them.

His observations and intellectual curiosity led to two major contributions to the science of geology, although, as is the wont of scientists, debate about the importance of both continues.[21] First, to explain the Green River's course through the Uinta Mountains, and not around them, he developed the concept of an *antecedent stream*, one that downcuts through a geologic structure as it is rising in response to forces deep within the Earth. In other words, the drainage preceded the mountains. He also developed the concept of *base level of erosion* to explain the end product of landscape erosion; although the ultimate base level is mean sea level, local base levels occur where bedrock impedes the downward erosion of rivers. The concept of base level is commonly used in geomorphology to address questions of downcutting rates and controls on the bed elevations of hillslopes and rivers, whether in bedrock or alluvium.[22] Finally, following Macomb, he was the second to map and define the "Plateau Province," now known as the Colorado Plateau.[23]

Some of Powell's contributions may have been more publicity of existing ideas than exposition of original ideas. John Strong Newberry, who viewed Canyonlands in 1858, developed many of the ideas more commonly attributed to Powell, but Powell presented those ideas to a wider audience. One undeniable contribution of Powell's was his major role in the establishment of the U.S. Geological Survey as well as his recruitment of highly talented young geologists—such as Clarence E. Dutton and Grove Karl Gilbert—who made fundamental contributions to science based in part on their association with the Powell Survey of the Colorado Plateau, including the Canyonlands region.[24] Later geologists refined Powell's ideas and added detail from better geologic mapping, topography, and modern age-dating techniques.

While details of the highlands are relatively well known, many details of the history of canyon cutting are unknown. Sedimentary strata may be dated directly with fossils or with a variety of isotopic, paleomagnetic, or mineralogic techniques. Intrusive or volcanic rocks can be dated using isotopic techniques based on radioactive decay. But erosion by wind and water cannot be directly dated unless deposits that result from the erosion are found and somehow correlated to the missing geologic record. This is one of the reasons why the details—and age dating—of the development of the Colorado River drainage are still so controversial and poorly understood.

Some details appear to be incontrovertible and contradict Powell's interpretation. Geologists now think that the east end of the Uinta Mountains subsided, allowing the lower Green River, which presumably drained from the Uintas to the lakes, to capture the upper Green, previously a tributary of the Platte River, which drains to the Mississippi.[25] Therefore, instead of Powell's idea of antecedence in the formation of Lodore and Split Mountain canyons, the modern interpretation is *stream capture* owing to a lowering of the topographic divide between two drainages. Stream capture, a concept of landscape development attributed to G.K. Gilbert, involves one drainage extending its length and area such that it subsumes another drainage. In the case of the Green River, stream capture resulted in less drainage area in the Mississippi River system and more in the Colorado River.

By about ten million years ago, the Colorado River drainage upstream from Canyonlands had cut through the block-faulted mountains thrown up in its path.[26] Although lakes were thought to be present over what is now Canyonlands and were believed to be impounded by the Henry Mountains and (or) Kaiparowits Plateau, no depositional evidence remains. What happened next is the subject of one of the great geological debates concerning the Colorado Plateau: the development of the Colorado River drainage and the age of Grand Canyon.[27]

When and how the Colorado River drainage became connected into its present course to the Gulf of California is, to a large degree, the story of lakes filling and emptying. A united Green River increased the flow into the lakes of the Uinta Basin, and, combined with millions of years of deposition, created conditions ripe for overflow. The best direction for overflow was southward towards Canyonlands and points beyond. In northern Arizona, Lake Bidahochi covered much of what is now the Navajo Indian Reservation between sixteen and six million years ago. Its presence is proof that the Colorado River was not connected to the Gulf of California until sometime after six million years ago. If more substantiation was needed, evidence in the western Grand Canyon suggests flow was to the northeast around the time that Lake Bidahochi began filling.[28] Some maps suggest that most of the flow from the vicinity of Canyonlands actually went to the Gulf of Mexico through the Rio Grande.[29]

Lake Bidahochi, plus other Tertiary volcanic and sedimentary deposits in western Arizona and southern Nevada, is widely considered the best constraint on the age of Grand Canyon. Did the Colorado River provide most of the water and sediment that filled Lake Bidahochi? If so, was its course along the present-day Colorado River through Cataract Canyon? Going further, then Cataract Canyon might be as old as sixteen million years. If not, Cataract Canyon might have formed after creation of Grand Canyon five to six million years ago. One extreme possibility is that the canyon could have been cut less than a million years ago if current ideas about a youthful Glen Canyon are correct.[30] This extremely large range in possible ages illustrates the problem

with dating erosion as opposed to deposits preserved on the landscape.

We still do not have a definite date on the age for the beginning of Cataract Canyon.[31] Instead, we have an evolving model of the Colorado River system that calls on some segments (*e.g.*, in Colorado) to be tens of millions of years old and others (the Grand Canyon) to be less than six million years old. In the Canyonlands region, there is no direct evidence that can be brought to bear on the age of canyon cutting. Any refinement of the age of Cataract Canyon from its current range from ten million to less than six million years old may require evidence from elsewhere or a creative new way of dating when the rock was eroded.

From evidence upstream and downstream from Cataract Canyon, one can infer that downcutting did not occur all at once. In Professor Valley, the canyon was 800 feet deep at the start of the Quaternary.[32] In Glen Canyon, five terrace levels suggest that downcutting was episodic and probably related to periods of glacial outwash.[33] Rincons and cutoff meanders at several points along the Green and Colorado rivers attest to their former channel levels being stable at a higher elevation than at present.[34] These bits and pieces of the larger story may eventually add up to the overall solution to the problem of determining the age of Cataract Canyon.

SALT, CLIFFS, AND SLIDING ROCKS

One simplistic way to look at Cataract Canyon is that downcutting created a blank canvas that geomorphic processes painted into the modern scenery. A more complex view would be that the walls adjusted as the canyon was downcut. Part of that adjustment involved large-scale faulting, which created the Grabens area of Canyonlands National Park. Another part created huge rotational slumps, known as *Toreva blocks*,[35] which dominate the walls along upper Cataract Canyon. What makes Toreva blocks unique as a geomorphic landform is that they are largely intact but rotated strata instead of sheared piles of rubble, as would result from an avalanche.

Salt domes, or anhydrite diapirs, have played a

large role in the origin of Cataract Canyon.[36] In the largest sense, the Meander Anticline, through which the Colorado River passes, is formed from the combination of salt deformation and unloading caused by removal of rock by the Colorado River.[37] Locally, some domes, such as the Prommel Dome at the mouth of Lower Red Lake Canyon,[38] have clearly deformed Permian strata, but the deformation probably occurred much later and perhaps even after Cataract Canyon began its existence.

The geomorphic processes are driven primarily by the presence of thick salt and shales in the Paradox Formation, which underlies all of Cataract Canyon, and to a lesser extent by percolating rainfall and river water. One visualization of the process likens the salt layers to a tube of toothpaste and the forces generated by the overlying cliffs to fingers squeezing that tube. What results are salt diapirs (the toothpaste exiting the tube) moving upwards or sideways and the cliff walls moving downward towards harder strata deeper in the Earth (like fingers moving closer together). Faulting occurs where joint patterns focus shearing between blocks.[39] The blocks, which rotate on the slippery surface, are called Toreva blocks if they remain intact or disintegrate into landslides if they do not.

Many of the larger Toreva blocks, such as those on both sides of the river at Tilted Park, may have resulted from a different process. The shales in the Paradox Formation provide an impermeable layer that stops downward percolation of rainwater. During Pleistocene climates this downward percolation was more appreciable than today, and the combination of high pore pressures on the top of the shales, the overlying weight of the Honaker Trail and higher formations, and the cliffs formed by downcutting created ideal conditions for rotational slumps. Similar rotational slumps are present along the Vermilion Cliffs west of Lee's Ferry, on the east face of Black Mesa in northern Arizona, and at discrete points in Grand Canyon, as well as in other parts of the world.

The key feature to understanding the broken walls of Cataract Canyon is the presence of tall cliffs pressing downward on strata that has a high potential to deform under pressure. The downcutting of Cataract Canyon removed an enormous amount of rock from the canyon's center, releasing pressure of the weight of the overlying rocks along the face of the cliffs. Because the now-eroded rocks no longer press against the cliffs, holding the rock in, the weight of the rocks in the cliffs can cause *unloading*, or movement of individual pieces of rock from the cliff or the entire mass of the cliff. The material underlying the cliffs may deform in response to the unloading depending upon the strength of the underlying strata; if the underlying strata is highly deformable, such as the salt lenses beneath the upper part of Cataract Canyon, then the overlying cliffs can slide towards the river. Some cliffs in Cataract Canyon—particularly on river right in the Big Drops—are near vertical and undeformed, suggesting that the underlying Paradox Formation has a relatively high structural integrity compared with other parts of Cataract Canyon, especially Tilted Park.

THE COLORADO RIVER AND ITS TRIBUTARIES

Raging Floods

Floods can occur in any season in Canyonlands, but most floods occur between May and October. These floods result either from snowmelt runoff on the major rivers in May and June or flash floods from thunderstorms in the summer. The largest historical flood in Cataract Canyon peaked at about 225,000 ft³/s in June of 1884.[40] No one was in Cataract Canyon at the time, but observers in Fruita, Colorado, and Lee's Ferry describe a deluge unprecedented in history. An even larger flood may have occurred in 1862; hydrologists estimate a peak discharge of 400,000 ft³/s for this flood on the Colorado River just downstream of Needles, California. Large floods in the Holocene reportedly approached half a million cubic feet per second in Grand Canyon,[41] but we do not have a good way of determining how much of that water came through Cataract Canyon.

The Colorado River has had many large floods in the twentieth century, particularly in the decade starting in 1916 (Figure 3-3). The largest recent flood occurred in 1984 and was about 115,000 ft³/s. Floods were relatively small in the 1950s, and in recent decades—except in 1983 and 1984—floods appear to be much smaller, perhaps because of flow regulation since the 1960s on the Green and Gunnison rivers. By one account, annual peak discharges on the Colorado and Gunnison rivers at Grand Junction, Colorado, have decreased by twenty-nine to thirty-eight percent since 1950.[42] Although Colorado River floods rarely affect Moab directly, except by inundating roads near the river, one of the largest concerns at present is the potential effect of floods on the Atlas Tailings Pile, the spoils from a uranium milling operation that are presently on the north bank of the Colorado River, across the river from Moab.

Floods on the smaller tributaries are another matter. For many decades, the one-day precipitation record for Utah was the 5.0 inches recorded in Moab on September 22, 1896. The resulting floods down Mill and Pack creeks carved deep channels, known as arroyos, into their floodplains. As a result, the channels of these creeks, which were narrow enough once to be crossed on fence planks, doubled or tripled their width.[43]

Floods in the Moab area were most numerous between the 1880s and 1930s, which to some extent mirrored what was happening in the Colorado River. Some observers believe that overgrazing was to blame,[44] and that floods decreased after the Taylor Grazing Act of 1932 reduced livestock grazing on public lands. Reduction in grazing almost certainly decreased the potential for floods, but rainfall— or more specifically the frequency of large, flood-producing storms—decreased after the early 1940s. But before large storms became less frequent, most of the rivers in the region had incised into their floodplains, creating the modern landscape of steep-walled arroyos.[45]

Although humans may have been on the landscape since the end of the Pleistocene, hunting mammoths and other large mammals now extinct, they either did not bother to measure river flow, or if they did, they did not write it down. While tree rings can be used to record prehistoric discharges, the oldest trees in the Colorado River basin are much younger than 11,000

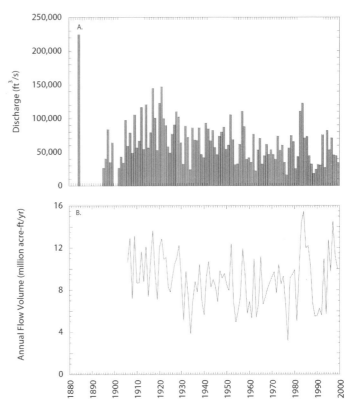

Figure 3-3. Flow in the Colorado River through Canyonlands National Park. A. The annual flood series represents the largest daily discharge for each year in the record. This series was developed by adding together the daily discharges for the Green River at Green River, Utah, and the Colorado River near Cisco, Utah, and looking for the highest value. The inputs of other rivers, such as the San Rafael and Dolores, which are downstream from these gaging stations, are insignificant. B. The annual flow volume is the amount of water that passes the gaging station each water year (October 1 through September 30). The data from 1906 to 1990 is from the Bureau of Reclamation and is corrected for water use and dam storage; the data from 1991-1999 is directly measured at gaging stations.

years old. The only record left of Pleistocene flow in the Green and Colorado rivers lies in cobble deposits, known as Pleistocene outwash terraces, perched along both rivers.[46] These deposits contain relatively large clasts of rocks that do not occur in the local, upslope environment; instead, these rocks were washed in from sources ranging from western Colorado to the peaks of the Front Range near Denver. While their presence suggests high discharges in the rivers, the bed of the river could have been higher also.

We do not know the glacial history of floods because little direct evidence remains. Indirect evidence from other regions suggests that the rivers of the Canyonlands region might have altered between raging and timid. During the full glacial period (about 18,000 years before present), most of the precipitation falling in the Rocky Mountains was trapped in glaciers, leaving only lowland areas as the source for snowmelt runoff to the Colorado River. The river likely had low flow during these periods. When those glaciers melted between about 13,000 and 11,000 years ago the river may have experienced tremendous floods. Periods of glacial melting may be when most of the downcutting through bedrock occurred in these canyons.

Because of major differences in air circulation patterns in the late Pleistocene, the summer thunderstorms, or monsoons, did not exist in the southwestern United States as we now know them. Lack of summer thunderstorms would reduce the potential for large flash floods on the tributaries; instead, flow in now-dry washes may have been perennial. Lack of high-energy rainfall also would reduce the potential for debris flows, which means the longitudinal profile of the river in the Pleistocene would have been drastically different than it is today.

Sources of Water and Sediment

The Colorado River in Cataract Canyon has somewhat of a split personality in terms of the sources of water and sediment. The water in the river, and particularly during the annual spring flood, comes from one part of the drainage basin, mostly the mountains of Wyoming, Utah, and Colorado above 10,000 feet. Water runs off during the spring warm up and flows towards the Gulf of California, accumulating in the bottleneck of Cataract Canyon. The largest floods tend to result from late spring rainfall on snowpacks that have not yet melted, and the combination runs off very quickly from high elevations.

Dendrochronologists, scientists who use tree rings to study climatic and hydrologic changes, have taken advantage of the high-elevation source of water to estimate long-term variations in Colorado River flow.[47] Using trees growing on poor sites, which are therefore more sensitive to climate and particularly to drought,

these scientists have used variations in the radial growth of coniferous species—particularly Ponderosa pine (*Pinus ponderosa*)—to estimate flow volumes downstream from roughly A.D. 1600 to the present. The average flow volume for the Green River at the town of Green River is 4.5 million acre-feet per year (1896-2000), and tree-ring reconstructions indicate the long-term average is approximately the same (392-year record). For the Colorado River near Cisco, the twentieth-century runoff volume is 5.4 million acre-feet per year, and the long-term average is 5.9 million acre-feet per year.[48]

The flow volumes for the Green and Colorado rivers have not been constant through time.[49] The period of about 1900 to 1930 is unusually high for the period of A.D. 1720 to 1960, and a low-water period from about 1870 to 1900 is unprecedented in the record. The average flow volume from 1906 to 1930 was 10.3 million acre-feet, and it was 8.3 million acre-feet from 1942 to 1965. Climate has overwhelmed the influence of dams; the flow volume from 1965 to 1999 is 9.0 million acre-feet, or roughly equal to the average flow volume of 9.1 million acre-feet for the twentieth century. Using streamside trees to estimate streamflow, annual flow volumes have been estimated back to the seventeenth century for Cataract Canyon (see Chapter 8).

Summer thunderstorms rarely raise the level of the Colorado River by a significant amount. Instead, their major contribution to the river is sediment eroded from the colorful Mesozoic and Cenozoic sandstones, mudstones, and shales that define Canyon Country's scenery.[50] While the water comes from the high mountains, the sediment comes from the Colorado Plateau. At Lee's Ferry, Arizona, before Glen Canyon Dam was built, the Colorado River had sediment concentrations of less than 10,000 parts per million (ppm) during the spring runoff floods, but floods caused by summer thunderstorms raised the sediment concentrations to 20,000 ppm or higher.[51] Spring floods carried coarser, mostly sand-sized sediment, while summer floods carried more silt and clay.

The spring floods scoured the bed in the alluvial reaches of the river, transporting those sediments in suspension or along the bed. At Lee's Ferry, the river bed dropped as much as twenty-seven feet as the flood wave passed, rebounding to its original level as the flood receded and during the summer.[52] At Green River, Utah, the bed of the Green River had much less scour (up to about five feet) during floods of much lower discharge.[53] Similar scour would be expected in other alluvial reaches of the Colorado River, such as near Moab, but scour in the bedrock reaches would be less and limited mostly to pools above or below rapids.[54] One thing is certain: scour and fill in these rivers occur seasonally in response to flood discharge and sediment input, and the long-term nature of scour and fill is dependent on the effects of upstream dams.

From Crystal Clear to Torrents of Mud

The word "flood" covers a wide range of processes in Cataract Canyon. For that matter, the ways that sediment is moved varies across the scale of processes that geologists ascribe worldwide.[55] Some perennial side canyons have clear water, while the Colorado River is generally muddy, particularly during the spring flood and summer flash floods. This sediment-transport process is called *streamflow*, the mechanics of which are relatively well understood. Some of the larger side canyons produce highly sediment-charged flows, "too thick to drink and too thin to plow." Some of these flows are in the rather nebulous category known as *hyperconcentrated flow*, a term originally ascribed to sediment-rich flows in the Paria River at Lee's Ferry and in some tributaries to the San Juan River in New Mexico.[56] Hyperconcentrated flow, if it does exist as a distinct fluvial process, is poorly understood.

Occasionally, torrents of mud flow down the small, steep side canyons in Cataract Canyon. As will be discussed in Chapters 8 and 10, this type of flood, known as a *debris flow*, has occurred recently in three sites along the river. Debris flows have sediment concentrations greater than about eighty percent by weight, meaning they have the consistency of wet concrete. The only real difference between debris flows and wet concrete is that you generally do not add huge boulders to concrete; however, in Cataract Canyon, those boulders are routinely picked up and transported by debris flows. Boulders appear to bob

on the flow surface, and because debris flows can move over surprisingly low slopes, boulders can be rafted into the center of the canyon and the river. Debris flows stop when they spread out over a wide surface, such as occurs when one reaches a debris fan on the Colorado River. In Grand Canyon, several debris flows have dammed the river for short periods of time.[57]

Debris flows have the highest sediment concentration of any water-based flow.[58] Hydrologists consider the continuum of flow—from streamflow to debris flow—to be the range of *fluvial processes*, or sediment-transport mechanisms dependent on water. Above this range are the *colluvial processes*, which may involve all three phases of sediment, water, and air, and typically are not completely saturated, if water is present at all. Colluvial processes include rockfalls, which are common in Cataract Canyon, avalanches, and landslides (explored further in Chapters 8 and 10); and rotational slumps (this chapter and Chapter 9). Although colluvial processes generally involve unsaturated sediments, landslides may slip on saturated sediments at their bases. A colluvial process such as landslide may change into a fluvial process such as debris flow if sufficient water is added to create a saturated water-based flow. This transition is a major initiation mechanism for debris flows on the Colorado Plateau.

The Hidden Tributaries in Cataract Canyon

In Cataract Canyon, it is easy to spot several tributaries as one moves downstream. These include Lower Red Lake, Cross and Y, and Range canyons on the free-flowing reach; while Gypsum, Clearwater, and Dark canyons are notable on the reservoir. By analyzing topographic maps, we have designated 177 tributaries in Cataract Canyon, from the Confluence down to Sheep Canyon, near the historical end of Cataract. The average tributary has a drainage area of 5.6 square miles, but that number is deceptive: they range in size from 0.04 square miles (the smallest unit we mapped) to 252 square miles (Dark Canyon).

Tributary canyons come in three varieties. Some simply drain the interior walls of Cataract Canyon, creating rills or gullies on the slopes between bedrock parapets. These steep tributaries, usually little more than high-angled chutes, produce small amounts of streamflow but are also capable of producing sizeable debris flows. An example of this type of tributary is on river right at the head of Rapid 1; the channel can be readily identified as a red-streaked gully leading to cliffs of Cedar Mesa Sandstone high above the river. The second type of tributary has significant drainage area on top of the Cedar Mesa Sandstone and has a similar behavior as the inner-canyon tributaries. An example of this type of tributary is the small canyon on river left at the head of Rapid 4.

The third type of tributary penetrates the landscape well beyond the walls of Cataract Canyon, draining sizeable areas of Canyonlands. These canyons can produce substantial streamflow floods and they also produce large debris flows. Range Canyon with a watershed of thirty-seven square miles is perhaps the best example of this type in Cataract Canyon, but other canyons have surprisingly large drainage areas as well. A good example is the small canyon on river right at Rapid 5; this innocuous-looking tributary has a drainage area of 13.7 square miles. Teapot (a.k.a. Calf) Canyon, which joins the Colorado at Big Drop 1, has a drainage area of 19.3 square miles. In the inundated Cataract Canyon, Dark Canyon is the largest tributary, followed by Gypsum (120 square miles) and Bowdie (75.5 square miles) canyons.

What is more interesting than the large number of tributaries is where they occur relative to the rapids in Cataract Canyon. Dark Canyon joins the Colorado where Dark Canyon Rapid used to roar. This rapid once was the single-largest drop on the Colorado River; now most of the time the current in the reservoir is impossible to detect. Teapot Canyon joins the river at the most significant remaining rapids, the Big Drops. Range Canyon has the largest remaining debris fan in the river corridor and forms the maelstrom known as Mile Long Rapid. All of the rapids of Cataract Canyon are either directly associated with tributaries or are indirectly associated by outwash from upstream.

THE ROCKS AND THE RIVER

Meanders and Bedrock

The process of river meandering has been of great interest to fluvial geomorphologists, and there is perhaps no other region where the meandering of the major rivers is as obvious as on the Colorado Plateau. Beginning with the observations and measurements of Powell, Gilbert, and Dutton, many researchers have tried to make geological and mathematical sense of the twists and turns in the region's canyons. Raymond C. Moore, a U.S. Geological Survey geologist, was one of the first to study the nature of meanders in the region.[59] He had firsthand experience, being the geologist on the 1923 expedition through Grand Canyon as well as a researcher in the region, but he did not accompany the expedition through Cataract Canyon in 1921. Nonetheless, he wrote that the Colorado River through Cataract Canyon is noteworthy because its meanders are poorly developed compared to those of either the Green River or the Colorado River upstream from the Confluence. He observed, correctly, that the extent of meandering is related to rock hardness at river level: the more resistant the rocks, the less meandering occurs.

Meandering, and particularly the phenomenon of cutoff meanders, is related to gradient, rock type, and to a lesser extent the regional dip of the strata.[60] Low gradient reaches of the Green, Colorado, and San Juan rivers meander more than high-gradient reaches. Meanders are more pronounced in less resistant strata than in more resistant strata. Less predictable is the effect of dip slope; rivers flowing against the stratigraphic dip (rising beds) meander more than those flowing with the dip (falling beds). Exceptions occur, however, and gradient exerts the strongest effect.[61] Meander cutoffs are insufficiently understood to predict their locations, although they clearly occur more frequently in low gradient reaches.

The formation of bedrock canyons, and possibly the development of meanders, is affected by *sapping processes*. Sapping consists of bedrock erosion by means of groundwater discharge at contacts between units, or bedding planes within units, where water movement is restricted vertically.[62] Although sapping may occur in any heterogeneous sedimentary rock type, it is most common in sandstones and may be the best explanation for the dramatic alcoves that occur in the Navajo and Wingate sandstones in Canyonlands.[63] Trin Alcove on the Green River, developed in Navajo Sandstone, and The Grotto, an alcove in Meander Canyon frequently used for musical performances, may be the best examples in the region of the effects of sapping on bedrock channels (see Chapter 5).

The Longitudinal Profile of the Modern River

The 1921 U.S. Geological Survey expedition collected invaluable long-term data in the form of a longitudinal profile of the river through Cataract Canyon (Figure 3-4). This profile clearly shows the nature of the river and its rapids through the approaches, the canyon itself, and downstream where the river once flowed into Glen Canyon. It is strange that in this era of satellite positioning systems and laser theodolites no one has duplicated this measurement.

Both the Green and Colorado rivers have low-gradient approaches to the Confluence (see Chapter 5). The gradient of the combined rivers increases for a few miles, then radically increases downstream from Rapid 1. At the end of Cataract Canyon, the gradient again is gradual as the Colorado River enters what once was Glen Canyon. In detail, Cataract Canyon is a series of closely-spaced drops between Rapid 1 and Gypsum Canyon, followed by a section of pools and drops that culminates in Dark Canyon Rapid, which formerly had a total drop of thirty feet over 1.2 miles. Rapid 47, 1.7 miles downstream of Dark Canyon Rapid, was reportedly bedrock-controlled,[64] with the river dropping over a ledge of Cedar Mesa Sandstone instead of flowing over a pile of boulders.

At the Confluence, the bed of the river is perhaps 125 to 150 feet above bedrock, based on holes drilled in the bed of the Colorado River in 1914.[65] Between Rapid 47 and the Confluence is the whitewater of Cataract Canyon, including both the current free-flowing reach and the section now submerged beneath the reservoir. The overall gradient through Cataract Canyon was 11.3 ft/mi, compared to a typical gradient

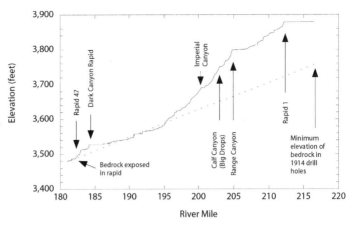

Figure 3-4. Longitudinal profile of the Colorado River through Canyonlands National Park.

of less than 1.1 ft/mi on the approaching Green and Colorado rivers. Most of the drop occurs in the rapids.

Meandering of the rivers in bedrock reportedly reflects this gradient change.[66] Because Cataract Canyon is controlling the gradient (or base level) of the Colorado River, both the Green and Colorado rivers may be widening their meander belts instead of cutting downward. This hypothesis would explain why there are cutoff meanders upstream of the Confluence (*e.g.*, Anderson Bottom on the Green, Jackson Hole in Meander Canyon) and sinuous canyons while the canyon through Cataract Canyon is relatively straight with no obvious meander cutoffs.

THE ROCKS AND THE RAPIDS

Two facts about the rapids of Cataract Canyon are readily apparent to any visitor: First, the rapids are huge and stand in stark contrast to the lack of rapids above the confluence, and second, these rapids are dotted with large boulders. The more astute river traveler will observe that the nature of the canyon walls changes downstream from the Confluence and then again in lower Cataract Canyon. Upstream, the walls are naked, solid rock; in Cataract Canyon, the walls are littered with boulders and broken rock. The giant Toreva blocks around Tilted Park stand as mute monuments to the difference between the reaches of the Colorado Rivers upstream and downstream from Cataract Canyon.

Many river runners, most of them geologists, have speculated on why Cataract Canyon has such fearsome whitewater. Large rapids affect people that way; indeed, it seems a natural curiosity that they want to know why those awesome spectacles of nature were put across the largest river in the arid southwest. Many observers have grasped at the seemingly strong associations between the geomorphology of the canyon and rapids for an explanation. Our answer involves a more subtle look at the processes that can leave boulders sitting in the middle of the Colorado River, instead of associating rapid with the unrelated, but impressive features, created by mass wasting in Cataract Canyon. Below we review the various hypotheses and discuss their strengths and weaknesses, and the competing hypotheses as to the origin of Cataract's rapids will be discussed throughout this book.

The Graben Hypothesis

Some geologists have seized upon the evidence of recent movement in the Grabens area of the Needles District as an explanation for the rapids in Cataract Canyon. According to this hypothesis, salt-induced deformation initiated by upward movement of anhydrite diapirs from the Paradox Formation fractures the upper Paleozoic bedrock, leading to Toreva blocks that rotate towards the Colorado River. This mechanism essentially is the "toothpaste squeeze" process.

Salt deformation of the overlying bedrock has caused faulting, as manifested by those grabens. Fracturing creates a ready supply of large boulders, but it does not explain how they get into the Colorado River. The timing and locations of the major deformations are out of sync with rapids, which appear to be relatively recent phenomena. Major rapids (*e.g.*, the Big Drops) are not at the rotational slumps; conversely, the Colorado River has a relatively low gradient adjacent to the largest rotational slumps at Tilted Park. The canyon is relatively wide where Toreva blocks occur, suggesting that the Colorado River has dealt with these obstructions and the blocks are not controlling the river's profile.

The Landslide/Rockfall Hypothesis

Another popular hypothesis is related to landslides, which many observers think they see throughout Cataract Canyon. According to this hypothesis, deformation by anhydrite diapirs has destabilized the cliffs, leading to large landslides and/or rockfalls. Sidney Paige, a geologist with the 1921 USGS Expedition, was one of the first proponents.[67] According to this idea, rockfalls and landslides are the primary source of large boulders in the river corridor. Rockfall- and landslide-controlled rapids do occur on western rivers, and a large "landslide" deposit is present at the former site of Gypsum Rapid as well as on river left at the Big Drops.

Landslides in the classical sense are not common in Cataract Canyon, although evidence for large landslides is present between Rapids 2 and 3 and just upstream from Rapid 5. A better term for these features might be "bedrock slumps," and they appear to be more related to Toreva block rotation than landslides. The problem with the idea of landslides creating rapids is that the river has fairly wide eddies in the vicinity of these landslides. At Gypsum Canyon, debris-flow outwash is pushing the Colorado River against an ancient deposit, which was actively eroding prior to filling of the reservoir. In other words, the river adjusted to the "landslide" on river right but was still being controlled by debris-flow deposition from the tributary on river left.

More commonly, avalanches and scattered rockfalls move fractured bedrock toward the Colorado River. Rockfalls occur throughout Cataract Canyon, but the canyon is wide enough that boulders typically do not reach the middle of the Colorado River. Instead, most of the talus is stored in aprons such as those present along the left margin of the Big Drops, the left side of Mile Long Rapid, and the right side of the river through Rapids 1 through 8. Isolated rockfalls have had major effects on rapids, particularly Rapid 18, as discussed in Chapter 8, but rockfalls alone do not explain the rapids of Cataract Canyon.

In addition, calling the commonly observed, poorly-sorted deposits in Cataract Canyon "landslides" is a questionable interpretation of geologic evidence. An alternative explanation is that they actually are large debris-flow deposits. They raised the bed of the Colorado River, which downcut through them at some unknown time, and their remnants are now stranded above the channel. Most of the purported rockfall/landslide deposits are not adjacent to the head of rapids; the Colorado River has removed their influence on its longitudinal profile and now concentrates its erosion process on deposits at the mouths of side canyons. Examples of now-stranded deposits are below Rapid 5, the pool below Rapid 7, the pool below Rapid 15—all on the right side—and the pool between Big Drops 2 and 3 on the left side. In the inundated Cataract Canyon, these deposits occurred where rapids were not present on the free-flowing river.

The Debris-Flow Hypothesis

Debris flows from major tributaries and small chutes deliver large boulders from cliffs and talus aprons to the river, creating debris fans that constrict the river at low discharges. Reworking leaves only the largest rocks, which form controls on major hydraulics at high discharges. Reworked material is transported downstream, forming islands and debris bars that create secondary riffles and rapids.

Debris flow evidence is especially abundant in Cataract Canyon where the Halgaito Shale is exposed in the cliffs above the river or in tributary canyons. This shale of terrestrial origin is very similar to shales in Grand Canyon that spawn debris flows.[68] Starting at Rapid 1, debris flow evidence is apparent everywhere along the river down to, or below, Gypsum Canyon. Shales similar to the Halgaito are known to be related to higher debris-flow frequency in Grand Canyon, where rapids also are associated with major tributaries. Salt deformation has destabilized cliffs, leading to formation of large talus aprons that provide a ready source of poorly sorted sediments for debris flows. Finally, wet landslides and rockfalls can mobilize into debris flows and transport boulders much further down slope than if the landslides or rockfalls are relatively dry.

Most rapids in Cataract Canyon are directly associated with major tributaries and debris fans. The locations of some of these tributaries, particularly in Mile Long Rapid, are not obvious from river level. These debris fans are more visible at low water, as most of these fans are overtopped during the spring runoff. Because of intense reworking by the Colorado River, and in some cases by the narrowness of the river corridor, some debris fans are not readily apparent (such as at Rapid 7) unless one looks carefully from the river bank at low water.

Secondary rapids are readily apparent in Cataract Canyon, including those that have received additional contributions from small chutes that produce debris flows. The best examples of secondary rapids are Big Drops 2 and 3, which are primarily created by outwash from the Teapot (Calf) Canyon debris fan and are secondarily affected by debris flows from chutes on river left. Less obvious is the extremely large debris-flow outwash and rapids associated with Range Canyon that are associated with Mile Long Rapid. Rapid 20, also known as Ben Hurt Rapid, flows around an island that terminates the outwash sequence that begins more than one mile upstream.

The best explanation of the rapids of Cataract Canyon is that various deformation processes—salt diapir formation and Toreva block rotation—create a geologic environment that is conducive to frequent debris-flow production. Further enhancing this process is the presence of a terrestrial shale—the Halgaito Shale—that has characteristics conducive to debris flow initiation and transport.

Notes

1. For particular information on the geology of Canyon Country, readers should see D.A. Sprinkel, T.C. Chidsey, Jr., and P.B. Anderson, editors, *Geology of Utah's Parks and Monuments* (Salt Lake City: Utah Geological Association Publication 28, 2000); L.F. Hintze, *Geologic History of Utah* (Provo, Utah: Brigham Young University Geology Studies, Special Publication 7, 1988); W.L. Stokes, *Geology of Utah* (Salt Lake City: Utah Museum of Natural History and Utah Geological and Mineral Survey, 1986); S.W. Lohman, *The Geologic Story of Canyonlands National Park* (Washington, D.C.: U.S. Geological Survey Bulletin 1327, 1974); F.A. Barnes, *Canyon Country Geology for the*

Layman and Rockhound (Salt Lake City, Utah: Wasatch Publishers, 1996); and D.L. Baars, *Canyonlands Country, Geology of Canyonlands and Arches National Parks* (Salt Lake City, Utah: University of Utah Press, 1993). The geology in map form is given in P.W. Huntoon, G.H. Billingsley, Jr., and W.J. Breed, *Geologic Map of Canyonlands National Park and Vicinity, Utah* (Moab, Utah: Canyonlands Natural History Association, 1983). The bedrock geology at river level is given in Bill Belknap, Buzz Belknap, and L.B. Evans, *Belknap's Revised Waterproof Canyonlands River Guide* (Evergreen, Colorado: Westwater Books, 1996).

2. D.L. Baars, "Paleozoic Rocks of Canyonlands Country," in *Geology of Cataract Canyon and Vicinity*, ed. J.A. Campbell (Durango, Colorado: Four Corners Geological Society, 1987), 11–17.

3. P.G. Griffiths, R.H. Webb, and T.S. Melis, *Initiation and Frequency of Debris Flows in Grand Canyon, Arizona* (Tucson, Arizona: U.S. Geological Survey Open-File Report 96–491, 1996), 35 p. Sidney Paige of the 1921 U.S. Geological Survey expedition repeatedly identified the bed as "Hermit Shale" in his notes.

4. Stokes, *Geology of Utah*, 120.

5. Barnes, *Canyon Country Geology*, 60.

6. G.M. Richmond, *Quaternary Stratigraphy of the La Sal Mountains, Utah* (Washington, D.C.: U.S. Geological Survey Professional Paper 324, 1962).

7. Stokes, *Geology of Utah*, 143.

8. Both the Laramide and Tertiary deformations left large and small structural features. Outcrop- to microscopic-scale deformations in the sandstones southwest of our region are discussed in G.H. Davis, *Structural Geology of the Colorado Plateau Region of Southern Utah* (Boulder, Colorado: Geological Society of America Special Paper 342, 1999), 157 p.

9. Ibid., 148.

10. R. Fillmore, *The Geology of the Parks, Monuments, and Wildlands of Southern Utah* (Salt Lake City: University of Utah Press, 2000), 116–119. Interestingly, this book completely ignores the Pennsylvanian Hermosa Group in its treatment.

11. H.H. Doelling, "Geology of the Salt Valley Anticline and Arches National Park, Grand County, Utah," in *Salt Deformation in the Paradox Region*, eds. H.H. Doelling, C.G. Oviatt, and P.W. Huntoon (Salt Lake City: Utah Geological and Mineral Survey, Bulletin 122, 1988), 41.

12. Stokes, *Geology of Utah*, 155.

13. Ibid., 189.

14. C.B. Hunt, *Geologic History of the Colorado River* (Washington, D.C.: U.S. Geological Survey Professional Paper 669, 1969), 59–130.

15. Hintze, *Geologic History of Utah*, 79.

16. Doelling, *Geology of the Salt Valley Anticline*, 43–50.

17. G.E. McGill and A.W. Stromquist, "Origin of Graben in the Needles District, Canyonlands National Park, Utah," in *Canyonlands Country*, ed. J.E. Fassett (Durango, Colorado: Four Corners Geological Society, 1975), 235–243; P. Walsh and D.D. Schultz-Ela, "Mechanics of Graven Evolution in Canyonlands National Park, Utah," *Geological Society of America Bulletin* 115(2003): 259–270.

18. Lohman, *The Geologic Story of Canyonlands*, 73–80; N.E. Biggar and J.A. Adams, "Dates Derived from Quaternary Strata in the Vicinity of Canyonlands National Park," in *Geology of Cataract Canyon and Vicinity*, ed. J.A. Campbell (Durango, Colorado: Four Corners Geological Society, 1987), 127–136.

19. I.G. Wong, J.R. Humphrey, A.C. Kollman, B.B. Munden, and D.D. Wright, "Earthquake Activity In and Around Canyonlands National Park, Utah," in *Geology of Cataract Canyon and Vicinity*, ed. J.A. Campbell (Durango, Colorado: Four Corners Geological Society, 1987), 51–58.

20. W.C. Darrah, "Geology Notes of John Wesley Powell," *Utah Historical Quarterly* 19 (1947): 134–139.

21. M.C. Rabbitt, *John Wesley Powell: Pioneer Statesman of Federal Science* (Washington, D.C.: U.S. Geological Survey Professional Paper 669–A, 1969), 7–8; G.P. Merrill, *The First One Hundred Years of American Geology* (New York: Hafner Publishing Company, 1969), 479–480; Wallace Stegner, *Beyond the Hundredth Meridian: John Wesley Powell and the Second Opening of the West* (Lincoln: University of Nebraska Press, 1953), 153.

22. Two seminal papers on base level and its significance to geomorphology are L.B. Leopold and W.B. Bull, "Base Level, Aggradation, and Grade," *Proceedings of the American Philosophical Society* 123 (1979): 160–202, and L.B. Leopold, "Base Level Rise: Gradient of Deposition," *Israel Journal of Earth Science* 41 (1993): 57–64.

23. Merrill, *The First One Hundred Years*, 544.

24. M.C. Rabbitt, *Minerals, Lands, and Geology for the Common Defense and General Welfare: Volume 1, Before 1879* (Washington, D.C.: U.S. Government Printing Office, 1979), 230.

25. W.R. Hansen, *The Geologic Story of the Uinta Mountains* (Washington, D.C.: U.S. Geological Survey Bulletin 1291, 1969).

26. Hunt, *Geologic History*, 59.

27. Little is more contentious than the age of Grand Canyon—and by association, Cataract Canyon—in the geological literature of the Colorado Plateau. See the discussions in Hunt, *Geologic History*, 63–65; E.D. McKee, R.F. Wilson, W.J. Breed, and C.S. Breed, *Evolution of the Colorado River in Arizona* (Flagstaff: Museum of Northern Arizona, 1967); Ivo Lucchitta, *Canyon Maker, a Geological History of the Colorado River* (Flagstaff: Museum of Northern Arizona, *Plateau* 59 (1988). As Lucchitta states, most of

the problem is created by negative evidence, or missing information, leading to reliance on conjecture, speculation, and circumstantial evidence that may have little to do with reality.

28. Lucchitta, *Canyon Maker,* 10.

29. McKee *et al., Evolution of the Colorado River,* 52.

30. One recent estimate holds that Glen Canyon is less than 500,000 years old; T.C. Hanks, Ivo Lucchitta, S.W. Davis, M.E. Davis, R.C. Finkel, S.A. Lefton, and C.D. Garvin, "The Colorado River and the Age of Glen Canyon," in *The Colorado River: Origin and Evolution,* eds. R.A. Young and E.E. Spamer (Grand Canyon, Arizona: Grand Canyon Natural History Association Monograph 12, 2002).

31. Most geologists evade the question of the age of Cataract Canyon; see Hunt, *Geologic History,* 83–85. Huntoon (p. 83) flatly states that Cataract Canyon is "younger than 5 million years old" with no direct evidence; P.W. Huntoon, "Late Cenozoic Gravity Tectonic Deformation Related to the Paradox Salts in the Canyonlands Area of Utah," *Utah Geological and Mineral Survey Bulletin 122* (1988): 79–93. Presumably, Huntoon is equating the age of Cataract and Grand Canyons.

32. Richmond, *La Sal Mountains,* 94.

33. M.E. Cooley, "Glen and San Juan Canyons Area," in McKee *et al., Evolution of the Colorado River,* 23–24.

34. Lohman, *The Geologic Story of Canyonlands,* 86–87.

35. The concept of Toreva blocks, developed from the Black Mesa area of northern Arizona, is discussed in J.A. Mabbutt, *Desert Landforms: An Introduction to Systematic Geomorphology* (Cambridge, Massachusetts, The MIT Press, 1979), 277.

36. Much of the discussion here is derived from Huntoon, "Late Cenozoic Gravity Tectonic Deformation," 81–93.

37. P.W. Huntoon, "The Meander Anticline, Canyonlands, Utah, an Unloading Structure Resulting from Horizontal Gliding on Salt," *Geological Society of America Bulletin* 93 (1982): 941–950.

38. H.W.C. Prommel and H.E. Crum, "Domes of Permian and Pennsylvanian Age in Southeastern Utah and Their Influence on Oil Accumulation," *Bulletin of the American Association of Petroleum Geologists* 11(1927): 373–393.

39. McGill and Stromquist, "Origin of Graben."

40. E.C. LaRue, *Water Power and Flood Control on the Colorado River below Green River, Utah* (Washington, D.C.: U.S. Geological Survey Water-Supply Paper 556, 1925).

41. J.E. O'Connor, L.L. Ely, E.E. Wohl, L.E. Stevens, T.S. Melis, V.S. Kale, and V.R. Baker, "A 4,500 Year Record of Large Floods on the Colorado River in the Grand Canyon, Arizona," *Journal of Geology* 102 (1994): 1–9.

42. M.M. Van Steeter and John Pitlick, "Geomorphology and Endangered Fish Habitats of the Upper Colorado River. 1. Historic Changes in Streamflow, Sediment Load, and Channel Morphology," *Water Resources Research* 34 (1998): 287–302.

43. F.M. Tanner, *The Far Country: a Regional History of Moab and La Sal, Utah* (Salt Lake City: Olympus Publishing Company, 1976), 269.

44. R.A. Firmage, *A History of Grand County* (Salt Lake City: Utah State Historical Society, 1996), 196–197.

45. R.H. Webb, *Late Holocene Flooding on the Escalante River, South-Central Utah* (Tucson: University of Arizona, unpublished Ph.D. dissertation, 1985), 3–21.

46. Richmond, *La Sal Mountains.*

47. Edmund Schulman, "Tree-Ring Hydrology of the Colorado River Basin," *University of Arizona Bulletin 16, Laboratory of Tree-Ring Research Bulletin 2* (1945): 1–51; C.W. Stockton and G.C. Jacoby, Jr., "Long-Term Surface-Water Supply and Streamflow Trends in the Upper Colorado River Basin Based on Tree-Ring Analyses," *Lake Powell Research Project Bulletin* 18 (1976): 1–70.

48. Stockton and Jacoby, "Long-Term Trends," 30–32.

49. *Ibid.,* 37.

50. W.V. Irons, C.H. Hembree, and G.L. Oakland, *Water Resources of the Upper Colorado River Basin* (Washington, D.C.: U.S. Government Printing Office, U.S. Geological Survey Professional Paper 441, 1965).

51. E.D. Andrews, "Sediment Transport in the Colorado River Basin," in *Colorado River Ecology and Dam Management,* ed. G.R. Marzolf (Washington, D.C.: National Academy Press, 1991), 54–74; D.J. Topping, D.M. Rubin, and L.E. Vierra, Jr., "Colorado River Sediment Transport 1. Natural Sediment Supply Limitation and the Influence of Glen Canyon Dam," *Water Resources Research* 36 (2000): 515–542.

52. D.E. Burkham, *Trends in Selected Hydraulic Variables for the Colorado River at Lees Ferry and Near Grand Canyon for the Period 1922–1984* (Springfield, Virginia: National Technical Information Service, Report PB88-216098, GCES/07/87, 1986); Topping *et al.,* "Colorado River Sediment Transport 1," 528.

53. T.M. Allred and J.C. Schmidt, "Channel Narrowing by Vertical Accretion Along the Green River near Green River, Utah," *Geological Society of America Bulletin* 111 (1999): 1757–1772.

54. Burkham, *Trends in Selected Hydraulic Variables.*

55. T.C. Pierson and J.E. Costa, "A Rheologic Classification of Subaerial Sediment-water Flows," in *Debris Flows/Avalanches—Process, Recognition, and Mitigation,* eds. J.E. Costa and G.F. Wieczorek (Boulder, Colorado: Geological Society of America, Reviews in Engineering Geology 7, 1987): 1–12.

56. J.P. Beverage and J.K. Culbertson, "Hyperconcentrations of Suspended Sediment," *American Society of Civil*

Engineers, Journal of the Hydraulics Division 90 (1964): 117–126.

57. R.H. Webb, T.S. Melis, P.G. Griffiths, J.G. Elliott, T.E. Cerling, R.J. Poreda, T.W. Wise, T.W, and J.E. Pizzuto, *Lava Falls Rapid in Grand Canyon: Effects of Late Holocene Debris Flows on the Colorado River* (Washington, D.C., U.S. Geological Survey Professional Paper 1591, 1999).

58. Pierson and Costa, "A Rheologic Classification," 1–12.

59. R.C. Moore, "Origin of Inclosed Meanders on Streams of the Colorado Plateau," *Journal of Geology* 34 (1926): 29–57.

60. D.R. Harden, "Controlling Factors in the Distribution and Development of Incised Meanders in the Central Colorado Plateau," *Geological Society of America Bulletin* 102 (1990): 233–242.

61. For a discussion of the effect of dip angle on meandering, see D.L. Baars, "Controlling Factors in the Distribution and Development of Incised Meanders in the Central Colorado Plateau: Discussion," *Geological Society of America Bulletin* 102 (1990): 1603–1605, and D.R. Harden, "Reply," *Geological Society of America Bulletin* 102 (1990): 1605.

62. Julie Laity, "The Colorado Plateau in Planetary Geology Studies," in W.L. Graf, Richard Hereford, Julie Laity, and R.A. Young, "Colorado Plateau," in *Geomorphic Systems of North America* ed. W.L. Graf (Geological Society of America, Centennial Special Volume 2, 1987), 288–297.

63. Julie Laity, "The Role of Groundwater Sapping in Valley Evolution on the Colorado Plateau," in *Sapping Features of the Colorado Plateau, A Comparative Planetary Geology Field Guide* ed. A.D. Howard, R.C. Kochel, and H.E. Holt (Washington, D.C.: National Aeronautics and Space Administration, NASA SP-491, 1988), 63–70.

64. Hugh Miser, unpublished notes, in the Marston Collection, Huntington Library, San Marino, California.

65. Secretary of the Interior, "Problems of Imperial Valley and Vicinity" (67th *Congress, 2d Session, Senate Documents*, v. 11, no. 142, 1922), Plate XLVII.

66. Moore, "Origin of Inclosed Meanders," 55.

67. Sidney Paige, Field notes, 32. U.S. Geological Survey Field Records Library, Denver, Colorado.

68. P.G. Griffiths, R.H. Webb, and T.S. Melis, *Initiation and Frequency of Debris Flows in Grand Canyon, Arizona* (U.S. Geological Survey Open-File Report 96–491, 1996).

4

A HARD PLACE TO MAKE A LIVING

The Plants and Animals of Canyonlands

Burning plains, barren even of sage—all glowing with bright color and flooded with blazing sunlight. . . . It is the extreme desolation, the blankest solitude, a superlative desert . . . the plain is barren, treeless, waterless.

– Clarence E. Dutton, 1880[1]

Cataract Canyon, a land of extremes, appears harsh and seemingly lifeless. The deep, fast-flowing river lined with lush vegetation distracts the mind from the true nature of this region. Step outside this thin, cool riverine line in the summer, and you slam full-force into a wall of heat, reminding you that this is a desert, a place to be taken seriously if you hope to survive independent of your drink cooler. In the same spot just six months later, the water can be frozen, the air bitterly cold, and there is little sign of living things. Life is there in Canyonlands, but it takes advantage of those times—usually in spring and fall—when conditions are favorable to show its presence. You just have to know when and where to look.

CLIMATE OF AN ARID REGION

Precipitation

Most of the Canyonlands region is arid, receiving less than ten inches of rainfall annually. Regional climate data have been collected since the late 1800s, giving this region one of the longest climatic records in the western United States. Moab, at 4,020 feet elevation, has an average annual precipitation of 8.99 inches, some of which falls in the winter months as snow (Figure 4-1). The highest rainfall occurs in October (1.16 in.) and the lowest in February (0.50 in.). Precipitation is distributed evenly throughout the year

with predictable short periods of drought in June and late September.[2]

The range in average annual precipitation across the region is large, with 5.32 inches of precipitation at Hanksville (4,310 ft) and 15.02 inches at Monticello (6,820 ft). Hanksville gets less precipitation than Moab in part because of the *rain shadow* induced by the Aquarius Plateau to its west, whereas Moab benefits in part from the *orographic lifting* associated with the La Sal Mountains to its southeast. Mountains affect precipitation by inducing more on the upslope side (orographic lifting), as moist air is forced to rise over the summit; because moisture is wrenched out of the clouds on the upwind side of the mountains, less moisture is available downwind in the rain shadow.

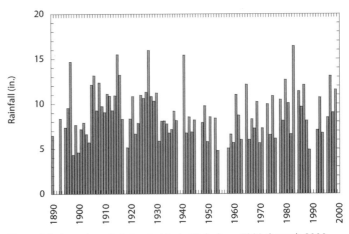

Figure 4-1. Annual precipitation in Moab, Utah, from 1889 through 2000.

63

Interannual variability of precipitation is large, underscoring that the average rainfall does not mean much in arid regions. Annual precipitation at Moab has ranged from a high of 16.42 inches in 1983 to a low of only 4.32 inches in 1898.

Precipitation on the Colorado Plateau is related to global circulation patterns in the atmosphere as well as conditions in the Pacific Ocean.[3] The El Niño–Southern Oscillation (ENSO) is a global-scale oceanic process that has its highest expression in sea-surface temperatures and pressures in the equatorial Pacific Ocean.[4] The so-called "warm phase" of ENSO is commonly known as El Niño conditions; conversely, the "cold phase" is known as La Niña. El Niño conditions typically cause above-average rainfall in the region, while La Niña conditions reliably result in drought. In the twentieth century, El Niño conditions recurred every four to seven years. Not surprisingly, some of the wettest years of the century (1905, 1941, 1965, 1983) experienced El Niño conditions while some of the most severe droughts (1956, 1989) occurred during La Niña conditions.[5] About one-quarter of the time, ENSO does not affect climate.

Another indicator of global-scale climate, called the Pacific Decadal Oscillation (PDO), integrates atmospheric-circulation conditions with those in the North Pacific Ocean to create an index that reliably predicts decadal-scale variations in climate.[6] On the Colorado Plateau, periods with positive PDO are generally wet while periods with negative PDO have sustained drought. El Niño interacts with PDO (the two are statistically related): the combination of El Niño conditions and a positive PDO results in very wet conditions on the Colorado Plateau.[7] Although the PDO does not perfectly explain climatic variation in the region, it is a good enough barometer of potential climate that some have predicted that, because the PDO went strongly negative in 1999, the region may experience sustained drought for roughly the first quarter of the twenty-first century.[8]

Temperatures

Temperatures are also highly variable in the Canyonlands region, and the seasonal difference is startling.

At Moab, the record high temperature of 114°F was recorded on July 7, 1989, and the record low was −24°F on January 22, 1930. As a result, the Colorado River may freeze over in winter, with mush ice common in the winter months, while water temperatures can reach 80°F in August. There is little doubt that the climate of Canyonlands has also been extreme in historic and prehistoric times. There is also plenty of evidence that the climate has changed considerably in geologic time. In the Pleistocene, we know that different types of vegetation communities were present, as well as some animals that are now extinct. By comparing past plant distribution patterns to those found today, paleoecologists have inferred that the latest Pleistocene period (about 22,000 to 11,000 years before present) was cooler and probably wetter.[9] Instead of desert shrubs in Cataract Canyon, pinyon pine trees and junipers dominated the slopes. Therefore, the Cataract Canyon of 11,000 years ago bore little ecological resemblance to the canyon that we know today.

COPING WITH HARSH ENVIRONMENTS

Organisms can adapt to most conditions as long as they fluctuate within a relatively constrained range. However, adjusting to the variable and extreme conditions found in the Colorado Plateau region is difficult. Temperatures are exacerbated within narrow canyon walls. Hot air is trapped in the summer, driving temperatures upward. In the winter, cold air and limited sunlight mean temperatures plummet and stay low for weeks on end. Rainfall is erratic, and both droughts and floods can occur in the same year. The tops of the shallow, nutrient-poor soils are extremely hot in summer yet freeze in winter. The shallow soils hold little moisture, dry quickly, and produce significant runoff when rains are intense. Burrowing invertebrates (*e.g.*, termites or ants) and vertebrates (*e.g.*, mice) require deep soils to avoid temperature and moisture extremes; consequently, numbers of these organisms are low. Aquatic organisms are also exposed to huge swings in habitat conditions when the fast, relatively clear and cold waters of winter and spring are replaced by sluggish, sediment-laden warm waters in summer and fall.

Plants and animals that live in this region have two options for survival. They can either avoid the extreme conditions or they can develop ways to tolerate them. Avoidance is a common strategy and can be accomplished by leaving reproductive material such as seeds or eggs to produce future generations, suspending activity during unfavorable times, or migrating. Many plant species in this region are avoiders: they reduce or cease activity during summer and winter and instead are most active in spring and fall when water is readily available and moderate temperatures prevail. Good examples of "avoider" plants are spring and late-summer annuals, which germinate, grow, and set seed while conditions are favorable. When soil moisture is depleted, they die. Some perennial plants, such as Indian ricegrass (*Stipa hymenoides*), sand dropseed (*Sporobolus* sp.), and galleta (*Hilaria jamesii*) have green shoots in spring and fall, and are mostly or completely brown during summer and winter. Most perennial shrubs are able to stay active during summer but are dormant in the winter. Only a few plants are photosynthetically active throughout the year, including pinyon (*Pinus edulis*), juniper (*Juniperus osteosperma*), yuccas (*Yucca* sp.), and Mormon tea (*Ephedra* sp.)

Most small animals either stash food and/or *estivate* (lower the metabolism to reduce energy requirements) during unfavorable conditions. A few larger species are able to tolerate extreme conditions and are active year-round, including coyotes (*Canis latrans*), bobcats (*Felix rufus*), mountain lions (*Puma [Felis] concolor*), badgers (*Taxidea taxus*), mule deer (*Odocoileus hemionus*), and desert bighorn sheep (*Ovis canadensis nelsoni*). While many birds leave the region to avoid winter, some species, such as Bald Eagles (*Haliaetus leucocephalus*), migrate in for the winter.

Because of these demanding conditions, Canyon Country is a sparsely-vegetated landscape dominated by a few species of perennial plants, mostly shrubs, with only a few annual plants. Canyonlands National Park has 637 plant species (Appendix 1). Some of these plants are highly specialized endemics that occur nowhere else. The Canyonlands Province of southern Utah has one of the highest rates of plant endemism in the United States and the world.[10] Most endemic and rare plants are found in isolated habitats, as in seeps on rock faces (hanging gardens), or in extremely demanding environments, such as highly saline or drought-susceptible soils developed on shales. Luckily, only a few of these endemic plants are rare or endangered, as this region is vast, relatively inaccessible, and has not felt the impact of human activities until recently. These harsh conditions also keep out many invasive non-native species.

PLANT ADAPTATIONS TO EXTREME ENVIRONMENTS

Water Use and Conservation

Desert plants have many water-conserving features that facilitate activity when water is limited and temperatures are high.[11] Most adaptations reduce water usage and/or heat loading. Stems and leaves can reflect light and thus heat via light-colored hairs or spines, by extruding light-colored salt crystals, or by orienting themselves parallel to the incoming light. Plants also use surface projections such as spines, hairs, and curled leaf margins to reduce evaporative losses by reducing air movement next to the plant surface. Air humidified by transpiration thus stays close to the leaf surface, reducing evaporative losses. Pores where the plants exchange gases are on the shady underside of the leaf, and these pores are often at the bottom of small pits; both features presumably reduce water loss. However, it is also possible these features also increase carbon dioxide intake required for photosynthesis.[12]

More leaves means more surface area from which to lose water, so many desert plants are deciduous, shedding their leaves every fall.[13] Other shrubs like blackbrush (*Coleogyne ramosissima*) are "drought-deciduous," dropping their leaves only if soils get too dry. This is a good compromise, as these plants do not need to produce new leaves every year. Other adaptations include plant leaves and stems that are narrow, thick, and/or covered with a waxy coating to reduce heating and evaporation. However, there are notable exceptions to these patterns, such as jimsonweed (*Datura* sp.) which has large, thin, dark leaves. Heat and water stress also play a large part in determining what a plant looks like: stems can act as water storage, as in cacti, or be arranged to maximize cooling, as in saltbush.[14]

Plants also have different root distribution patterns to deal with water stress. The roots of desert plants often extend further laterally and deeper and are better able to extract water from dry soils than plants that grow in moister regions. In the Canyonlands region, plants mostly have a combination of deep taproots and fibrous shallow roots (blackbrush, grasses), or deep taproots only (pinyon).[15]

On average, the Canyonlands region receives about two-thirds of its annual precipitation in winter and the rest in summer thunderstorms. Unfortunately, summer rainfall is unreliable and patchy. As a result, plants in this region do not have many roots at the soil surface, as these roots die during long, hot summers. This is in contrast to other deserts that receive reliable summer precipitation, such as the Sonoran Desert, where plants have numerous surface roots.[16] Some plants—such as rabbitbrush (*Chrysothamnus nauseosus*), Gambel's oak (*Quercus gambelii*), fourwing saltbush (*Atriplex canescens*), and juniper—do not use summer precipitation even if it is available, but instead depend on winter rainfall stored deep in soils.[17] Other plants rely almost exclusively on summer rains, including yucca, most cacti, locoweed (*Astragalus* sp.), Wright's birdbeak (*Cordylanthus wrightii*), yellow cryptantha (*Cryptantha flava*), globemallow (*Sphaeralcea* sp.), sand dropseed, and scrub oak (*Quercus* sp). The majority of plants utilize both summer and winter precipitation, including snakeweed (*Gutierrezia sarothrae*), blackbrush, pricklypear cactus (*Opuntia* sp.), sand sage (*Artemisia filifolia*), Mormon tea, shadscale (*Atriplex confertifolia*), and most perennial grasses.

Plant Fuel

Plants have three ways of utilizing sunlight for energy. These *photosynthetic pathways* have been called C_3, C_4 and CAM, referring to the process by which atmospheric carbon dioxide is converted to carbon within the plant.[18] Most shrubs and grasses in this region use the C_3 photosynthetic pathway. These species

are the least water efficient and are predominantly active from early spring to early summer. A few grasses (*e.g.*, galleta and dropseed) and shrubs (saltbush) are C_4 plants. These species are more water efficient and are predominantly active in the late summer and fall. The CAM pathway typically is used by cacti and other succulents, which are the most water-efficient species of all and are active from spring through fall.

Despite their carbon pathways, the peak activity times of plants do not always occur in what is "supposed" to be their optimal season. In the Canyonlands region, for instance, most plants are active when temperatures are warm and sufficient soil moisture is available, regardless of the calendar date. Therefore, while the dominant activity time for C_3 plants is springtime, these plants also green-up with the late summer rains. Indeed, if summer rains are above average, above-ground biomass of these plants in late summer can exceed that of spring. The same is true for the C_4 plants: although their main activity time is from late August through October, they are also green from March through June. Generally, however, C_3 plants set seed in early summer while C_4 plants set seeds in late summer.

Some plants do not use chlorophyll and sunlight to obtain their energy or carbon but instead are parasitic on other plants.[19] Broomrape (*Orobanche* sp., from two Greek words meaning "strangle" and "vetch") is the most common parasitic plant in the Canyonlands region. Broomrapes lack chlorophyll, have white stems and scale-like leaves, and are completely dependent on their host for energy. Indian paintbrush (*Castilleja* sp.) is a hemi-parasite that often infects sagebrush (*Artemisia tridentata*). This plant obtains carbon on its own (and thus is green), and also steals it from the host.

Both of these parasitic species have tiny seeds with elaborately-carved seed coats. These seeds ride along with water as it flows through cracks into the soil. If these seeds germinate near a host plant, cells of the parasite grow towards the host plant root and penetrate it to obtain carbon, minerals, and water from the host. Being a parasite is a challenge: they want to get as much as they can from their host without killing it, at least until they are able to complete their life cycle.

Clearly this is a very successful way to make a living, as there are a huge number of parasites at all levels in ecosystems worldwide.

Herbivory Protection

Plants have many ways to protect themselves from being stepped on or eaten. Blackbrush and yucca have branches with very sharp tips that keep animals away. Most cacti have long spines. Pricklypear pads, in addition to having spines, also have very high levels of oxalic acid that can cause kidney disorders in animals.[20] Jimsonweed has very high levels of toxic alkaloids that can be fatal to animals and people. Despite these defenses, however, it is interesting to note that relatively few plants in this region have physical defenses compared to those of the Sonoran Desert. In fact, there are spineless varieties of both pricklypear and hedgehog cactus in the Canyonlands region.

The lack of armoring on plants in Canyon Country, compared to other deserts such as the Sonoran, may result from several factors. First, there are far fewer herbivores in this region compared to the Sonoran Desert, so herbivory may be a major factor in determining the success of a plant. Secondly, most plants on the Colorado Plateau are northern plants that have adapted to warmer temperatures, while most Sonoran Desert plants are southern plants that have moved north.[21] Thus, genetic material to provide for physical protection may not be present in plants of the Colorado Plateau.

Nutrients and Water

Desert soils are low in nutrients and seasonally dry, providing plants with a survival challenge. In most desert soils, water and nutrients are not spread homogeneously across and through soils but instead are concentrated into "islands of fertility" underneath plant canopies.[22] This concentration of water and nutrients occurs because: (1) plant canopies intercept and funnel water to the plant base; (2) plant canopies shade the soil surface and reduce evaporation; (3) organic matter and wind-blown fine particles of soil collect under the plant, resulting in soils with greater capacity to absorb water than the coarser soils in the interspaces between plants; (4) plants slow the velocity of runoff water, resulting in higher infiltration rates under the plant; (5) plant roots "mine" the surrounding soils and incorporate nutrients and water into the plant tissue. This tissue is then dropped directly under the plant and so nutrients accumulate there; and (6) decomposition rates are faster under plants because of greater soil moisture and greater amounts of plant litter. This process results in more nutrients being available faster under plants compared to soils between the plants. These fertile islands can persist for many years after the plant dies.

Root structure influences how a plant obtains nutrients and water. Many desert shrubs have U-shaped roots that go straight down from the plant to a deep soil layer (with short side branches along the way), turn 90° to the right or left, grow laterally for some distance, and then go straight back up to the surface.[23] In this way, the plant can exploit the whole soil volume around itself for nutrients and water. Moreover, roots of a given plant "share" their water with other roots of the same plant by actively pumping water to roots that lack water. The receiving roots, in turn, pump the water *out* into the surrounding soil at night, which helps to dissolve available nutrients. This nutrient-rich water is then reabsorbed the next morning.[24] This incredibly clever idea has one major drawback: water that is pumped out may get stolen by other plants, so it is important that other plant roots be kept away. Some plant roots exude secretions to do just that. Many do not, however; and there is some evidence that other plants do take their water.

Salt Tolerance

Many desert soils are very salty because of low amounts of precipitation and high evaporation rates. This can create severe problems for plants. First, dilute solutions tend to flow towards more concentrated ones, so if salt concentrations are greater in the soil than inside the plants, it is difficult for the plants to retain water.[25] Secondly, because salts are often dissolved in the soil water, it is difficult for plants to obtain water without also acquiring the toxic salts.

Plants have three solutions to the soil salinity problem. First, they can prevent uptake of salty water at the root surface, a technique employed by salt grass (*Distichlis* sp.) and winterfat (*Ceratoides lanata*). However, this often only works where the salt buildup is frequently washed away, such as along streambanks and in floodplains. Secondly, plants can store salt in small, liquid-filled sacks inside the leaves called *vacuoles*, making their leaves plump and liquid-filled. Plants in the saltbush family, such as greasewood (*Sarcobatus vermiculatus*) and pickleweed (*Allenrolfea* sp.), employ this mechanism. Finally, plants can exude salt either directly onto their leaves (*e.g., Tamarix* sp.) or into hairs on the leaves (*e.g.,* saltbushes).

Plant Architecture

The growth forms of plants can affect both the plant itself and the habitat it creates. All plant shapes are a cost-benefit game. For example, the shape and size of a plant's branches can enhance water harvesting. Large, spread-out canopies and horizontal branches are the best at intercepting the most rain.[26] This captured water is then transported to the central stem and into the soil around the base of the plant where the roots are concentrated and the soil is shaded to minimize evaporation. Most desert plants have slightly inward-sloping branches to optimize this process. However, this same spreading architecture can increase air flow and thus evaporation rates from the leaves.

Light is not a limiting factor in the desert, and so unlike trees in a forest, desert plants can expend energy to grow out rather than up. With so much light, they can also afford to be bushy, as self-shading is less of a problem for them than it is for their forest counterparts. There are other design constraints on desert plants. In addition to extreme temperatures, deserts often have high winds. In response, plants such as blackbrush and cottonwood (*Populus frémontii*) can be very stiff, with the strategy that the wind is not so strong that it breaks the branches; or, like rabbitbrush they can be very limber and sway with the wind; or, like juniper and sagebrush, they can twist as they grow. Some tall species such as cottonwood are able to regenerate vegetatively, so limited wind damage can be beneficial by creating the opportunity for fallen branches to take root nearby and clone the parent tree.

Because animals depend on plants for food and shelter, the architecture of plants heavily influences the type and number of animal species in a given community.[27] What a plant looks like, tastes like, and when it is active will determine who can live in, around, or off of it. The architecture of a plant is so important to some species of birds and spiders that they will inhabit a stick imitation of a shrub, ignoring the fact it is quite dead and lacks leaves. Some lizards are "sit and wait" predators.[28] These animals lie still under shrubs, waiting for their prey to walk by, and then leap out to catch them. This requires that they wait under plants that have branches low enough to hide them, while sufficiently high enough off the ground to provide a clear line of sight and unencumbered access to their prey. Many birds require perches of a certain height and select plant communities accordingly.[29]

Genetic Controls on Adaptation

As previously discussed, organisms can only work within the constraints of their evolutionary history. If there is no genetic material orchestrating leaf-drop response to drought, a plant will not be able to adopt this strategy. Many of the plants we see growing in deserts today did not originally evolve in a desert setting.[30] Thus, many features in a given species may not be an adaptation to desert living at all but left over from some other set of conditions. For example, many conifers have a conical shape that enable them to keep their leaves all winter while not losing branches to excessive snow loads, yet they occur in deserts where snows generally are light.

HOW ANIMALS COPE WITH THERMAL STRESS

The biggest problem facing animals in deserts is the same one facing plants: how to survive in a place with limited access to water during time of very high air temperatures. Animals avoid thermal stress and conserve water in many ways, using both physiological and behavioral mechanisms.

Behavioral Mechanisms

The main way animals keep their body temperatures optimal is by moving back and forth from heat sources to heat sinks. If not allowed to move out of direct sunlight on hot days, they quickly die.[31] When not thermally stressed by either cold or heat, lizards move through their home ranges in a random fashion; when they are temperature or moisture stressed, they more often are found in microclimates where the stressful climatic conditions are ameliorated to some degree.[32] Insects under thermal stress will first select microhabitats with lower temperatures; if there are several microhabitats of similar temperature to choose from, they will then select those with greater humidity. When cold, most animals orient their bodies perpendicular to the sun to maximize solar radiation gain or press their bodies to warm objects such as the ground, rocks, or plants.[33] When overheated, animals employ one or several strategies, including orienting their bodies parallel to the sun, lifting their bodies off the hot surface (*stilting*), and changing the height at which they are perched off the ground. They may also pant or salivate on themselves, seek the shade of a plant or a rock, fly a short way to take advantage of cooling by moving air, and/or enter burrows.

Burrows are the main refuge from the heat for smaller animals. While surface temperature can fluctuate 75°F or more on a hot summer day, the temperature of subsurface soils stays relatively constant throughout the day.[34] At a six-inch depth, soils can be as much as 36°F cooler than the surface; at twenty inches, there is little variation in soil temperature throughout the year. Luckily for burrowers trying to escape the heat, there is lag time between when sun hits and warms the surface and when temperature rises in soils below the surface. Therefore, burrows six inches deep are actually warmest at night, minimizing heat loss of animals nestled in for sleep. Larger animals dig burrows from eight to twenty-eight inches below the surface. In contrast, many arthropods

(spiders and insects) are weak burrowers and instead utilize holes made by other animals (*e.g.*, large beetles often occupy scorpion burrows) or rely on small holes under rocks. The temperature under rocks is mostly dependent on the size of the rock: the bigger the rock, and the bigger the cavity underneath the rock, the cooler the temperature of the burrow. Rock color only makes a difference when the rock is less than about an inch thick.

The time of day when foraging takes place is a very important way animals regulate their body heat, and foraging times can vary according to season.[35] Whereas most day-active arthropods and reptiles are active only in the early morning and late afternoon during the hot summer months, these same species are often active midday in cooler months. Some beetles that are day-active in spring and autumn plug their burrows during summer days and are active only at night. There are also some species such as deer that are strictly active during the day (*diurnal*), and others such as bats that are only active at night (*nocturnal*), regardless of the season. Centipedes and scorpions are more strictly nocturnal and overall are more active than their temperate-climate relatives. Most birds tend to be active in the morning, especially during the breeding season (spring-early summer).[36] During the day, they sit in the shade with their wings held away from the body and can pant if they get too hot. Some species of birds such as nighthawks and owls forage in the twilight and nighttime hours, thus avoiding activity during the daytime heat.

Lizards in the Canyonlands region are day-active and have two types of activity patterns.[37] Sit-and-wait predators are intermittently active and include sagebrush lizards (*Sceloporus graciosus*), side-blotched lizards (*Uta stansburiana*), and horned lizards (*Phrynosoma platyrhinos*). Pursuit predators run about nearly continuously, as demonstrated by the whiptail lizard (*Cnemidophorus tigris*). While the latter activity pattern results in a greater food reward and thus faster growth rates, whiptails have metabolic rates twice that of the other lizards, lose much more water, and are more exposed to predation.

However, while there are lifestyle tradeoffs that affect water conservation and thermal stress, it should be kept in mind that other factors may influence selection of habitats or activity times, including maximizing reproduction, avoiding predators, niche separation, or optimizing feeding. Many animals, including lizards and ants, avoid intraspecific competition by foraging at different temperatures.[38] Places where conditions are optimal for *thermoregulation* (regulating of body temperature) may not always be optimal for locating food. When food is easy to find, or competition for resources such as shelter or food is low, animals are more likely to seek out habitats where they can more precisely regulate their body temperature. When food or shelter is scarce, the animals are often no longer so choosy.

Physiological Mechanisms

General physiological factors that influence thermal stress and water conservation include the size and shape of the organism; the color and nature of their outer coverings, whether it be scales, feathers, fur, or exoskeleton; the way the body absorbs and stores water; the ability to adjust reproduction to current conditions; tolerance of high temperatures and dehydration; specialized respiratory patterns; reduction of water lost by respiration and excretion; reduced metabolic rates; and modifications in digestive physiology.[39] Some organisms such as certain midges are an extreme example of drought adaptation: they can survive complete desiccation (drying out) and yet become active within an hour after rain.[40] Most animals use a combination of mechanisms to survive.

Because of limited food and water in deserts, most resident animals are fairly small, which means they are more likely to experience temperature and water stress. Being smaller takes less food and water, but it also means a greater potential for water loss and thermal stress. Most lizard and snake species in deserts are smaller than their counterparts in other regions.

Many animals pant (mammals), gape (lizards), or use *gular fluttering* (birds) to dissipate heat via the mouth. Gular fluttering is a rapid vibration of the upper throat and thin floor of the mouth and is similar to panting, only with less energy expenditure. Long extremities also help in heat loss. Some reptiles

can alter blood flow patterns to avoid extra-warm blood flowing to their brains. Some mammals actually cool the blood going to the brain. Fat layers in small animals, such as arthropods, are evenly distributed over the body so they can stay warm, while in larger animals, fat is stored in clumps (camel humps, lizard tails) so the rest of the body can easily gain and disperse heat.[41]

Another important way to regulate temperature and water loss is through what covers the outer body, and this is a major difference between birds and mammals on the one hand, and reptiles and arthropods on the other. Larger mammals have skins that readily lose water through sweating. This reduces body temperature by evaporative cooling, the same principal used in "swamp" coolers throughout buildings in the Southwest. However, the sweat needs to evaporate on the skin to produce the desired result. Therefore, animals with coarse or thin hair can utilize sweating, while those with dense hair do not.[42] Small rodents do not sweat, as it is too expensive: for a kangaroo rat to maintain a normal body temperature at 104°F would require losing twenty percent of their body weight per hour.[43] When extremely thermally stressed, both kangaroo rats and ground squirrels will salivate onto their necks and chests to cool down.

Feathers both insulate and facilitate convective and radiative heat loss. In deserts, long and sparse feathers are a good compromise between insulation and heat loss. When hot, birds can erect their hair or feathers and both increase the barrier between solar radiation and the skin and let cool air in next to the skin. Although birds do not have sweat glands, they can still utilize evaporative cooling by panting or gular fluttering. Birds that fly high, such as raptors and ravens, often soar in the cool upper air currents during the heat of the day. Coarse fur on mammals acts somewhat like feathers. It can insulate, yet facilitate heat loss when held erect by increasing the solar barrier and allowing cool air next to the skin. Rabbits—particularly jackrabbits—lose excess heat through their large ears, which have blood veins close to the skin surface.

In contrast, most reptiles and arthropods have relatively impermeable skins covered with the hard substance *chitin* (creating the shell-like *exoskeleton*), wax, thick scales, or other water barriers.[44] These animals cannot use evaporative cooling. There are some exceptions, such as some grasshoppers, beetles, bees, and locusts that use limited evaporative cooling, and some beetles and cockroaches that have a more permeable outer covering that can absorb water vapor. Interestingly, reptile skin is more impermeable to water loss than insect exoskeletons, while bird and mammal skin is several times more permeable than reptile skin. Even with their sealed covering, over fifty percent of the water lost by nonheat-stressed reptiles occurs through their skin.[45]

Because most amphibians have highly permeable skin, both water loss and gain occur quickly, meaning they are restricted to places with year-round available water. A few amphibians such as spadefoots (*Scaphiopus intermontanus*) have less permeable skin, and lose only one to five percent of the water lost by most amphibians.[46] Spadefoots, however, spend nine months or more buried in deep soils that maintain moisture most of the year. In addition, they cover themselves with multiple layers of dead skin and mud to reduce water loss during hibernation.

An animal's color can be used to conceal, to advertise for mates, or to warn away competitors or predators. It is also thought to be a handy way to reduce unwanted heat by increasing or decreasing heat load, depending on conditions, or creating opportunities for convective cooling. However, the diversity of color seen in most ecosystems is markedly absent in deserts,[47] where most animals are either cryptically-colored to blend into their surroundings or are black. The reason for being cryptically-colored seems needed for predator avoidance, but why be black in a hot place?

There are several theories as to why so many different types of desert dwellers, such as ravens, beetles, and even lichens, are dark colored.[48] First off, black makes for great camouflage for creatures that are active at night. Black is also distinctive and may warn away potential predators, and being black for basking animals means they warm up faster when temperatures are cold. Compounds that confer waterproofing or sunscreen may be black, so if the body requires

them, then it has no choice about color. If there is an airspace under the black covering, the temperature difference between the outer covering and the underlying body can create cooling convective air currents. For example, while a raven's outer feathers can be 176°F, it's skin remains a comfortable 104°F (at least comfortable for it!). Interestingly, many Bedouin tribes in the Sahara desert wear black robes for this reason.

Colors can be also deceptive: what appears to be black can appear differently depending on the sun angle (see the discussion on tenebrionid beetles in Chapter 7), or what appears black to the human eye may be a different color to a predator's eye.[49] Light penetrates further into light-pigmented fur and feathers than dark ones, lessening their insulation value against the sun's heat. A study on pigeons showed that black pigeons acquire a much greater heat load at low wind speeds than white pigeons. However, the penetration of radiation was much greater for white pigeons and there was less convective cooling, so the skin was hotter. As wind speeds increased, the heat loads between the two colors converged.[50] At speeds greater than ten feet per second, black pigeons actually acquired less heat than white pigeons. In addition, some black-colored animals—tenebrionid beetles and some lizards—can change their black color to a lighter color when temperatures are hot.[51]

Another adaptation to thermal stress is to reduce the water loss that accompanies excretion of body wastes or during respiration.[52] Birds and mammals excrete very concentrated (*hypertonic*) urine and relatively dry fecal pellets. Reptiles and arthropods cannot concentrate their urine, but their fecal pellets are very dry and made of insoluble nitrogenous waste. These animals can also tolerate much greater changes in the volume of body fluids and the osmotic concentration of these fluids than birds and mammals. Amphibians, when dehydrated, can decrease urinary water loss and increase water uptake through their skin. During this time, little urine is produced and urea is stored in the body, meaning these animals can tolerate high concentrations of urea in blood and tissues while estivating or hibernating. In general, desert amphibians can also extract higher amounts of water from their feces before excretion than their humid-climate relatives.[53] While desert insects and arachnids (spiders) are not able to tolerate greater water loss than their more temperate counterparts, they can reduce water loss by excreting insoluble uric acid.[54] Insects such as cicadas and aphids are an exception: because they feed on plant sap, they have constant access to water and thus do not need to conserve water in their waste. Some species of cicadas, cockroaches, grasshoppers, locusts, beetles, and bees even extrude water through pores onto their body surface to cool down, similar to sweat in mammals; however, these are exceptions and not the rule.[55]

Having a high basal temperature is another way to deal with thermal stress, as the animal can then rely more on conduction and radiation to dissipate heat. Most birds employ this strategy since their body temperatures are generally 104-108°F, giving them a distinct advantage over mammals in deserts. Mourning doves can tolerate temperatures up to 116°F, hyperthermia, and extensive dehydration;[56] they also can fly long distances, making them superb desert dwellers. Given these characteristics, it is surprising that temperate regions, not deserts, are the dove's primary habitat. Among desert reptiles, desert lizards are able to tolerate much higher temperatures than desert snakes.[57] Many insects (*e.g.*, ants, beetles, termites, antlions) and scorpions can tolerate higher body temperatures than vertebrates, and desert lizards have higher body temperatures than nondesert lizards. Diurnal species tend to have greater basal body temperatures than nocturnal animals.[58] In addition, the upper thermal limits in desert insects are often higher than in relatives inhabiting cooler regions.[59]

Flight in deserts creates special problems.[60] The thoracic muscles used during flight generate considerable heat. In small insects, most of this heat is dissipated rapidly due to their high surface-to-volume ratio. In larger insects (bees, moths, locusts) and birds, flight can increase body heat 86°F above the ambient air temperature, restricting flight to the cooler parts of the day. Flight also requires huge amounts of oxygen, so the greater respiration associated with flight increases both cooling and water loss. Insects often spread the heat concentrated in the thorax to the abdomen to help dissipate it more rapidly. Locusts are especially well-adapted to deserts: they have a relatively low metabolic rate in flight and, more importantly, they have holes called *spiracles* in their exoskeletons that they can open and close at will to help regulate body heat, unlike most insects whose spiracles are always open.[61]

Reproduction generally is timed for when water and other resources are most abundant, thus reducing water use during this otherwise stressful time. For example, androgen production, which stimulates reproduction, is controlled in many lizards by temperature, precipitation, or humidity so that the young are born during the cool rainy season.[62]

Animals can also deal with thermal or water stress through avoidance. Soil-inhabiting creatures often make cysts, spores, or can dry completely when soils become dry. Many larger animals hibernate or estivate when conditions are unfavorable. Birds such as the poorwill hibernate in the dry season when food is scarce. Spadefoots spend most of their lives hibernating, waiting for rainfall before becoming active. Reduced activity or estivation is also a great way to avoid cold temperatures and is used by hummingbirds and most small mammals.

Evolutionary Similarities

There are some interesting parallels in how plants and animals deal with heat and water stress.[63] Both use solar orientation for thermoregulation: while locusts, lizards, and snakes actively line their bodies up appropriately, some plants change the angle of their leaves towards the sun throughout the day. Plant leaves and arthropods both secrete surface waxes to reduce water loss. Plant stomata and insect spiracles are especially efficient in desert species, and restrict water loss. Cactus spines act like coarse fur, feathers, and scales, as they protect the succulent from direct radiation while allowing cool air to reach the organism's surface. In addition, many plants and animals choose to avoid, rather than tolerate, the heat.

Many animals in deserts on different continents also have evolved a similar appearance. The kangaroo rat has close structural affinities to the jerboas of the

Old World; jackrabbits are similar to the hares and the quokka of Australia. The horned lizards are very similar in appearance to the thorny devils of Australia. The sidewinder of U.S. deserts is almost identical to the Saharan sand viper, except that the viper lacks a rattle. Many ant species are similar on different continents. In addition, many plants share similar characteristics, regardless of the desert in which they occur.

DESERT BIRDS

The number of resident bird species is fairly limited in deserts. Most birds do not have any unique adaptations to desert conditions as discussed above, and the heat created by flying is especially problematic for unadapted species. To escape undesirable environments, most birds rely on migrating from where conditions are no longer favorable. Despite the harsh environment, 218 species of resident and transitory birds have been observed in Canyonlands National Park.[64]

Birds do have a few advantages over other vertebrates when temperatures are hot. They have higher average body temperatures than mammals (104 versus 99°F), so they can better utilize conduction and radiation to cool down. Also, birds are more tolerant of increased body heat than mammals, as they can reach 110°F before needing to cool down.[65] In most deserts on most days, temperatures in the shade are less than 110°F, so birds generally do not need to expend energy cooling down. In addition, many birds can fly to places with cooler air temperatures, such as stream edges, to spend the day. However, because flying generates a lot of body heat, most birds cannot fly far during hot midday temperatures. The exception to this are birds that fly at high altitudes, such as raptors, ravens, and swifts, as air temperatures are cooler at such altitudes.

Birds conserve water in many ways. To keep temperatures low, birds are most active in morning and evening and sit in shade during the day. As with reptiles, birds conserve more water than mammals by excreting uric acid as small pellets instead of liquid urine. Some species can lose tremendous amounts of body mass before being water stressed: house finches can lose as much as twenty-six percent of their body

weight, while quail can lose up to fifty percent.[66] Feathers also help cooling by reducing the direct solar radiation that reaches the skin, and feathers can be raised to let cooling air in next to the skin. In addition, most birds have thinly-feathered sides and raise their wings during the day to allow heat to escape. Birds use gular fluttering and can dilate the blood vessels in their legs to dump heat. Vultures urinate on their legs if temperatures are over 70°F, which is why their legs are white in summer, but not in the winter.[67]

Large body mass, which decreases relative surface area where water loss occurs, also helps conserve water. This is well-illustrated by doves: White-winged Doves weigh 5 ounces, Mourning Doves weigh 3.5 ounces, and Inca Doves weigh 1.5 ounces.[68] If you compare body weight lost per day when these birds are deprived of water (at 68–75°F), the largest bird loses 4 percent, the midsize loses 4.8 percent, and the smallest 6.1 percent of their body weight. As a result, desert upland birds that live in drier conditions weigh 1.4 times more than their riparian counterparts living in more humid and cooler conditions.

Despite all of these ways to reduce heat and water stress, most desert birds still lose up to 2.4 time more water through gular fluttering and evaporation than they produce metabolically; thus, they must obtain fluids in other ways. While some birds (*e.g.*, Black-throated Sparrows) obtain all of their water from foods such as insects and plant parts, most birds, especially seed eaters, flock to waterholes each day. However, desert bird species typically need to drink only half as much as their nondesert relatives.

The ability to fly has required some extreme modifications in birds, especially in the arena of weight reduction.[69] Modified features include large bones that are hollow and thin; other bones that are fused or reduced in size; feathers (a body covering that is light, yet strong); no teeth or heavy jaws; air sacs; atrophy of reproductive organs between breeding seasons; one ovary; feeding on high calorie, compact food; rapid and efficient digestion; no bladder; and the excretion of dry, lightweight uric acid.[70] While being able to fly has its advantages, there are disadvantages are well. Reduced weight necessary for flight means that fat storage is limited, thus birds have low tolerance for cold and times of low food supply. Some birds in this region, such as Lesser Nighthawks (*Chordeiles acutipennis*), Violet-green Swallows (*Tachycineta thalassina*), Hummingbirds, and White-throated Swifts (*Aeronautes saxatalis*), regularly use *torpor* (slowing down activity) to deal with such situations.

REPTILES AND AMPHIBIANS

So why are reptiles and amphibians so successful in deserts?[71] First, reptiles and amphibians have low metabolic rates, which means that they do not need to eat or drink as much as other vertebrate life forms. This makes living in a region where food and water is limited less of a problem. Second, *ectothermy* (cold-bloodedness) and thermoregulation of reptiles and amphibians result in a significantly higher metabolic efficiency than birds or mammals of the same size. Third, if you add in energy savings due to inactivity by reptiles and arthropods, they use only one to five percent of the energy that birds and mammals require.[72] Fourth, reptiles and amphibians also conserve water by excreting bodily waste in dry, insoluble forms, and they have a wider tolerance of fluctuations in internal water conditions than birds and mammals. Finally, they avoid behavior and activities in the hot sun that increase their heat stress or result in a high consumption of water and/or energy. Taken together, these five points suggest why deserts can support a much greater biomass of reptiles and amphibians than birds and mammals.[73]

DOMINANT PLANT AND ANIMAL COMMUNITIES OF CANYONLANDS

Most communities found in the Canyonlands region are combinations of plants and animals colonizing from surrounding regions.[74] Great Basin plants are represented by sagebrush, shadscale, and grama grass (*Bouteloua gracilis*). Much of the succulent flora, including pricklypear (*Opuntia phaeacantha*) and hedgehog cactus (*Echinocereus engelmanni*), is from the Sonoran Desert. The Mojave Desert contributes blackbrush and other succulents such as beavertail (*Opuntia basilaris*) and Mojave pricklypear (*Opuntia erinacea*).

Riparian Vegetation

Plants that grow within riparian areas have a limited tolerance of drought and are generally only found along perennial sources of water. Riparian vegetation collects sediment and plant litter flowing from adjacent slopes and alluvial sediments deposited during floods, making riparian soils much more fertile than adjacent upland soils. There is also a positive feedback loop at work: the more fertile the soils, the closer plants can grow together; and the closer plants grow together, the better they capture sediment. Riparian plants tend to be fast growing and have large leaves, high transpiration rates, and thick growth. Most of the native *overstory* plants are insect-pollinated (except cottonwoods) and all have tiny seeds that are dispersed by the winds that often blow along the river corridor.

Above the confluence of the Green and Colorado rivers, the channel gradient is low and the river is wide, resulting in slow-moving water. Slower water allows for flooding with less scouring and thus a much wider and better-developed riparian community. In the past, banks along this slow-moving water were dominated by native overstory plants that included up to three species of cottonwoods (*Populus* sp.), six species of willow (*Salix* sp.), water birch (*Betula occidentalis*), boxelder (*Acer negundo*), and desert olive (*Forestiera pumila*).[75] However, some of these plants are now uncommon, inundated in a sea of tamarisk (*Tamarix* c.f. *chinensis*).[76]

Riparian communities along both rivers (Figure 4-2) have many *understory* herbaceous species, such as necklacepod (*Sophora nuttalliana, S. stenophylla*), emory seepwillow (*Baccharis emoryi*), wood rose (*Rosa woodsii*), dogbane (*Apocynum* sp.), coyote bush (*Nicotiana attenuata*), tall thelypody (*Thelypodium integrifolium*), wild licorice (*Glycyrrhiza glabra*), goldenrod (*Solidago* sp.), cocklebur (*Xanthium strumarium*), golden currant (*Ribes aureum*), and water birch. A rare plant, rusby milkweed (*Asclepias rusbyi*), occurs along the Green River corridor. The most common birds include Bewick's Wrens (*Thryomanes bewickii*), Mockingbirds (*Mimus polyglottos*), Orange-crowned Warblers (*Vermivora*

Figure 4-2. Below Castle Creek (White's) Rapid (mile 77.1)

A. 1926. This downstream view of the Colorado River shows the unnamed narrow canyon below Professor Valley and upstream from Spanish Valley. Extensive sand deposits along the banks were probably deposited during the 1905 flood, one of the largest of the twentieth century. Essentially no riparian vegetation occurs below the top of this sand line. Higher on the slopes, a line of what appears to be willows is nearly continuous down the left bank and broken on the right. The dirt road that would become Utah 128 appears in the left foreground with a rock wall as its riverside face. (A.A. Baker 159, courtesy of the U.S. Geological Survey Photographic Library)

B. October 7, 1999. The channel of the Colorado River is constrained by dense lines of native and non-native vegetation; most of this vegetation is tamarisk. Several individual trees persist for the ninety-four intervening years. The modern Utah 128 with its soil berm is in the left foreground. (Dominic Oldershaw, Stake 3901)

celata), yellow chats (*Icteria virens*), Yellow Warblers (*Dendroica petechia*), Yellow-rumped Warblers (*Dendroica coronata*), House Finches (*Carpodacus mexicanus*), Purple Finches (*Carpodacus purpureus*), Green-tailed Towhees (*Pipilo chlorurus*), Spotted Towhees (*Pipilo erythrophthalmus*), and Gray-headed Juncos (*Junco hyemalis*).

Within Cataract Canyon, the steep, narrow canyon walls and high gradient result in fast-moving water and frequent floods. As a result, the wide continuous band of riparian vegetation and river bottoms is replaced by a thin, discontinuous line of vegetation. Hackberry (*Celtis reticulata*)[77] is commonly found (see Chapter 7), marking the high-water line along canyon

Figure 4-3. Bonita Bend (mile 30.9)

A. September 13, 1871. Powell was so impressed with the beauty of the Green River bend at mile 30 that he named it Bonita Bend (*bonita* means beautiful in Spanish) in 1869. The Green River flows from left to right in this view from the outside of the bend on the downstream end of Anderson Bottom. This view shows the diversity of pre-settlement bottomland vegetation. Willows are at the water's edge on the upstream side of the bend, and willows and desert olive mantle the top of the bank. The trees well behind the river banks are cottonwoods, some of which appear to be white and look as if they have recently died. Between these trees and the river banks is a zone dominated by greasewood. Some more xeric shrubs appear in the lower right foreground. (E.O. Beaman 446, courtesy of the U.S. Geological Survey Photographic Library)

slopes. The desert olive found upstream is no longer present, and Apache plume (*Fallugia paradoxa*) appears, probably preferring the faster water velocity and warmer air temperatures.

River Bottom Vegetation

Low-gradient rivers meander back and forth within their channels. When the river shifts, it leaves behind low, flat-lying terraces with deep, silty, alluvial soil. These silty soils are usually highly saline and are able to hold more water than upland sandy soils. These bottomlands are commonly flooded, so occupying plants must be able to tolerate standing water for long periods of time. In addition, the proximity of the river means the water table is fairly shallow. Unlike riparian plants that grow directly adjacent to the river, plants growing in river bottoms do not need to withstand fast-moving flood waters. Because of these factors, bottomland plant communities are very different from upland or riparian vegetation (Figure 4-3). They are dominated by greasewood (*Sarcobatus vermiculatus*), sagebrush (*Artemisia tridentata*), curly dock (*Rumex hymenosepalus*), pickleweed (*Allenrolfea occidentalis*), rabbitbrush, four-wing saltbush, and

flexible dropseed (*Sporobolus flexuosus*). Deer mice, packrats, and sparrows are common here.

Many river bottoms along the Green River have been and continue to be used for agriculture. During the past century, bottomlands between the town of Green River and Mineral Bottom were used to grow watermelons and potatoes as well as for cattle grazing. Unfortunately, the fertile soils of river bottoms are also prime places for exotic plant invasion, and agricultural activities have undoubtedly contributed to the introduction of non-native plants into these areas.

Upland Plant Communities

Talus-Slope Communities. Soils on talus slopes are very rocky and soil depth is highly variable. As a result, many different species are found in this habitat. The most common shrubs include four-wing saltbush, shadscale, snakeweed, Mormon tea, and yuccas. Cactus species include pricklypear, claretcup (*Echinocereus triglochidiatus*), and fishhook cactus (*Sclerocactus whipplei*). Common grasses are sand dropseed and Indian ricegrass, while common herbaceous plants include wirelettuce (*Stephanomeria* sp.),

B. August 19, 1968. The channel of the Green River has narrowed in both the upstream and downstream segments. By 1968, tamarisk dominated the banks of the Green River, including Bonita Bend. However, the pattern of tamarisk establishment suggests a relationship between water flow, geomorphology, and the preferred sites for this non-native tree. Tamarisk is dense directly across the river from the camera position in a low-velocity section of channel bank. Upstream (at left), where water flow along the bank is relatively swift at flood stage, willows dominate the vegetation on the new, lower banks, with tamarisk sharing the former river banks with desert olive. Cottonwoods are restricted to a narrow band of scattered but larger individuals, some of which persist from 1871. The area of white trees in 1871 is now occupied by saltbush and greasewood on the edge of a playa that periodically fills with saline runoff from the uplands at center. The water level of the Green River is similar in the 1871 and 1968 views, and the pattern of sandbars has changed slightly adjacent to the ever-shifting channel. An old cattle trail passes through the center of the slope at lower right; this trail follows the river for several miles to Valentine Bottom. (H.G. Stephens, Y-4)

C. October 13, 1999. The width of the Green River is about the same as in 1968, and the spatial structure of the riparian ecosystem is similar although many individuals are larger. The playa may have grown slightly in size, and non-native halogeton (*Halogeton glomeratus*) grows on its edges. The water level of the Green River is lower, exposing more sandbars that are in different positions from those in 1871 and 1968. At lower right, mountain mahogany has persisted since 1871. (Dominic Oldershaw, Stake 3896)

desert trumpet (*Eriogonum inflatum*), and prince's plume (*Stanleya pinnata*). Rock squirrels (*Spermophilus variegatus*), packrats (*Neotoma* sp.), and deer mice (*Peromyscus maniculatus*) are commonly found here as well. Common birds include sparrows, Rock Wrens (*Salpinctes obsoletus*), and Canyon Wrens (*Catherpes mexicanus*).

Figure 4-4. Trin Alcove (mile 90.9)

A. September 8, 1871. John Wesley Powell and his photographer, E.O. Beaman, were fascinated by the landforms in the vicinity of Trin Alcove on the Green River. In his diary, Powell marveled at the "naked rocks" and undoubtedly instructed Beaman to record them on film. In addition to photographs within Three Canyon on river right, they crossed to river left and climbed onto the top of the mesa in the center of the bend for several photographs, including this view back towards the mouth of Three Canyon. The photograph documents the swirling nature of the sedimentary strata in the top of the Navajo Sandstone. The dark areas in the foreground are patterns in lichens and mosses growing on the bedrock. (E.O. Beaman 727, courtesy of the U.S. Geological Survey Photographic Library)

Pinyon-Juniper Communities. In Cataract Canyon and immediately adjacent uplands, pinyon-juniper communities are generally found on shallow, nutrient-poor sandy soils. These two trees may dominate a plant community to the exclusion of other species, but in the Canyonlands area pinyon-juniper communities are more open than in other regions, allowing shrubs and other plants to coexist. Shrubs dominate the understory and include roundleaf buffaloberry (*Shepardia rotundifolia*; on the Maze District side only), singleleaf ash (*Fraxinus anomala*), Frémont Barberry (*Mahonia frémontii*), mountain mahogany (*Cercocarpus* sp.), skunkbush (*Rhus trilobata*), and cliff rose (*Purshia mexicana*). These communities have a very high diversity of herbaceous plants. Some common species include Newberry's twinpod (*Physaria newberryi*), bastard toadflax (*Comandra umbellata*), lomatium (*Lomatium* sp.), pinyon-juniper lousewort (*Pedicularis centranthera*), woody tiquilia (*Tiquila latior*), little and heartleaf twistflower (*Streptanthus cordatus*), buckwheat (*Eriogonum* sp.), several species of gilia (*Gilia* sp.), Indian paintbrush (*Castilleja* sp.), locoweed (*Astragalus* sp.), penstemon (*Penstemon* sp.), and milkweed (*Asclepias* sp.).[78]

Pinyon-juniper communities have a large rodent contingent. Common rodents include rock squirrels, packrats, antelope ground squirrels (*Ammospermophilus leucurus*), chipmunks (*Eutamias* sp.), pinyon mice (*Peromyscus truei*), and deer mice. The bird life in pinyon-juniper communities is also diverse and distinctive, with some birds dependent on the particular structure of this habitat. Common birds include the Blue-gray Gnatcatcher (*Polioptila caerulea*), Grey Vireo (*Vireo vicinior*), Western Scrub Jay (*Aphelocoma coerulescens*), Pinyon Jay (*Gymnorhinus cyanocephalus*), Juniper Titmouse (*Parus inornatus*), bushtit (*Psaltriparus minimus*), Black-chinned Hummingbird (*Archilochus alexandri*), Broad-tailed Hummingbird (*Selasphorus platycercus*), and Rufous Hummingbird (*Selasphorus rufus*).

B. August 18, 1968. The large, split rock in the right mid-ground is gone without a trace. This photograph documents a recent rockfall (under the cliff at right center) and the persistence of a shrub (probably singleleaf ash, at right). At center, the island of soil in a sea of rock is light-colored, as if the density of the heavy crusts apparent in 1871 had decreased. The plants in this soil island are more numerous and are larger in size than in 1871. (H.G. Stephens, V-7)

C. October 9, 1999. Several important changes have occurred since 1968. The riparian zone beneath the cliff at right center burned in 1994-1995, decimating a stand of Gambel's oak and scattered cottonwoods. The shrub is dead and no carcass remains. In the soil island, we identified numerous individual plants that are persistent from 1871, including singleleaf ash, blackbrush, and Mormon tea. (Dominic Oldershaw, Stake 3891)

Blackbrush Communities. Blackbrush communities generally have very low diversity, as this plant often dominates to the near-exclusion of other species (Figure 4-4). Where present, other species include Indian ricegrass, sand dropseed, shinnery oak (*Quercus harvardii*), twistflower, yellow cryptantha, sixweeks fescue (*Festuca octoflora*), and yucca. Common birds include the Common Raven (*Corvus corax*), flycatchers (*Empidonax* sp.), Black-throated Sparrows (*Amphispiza bilineata*), Western Scrub Jays, Grey Vireos, and Rufous and Black-chinned Hummingbirds. The most common rodents are deer mice, pocket mice (*Perognathus apache*), and kangaroo rats (*Dipodomys ordii*).

Grassland Communities

Grasslands in this region have two dominant associations: galleta grass, and a mixed-grass community consisting of needle-and-thread (*Stipa comata*), Indian ricegrass, and sand dropseed. Interspersed shrubs include Mormon tea, snakeweed, winterfat, and fourwing saltbush. Disturbed grassland soils are often dominated by cheatgrass (*Bromus tectorum*) or Russian thistle (*Salsola kali*). Many small mammals live in these vegetation communities, including deer mice, pocket mice, grasshopper mice (*Onychomys leucogaster*), and kangaroo rats. Grassland birds include Black-throated Sparrows, Western Meadowlarks (*Sturnella neglecta*), Lark Sparrows (*Chondestes grammacus*), Sage Sparrows (*Amphispiza belli*), and White-crowned Sparrows (*Zonotrichia leucophrys*).

Hanging Gardens

Hanging gardens are created by water seeping out of the sandstone, creating a moist micro-environment of higher humidity and somewhat lower temperatures than is found in the immediately-surrounding area. As a result, these unique ecosystems are associated with sites affected by the sapping process discussed in Chapter 3. Calcium carbonate creates the often-seen white streaks on the rock faces, while the dark streaks are desert varnish (for more detail on desert varnish,

see Chapter 10). Plants in hanging gardens typically are highly tolerant of calcium-rich, calcareous soils. Most of the plant species in these gardens are rare and restricted to stable, moist habitats, and include alcove death camas (*Zygadenus elegans*), stream orchid (*Epipactus gigantea*), maidenhair fern, alcove bog-orchid (*Habenaria zothecina*), scarlet monkeyflower, cave primrose (*Primula specuicola*), and columbine. Other plants that are more common elsewhere include poison ivy (*Toxicodendron rydbergii*), emory seepweed, birchleaf buckthorn (*Rhamnus betulifolia*), and assorted grasses. Liverworts and mosses are also well-developed on soils and rocks in these gardens.

Sand Dunes

In a few places, soils are extremely sandy, and small sand dunes have formed. Common plants in these habitats include purple sage (*Poliomintha incana*), Indian ricegrass, hyalineherb (*Hymenopappus filifolius*), dwarf lupine (*Lupinus pusillus*), locoweed, globemallow, and shinnery oak. Kangaroo rats are the most common rodents; rabbits are common as well.

Communities on Gypsum Soils

Gypsiferous soils are dominated by plants that can tolerate high alkalinity and include shadscale, scattered woody tiquila, phlox (*Phlox* sp.), and Mormon tea. There is a notable absence of grasses, although biological soil crusts are especially well-developed on gypsum soils. These gypsic areas occur as small pockets, therefore no birds or mammals are specific to them.

Side Canyons

Side canyons both above and below Cataract Canyon contain mixtures of riparian and upland vegetation. This type of vegetation is dependent on width of the side canyon, flood frequency and intensity, and soil depth. In general, scattered tamarisk, willows, and cottonwoods grow alongside pinyon, squawbush, juniper, blackbrush, ricegrass, and other sand-loving plants.[79]

PLANT AND ANIMAL COMMUNITIES OF THE PAST: THE SECRETS OF PACKRAT MIDDENS

Neotoma, the wood rat or packrat, plays a unique and critical role in understanding long-term change in desert ecosystems.[80] Packrats are highly inquisitive and acquisitive, giving rise to the anthropomorphic meaning of the name. Packrats will drag in almost anything that catches their eyes—especially if it is shiny—within a few hundred feet of their nest. The nests are mostly made up of plant material: needles, leaves, shredded bark, and twigs. However, the nests also contain plentiful amounts of animal droppings, insects, bones, rocks, and other objects; including bottle tops, aluminum cans, metal tags left by researchers to mark study plots, wires connecting probes to weather stations, chewing gum wrappers, car keys, you name it. If an object is shiny and left unattached, packrats take it. After collecting these objects into a midden, packrats then urinate and defecate on them. After a fairly short time, the piles solidify into a hard, dark-colored mass. You can often see hardened packrat middens on cliff faces, wedged between loosened rocks, or on the floor of rock alcoves.

It turns out that solidified urine is an excellent preservative. In places protected from rain, packrat middens can last more than 40,000 years, preserving a record of the flora and fauna of the area immediately surrounding the nest location. Using these middens, scientists have been able to reconstruct past climates of the desert southwest.[81] Middens tell a consistent story of regional change. During the latest Pleistocene (11,000 to 22,000 years ago), the climate was much cooler and wetter across this region. In the Sonoran Desert, old middens contain the remains of pinyon, juniper, oaks, and other species that now occur 4,000 feet higher in elevation in moister and cooler conditions. At lower elevations on the Colorado Plateau, middens contain remnants of limber pine, ponderosa pine, and other plants that currently occur thousands of feet above the midden location.

Therefore, these middens tell us that the desert plant communities we see now are fairly recent, and it was not so long ago that our current shrub-dominated communities were dominated by trees. Still, plants we see today were also part of these ancient communities. Remains of shadscale, Mormon tea, and many of the current grasses are commonly found in middens. Though scientists once viewed plant communities as more or less fixed assemblages that moved through time and space as a unit, the prevalent view held today is quite different. Instead, species are believed to respond as individuals to changing conditions. Thus, it would not surprise most scientists to find many of the components present in these deserts long ago still here today, in spite of the landscape going from a tree-dominated landscape to one dominated by shrubs and grasses.

Packrat middens and protected alcoves also tell us that the cooler climates and forested environments once supported a very different fauna than is currently present. We have no indication of their abundance or density; however, we have bones and dung to tell us what animals were present. Moreover, when only a few bones are found, it is impossible to tell if the animals were actually present, or if the bones were trade items from other regions. Records from the Grand Canyon indicate the prehistoric presence of Shasta ground sloths that ate globemallow and Mormon tea; Harrington's mountain goat that ate herbs and grasses; and ancient equids, mountain sheep, and deer.[82] Remains of mammoths and camels have been found on the Kaibab Plateau (northern Arizona), and remains of mammoths in Arches National Park. Remains of extinct condors and Merriams's terratorns, which were enormous vultures, have also been found. Stanton's Cave in the Grand Canyon contains remains of seventy-five bird species, fourteen of which are extinct.[83]

The large mammals that were found during the Pleistocene went extinct rather abruptly 11,000 years ago, and it is not known why. One guess is that vegetation changed as the climate began to warm, which began to occur several millennia before the extinction. However, because many food plants of these animals are still present today this seems an unlikely explanation. Another theory is that these animals depended on a forest habitat that no longer exists. Yet another theory is that the disappearance of the *megafauna* (large animals) coincided with the arrival of people.[84] Large kill sites have been found with projectile points embedded in the rib cages of mammoths. Some competition from other similar animal species also may have been responsible; for example, bighorn sheep arrived just when Harrington's mountain goat disappeared.[85]

A commonly asked question is this: If large grazing herbivores such as mammoths and camels were roaming the Colorado Plateau long ago, how can we say these ecosystems did not evolve with grazing? The answer: the ecosystems now present under the current warmer and drier climate are not the same as those that were present during the Pleistocene. Although some of the same plant species are present today, the structure and function of the systems as a whole were very different more than 11,000 years ago. Modern-day shrubs replaced forests, and grasses became more abundant. In addition, bunchgrasses much less tolerant of grazing replaced grasses that are tolerant of grazing (see Chapter 5). Another factor to keep in mind is that the animals found in these prehistoric records were not part of large thundering herds. Bison, for example, grazed in small family groups. This is quite unlike livestock herds that currently graze landscapes in this region.

READING THE LANDSCAPE

The distribution of plant communities is controlled by a variety of factors: how much light and space is available, the intensity and frequency of disturbance, soil characteristics, and climate. Perennial vegetation is dense in regions where rainfall is plentiful, such as in the central and eastern United States. In contrast, low rainfall in deserts limits the amount of vegetation present, and competition for light and space are seldom important factors in determining what grows where in this landscape. Instead, plant community composition is mostly determined by soil characteristics that include texture, depth, and chemistry. Along the river's edge, most plants have access to lots of water and nutrients and as a result, the vegetation is lush. Just in from the water's edge are habitats that used to be along the river's edge and are filled with flood-deposited silt; these soils are fertile and have a high water-holding capacity. Many of these river bottoms are now isolated vertically from the water table, so plants that grow here cannot tap into river water. A few feet further in from the river are coarse-textured upland sandy soils that receive sediments from the surrounding cliffs instead of the river.

Comparisons between the vastly different vegetation that grows on these three soil types, which can occur within a few feet of each other, point out how important water availability and soil characteristics are in determining plant community composition. A certain type of vegetation grows in abundant river water. If river water is not available, soil characteristics determine what type of vegetation is present.

Within a given soil type (*e.g.*, sandy or fine-textured soils), the interaction between soil depth and texture generally determines whether a plant community is grass or shrub-dominated.[86] Because stiff shrub roots can transport water along a much greater vertical distance than grass roots, shrubs can send roots down through cracks in the bedrock to find deep water. This ability enables them to grow on very shallow soils and simultaneously tap water deep from within the bedrock; also, they can grow on deep alluvial soils and still access the deep water table. Perennial grasses, on the other hand, do not have stiff enough roots to transport water very far and thus require the soils on top of the bedrock to be deep enough to contain all the water and nutrients they need to grow. Wherever a grass-dominated community is present, the soils there are at least several feet deep.[87] The erosional nature of this environment results in only a few small pockets of deep soils, meaning that the Colorado Plateau is a heavily shrub-dominated region.

Fine-textured soils have smaller particles with a higher negative electrical charge than sandy soils,[88] allowing them to hold onto positively-charged nutrients (most nutrients that plants need are positively-charged) that would otherwise be leached away with rainfall. As fine particles also absorb and hold more water than sand particles, plant roots in fine soils have an easier time finding water. However, water is also more readily evaporated from fine soils as it is held closer to the surface. Desert plants that grow on fine-textured soils generally find less water in the upper and mid-portions of the soil profile during dry periods than plants that grow on sandy soils. Therefore they have to have very long roots that can grow through the drier top and middle soil profiles to reach deep water tables. For this reason, deep-rooted shrubs dominate fine-textured soils.[89]

In river bottoms where soils are deep but the water table is relatively shallow, the poorly aerated soils will also support some grasses. Aside from river bottoms, only a few other habitats in Cataract Canyon have fine-textured soils: the gypsic soils in Lower Red Lake Canyon, Tilted Park, and Gypsum Canyon, and some occasional shale outcrops. In these places, soils are often shallow and the water table is very deep. Thus, these soils are dominated by small shrubs with very few, if any, grasses.

With these concepts in mind, you can "read this landscape" and understand some general concepts as to where plants and animals live. If perennial grasses are dominant, the soils are sandy and deeper than a few feet. If shrubs dominate the landscape, the soils are either shallow and sandy or fine-textured with deep water. If you see a mix of shrubs and grasses, the soils are either sandy and of immediate depth or are fine-textured with a shallow water table. If the plants are mostly annuals, either the soils are more fertile and fine-textured than adjoining soils or there has been a recent disturbance.

BIOLOGICAL SOIL CRUSTS

Several years ago, a visitor walked into the headquarters of Natural Bridges National Monument, in a state of great excitement. "Your soil is so wonderful!" he exclaimed to the ranger behind the desk. "It crunches just like snow in the winter at my home. But it's not cold out, so it's much more fun!" The astonishment of the ranger quickly turned to chagrin. Patiently, she explained to the visitor that the soil he was crunching was not at all what he thought it was: instead of walking over lifeless dirt, his feet had been destroying an intricate and astonishing microcommunity that is full of bustling activity whenever it rains and that is critical to the health of this ecosystem.[90] Biological soil crusts occur in all of the plant communi-

ties found in Canyon Country and especially in Cataract Canyon. If you spend any time in Moab, you will notice brochures in all the stores, signs at the trailheads, guides talking on trips, and t-shirts in the shops telling you to not "bust the crust."

Biological soil crusts are found on all continents, and they live in the harshest conditions imaginable. They can survive the extreme cold of the Arctic and the extreme heat of the Sahara. They consist of microscopic *cyanobacteria* (once called blue-green algae), fungi, green algae and bacteria, and macroscopic mosses and lichens. The appearance of biological crusts varies among deserts. In very hot hyperarid deserts like the Sahara, there is not enough water to support lichens and mosses, and so the crusts are flat and contain only cyanobacteria. Hot deserts, like the Sonoran Desert, have enough rainfall for a few scattered mosses and lichens but still no frost-heaving, so the crusts are roughened, or *rugose*. In areas where winter temperatures freeze the soil, one finds pinnacled and rolling crusts. Pinnacled crusts occur where cyanobacteria dominate frost-heaved crusts, as found on the Colorado Plateau and the southern Great Basin. As moisture increases, such as in the northern Great Basin and farther north, so do the cover and diversity of mosses and lichens. These organisms are much more resistant to micro-erosion, and so the crusts there have a smooth, rolling appearance.

Seasonality of rainfall can also determine crust cover and composition. Quick-drying summer rainfall events can actually harm some lichen and moss species. Upon wetting, they begin using up their food stores, but in summer often dry before they have an opportunity to replace these stores. Consequently, soil lichen diversity is lower in summer-rainfall regions, such as the Sonoran Desert, than in regions without summer rainfall, such as the northern Great Basin.

In most deserts, crust cover is inversely related to vascular plant and rock cover. In other words, biological soil crusts will cover almost all undisturbed soil surfaces not otherwise occupied. This relationship holds until precipitation is high enough for vascular plant cover to preclude the presence of soil crusts, as in the nearby La Sal Mountains of Canyon Country. Exceptions are actively disturbed areas such as wash bottoms, moving sand dunes, or places where recurring human or animal activities disturb the soil surface. Until the plant cover and litter excludes crusts, the shading provided by plant cover can enhance development of soil crusts through increased soil moisture. Soils under shrubs tend to be dominated by mosses, while interspaces tend to be dominated by cyanobacteria and lichens. Invasive exotic plants generally decrease the structural diversity of native vascular plant communities and often fill previously biologically crusted interspaces, resulting in less cover and lower species richness of soil crusts.

Soil texture can strongly influence the species composition of crust communities. Fine-textured soils, such as those derived from gypsum and shale or found on river bottoms, support greater cover and more varied populations of cyanobacteria, lichens, and mosses than less stable, coarse-textured sandy soils. Embedded rocks near or at the soil surface can increase crust cover by providing additional water and protection from disturbances. Very shallow soils (less than six inches) often support a wide variety of cyanobacteria, lichens, and mosses relative to adjacent deep soils. Physical and chemical crusts can also enhance cover of biological crusts because they are a stable surface on which water pools.

Soil chemistry can also influence crust cover and composition. Some soil lichens are indicative of soils with low and high levels of calcium carbonate. Overall, crust cover and lichen diversity increases on highly calcareous soils. In the North American deserts and other deserts worldwide, highly calcareous soils derived from limestone or gypsum can support up to eighty percent lichen cover, while adjoining, less calcareous substrates may have less than ten percent cover.

In the cold deserts of the Colorado Plateau region, including parts of Utah, Arizona, Colorado, and New Mexico, biological soil crusts are extraordinarily well developed and typically account for over seventy percent of the living ground cover. The most common species of cyanobacteria in Colorado Plateau soils crusts is *Microcoleus vaginatus*. The most common lichens include the black gelatinous lichens *Collema tenax* and *C. coccophorum*, and the dark-brown plate

lichen *Catapyrenium squamulosum*. Other common species include *Psora decipiens* (red plates), *Toninia sedifolia* (gray dots), *Fulgensia bracteata* (yellow dots), and *F. desertorum* (orange dots), *Squamarina lentigera* (greenish-white, continuous), and *Diploschistes muscorum* (greyish-white, hard, continuous). The most common mosses encountered are *Syntrichia ruralis* (long and dark brown) and *Bryum argenteum* (short and green).

We owe just about everything to cyanobacteria, for without them, our current life form might have never evolved. For almost two billion years, the world was dominated by cyanobacteria. By taking in carbon dioxide and releasing oxygen over vast amounts of time, the huge oceanic mats of cyanobacteria slowly filled the atmosphere with sufficient oxygen for oxygen-dependent life forms to evolve. By 900 million years ago, cyanobacteria had made their way onto land. This was a good thing, as the then-forming soils needed something to hold them in place, since plants had not yet appeared. By 600 million years before present, the atmosphere was approaching what exists today. And finally, at 400 million years ago, vascular plants became established in those soils so nicely held in place by the cyanobacteria.

Cyanobacterial communities in desert soils are often layered, with dark-colored species (*Nostoc, Scytonema*) growing right at the soil surface and light-colored species (*Microcoleus, Oscillatoria*) just below them. Many species grow as long filaments surrounded by a nonliving sheath that is secreted for protection from desiccation and abrasion. When moistened, cyanobacterial filaments move through the soils and leave behind a trail of the sticky, mucilaginous sheath material, which sticks to rock and soil particles, forming an intricate web of fibers in the soil. Loose soil particles are joined together and otherwise unstable and highly erosion-prone surfaces become resistant to both wind and water erosion. This soil-binding action is not dependent on the presence of living filaments: layers of abandoned sheaths can build up over long periods of time and will remain clinging tenaciously to soil particles until disturbed. Cyanobacterial communities provide cohesion and stability in these loose sandy soils, even at depth.

Experiments have shown that well-developed, undisturbed crusts protect soil surfaces from erosion while disturbance to these crusts leaves surfaces vulnerable. Even ten years after impact disturbance soils can still be susceptible to wind erosion during the high winds of spring. Many soils in this area are thin and easily removed unless protected by crusts. As most crustal biomass is concentrated in the top eighth-inch of soil, it does not take much erosion to show profound consequences.

In addition to stabilizing the slow-forming and thus precious desert soil, crusts perform other ecosystem functions as well. They are important in absorbing rainfall. When moistened, the sheaths absorb up to ten times their volume of water. The roughened surface of the crusts slows water runoff, increasing the amount of water that enters the soil and is available to plants. Crusts also contribute nitrogen and organic matter to ecosystems, as well as make other nutrients more available to vascular plants. Vascular plants growing in crusted areas have higher levels of most essential nutrients than plants growing in areas without crusts. This is especially important in desert ecosystems, where nutrient levels are low and often limit plant productivity.

Unfortunately, many recreational and economic activities are incompatible with the presence and well-being of these cyanobacterial crusts. The cyanbacter-ial fibers that confer such tensile strength to these crusts are no match for the compressional stress placed on them by footprints (cows or people) or machinery, especially when the crusts are dry and brittle. Crushed crusts contribute less nitrogen and organic matter to the ecosystem, and soils are left highly susceptible to both wind and water erosion. Wind blows pieces of the pulverized crust away and also buries nearby living crusts. Since crustal organisms need to photosynthesize, burial can mean death. When large sandy areas are disturbed in dry periods, previously stable areas can become loose sand dunes in only a few years.

Large areas that are severely impacted recover slowly. While a thin veneer of cyanobacteria may return in five to seven years, lichen and moss growth can take hundreds of years. Even a single footprint has a long-lasting effect when nitrogen fixation stops and underlying sheath material is crushed. Damage done to the abandoned sheath material underneath the surface cannot be repaired since the living organisms are only on the surface. Instead, sheaths must build up slowly as a result of many years of cyanobacterial growth.

There are many different names for soil crusts (see Sidebar). At least six terms—most commonly cryptogamic, microbiotic, microphytic—have been used to describe soil crusts, and their usage can be confusing. Names are very important in science, as they establish

---

THE DIFFERENT NAMES FOR BIOLOGICAL SOIL CRUSTS

Dear Ms. Belnap:

I just got back from Canyonlands. It was beautiful. Thank you. I've visited many times over the past fifteen years—enough to watch the crusty desert soil have its name changed at least three times over the years. Cryptogamic, microbiotic, cryptobiotic. . . . What's the deal? Is this crust in the witness protection plan or something?

I understand that you're at least in part responsible for the name changes. Since the name is obviously not set in stone, I'd like to offer my suggestion. Let's face it. The crust is not grand like the rock formations or cute like the bunnies or beautiful like the flowering cacti. I'm sure it's fascinating to study, but in the whole scheme of things I'm afraid it's kind of ugly. Plus it lives with the danger that people who don't know better might step on it, the Rodney Dangerfield of crusts. It plays an important role, but it's hard for people to relate to.

Anthropomorphizing it is not a bad idea. In that same vein, we could give it a name that people could easily relate to, the kind of name their best friend might have; something short and sweet with instant name recognition. Drumroll please. How about this: Bob. Cryptobiotic crust is relatively easy to step on compared with Bob. I know what you're thinking: the name has to have a scientific bent. Don't worry! I've addressed that, too. It's also an acronym for our "Bio-Organic Buddies." Can't you just hear the hikers saying "don't step on Bob! He's our buddy."? It puts a human face on a crusty situation. If you have time, let me know what you think of my idea.

Sincerely,
Chris Keener

relationships among organisms and give scientists a way to structure their thinking about them. Thus, scientists invest a lot of time and energy in making certain names of organisms are correct. Whenever scientists come up with more precise ways of establishing relationships among organisms, they update the names accordingly. That, in a nutshell, is why biological soil crusts have been called so many names.

Cryptogam is the scientific term for plants that do not have flowers. Cryptogams also lack sophisticated systems by which to transport water and nutrients. Thirty years ago when cryptogamic crusts were named, scientists generally believed there were only two kingdoms in nature: plants and animals. Under this system, all the dominant components of the crusts—cyanobacteria, green algae, mosses, fungi, and lichens—were all considered plants. Since all these organisms were nonflowering and without vascular systems, they were all considered cryptogams. Hence, the name "cryptogamic crusts" was adopted.

Since then, it has been well accepted among scientists that there are at least *five* kingdoms out there. Rather than dividing life according to plant and animal, the initial division is now between *prokaryotes* (organisms without membrane-bound structures inside their cells) and *eukaryotes* (those that contain such structures). Further divisions divide the prokaryotes into two kingdoms and the eukaryotes into three kingdoms. Within this new system, only mosses and green algae remain in the plant kingdom. The prokaryotic cyanobacteria are combined with bacteria. Fungi inhabit a separate kingdom. Lichens straddle both worlds: they are a combination of fungi and either a cyanobacteria or a green algae.

Suddenly, cryptogamic crusts had very few cryptogams left in them. A Pandora's Box was opened as the search for a new name began. Names popped up everywhere, with each scientist adopting a favorite term. As with other objects of scientific interest, these multiple names will undoubtedly persist for some time until a majority of scientists settle on one term. Therefore, the answer to the question "which name is correct?" is, well . . . you can avoid the whole dilemma by calling them the generic name, "biological soil crusts."

THE PROBLEM OF NON-NATIVE VEGETATION

Call them what you will: introduced species, non-native species, exotics, invasives, or aliens. We will use these terms interchangeably in this book as a reflection of our ambivalence toward the value judgments that are implied. Some of these terms have more pejorative connotations than others, but they refer to plant and animal species that have been introduced deliberately or inadvertently by humans. Here, we discuss non-native plant species in Canyonlands; bullfrogs will be discussed in Chapter 5 and non-native fish and aquatic species will be discussed in Chapter 7. Other than feral cats, peacocks, and the occasional pig near Moab, there are few significant exotic terrestrial mammals or birds in the region.

There are two classes of exotic species found along the river corridor. The first types are those exotics that appear to pose little threat to the native ecosystem. These include plants such as goosefoot (*Chenopodium album*) and perennial pepperweed (*Lepidium latifolium*). At present, only a few individuals of these species are found in the habitats that they prefer. The second types are much more aggressive and problematic for land managers. They generally prefer habitats disturbed by land use, although once established they can invade undisturbed habitats as well. Fire and heavy grazing kills many native species, facilitating the invasion of cheatgrass (*Bromus tectorum*) into river bottoms and adjacent communities. Fire combined with lack of flooding gives tamarisk a competitive advantage over native riparian species. Livestock grazing transports the seeds of cheatgrass into many communities. Russian knapweed (*Centaurea repens*) now dominates many river bottoms. Unfortunately, we know little about what simulates invasions by this species, although fire, livestock grazing, and lack of flooding are the most likely factors.

Cheatgrass

One of the major legacies of livestock grazing is the cheatgrass invasion. Cheatgrass appeared in the United States from Eurasia sometime in the late 1800s[91] in packing material received in Denver.[92] In the Inter-mountain West, one of the first recorded locations of cheatgrass was Provo, Utah. Cheatgrass now dominates almost seventeen million acres of the western states, with an additional sixty-two million acres at high risk of invasion.[93] Even where it is not dominant, it is present to some extent in most low-elevation vegetative communities. The range of this diminutive plant is still expanding, as it manages to newly invade hundreds of thousands of acres of western rangeland yearly, reducing previously rich native plant communities to monoculture wastelands. This expanding empire is helped along by multiple factors including increased fire frequency, livestock grazing, and the empty ecological niches exploited by this incredible plant.

As with tamarisk, fire cycles in cheatgrass-dominated systems are far more frequent than native-dominated ecosystems. The fine fuels created by cheatgrass ignite easily, creating huge rangeland fires every few years in ecosystems that previously burned only every few hundred years, if ever. The native plants in these ecosystems are not adapted to such frequent fire, and are often extirpated as a result, leaving the ecosystem open to dominance by cheatgrass.[94]

Livestock grazing of western rangelands has also helped the expansion of cheatgrass. Cheatgrass has evolved alongside domestic livestock for thousands of years and is well adapted to the various types of disturbance associated with livestock. The seeds travel on the animals, and hoof action helps "plant" cheatgrass seed by churning and turning the soil. Churning of soils by animal hooves results in the death of microorganisms, which in turn creates nutrient pulses that favor the annual grass over the natives. Because it is a fast-growing annual plant, it is more adapted to exploit nutrient pulses than slow-growing native perennials. In addition, cattle prefer to eat native grasses instead of cheatgrass. Consequently, the increased herbivory pressure on the native plants keeps them stressed and less able to compete with cheatgrass.

Cheatgrass has filled an ecological niche seemingly never filled by native plants. Cheatgrass germinates in the fall, unlike most of our native plants. During the winter months, it develops as a rosette of leaves pressed closely to the soil surface. However, the small rosette is deceiving: cheatgrass is actually forming a deep and extensive root system while it appears above ground to be quite harmless. This means that in the spring, when the natives are either just germinating or coming out of dormancy, cheatgrass is up and running with a well-developed root system in place. Early spring is when the most soil moisture is available and cheatgrass often uses up much of the limited soil moisture before the natives are even active.[95]

The cheatgrass invasion has had profound negative consequences for native plant and animal diversity in the western United States. It has obliterated many native plants. Native animals, adapted to the structurally-complex and year-round habitat perennial plants created, have been suddenly confronted with a greatly simplified habitat that is there one day and gone the next. Smaller amounts of food that were once available year-round are suddenly replaced by a huge burst of food that is present for only eight or so weeks. Species that rely on seeds are often able to take advantage of this sudden inundation of food by caching seeds; other species that do not horde seeds are often out of luck.

Perennial plants offer lots of hiding places year-round for many sizes of rodents and rabbits; short, stubby annual grasses are unable to hide these animals or provide protection from wind, heat, or cold.[96] Thus, larger animals, once able to hide, have become easy pickings for predators in such an altered landscape. Conversely, some insects find additional hiding places in cheatgrass, thus making the hunt more difficult for those that eat them. For instance, lizards that hide under bushes waiting to ambush prey suddenly find themselves unable to see through the thick cheatgrass.[97] Thus, the presence of cheatgrass reduces both the abundance and diversity of native plant and animal communities.

However, cheatgrass is not unwelcome everywhere; it is nutritious when green. Ranchers in areas of higher and more predictable rainfall, such as northern Montana, find it a good forage item for livestock. However, cheatgrass is at the southern edge of its distribution in the Canyonlands region, and it performs poorly during drought years; in a very wet year there will be 100 plants per square foot, while in the next dry year the same spot might support only 0.5 plants per square foot.[98] This unreliability makes it a very poor forage source for livestock or wildlife. Despite drought, cheatgrass can regain its former biomass within a few years, as it can have many long-lived seeds in the soil.

Much research has delved into the dynamics of the invasion and dominance by cheatgrass. Studies have focused on site disturbance histories, genetic plasticity, life history strategies, favorable associations with fungi (*mycorrhizal associations*), water relations, nitrogen relations, and environmental tolerances of exotic grasses relative to other plants in the community. These grasses have been found to have most of the characteristics generally associated with successful weedy annual plants; including quick invasion of disturbed sites, high rates of germination and seedling establishment under a wide range of conditions, and rapid seedling growth.[99] However, what makes one ecosystem susceptible to invasion, while an adjacent community is not, is only partially understood. Looking at the cheatgrass communities along the rivers, it is possible to see that they are concentrated in the flat and frequently flooded areas found just behind the riparian vegetation. Cheatgrass does best on fine-textured soils in this region and this is probably partially explained by the greater moisture-holding capacity of the soils. However, once the ground starts to rise and the soils get shallow, sandy and rocky, there are fewer cheatgrass plants to be found. Thus, soil characteristics clearly play an important role in determining where these plants are found.[100]

Recovery trajectories of disturbed areas are also puzzling: when areas are released from disturbance such as livestock grazing, cheatgrass sometimes remains dominant while in other sites, sometimes only a few feet away, natives are able to completely or partially reinvade sites. Again, this implies that local factors such as soil characteristics, microhabitats, or rodent activity are influencing the recovery outcome. Most efforts to reestablish natives into annual grass stands have failed, especially in areas receiving less than ten inches of rain annually. Attempts to encourage the natural spread of native plants or to interseed selected species into cheatgrass stands have generally

not been effective. Instead, complete site renovation has often been required for successful native establishment. This remedy is expensive, results in the loss of other resource values, and is not feasible for restoration of vast acreages infested with these weeds.

Russian Knapweed

Russian knapweed poses a serious problem for land managers. Introduced to North America in 1898 from Eurasia,[101] Russian knapweed did not invade river bottoms along the Green River until the early 1990s, showing that the problem can come long after the introduction. This species has since spread rapidly, eradicating native vegetation locally and forming monospecific stands. Russian knapweed spreads from adventitious shoots that rise from its spreading roots and can penetrate to a depth of over eight feet. The National Park Service has spent much money and effort trying to control the spread of Russian knapweed along the river corridor, but unfortunately, this is an expensive, long-term task that may inevitably be unsuccessful. At this writing, Russian knapweed can be seen on river left across from Spanish Bottom and at Rapid 10 on river right in Cataract Canyon; it is also very common in the vicinity of Moab.

Tamarisk

Tamarisk, a native of the Mediterranean, first appeared in the United States sometime in the early 1800s.[102] By 1852 it was being sold as an ornamental in California nurseries, as people were attracted to the beautiful, pale pink flowers and fine feathery foliage. Tamarisk appears to have escaped cultivation sometime in the 1870s, and colonized the banks of the lower Colorado River sometime in the late 1880s. It has been reported that tamarisk was deliberately planted along the Paria River in southern Utah in 1870 and in Green River, Utah, around 1900.[103] Its ability to stabilize streambanks attracted engineers, and massive plantings were done in the early 1900s along many western waterways. Botanical surveys from 1933 and 1938 found it along the San Juan River in southern Utah, and photos record its presence along the Colorado and Green rivers in 1941.[104] The spread of tamarisk has been rapid: in 1920, it covered only fifteen square miles in the western United States; by the late 1960s, tamarisk covered 580 square miles.[105]

Tamarisk is prolific. A single adult plant is capable of producing over a billion seeds a year.[106] These tiny seeds travel easily on the ever-present desert winds, sending tamarisk seeds to just about every low-elevation, western river, stream, and spring. Seeds are produced during high-water times and plants readily colonize after flood waters recede by germinating within twenty-four hours on wet sands. Seedlings can grow up to two inches a day.[107] Tamarisk seeds can germinate under much saltier conditions than native riparian species such as willows, and therefore have an advantage in saline watersheds and springs. The adult tamarisk can also survive in very salty soils (up to 35,000 ppm) by actively excreting salts onto leaf surfaces. When these leaves fall salts accumulate on soil surfaces. Unless these soils are periodically flooded the resultant salty soils retard or prevent seed germination in willow and cottonwood plants, as they can only tolerate salinities up to 1,500 ppm. Thus, the long-term presence of tamarisk can exclude the germination of other species. However, if soils get too salty even tamarisk will not germinate, leaving barren soils.[108]

Tamarisk generally uses more water than native species. The rate at which water is lost through evaporation and plant respiration for a given area of tamarisk leaf surface is the same as for native plants, but the larger leaf surface area of tamarisk results in about thirty percent higher water usage.[109] Accordingly, tamarisk has been reported to dry up springs and/or lower water tables along springs or intermittent streams. Tamarisk is also able to out-compete native cottonwoods and willows in water-limited soils, giving the plant an edge in drought conditions. In addition, tamarisk grows in thick clumps, often excluding light necessary for the germination and growth of other species. Removal of tamarisk can have a positive effect on willow growth and water availability.[110] Water is costly in the desert, and savings from the complete removal of tamarisk from the West is estimated at sixteen billion dollars over a fifty-five-year span.[111]

Tamarisk has deep taproots (up to thirty-five feet) and flexible stems that can resist flooding. Individuals can withstand prolonged submersion, with reports of survival after 100 days under water.[112] However, tamarisk thickets are best developed in areas of lower water velocity and stable flow levels. This can be seen vividly as the huge tamarisk thickets along the slower, fairly stable stretches of the Green River (due to upstream dams and a meandering course) disappear once the river enters Cataract Canyon, where water velocity increases dramatically and flow levels are highly variable. In addition, instream island banks have willows on the banks where water velocity is the highest, while tamarisk is generally found on the more protected sides, in backwaters, and the upstream edges of eddies.

Where tamarisk occurs, riparian areas are generally much wider than they were 100 years ago. According to one study, tamarisk took advantage of new habitat created by reduction in flood discharges, colonized open banks, and trapped sediment to build new, stable floodplains.[113] Alternatively, tamarisk may have simply followed narrowing induced by physical processes.[114] Whatever the reason, the widening of the riparian communities in towards the river has resulted in the narrowing of the river channel and stranding of native vegetation far from the river's edge.[115] As the channel narrows, stream power is concentrated and downcutting occurs. Channel narrowing results in a lowering of the water table, making saturated alluvium more difficult for roots to reach. This is especially apparent in areas like Bonita Bend, where the old cottonwoods are now high above the current river level. Downcutting also decreases the frequency of inundation and the attendant desalinization of the soils. Thus, the longer the tamarisk is present, the slower the natives are to return—if they can return at all.

Flow regulation and large-scale water use exacerbate this situation. Flood control, which is a common justification for dams, reduces peak discharges and the amount of water available to riparian systems. Because flood peaks are lower, groundwater tables in the alluvial floodplains are also lowered, killing or retarding growth of established cottonwoods and other native trees. Water use for agriculture can also lower

Figure 4-5. Millard Canyon (mile 34.0)

A. September 12, 1871. The Buttes of the Cross, described by the first Powell expedition in 1869, are formed by the intersection of two blade-like ridges in the Moenkopi Formation that are not actually connected. As a result, the Buttes of the Cross can only be seen from a narrow angle along the Green River. Powell was enamored of this topographical coincidence and had his photographer, Beaman, document the Buttes from a point on the undulating surface of the White Rim Sandstone. The Green River and its bottomlands appear at left center, and Millard Canyon enters the Green at right center. (E.O. Beaman 733, courtesy of the U.S. Geological Survey Photographic Library)

river flows, particularly during summer months, and thereby stress riparian plants in the season when they need water most. Scouring floods are reduced, thus further encouraging tamarisk growth, and leading to the senescence of riparian systems which require periodic disturbance for renewal.

The presence of tamarisk has altered many aspects of the riverine environment (Figure 4-5). It can form almost impenetrable thickets, increasing the difficulty of gaining access to water for larger mammals such as bighorn sheep, deer, and river runners. As mentioned above, tamarisk can dry up isolated water sources critical to the well-being of many species of desert fauna. Thickets can conceal predators, making river access dangerous. The lack of palatable fruits and seeds results in few animals using tamarisk for forage. Lack of diversity in height, unlike cottonwood-willow stands, reduces the numbers of animals that use it for cover and nesting. In some areas, beaver prefer native vegetation over tamarisk; however, in the Grand

Canyon, tamarisk appears to be the preferred target.[116] Many native insects avoid tamarisk, and diversity is lower on tamarisk than willow, which may reduce pollinator services where tamarisk occurs.[117] However, the density of insects, especially for nonnatives such as honeybees, can be significantly higher on tamarisk than native vegetation.[118] Reptile density (the number of individuals per unit area) and diversity (the number of species per unit area) is higher in native stands compared to tamarisk stands.[119]

Many studies have suggested that tamarisk has little value to native birds, except where tamarisk is the dominant, or only, plant available.[120] The thinness of the branches eliminates use by woodpeckers and raptors. Many birds that nest in willows and cottonwoods avoid tamarisk and overall numbers of species and individuals are lower in tamarisk compared to native stands.[121] However, some birds utilize the additional habitat that tamarisk has created, including the endangered Southwest Willow Flycatcher (see

B. August 21, 1968. In 1964, this site became part of Canyonlands National Park. The main change between 1871 and 1968 is the invasion of tamarisk on the floodplain of the Green River. Some minor changes have occurred in the shrubs on the soil islands throughout the fore- and midground. (H.G. Stephens, W-4)

C. October 13, 1999. The surface of the White Rim Sandstone supports some of the most biologically diverse plant assemblages in Canyonlands National Park. In our brief survey, we found twenty-seven perennial plant species in the foreground area and an additional eight riparian species in the left midground. Many individuals persist from 1871 to 1999, including blackbrush, Bigelow sagebrush, and Mormon tea. Some of the soil pockets have shifted, but some of the surfaces covered by biological soil crusts at lower right are remarkably similar. The only grazing at this site may have come from cattle and sheep herds being moved through the area from one range to another, sometimes using a ferry that operated about a half mile upstream from this site. (Steven Young, Stake 3894)

below), Mourning Doves, and Black-chinned Hummingbirds.[122]

Tamarisk is highly resistant to the common disturbances that occur in riparian ecosystems, including flooding and fire. It quickly resprouts when cut or burned. The presence of tamarisk has increased the frequency and intensity of fires along the river corridor, as the fine foliage of tamarisk ignites easily, and the thick duff burns readily. As a result, several fires a year occur along this stretch of river, caused primarily by human activities such as campfires and burning toilet paper. Tamarisk doesn't mind much; each trunk cheerfully sends up multiple shoots the next spring. However, most native streamside plants die when they burn, with the exception of the coyote willow, leaving tamarisk to win the race of reestablishment. Deep ash, salty soils, vertical and horizontal stranding from the water table, and thick, newly sprouted tamarisk cover often keep the native plants from returning quickly.

Management of tamarisk is currently a contentious issue. With the exception of a few leaf-sucking aphids, there are few critters that eat or harm tamarisk. Tamarisk removal is a daunting task, and neither fire nor cutting is effective on a large scale. Moreover, eradication cannot succeed over the long term if all individuals are not found and killed. Eradication appears to require a biological control imported from tamarisk's native realms. Years of research have gone into finding such a control, and two have been found: the manna mealybug and the saltcedar leaf beetle.[123] Both insects are able to kill adult tamarisk within a few years, and both refrain from eating native species. These insects were ready for release by land managers several years ago; however, concerns about what might happen to Southwest Willow Flycatchers, as well as fears of what effect any new organism might have on native plants, have dampened enthusiasm for this mechanism of biocontrol.

It is hard to believe, but here we finally find a good species to get the bad species and then we find out the good species might actually harm another good species. The Southwest Willow Flycatcher is a small, unobtrusive bird that has the misfortune of being historically restricted to highly desirable human habitat: southern California streamside property. Now that

houses have replaced willows and other vegetation along vast stretches of semiarid streams in southern California, the flycatcher has moved into other regions where dense streamside vegetation remains, and tamarisk forms the densest stands. Thus, eradication of tamarisk could eliminate what little habitat is left for the flycatcher. Some studies have shown that Southwest Willow Flycatchers nest preferentially in tamarisk in the Grand Canyon.[124] That said, however, other studies have shown that Southwest Willow Flycatchers that live in tamarisk have smaller body biomass, lower fat stores, and reduced numbers when compared to birds in adjacent willow and cottonwood stands.[125]

Management of exotic species is a dilemma, to be certain. However, there are several factors to mitigate the possible negative effects of biocontrol of tamarisk. First, in areas that flood frequently, the most likely outcome of revegetation is recolonization by native willows, an outcome that can be hastened by replanting. Secondly, these insects take several years to kill an individual tamarisk and they will not be able to kill 100 percent of the established plants. Thus, release will not result in an immediate or a complete loss of habitat. Finally, tamarisk is negatively affecting other species of concern such as cottonwoods. On the downside, biocontrols always carry the risk of unintended consequences, as we humans are good at intending good and producing ends we never thought possible.

There is one piece of good news on the horizon about exotic riparian species. Long-time tamarisk watchers report stretches of streams where willows are increasing, in spite of the fact that tamarisks share the same habitat.[126] Willows along the banks of dam-created lakes are more likely to establish themselves than tamarisk if water levels are lowered when willow seed, not tamarisk seed, is flying about. In addition, we have ways to remove localized stands of tamarisk, using carefully timed applications of fire, chainsaws, and herbicides.

Russian Olive

Russian olive (*Elaeagnus angustifolia*) is a non-native species that is present along the Green and Colorado rivers. This thorny tree has a grey ghost-like appearance and occurs on reaches with very slow-moving water and is very common near the towns of Green River and Moab. Planted extensively as an ornamental, Russian olive has spread down local Pack and Mill creeks, and Courthouse Wash in Arches National Park is clogged with Russian olive near its juncture with the Colorado River. Although Russian olive is spreading quickly along the San Juan River, it is spreading very slowly, if at all, along either the Green or Colorado river corridors. If it does invade at a faster pace, it could present severe problems to riparian ecosystems on both approaches to Cataract Canyon.

THE STRUGGLES OF DESERT LIVING

Life for desert residents is challenging for different reasons than those facing plants and animals in wetter regions. Factors such as lack of water, extreme temperatures, and shallow, infertile or saline soils shape the lives of desert creatures. Relatively few organisms have been able to adapt, particularly in an evolutionary sense, to such inhospitable conditions. Thus the number of species and the number of organisms of a given species are relatively low in these regions. In contrast, the teeming numbers of organisms living in less extreme environments are mostly concerned with each other: who eats who and/or who is most effective in competing for resources.

Life in the desert will always be a struggle against the ever-changing environment. However, the lifeforms of this region have demonstrated that they are quite capable of adapting to current conditions. On the other hand, rapid change induced by humans is far more difficult for them to handle. Of these changes, increased land use is of the most immediate concern, and directly and obviously impacts Cataract Canyon's ecosystems. These human-related changes are addressed throughout the following chapters of this book. Longer-term impacts, such as atmospheric deposition of anthropogenically-produced nutrients and alteration of the amount and/or timing of rainfall, are not addressed directly in this volume. These impacts may profoundly affect Cataract Canyon's

ecosystems in the future, thus increasing the challenge of living within its walls.

Notes

1. C.E. Dutton, *Report on the Geology of the High Plateaus of Utah* (Rocky Mountain Region: U.S. Geological and Geographical Survey, 1880), 284–291.

2. Dan Pope and Clayton Brough, eds., *Utah's Weather and Climate* (Salt Lake City: Publisher's Press, 1996), 168–169.

3. Richard Hereford, R.H. Webb, and Scott Graham, *Precipitation History of the Colorado Plateau Region, 1900–2000* (Flagstaff: U.S. Geological Survey Fact Sheet 119-02, 2002).

4. D.B. Enfield, "El Niño, Past and Present," *Review of Geophysics 27* (1989): 159–187.

5. Hereford et al., *Precipitation History*, 2.

6. N.J. Mantua and S.R. Hare, "The Pacific Decadal Oscillation," *Journal of Oceanography 58* (2002): 35–42.

7. Hereford et al., *Precipitation History*, 4.

8. K.M. Schmidt and R.H. Webb, "Researchers Consider U.S. Southwest's Response to Warmer, Drier Conditions: *EOS, Transactions of the American Geophysical Union 82* (2001): 475, 478.

9. S.A. Elias, *The Ice-Age History of Southwestern National Parks* (Washington, D.C.: Smithsonian Institution Press, 1997).

10. Arthur Cronquist, N.H. Holmgren, and P.K. Holmgren, *Intermountain Flora* (New York: New York Botanical Garden, 1997), 19–39.

11. R.W. Pearcy, J. Ehleringer, H.A. Mooney, and P.W. Rundel, *Plant Physiological Ecology* (New York: Chapman and Hall, 1989); S.D. Smith, R.K. Monson, and J.E. Anderson, *Physiological Ecology of North American Desert Plants* (Berlin: Springer, 1997), 57–59; John Sowell, *Desert Ecology* (Salt Lake City: University of Utah Press, 2001), 24–46.

12. Sowell, *Desert Ecology*, 34.

13. Smith *et al.*, *Physiological Ecology,* 59–64

14. Sowell, *Desert Ecology*, 24–46.

15. P.W. Rundel and P.S. Nobel, "Structure and Function in Desert Root Systems," in *Plant Root Growth: an Ecological Perspective*, ed. D. Atkinson (Oxford, England: Blackwell, 1991), 349–378; J.A. Ludwig, "Distributional Adaptations of Root Systems in Desert Environments," in *The Belowground Ecosystem: A Synthesis of Plant-Associated Processes*, ed. J. K. Marshall (Fort Collins, Colorado: Colorado State University, Range Science Department Science Series, Vol. 26, 1977), 85–91.

16. M.A. Dimmitt, "Plant Ecology of the Sonoran Desert Region," in *A Natural History of the Sonoran Desert*, 127–152; J.R. Ehleringer, S.L. Phillips, W.S.F.

Schuster, and D.R. Sandquist, "Differential Utilization of Summer Rains by Desert Plants," *Oecologia* 88 (1991): 430–434.

17. Ehleringer *et al.*, "Differential Utilization," 430–434; D.R. Sandquist, W.S.F. Schuster, L.A. Donovan, S.L. Phillips, and J.R. Ehleringer, "Differences in Carbon Isotope Discrimination Between Seedlings and Adults of Southwestern Desert Perennial Plants," *Southwestern Naturalist* 38 (1993): 212–217; G. Lin, S.L. Phillips, and J.R. Ehleringer, "Monsoonal Precipitation Responses of Shrubs in a Cold Desert Community on the Colorado Plateau," *Oecologia* 106 (1996): 8–17.

18. Smith *et al.*, *Physiological Ecology*, 45–57.

19. John Alcock, *Sonoran Desert Summer* (Tucson: University of Arizona Press, 1990), 26–29.

20. M.A. Dimmitt, "Flowering Plants of the Sonoran Desert," in *A Natural History of the Sonoran Desert,* 153–264.

21. Arthur Cronquist, "The Biota of the Intermountain Region in Geohistorical Context," *Great Basin Naturalist Memoirs* 2 (1978): 3–15.

22. J.L. Charley and N.E. West, "Plant-Induced Soil Chemical Patterns in Some Shrub-Dominated Semidesert Ecosystems of Utah," *Journal of Ecology* 63 (1975): 945–964.

23. L.H. Giles, R.P. Gibbens, and J.M. Lenz, "Soils and Sediments Associated with Remarkable, Deeply-Penetrating Roots of Crucifixion Thorn (*Koeberlinea spinosa* Zucc.)," *Journal of Arid Environments* 31 (1995): 37–15; L.H. Giles, R.P. Gibbens, and J.M. Lenz, "The Near-Ubiquitous Pedogenic World of Mesquite Roots in an Arid Basin Floor," *Journal of Arid Environments* 35 (1997): 39–58.

24. M.M. Caldwell and J.H. Richards, "Hydraulic Lift: Water Efflux from Upper Roots Improves Effectiveness of Water Uptake by Deep Roots," *Oecologia* 79 (1989): 1–5; M.M. Caldwell, T.E. Dawson, and J.H. Richards, "Hydraulic Lift: Consequences of Water Efflux from Roots of Plants," *Oecologia* 113 (1998): 151–161; C.K. Yoder and R.S. Nowak, "Hydraulic Lift Among Native Plant Species in the Mojave Desert," *Plant and Soil* 215 (1999): 93–102.

25. Sowell, *Desert Ecology*, 43–45.

26. Bernd Heinrich, *The Trees in My Forest* (New York: Harper Collins, 1997).

27. C.E. Bock, J.H. Bock, W.R. Kenney, and V.M. Hawthorne, "Responses of Birds, Rodents, and Vegetation to Livestock Exclosure in a Semidesert Grassland Site," *Journal of Range Management* 37 (1984): 239–242; R.H. MacArthur and J.W. MacArthur, "On Bird Species Diversity," *Ecology* 42 (1961): 594–598; J.V. Robinson, "The Effect of Architectural Variation in Habitat on a Spider Community: an Experimental Field Study," *Ecology* 62 (1981): 73–80; W.G. Whitford, G.S. Forbes, and G.I. Kerley, "Diversity, Spatial Variability, and Functional Roles of Inverte-brates in Desert Grassland Ecosystems," in *The Desert Grassland,* eds. M.P. McClaran and T.R. Van Devender (Tucson: University of Arizona Press, 1996), 153–195.

28. David Williams, *A Naturalist's Guide to Canyon Country* (Helena, Montana: Falcon Press/Canyonlands Natural History Association, 2000), 149.

29. MacArthur and MacArthur, "On Bird Species Diversity"; J.T. Rotenberry, "The Role of Habitat in Avian Community Composition: Physiognomy or Floristics?" *Oecologia* 67 (1985): 213–217; R.R. Roth, "Spatial Heterogeneity and Bird Species Diversity," *Ecology* 57 (1976): 773–782; R.B. Huey, E.R. Pianka, and T.W. Schoener, *Lizard Ecology* (Cambridge, Massachusetts: Harvard University Press, 1983).

30. Arthur Cronquist, A.H. Holmgren, N.H. Holmgren, and J.L. Reveal, *Intermountain Flora: Vascular Plants of the Intermountain West, U.S.A., Volume One* (New York: The New York Botanical Garden, Hafner Publishing, 1972), 19–39.

31. R. Cowles and E. Bakker, *Desert Journal: A Naturalist Reflects on Arid California* (Berkeley: University of California Press, 1977), 91–92.

32. *Ibid.*

33. Sowell, *Desert Ecology*, 59–101; J.L. Cloudsley-Thompson, *Ecophysiology of Desert Arthropods and Reptiles* (Berlin: Springer-Verlag, 1991).

34. Sowell, *Desert Ecology,* 59–101.

35. *Ibid.*; Cloudsley-Thompson, *Ecophysiology of Desert Arthropods and Reptiles*; J.L. Cloudsley-Thompson, *Diversity of Desert Life* (Jodhpur, India: Pawan Kumar Scientific Publishers, 1993), 31.

36. F.A. Ryser Jr., *Birds of the Great Basin: A Natural History* (Reno, Nevada: University of Nevada Press, 1985), 15–37.

37. Cloudsley-Thompson, *Ecophysiology of Desert Arthropods and Reptiles,* 154–155.

38. Cloudsley-Thompson, *Diversity of Desert Life,* 79.

39. *Ibid.*, 37; Sowell, *Desert Ecology,* 59–101; Cloudsley-Thompson, *Ecophysiology of Desert Arthropods and Reptiles*; Ryser, *Birds of the Great Basin,* 15–50; Peter Siminski, "The Desert Adaptations of Birds and Mammals," in *A Natural History of the Sonoran Desert*, eds. S.J. Phillips and P.W. Comus (Tucson: Arizona-Sonora Desert Museum/University of California Press, 2000), 367–372.

40. MacArthur and MacArthur, "On Bird Species Diversity"; J.T. Rotenberry, "The Role of Habitat in Avian Community Composition: Physiognomy or Floristics?" *Oecologia* 67 (1985): 213–217; R.R. Roth, "Spatial Heterogeneity and Bird Species Diversity," *Ecology* 57 (1976): 773–782; Huey *et al.*, *Lizard Ecology*.

41. G. N. Louw and M. K. Seely, *Ecology of Desert Organisms* (New York: John Wiley and Sons, 1990), 55.

42. Cloudsley-Thompson, *Diversity of Desert Life,* 29.

43. *Ibid.*, 47.

44. Cloudsley-Thompson, *Ecophysiology of Desert Arthropods and Reptiles*, 80–101; Sowell, *Desert Ecology*, 88.

45. Sowell, *Desert Ecology*, 59–101.

46. Cloudsley-Thompson, *Diversity of Desert Life*, 41.

47. Cloudsley-Thompson, *Ecophysiology of Desert Arthropods and Reptiles*, 128–133.

48. Sowell, *Desert Ecology*; Peter Siminski, "The Desert Adaptations of Birds and Mammals," in *A Natural History of the Sonoran Desert*, 367–372; Cloudsley-Thompson, *Diversity of Life*, 57; Ryser, *Birds of the Great Basin*, 16–44; Alcock, *Sonoran Desert Summer*, 8–11.

49. Louw and Seely, *Ecology of Desert Organisms*, 47–49.

50. *Ibid.*

51. Knut Schmidt-Nielsen, *Desert Animals: Physiological Problems of Heat and Water* (London: Oxford University Press, 1964), 231.

52. Cloudsley-Thompson, *Ecophysiology of Desert Arthropods and Reptiles*, 80–101; Ryser, *Birds of the Great Basin,* 44–45; Knut Schmidt-Nielsen, *Animal Physiology: Adaptation and Environment* (Cambridge: Cambridge University Press, 1983), 340–372; Sowell, *Desert Ecology,* 92–98; Cloudsley-Thompson, *Diversity of Life*, 42.

53. Cloudsley-Thompson, *Diversity of Life*, 30, 42.

54. *Ibid.*, 28–30.

55. *Ibid.*, 38.

56. Ryser, *Birds of the Great Basin*, 16–37.

57. Cloudsley-Thompson, *Ecophysiology of Desert Arthropods and Reptiles*, 52–79; Cloudsley-Thompson, *Diversity of Life*, 49.

58. Sowell, *Desert Ecology*, 59–80.

59. Cloudsley-Thompson, *Diversity of Life*, 49.

60. Ryser, *Birds of the Great Basin*, 15–35; Cloudsley-Thompson, *Ecophysiology of Desert Arthropods and Reptiles,* 71; Schmidt-Nielsen, *Animal Physiology*, 195–196, 415–416.

61. Cloudsley-Thompson, *Ecophysiology of Desert Arthropods and Reptiles*, 89; Cloudsley-Thompson, *Diversity of Life*, 46.

62. Cloudsley-Thompson, *Diversity of Life*, 32.

63. *Ibid.*, 28, 67–70.

64. National Park Service records, Canyonlands National Park, Moab, Utah, 2002. These records are continually being updated, and supercede those published in Charlie Schelz, comp., "Species Numbers for Vertebrates," *The Confluence* 7 (2000): cover.

65. Ryser, *Birds of the Great Basin*, 15–34; K. Long, *Hummingbirds, A Wildlife Handbook* (Boulder, Colorado: Johnson Books, 1997), 110–113; Siminski, "The Desert Adaptations of Birds and Mammals;" Sowell, *Desert Ecology*, 64–80; Cloudsley-Thompson, *Diversity of Life*, 49.

66. Ryser, *Birds of the Great Basin*, 41–44; Siminski, "The Desert Adaptations of Birds and Mammals," in *A Natural History of the Sonoran Desert*.

67. Siminski, "The Desert Adaptations of Birds and Mammals," in *A Natural History of the Sonoran Desert*.

68. Ryser, *Birds of the Great Basin*, 39–50.

69. Chris Elphick, J.B. Dunning, and D.A. Sibley, eds., *Sibley Guide to Bird Life & Behavior* (New York: Alfred Knopf, 2001), 15–38.

70. *Ibid.*; Ryser, *Birds of the Great Basin*; Long, *Hummingbirds, A Wildlife Handbook,* 92–106; Schmidt-Nielsen, *Animal Physiology,*195–196, 415–416.

71. Cloudsley-Thompson, *Ecophysiology of Desert Arthropods and Reptiles*; Schmidt-Nielsen, *Desert Animals: Physiological Problems of Heat and Water*.

72. Cloudsley-Thompson, *Ecophysiology of Desert Arthropods and Reptiles*; A.F. Bennett and K.A. Nagy, "Energy Expenditure of Free-Ranging Lizards," *Ecology* 58 (1977): 697–700; Huey *et al.*, *Lizard Ecology*.

73. Cloudsley-Thompson, *Ecophysiology of Desert Arthropods and Reptiles*.

74. Cronquist *et al.*, *Intermountain Flora*, 19–39.

75. B.J. Albee, L.M. Shultz, and Sherel Goodrich, *Atlas of the Vascular Plants of Utah* (Salt Lake City: Utah Museum of Natural History, Occasional Publication No. 7, 1988), 552.

76. In this book, the name "tamarisk" is used to refer to a plant that may be one of several, closely related species or even a hybrid swarm among these species. This tree is also known as saltcedar, a name we do not use. We do not offer any new insights into the botanical classification of this invasive species in Canyonlands.

77. *Ibid.*, 601.

78. Albee *et al.*, *Atlas of the Vascular Plants of Utah,* 129.

79. *Ibid.*, 534 and 552.

80. J.L. Betancourt, "Late Quaternary Biogeography of the Colorado Plateau," in *Packrat Middens*, eds. J.L. Betancourt, T.R. Van Devender, and P.S. Martin (Tucson: University of Arizona Press, 1990), 259–292.

81. See individual chapters in Betancourt *et al.*, *Packrat Middens*, for information on late Quaternary floral and ecological changes in the Southwest inferred from packrat middens.

82. J.I. and A.M. Phillips, III, "The Late Pleistocene and Holocene Fauna of Vulture Cave, Grand Canyon, Arizona," *Southwestern Naturalist* 26 (1981): 257–288; A.M. Phillips, III, "Shasta Ground Sloth Extinction: Fossil Packrat Midden Evidence from the Western Grand Canyon," in *Quaternary Extinctions*, eds. P.S. Martin and R.G. Klein (Tucson: University of Arizona Press, 1984): 148–158.

83. E.I. Robbins, P.S. Martin, and Austin Long, "Paleoecology of Stanton's Cave," in *The Archaeology, Geology, and Paleobiology of Stanton's Cave, Grand Canyon Na-*

tional Park, Arizona, ed. R.C. Euler (Grand Canyon, Arizona: Grand Canyon Natural History Association, Monograph Number 6, 1984), 115–130.

84. For discussions of the human overkill theory, see chapters in Martin and Klein, eds., *Quaternary Extinctions.*

85. J.I. Mead, *Harrington's Extinct Mountain Goat (Oreamnos harringtonii) and Its Environment in the Grand Canyon, Arizona* (Tucson: University of Arizona, unpublished Ph.D. dissertation, 1983).

86. W.L. Loope, *Relationships of Vegetation to Environment in Canyonlands National Park* (Logan: Utah State University, unpublished Ph.D. dissertation, 1977), 39–118.

87. *Ibid.,* 48.

88. H.L Bohn, B.L. McNeal, and G.A. O'Connor, *Soil Chemistry* (New York: John Wiley & Sons, 1985), 153.

89. Loope, *Relationships of Vegetation to Environment,* 69; John Sowell, *Desert Ecology* (Salt Lake City: University of Utah Press, 2001), 29–32.

90. K.T. Harper and J. Belnap, "The Influence of Biological Soil Crusts on Mineral Uptake by Associated Vascular Plants," *Journal of Arid Environments* 47 (2001): 347–357. For complete references on biological soil crusts and further information, see J. Belnap and O.L. Lange, eds., *Biological Soil Crusts: Structure, Function, and Management* (Berlin: Springer-Verlag, Ecological Studies Series Vol. 150, 2001); and *www.soilcrust.org.*

91. R.N. Mack, "Alien Plant Invasion into the Intermountain West: A Case History," in *Ecology of Biological Invasions of North America and Hawaii,* eds. H.A. Mooney and J.A. Drake (New York: Springer-Verlag, 1986), 191–213.

92. T.D. Whitson, ed., *Weeds of the West* (Newark, California: Western Society of Weed Science, 1992), 433.

93. *Ibid.*; S.G. Whisenant, "Changing Fire Frequencies on Idaho's Snake River Plains: Ecological and Management Implications," in *Proceedings: Symposium on Bromus Invasion,* eds. E.D. McArthur, E.M. Romney, S.D. Smith, and P.T. Tueller (Washington, D.C.: U.S. Department of Agriculture, General Technical Report GTR-INT-276, 1990).

94. Whisenant, "Changing Fire Frequencies."

95. J.O. Klemmedson and J.G. Smith, "Cheatgrass (*Bromus tectorum*)," *Botanical Review* 30 (1964): 226–262.

96. S.B. Monsen and S.G. Kitchen, eds, *Proceedings, Ecology and Management of Annual Rangelands* (Washington, D.C.: U.S. Department of Agriculture, Forest Service, General Technical Report INT-GTR-313, 1994).

97. Jeff Lovich, personal communication.

98. Canyonlands National Park, Long-term Vegetation Monitoring Program (Moab, Utah: Canyonlands National Park, unpublished report, 2000).

99. S.B. Monsen and S.G. Kitchen, eds, *Proceedings: Ecology and Management of Annual Rangelands* (Ogden, Utah: U.S. Forest Service, INT-GTR-313, 1994).

100. J. Belnap and S.L. Phillips, "Soil Biota in an Un- grazed Semi-arid Grassland: Response to an Exotic Annual Grass (*Bromus tectorum*) Invasion," *Ecological Applications* 11:5 (2001): 1261–1275.

101. T.D. Whitson, ed., *Weeds of the West* (Newark, California: Western Society of Weed Science, 1992), 92–93.

102. I. Tidestrom, *Flora of Utah and Nevada* (Washington, D.C.: Contributions from the United States National Herbarium 25, 1925), 665; T.W. Robinson, *Introduction, Spread, and Areal Extent of Saltcedar (Tamarix) in the Western States* (Washington, D.C.: U.S. Geological Survey Professional Paper 491-A, 1965); B.R. Baum, "Introduced and Naturalized Tamarisks in the United States and Canada (Tamaricaceae)," *Baileya* 15 (1967): 19–25.

103. R.H. Webb, *Grand Canyon, A Century of Change* (Tucson: University of Arizona Press, 1996), 112.

104 S.W. Carothers and B.T. Brown, *The Colorado River through Grand Canyon* (Tucson: University of Arizona Press, 1991), 120–121.

105. Robinson, *Introduction, Spread, and Areal Extent of Saltcedar*; Graf, "Fluvial Adjustments to the Spread of Tamarisk," 1491.

106. L.R. Walker and S.D. Smith, "Impacts of Invasive Plants on Community and Ecosystem Properties," in *Assessment and Management of Plant Invasions,* 1997, eds. J.O. Luken and J.W. Thieret (New York: Springer-Verlag, 1997): 69–86; E. Zavaleta, "Valuing Ecosystem Services Lost to *Tamarix* Invasion in the United States," in *Invasive Species in a Changing World,* eds. H.A. Mooney and R.J. Hobbs (Covelo, California: Island Press, 2000), 261–301.

107. L.L. Loope, P.G. Sanchez, P.W. Tarr, L.L. Loope, and R.L. Anderson, "Biological Invasions of Arid Land Reserves," *Biological Conservation* 44 (1988): 95–118.

108. J.J. Jackson, J.T. Ball, and M.R. Rose, *Assessment of the Salinity Tolerance of Eight Sonoran Desert Riparian Trees and Shrubs* (Yuma, Arizona: Bureau of Reclamation, 1990).

109. Zavaleta, "Valuing Ecosystem Services," 269.

110. Walker and Smith, "Impacts of Invasive plants"; Zavaleta, "Valuing Ecosystem Services."

111. Zavaleta, "Valuing Ecosystem Services," 273.

112. D.K. Warren and R.M. Turner, "Saltcedar Seed Production, Seedling Establishment, and Responses to Inundation," *Arizona Academy of Sciences* 10 (1975): 131–144.

113. Graf, "Fluvial Adjustments to the Spread of Tamarisk," 1499–1501.

114. Allred and Schmidt, "Channel Narrowing along the Green River," 1757.

115. Carothers and Brown, *The Colorado River.*

116. L.E. Stevens and T.J. Ayers, "The Biodiversity and Distribution of Alien Vascular Plants and Animals in the Grand Canyon Region," in *Invasive Species in Sonoran Desert Ecosystems, Symposium Proceedings,* ed. Barbara Tellman (Tucson: University of Arizona Press, in press).

117. Carothers and Brown, *The Colorado River*, 141.

118. Stevens and Ayers, "The Biodiversity and Distribution of Alien Vascular Plants and Animals."

119. Zavaleta, "Valuing Ecosystem Services," 277.

120. B.W. Anderson, R.D. Ohmart, and J. Disano, "Revegetating the Riparian Flood Plain for Wildlife," in *Strategies for Protection and Management of Floodplain Wetlands and other Riparian Ecosystems*, eds. R.R. Johnson and J.F. McCormick (Washington, D.C.: USDA Forest Service Technical Report WO-12, 1979), 318–331.

121. Fleischner, *Singing Stone,* 59; Zavaleta, "Valuing Ecosystem Services," 277–283.

122. Anderson *et al.*, "Revegetating the Riparian Flood Plain"; Carothers and Brown, *The Colorado River*; Jack De-Loach, "Saltcedar Biological Control: Methodology, Exploration, Laboratory Trials, Proposals for Field Release, and Expected Environmental Effects," (Portland, Oregon: U.S. Fish and Wildlife Service, unpublished report, 1996).

123. DeLoach, "Saltcedar Biological Control."

124. Stevens and Ayers, "The Biodiversity and Distribution of Alien Vascular Plants and Animals."

125. W. Yong and D.M. Finch, "Migration of the Willow Flycatcher along the Middle Rio Grande," *Wilson Bulletin* 109 (1997), 253–268.

126. David Williams, *A Naturalist's Guide to Canyon Country* (Helena, Montana: Falcon Press/Canyonlands Natural History Association, 2000), 37; L.E. Stevens, *Mechanisms of Riparian Plant Community Organization and Succession in the Grand Canyon, Arizona* (Flagstaff: Northern Arizona University, unpublished Ph.D. dissertation, 1989); Jayne Belnap and R.H. Webb, personal observation.

5

VERY FLAT WATER

The Green and Colorado Rivers above the Confluence

This part of the cañon is exceedingly grand and beautiful, both from the form and coloring of its walls. A few piñons and cedars cling to the side and crown the summits of the walls, while scattered cottonwoods and thickets of willow, with here and there a small tree of a new and peculiar species of ash, form a narrow thread of vegetation along its bottom.

— John S. Newberry, 1859[1]

River trips on the Green or Colorado rivers usually begin at one of several possible boat ramps, but most commonly at either Green River State Park or the Potash ramp in Meander Canyon (Figure 5-1). Wherever you put in, the water in both rivers is slow-moving, even sluggish at times. These rivers flow in relatively wide reaches, choked by sediment and riparian vegetation, as they meander through their bedrock confines. Humans, prehistorically and historically, have used the calmer stretches above the Confluence more than the swift-flowing and menacing waters in Cataract Canyon. Not surprisingly, many plants and animals prefer slower rivers, too. Riparian vegetation thrives adjacent to low-energy rivers, forming dense thickets that are havens for certain wildlife. Some geologic evidence suggests that Cataract Canyon forms a sort of low-head dam or *weir* that backs water up, nearly as far upstream as Moab along the Colorado side and to the mouth of the San Rafael River along the Green. The riverine environment, and the humans who use it, benefit from this geological phenomenon.

MUDDY WATER

Flow in both the Green and Colorado rivers can be accurately described as muddy. Sediment records collected at gaging stations at the town of Green River and near Cisco provide the definition of "muddy."[2]

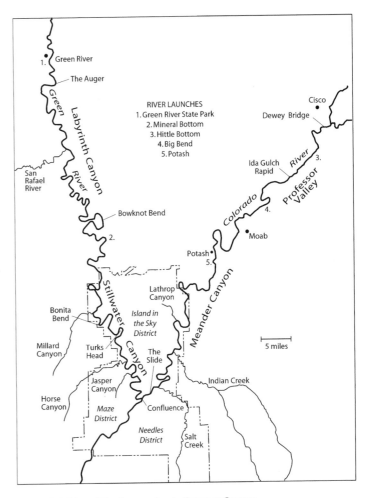

Figure 5-1. Map of the Approaches to Cataract Canyon.

The record daily loads past these gaging stations are 2.2 million tons on the Green River on July 11, 1936, and 2.8 million tons on the Colorado River on October 14, 1941. Even the lowest daily sediment loads are large: fifty-four tons on the Green and fourteen tons on the Colorado River. All that sediment is the reason that the rivers seldom transmit light, minimizing the ability of aquatic organisms to photosynthesize and sustain a food base in the river.[3]

On an annual basis, these rivers transport a prodigious amount of sediment downstream. Between 1930 and 1982, the Colorado River transported an average of 11.4 million tons per year past the Cisco gaging station; similarly, the Green River transported 15.6 million tons per year. This illustrates a fundamental difference between these rivers: the Colorado River moves more water—5.4 versus 4.5 million acre-feet per year—and the Green River moves more sediment. This difference reflects the nature of the upstream watersheds, which are lower with more sedimentary rocks on the Green and higher with more igneous rocks on the Colorado.

Sediment entering the rivers originates on hillslopes at the heads of tributaries, and then passes through a complex of channels en route to the two rivers. These channels appear to have different channel storage capabilities, which change with time.[4] Channels draining small tributaries (less than one square mile) transport sediment into larger systems (1 to perhaps 1,000 square miles), where a complex shifting between erosional and depositional processes occurs. During some periods, such as what happened during the Little Ice Age, deposition dominates; in other periods, erosion dominates. The sediment evacuation from tributaries is a process known as arroyo cutting, where channels quickly deepen and widen. Deposition is a slower process, and the Holocene history of these channels is one dominated by long periods of deposition. Larger rivers, such as the Green and Colorado, primarily transport sediment with little storage, although stored sediments locally narrow these rivers (see below).

The sediment load on both rivers has changed through time.[5] High sediment loads in the early twentieth century are thought to be the result of arroyo cutting, which began shortly after settlement in the late nineteenth century. By many accounts, arroyo cutting ceased in the early 1940s,[6] and sediment was stored in floodplain terraces in tributaries, decreasing the sediment loads in the larger rivers. The combination of climate, expressed as low runoff years, and reservoir construction decreased the annual sediment loads forty to sixty-five percent on the Colorado and Gunnison rivers near Grand Junction, Colorado, between 1964 and 1978.[7] Construction of floodplain terraces is thought to be the first phase in arroyo filling, suggesting that we are returning to the long-term Holocene trend of deposition. Sediment loads on both rivers decreased further in the 1960s because of reservoir construction upstream.[8]

The large sediment loads of the rivers are the reason for all those shifting sandbars, because the low channel slopes of the approaches encourage deposition of sediment. Sediment is stored in channel banks downstream, either as sandbars in Cataract Canyon or riparian habitat along the approaches, or it is transported into the delta of Lake Powell. The decreases in sediment load attributed to reservoir construction upstream of Canyonlands raise the possibility that sandbars in Cataract Canyon may be decreasing in size, as they have in Grand Canyon.[9] We will address this question in Chapter 7.

THE GREEN SIDE

When rigging boats at Green River State Park, or other possible put-in sites in and near Green River, Utah, river runners might imagine Beale's expedition, in 1853, building a boat of skins and rubber blankets stretched over a wood framework to cross here.[10] Instead of primitive boats, the most likely sights here these days are whitewater rafts, canoes, and powerboats, particularly when the river is high. Shoving off from the ramp, boats pass first beneath the historical railroad bridge, then under the Interstate-70 freeway bridges, and then they approach the bedrock walls that mark the start of Labyrinth Canyon. Keen observers will notice something else before the town of Green River disappears into the distance: a cable across the river and a little house on the bank with a satellite antenna on the roof mark one of the longest-term gaging stations in the western United States. Gaging stations like this one provide much information on environmental changes in Canyonlands.

Channel Narrowing

Before entering that canyon downstream from Green River town, one might consider that the channel does not resemble the scene that Beale and his contemporaries saw in 1853. Three major factors have caused the channel of the Green River to decrease significantly in width.[11] First, tamarisk became established along the river, probably as a result of seeds wafting to the river from the gardens of the nineteenth-century Green River town. Second, climate has affected floods on the Green River, reducing flood flows after the early 1940s. Finally, Flaming Gorge Dam has regulated flow downstream since 1962, leaving the Yampa River and other smaller tributaries to provide the only unregulated flows to sculpt the channel. These three factors create inseparable effects that must be considered together.

At the Green River gaging station in the town of Green River, channels began to narrow in the 1930s. The channel width was stable in the 1940s and 1950s, in part because of reductions in discharge attributable to a dry period of climate and despite large increases in non-native tamarisk on the banks. Channel width again decreased after 1959, because tamarisk stabilized banks and trapped sediments and completion of Flaming Gorge Dam in 1962 caused additional decreases in discharge. Downstream at Bowknot Bend (miles 63 to 70), channel narrowing is obvious in repeat photography taken from the saddle in the bend (Figure 5-2).[12] By one account, the channel of the Green River has decreased in width by an average of twenty-five percent from Green River, Utah, to the Confluence.[13] Channel narrowing has eliminated some backwater habitat, stabilized islands, and joined some former islands to the banks.

The effects of Flaming Gorge Dam, while more pronounced immediately downstream in Lodore Canyon, are still felt in Canyonlands and in some respect are more severe. The sizes of flood flows, which sculpt the channels of desert rivers, have decreased significantly.[14] At the same time, the annual sediment discharge past Green River town has decreased by more than half. The combination of effects, along with the sediment-trapping influence of non-native tamarisk and native riparian species, leads to *vertical accretion* of channel banks, causing former channel bars and channel margins to rise as sediment is trapped, instead of growing laterally into the river.[15]

Oil and Gas

After passing under the bridges, boats move between walls of Upper Cretaceous rocks, mostly sandstones, siltstones, and mudstones that look pretty nondescript. On river right at river mile 115.4, four and a half miles downstream from Green River, a broad, denuded area gleams with the yellow-orange sheen most commonly associated with hot springs. But this is neither a natural spring nor is it even hot; it is Crystal Geyser, one of the relics of oil and gas exploration along the rivers of Canyonlands. This was an unsuccessful oil well with an unpredictable result.

Oil and gas are trapped in the Pennsylvanian Hermosa Group—particularly the Honaker Trail and Paradox Formations—that underlie much of Canyon Country.[16] The first oil well in Utah was drilled in 1891 near the once-abandoned town of Elgin, on the east side of the Green River opposite the town of Green River.[17] In the thirty years that followed, oil drilling generated more profits locally than oil production. An oil well that became known as Frank Shafer No. 1 well at mile 46.2 on the Colorado River gushed oil 200 to 300 feet in the air, but after a series of setbacks, including fire and water seepage, the 5,000-foot well was abandoned, never having produced oil for shipment.[18] Because of the pervasive nature of the two dominant formations, as well as the abundance of appropriate geologic structure in the region, oil and gas exploration remains common in Canyon Country, particularly near Moab.

Crystal Geyser was an unsuccessful oil well drilled in September 1936 that was never plugged.[19] The drilling intersected the water table, then a pocket of carbon dioxide. This combination resulted in a cold

Figure 5-2. Bowknot Bend (mile 70.1)

A. September 10, 1871. John Wesley Powell had discovered Bowknot Bend on the Green River during his 1869 expedition. In 1871, he had photographer E.O. Beaman climb to the western end of the bend as high as he could and photograph the bend with the river flowing away at left and toward the photographer at right. To capture this effect, Beaman used an extremely wide-angle lens. Prominent sandbars are barren in the wide channel, and desert olive lines the high-water banks. (E.O. Beaman 476, courtesy of the U.S. Geological Survey Photographic Library)

B. October 23, 1911. The Kolb Brothers took Major Powell's account of his 1869 trip along when they reenacted the Powell Expedition in the fall of 1911. They matched many of the images (lithographs of photographs) in Powell's book, including this downstream view from the saddle in Bowknot Bend. (Kolb 1061, courtesy of Cline Library, Northern Arizona University)

C. September 21, 1914. Eugene C. LaRue also photographed this view in 1914 as part of his basin-wide survey for potential dam sites. It is unknown whether he knew of Beaman's photograph or not, but LaRue used a panoramic camera for this view instead of a wide-angle lens. As it was forty-three years earlier, the Green River was relatively wide with numerous barren sandbars. (E.C. LaRue 9, courtesy of the U.S. Geological Survey Photographic Library)

D. August 19, 1968. Hal Stephens climbed to this point to repeat Beaman's view during the Shoemaker-Stephens reenactment of the first Powell expedition. By 1968, fifty-four years after LaRue stood here, riparian vegetation had encroached onto the formerly barren sandbars, narrowing the channel significantly. (H.G. Stephens W-3)

E. October 10, 1999. Little additional channel narrowing has occurred on the upstream section of channel, which appears at left. However, on the right side, the island that is prominent in Stephens's view has become connected to the bank. On both visible sections of river, the riparian vegetation appears much taller. (Steve Young, Stake 3893c)

Figure 5-3. Hell Roaring Canyon (mile 55.5)

A. May 28, 1889. The Brown Expedition, funded by the Denver, Colorado Cañyon, and Pacific Railroad Company, made their Camp 4 on the right side of the Green River opposite the mouth of Hell Roaring Canyon. In this downstream view of the camp, Nims's camera documents an open sandbar lined with desert olive, a riparian shrub that forms dense thickets along most of the Green River. His view is across the point bar on the inside of a river bend and into the mouth of Hell Roaring Canyon, which enters the Green from the left. (F.A. Nims 7, courtesy of the National Archives)

B. October 11, 1999. Channel narrowing on the Green River is most pronounced on bends where previously barren point bars have become densely vegetated and are now extended into the former river channel. At this site, we hiked about fifty yards through dense riparian vegetation to arrive at a point near the former camera station. Desert olive trees on the former river bank appear at right, although they are not the same individuals shown in the 1889 view. Tamarisk trees mostly block the view and cover the former sandbar, although river cane and willows are also present. Only the tops of some cliffs serve as reference points for the photograph. (Steve Young, Stake 3907)

water geyser, which occasionally erupts a column of mineral-laden water. On occasion, the eruption reportedly has reached fifty-feet high, although much lower heights are more common.

Agriculture and Manganese

Downstream from Crystal Geyser, The Auger, an infamous "rapid" on the Green, is the last real piece of whitewater on the Green River approach. Once feared by the locals, who warned historical river runners of their impending death here, this is a minor riffle around a cobble bar. Below the Auger, the river flows through relatively open country that marks the approach to Ruby Ranch. Ruby Ranch and many of the bottomlands in this area have a rich history.[20] For instance, during the Great Depression, many local residents of the town of Green River raised gardens along the Green River bottoms (*e.g.*, Anderson Bottom, Potato Bottom) to supplement their meager supplies. Today, many ditch and irrigation works can be seen at places such as June's Bottom (mile 89).[21]

On river right, opposite this large ranch, the mouth of the San Rafael River is difficult to observe from the river owing to channel narrowing and a maze of tamarisk. Near White Wash (mile 96, river left), large banks of river cobbles begin to rise above the river. These cobbles were deposited during the Pleistocene, possibly during large floods that occurred when glaciers rapidly melted. If one lands on river left and climbs onto these banks—also known as *river cobble terraces*—the remnants of mining activity shreds large areas of the landscape.

Manganese, an element used in the steel industry, was valued during the wartime periods of the first half of the twentieth century. In Canyon Country, manganese can either occur in sedimentary rock or as desert varnish on cobbles or boulders. Just downstream from the San Rafael River juncture with the Green River, Pleistocene gravels were mined for manganese as part of a larger manganese operation based out of Green River, Utah.[22] The most obvious abandoned workings are on river left, but test pits are present on most of these terraces on both sides of the river.

Uranium

The Green flows peacefully through Labyrinth Canyon, where cliffs of orange and red sandstone rise to towering heights. Trin Alcove (mile 90.0, river right) is a popular side-canyon hike, and Three Canyon well-illustrates the results of the sapping process discussed in Chapter 3. The Chinle Formation, dominated by grey and red shales, rises and causes cliff retreat, broadening the canyon. Tamarisk is dense in these wide sections and has contributed to channel narrowing (Figures 5-2, 5-3).

Beginning at Hey Joe Canyon, and increasing around Bowknot Bend, new signs of mining activity are seen. Uranium, commonly found in the Moss Back Member of the Chinle Formation, was mined heavily in the 1950s. Many of the mines required ferries to transport ore. The known ferry sites on the Green River are on the inside of Bowknot Bend (mile 67.5), between Point and Woodruff bottoms (mile 49.2), at Queen Anne Bottom (mile 33.5), and Anderson Bottom (mile 32.5). The latter ferry was originally built to move livestock and agricultural products. The ferry between Point and Woodruff bottoms flipped during "reasonably high water," dumping a bulldozer into the river. The remains of the ferry are stranded on the right bank at mile 43.3.[23]

Uranium was first extracted by the Native Americans. They used it mostly as a yellow dye for paint. Prospectors rediscovered the large deposits of uranium ore on the Colorado Plateau around the beginning of the twentieth century. Initially, uranium was used in the ceramic and glassware industry, until the danger of radioactive materials was understood and uranium oxides ceased to be used as coloring agents.[24] Madame Marie Curie, a French scientist conducting experiments with radiation, came to Grand Junction, Colorado, in 1899 to purchase uranium ore for her experiments.[25] At that time, uranium was easily obtained as a waste product of vanadium extraction, a mineral used to harden steel. The search for vanadium on the Colorado Plateau focused primarily on outcrops of Chinle and Morrison shales, which are widely distributed across the Plateau.

Once both the energy-production and destructive uses for uranium were discovered, miners eagerly sought its ore. The first mining occurred between 1910 and 1912 on Poverty Flats, just south of Moab.[26] After the detonation of nuclear bombs during World War II and the start of the Cold War, nuclear technology spread to other countries, spurring mining activities on the Colorado Plateau. Ironically, vanadium became merely a by-product of uranium mining. The U.S. Atomic Energy Commission essentially paid a bounty for the discovery of new sources of uranium and, as a result, great numbers of prospectors began combing Canyon Country.

In 1952, a man named Charlie Steen discovered a large deposit of uranium ore in San Juan County, making him a regional legend.[27] The uranium industry on the Colorado Plateau blossomed like the mushroom clouds that soon followed the detonation of nuclear bombs. Prospectors were everywhere and people got rich from even small grubstakes, selling their claims for millions of dollars, thus making Moab the "Uranium Capital of the World." By 1956, Moab was "the richest town in America" with one millionaire for every 250 residents.[28] Investment was high, and prospectors now had the resources they needed to blaze new roads into isolated areas. The uranium industry was largely responsible for the proliferation of roads that opened Canyon Country to other kinds of exploitation, including tourism. Controversy continues to rage about whether those roads should remain open or be allowed to return to the desert.

Incidental river expeditions were launched in the 1950s by government, amateur, and professional geologists, usually with Geiger counters in hand, measuring radiation to help locate the ore.[29] Claim markers and inscriptions still remain from those days and are visible by those who hike, bike, and jeep around this region. Uranium ore processing requires tremendous amounts of water, so processing mills were established on the river banks throughout Canyon Country. Almost all of the now-defunct mills have since been reclaimed by capping the waste pile in place or by removing the waste to more stable sites and capping it in place at the new location. One processing plant at the mouth of White Canyon was inundated by the reservoir.[30] The largest remaining waste pile on the

Colorado Plateau is the tailings pile attributed to the Atlas Mining Corporation on the north bank of the Colorado River at Moab. This processing plant, begun by Steen in 1957, closed in 1984 without a cleanup.[31] At the time of this writing, there are plans to move this pile seventeen miles from the river to a site where thick shale deposits will help shield the ground water from contamination.[32]

The uranium industry declined in the 1960s and was effectively eliminated when the passage of the North American Free Trade Agreement (NAFTA) allowed Canadian uranium to flood the U.S. market. Uranium mining left many legacies on the Colorado Plateau. These include heavy metals and toxic chemicals that now enter the Colorado River and are incorporated into sediments in the reservoir,[33] thousands of miles of unpaved roads leading to abandoned mines and mine camps, tailings piles and mine shafts scattered throughout the region, and abandoned mills. River runners can see remains of uranium mining along the Green River; however, the Chinle Formation, the strata most commonly mined for uranium, does not have significant outcrops along the Colorado River in Meander Canyon.

The Record in Stone

Observant river runners, peering past the tamarisk jungle, may see faint and occasionally bold markings on rock faces. Three distinct kinds of human marks have been left on rock faces in Canyonlands: prehistoric Indian rock art, historic inscriptions, and recent vandalism. The Fremont and Ancestral Puebloan peoples carved *petroglyphs* or painted pictographs on the rocks. Petroglyphs are commonly found where travel was focused, such as at the mouths of important side canyons and points where aboriginals climbed to higher benches. Notable panels are found on the Green River at river mile 83 and 24 and in Meander Canyon on the Colorado River at river miles 52 and 59.5. Pictographs are rarer, with significant panels at Colorado River mile 23.5. There are no known petroglyphs or pictographs in Cataract Canyon downstream from Rapid 1.

Historical inscriptions abound in the Canyonlands

Figure 5-4. Hell Roaring Canyon (Green River mile 55.5) October 11, 1999. Denis Julien was a French-speaking fur trapper who traveled the Green and Colorado rivers in the 1830s and 1840s. His biggest claim to fame is his penchant for carving his name on rock faces in an elaborate script. His inscriptions are the earliest in the Canyonlands and are considered valuable historical artifacts. Some recent visitors to this site have vandalized this panel. This site is now on the register of National Historic Places and is clearly marked by signs erected by the Bureau of Land Management. Despite this designation, a recent addition appears above the "D" in the inscription. (Dominic Oldershaw, Stake 3908)

region,[34] with most found on the Green River. In addition to the two Denis Julien markings (the most familiar of which is given in Figure 5-4), prominent inscriptions commemorate the launch *Marguerite* (on river left near mile 72); the "river register" on river left at mile 77.6; the inscriptions at the narrowest part of Bowknot Bend (mile 70); the Wolverton family; and innumerable sheep herders, ranchers, river explorers, and miners. Some inscriptions, such as a reported Denis Julien inscription on the Green River just upstream from the Confluence, were once visible but now may be lost to the tamarisk jungles or rolling rocks.

The "river register" contains carvings from many historical river runners. Unfortunately, this panel—as well as other historic and prehistoric inscriptions like it—has been defaced by more recent visitors. Visitation to the Canyonlands region has boomed in recent years with the widespread ownership of whitewater boats and improved equipment. The present-day high usage of the rivers in the Canyonlands region is such that if everyone who used the area for recreational purposes decided to sign his or her name in stone, few unmarred faces would remain. While many are careful not to leave their marks behind, some are less so; and continued disrespect of our historic landmarks, some of which are federally registered, will result in the eventual cordoning off of these locations. These sites must be visited, for preservation's sake, with the same courtesy normally given to museums of antiquity or aboriginal rock art. Not touching petroglyphs and inscriptions is especially helpful in their preservation, because skin oils can accelerate deterioration of the rock.

Flat Water and Mosquitoes

As the river moves downstream from Bowknot Bend, first the prominent palisades herald the presence of Hell Roaring Canyon (mile 55.4, river left), site of the most well-known Denis Julien inscription, and then a broad expanse on river left yields to a boat ramp, signaling Mineral Bottom (mile 52.2). Mineral Bottom is a boat ramp that provides another means for accessing the Green River. From Green River town to this point, permits are not required for river runners (as of this writing), but Canyonlands National Park rangers do require permits from those who wish to go downstream.

It does not matter when exactly—whether taking out, putting in, or continuing downstream—but at some point river runners are likely to experience the plague of the Green River: mosquitoes. River runners find themselves either slapping their exposed skin, wearing full-body clothing, or using smelly insect repellents in this area. Mosquitoes have been around for fifty million years and now number 2,700 species.[35] They are found on every continent from arctic tundra to the Sahara, but they appear to prefer tropical rainforests and the Green River in Utah. Mosquitoes thrive in the Uinta Basin upstream from Desolation and Gray canyons. They are present in far fewer numbers in the canyons downstream, but they still thrive there.

Mosquitoes hatch and grow to maturity in standing water, a common occurrence in bottomlands. The young are legless, and move by wriggling. They hang upside down from the water surface, suspended by a tube that projects from near the end of their bodies. The tip of this tube, which allows the larvae to breathe, protrudes just above the water surface and has a small circle of flaps spread out to keep the larvae afloat. The mosquito larvae use facial bristles to comb the water for food.

Both male and female mosquitoes live on plant sap and nectar from flowers. However, when it comes time to reproduce, females rely on the blood of vertebrates (mostly warm-blooded ones) to obtain the protein needed to produce eggs. Females can lay up to ten batches of 200 eggs.[36] They can develop the first batch of eggs without vertebrate blood, but blood is required for subsequent batches. The average blood intake per bite is 2.5 times the original weight of the mosquito, yet they still manage to fly away. Mosquitoes will also suck blood from newly dead carcasses.

Mosquitoes on the Green River in Canyon Country earned dubious historical distinction among early explorers such as John Wesley Powell and his men, who cursed their existence. Said crew member George Bradley, upon entering the Colorado Plateau on the Green River in 1869, "Our camp tonight is alive with the meanest pest that pesters man—mosquitoes. Yet they will be as quiet as death in an hour or so for the night wind is too cool for them and they take shelter in the grove."[37] The nuisance still exists but some years are not as bad as others; it depends on whether the spring flood is high enough to go over the river banks to pool in stagnant ponds. In drought years, when the river does not spill over onto the banks, mosquitoes are not much of a problem. In areas where the river gradient is steep, as in Cataract Canyon, stagnant pools are nonexistent and therefore the mosquitoes are few and far between.

Mosquitoes are believed to locate their victims by sensing heat, carbon dioxide, the smell of perspiration, and/or warm, moist air. However, no one can determine the dominant mechanism. In Italy, folklore instructs people to sleep with pigs, as pigs have higher body temperatures and so supposedly they will get bitten instead of the humans. On the Green River, some river runners carry dry ice for the express purpose of attracting mosquitoes away from their work areas to the coolers placed a discrete distance away. Unfortunately, this strategy does not really work because there are too many of these nuisances around to be completely lured away by dry ice.

Bottomlands

While floating along the flat water, one's view is often dominated by riverside vegetation. Riparian areas are the lifeblood of most desert communities, including human communities. Although these ecosystems make up only two percent of the landscape, over eighty percent of the local animal species are directly dependent on riparian communities for food, water, and shelter.[38] Human settlement in the West has always centered on free-running water, especially large rivers. Above Cataract Canyon, those human activities that are associated with settlements—including livestock grazing, agriculture, and harvesting of vegetation for firewood and timber—have profoundly affected many of the riverine communities, especially river bottoms.

River bottoms are especially prominent on the Green River between Mineral Bottom and the rise of the White Rim Sandstone near the start of Stillwater Canyon. Bottomland vegetation is usually dominated by greasewood, ranging in size from shrubs to small trees with deep roots that can be up to sixty-feet long. Greasewood tolerates salt by sequestering the salt in internal vacuoles within the leaves. It is *monoecious*—both female and male parts are on the same plant—which is unusual in the saltbush family. To avoid self-pollination the stamens on a given individual plant mature and dry up before the flowers are mature.

Sagebrush and rabbitbrush, both members of the aster family, are common in river bottoms, growing quickly on the flood-deposited alluvial soils. Before white settlers arrived, the western United States contained much less sagebrush. However, livestock soon changed this situation, because cows prefer grass over sagebrush. This selective feeding resulted in a rapid replacement of grasses with sagebrush. Sagebrush is wind dispersed, and each plant sends out up to one million seeds annually.[39] These seeds can be found everywhere: floating on water, wafting on the wind, or being carried in the fur of animals. Because of the large number and the wide distribution of seeds, sagebrush is poised to increase in areas where other plants are removed, whether by grazing or clearing. Sagebrush is intolerant of fire, so fire suppression throughout the West has helped promote its spread.

Rabbitbrush has composite flowers (many tiny flowers make up what appears to be one flower).[40] There are two species of rabbitbrush found in the Canyonlands area: the most common is rubber rabbitbrush, and less common, but with many subspecies, is low rabbitbrush (*Chrysothamnus viscidiflorus*).[41] Rabbitbrush is typically thought of as a short-lived plant that colonizes disturbed areas and grows very quickly. However, both species can also grow quite old; in our repeat photographs they live between eighty and 104 years old. Rabbitbrush produces a prodigious amount of pollen, much to the discomfort of allergy sufferers, when it flowers in late summer. Rabbitbrush seed is wind dispersed, and the seeds remain viable for years. Members of this genus easily colonize disturbed sites and are common in many diverse habitats throughout the western United States. Interestingly, rubber rabbitbrush, the most common of the rabbitbrushes in Canyonlands, was farmed during World War II for tire rubber production. It also makes a huge variety of chemical compounds, and Native Americans used it to treat everything from fever to rheumatism.

Insect galls are very common on both sagebrush and rabbitbrush. While many sagebrush galls are the result of wasp larvae, the more frequently seen galls on rabbitbrush are cotton-like balls created by the presence of fruit fly larvae encased in spittle. These fruit flies can be very picky: if two subspecies of rabbitbrush are growing together, one species of fruit fly will invade only one of the subspecies of rabbitbrush, while another fruit fly will invade the other.[42]

The Wall of Riparian Vegetation

River runners floating down the slow-moving Green River have ample time to study the banks, looking for the telltale sign of a path through the riparian vegetation that provides access to the landscape beyond. If you watch the streamside vegetation as you float down the calm water, you will see that what appears to be a continuous strip of uniform vegetation is actually several distinct communities all jumbled together. This is due to two things: the parent material from which the soil is derived (which determines chemistry and texture), and river characteristics. While tamarisk can out-compete most native plants along slow-water stretches, willows dominate where currents are fast. Cottonwoods have an advantage when soils are derived from the calcareous Navajo Sandstone or Kayenta Formation, but they need soils wetted by floods for germination and establishment. The crumbly soils developed on Chinle Formation favor tamarisk, partially because it can tolerate the additional salts derived from the bedrock. While willows are found on all substrates, they often dominate on soils derived from Wingate Sandstone.[43]

Desert Olive. Desert olive (*Forestiera pubescens*) is one of the most interesting species along the Green River, although it is sometimes difficult to spot despite its yellow-green leaves. One of the few native species that once was prominent, this member of the olive family is now engulfed in a sea of other species, mostly tamarisk and willows. Unlike the popular perception, however, desert olive has not been eliminated; in fact it is possible that its distribution has not even been reduced. It is just not as obvious now. When you do find desert olive, it appears to indicate a former river bank reliably and can give the observer an idea of how much channel narrowing has occurred. Although individuals are difficult to distinguish, our repeat photography indicates that this species can live at least 128 years.

Gambel's Oak. Gambel's oak (*Quercus gambelii*) is common along the Green River upstream from Mineral Bottom. The casual observer may confuse it with other large riparian trees, but closer examination (if one can penetrate the thicket on the banks) reveals the large, lobate leaves that most associate with the oaks. Gambel's oaks have several forms; some grow as single-stemmed, large trees, while others grow in clonal clumps consisting of stems with subequal diameters. Our repeat photography shows that this species, or at least its clones, can live for at least 131 years, and probably much longer.

Willows. Willows are the most common native plant along the river corridor, and are also common nationwide, with ninety species reported in the United States and twenty-five species in Utah.[44] While most of the willows along the river edges are sandbar willows (*Salix exigua*), there are other types as well, including peachleaf (*S. amygdaloides*), yellow (*S. lutea*), and black willow (*S. gooddingii*). All of these species tend to grow in clumps on the edge of the river. Willows are *dioecious* plants, meaning that individual plants are either male or female but not both. Pollen and flowers, made by male and female plants respectively, are both produced on catkins. These plants are pollinated mostly by bees and the small seeds are dispersed by the wind. The Southwest Willow Flycatcher (*Empidonax traillii extimus*), one of the few rare bird species in Canyonlands, inhabits dense willow thickets and tamarisk along both the Green and Colorado rivers.

Native Americans used willow for many things, including making cloth, baskets, bows, and treating lumbago and headaches. Individual peachleaf willow has persisted for 108 years in our repeat photography. Although it is impossible to identify individual sandbar willows in photographs, clumps of this species appear in the same places in photographs spanning eighty years.

Cottonwoods. Cottonwoods are the most conspicuous native trees along the river corridor. Although there are several species of cottonwood in Canyon Country, almost all are Frémont cottonwood, named for John Charles Frémont.[45] Frémont cottonwoods have broad triangular leaves, huge spreading crowns, and massive trunks. As with willows, cottonwoods are dioecious: both male pollen and female flowers occur on drooping catkins that appear before the leaves. Unlike willows, cottonwoods are pollinated by the wind. The fruit is a capsule containing seeds with tufts of hairs attached (the "cotton" for which the tree is named), which waft with river breezes up and down the canyon. The trees can be long-lived: trees along the Escalante River and its tributaries west of Canyonlands have been tree-ring dated at 200 to 300 years old.[46] Because of their fast growth rate, many of the large cottonwoods in Canyonlands may actually be less than 100 years old.

Cottonwood trees provide great comfort to people, especially in a desert setting. Their presence, often seen at a distance, promises both water and shade.[47] The inner bark is edible by horses, and Hopi Indians prefer cottonwood roots for carving their distinctive kachinas. Because it is such a beautiful tree and branch cuttings are easily rooted in soil, many cottonwoods have been planted along stream corridors and in people's yards. Cottonwoods occasionally are infected by mistletoe, but this seldom causes mortality; however, they are often severely defoliated by tent caterpillars. If this happens in consecutive years, the tree can die. Populations of cottonwoods along the mainstem rivers have been drastically reduced in recent years due to fire, flood control, and channel downcutting. In addition, competition with tamarisk and consumption by livestock limits reestablishment of cottonwoods.

Boxelder. Boxelder is also common along the river. This tree is familiar to many people, and is often grown as an ornamental because it can withstand extreme temperatures and drought. Rather than being related to elders, it is actually in the maple family, and is the only maple in North America with *compound* (each leaf made of multiple leaflets) leaves.[48] Boxelders were tapped by both Native Americans and western settlers to make syrup. The story goes that boxelders got their name because the pioneers put boxes around the trees to collect the sap. Boxelder trees are also famous for their seemingly ever-present boxelder bugs (little brown insects with orange stripes). Individual boxelders are long-lived, persisting for 128 years in our photography.

When growing wild, boxelder is found along streams or in habitats with moist soils. This plant is *dioecious* (male and female flower parts occur on sep-

arate plants), and as with many dioecious plants the male plants occur in drier, less fertile habitats while female plants occur in moister and more fertile habitats. This may be because producing pollen is much less demanding on available water and nutrients than producing seeds. If the habitat characteristics change, the plants can respond by changing sexes.[49] Interestingly, the males are more water efficient but have a lower photosynthetic rate than the female plants. This may be from necessity, as there is less water available in the drier habitats. However, it may also actually aid in pollen dispersal, as the pollen can spread more widely when soils and plants are drier and where individual plants are spaced further apart. This species produces winged fruit, presumably an adaptation to help the seeds get away from the parent tree, where competition for resources is stiff.

Boxelder trees have small-scale internal plumbing. While this means their capacity to transport water and nutrients is lower, it also means that they suffer less from *air embolisms*, a problem that all plants have to face.[50] Air embolisms are formed when drought or freezing conditions occur, and the continuous bead of water in the vessels that transport water within the plant is broken. When this occurs, the air embolism can prevent water movement and the branch or leaf can die. Smaller vessels are less likely to form embolisms, and if they do form, they are easier to push out. The upshot of this is that when spring arrives, boxelders can push the embolisms out and reuse the vessels. Because they do not need to rebuild damaged tissue, boxelders can get their leaves out ahead of those plants that have larger tubes that need reconstruction.

While it would seem obvious that trees growing alongside streams are using water from the stream, this is not always true for established boxelders or cottonwoods. When seedlings, these trees use the water of the adjacent stream or river. However, as soon as their roots are deep enough, these plants stop using the stream water and rely almost exclusively on deeper ground water.[51] While this might not make sense in the short term, it might be a positive strategy for a long-lived species. Streams meander, creating new channels literally overnight or downcutting to a level the roots may not be able to reach. If long-lived trees were exclusively dependent on surface water, there is a strong likelihood they would eventually find themselves without a water supply.

Water Birch. Water birch is the only native birch tree in desert regions, growing in moist soils along stream-banks.[52] It is a diminutive tree, with reddish bark and small sharp-toothed leaves. Water birch has many dormant buds at the trunk base under the bark. When the top of the tree is damaged, these buds sprout, producing massive clumps of stems. Birches are very shallow rooted, and unlike many other streamside trees they depend on stream water both as a seedling and an adult. Because of this, birch grows only where the water table is close to the surface. Birds love to perch and nest in these trees. In this *monoecious* species (both sexes on the same plant), the male flowers are tiny and arranged on stiff catkins that form during the summer and winter over. In the spring, these catkins become long and pendulous, and then shed their pollen. The female flowers, on short thick catkins that emerge in spring, become cone-like when fertilized. This species does not appear in our repeat photography.

Landmarks in the Canyon

Launching at Mineral Bottom starts an easy flat-water trip. The Green River slowly winds downstream through low banks and bottomlands. The cliffs of Wingate Sandstone open out, exposing distant spires and cliffs. John Wesley Powell named this place Tower Park in his diary, as a short demarcation between Labyrinth Canyon upstream and Stillwater Canyon downstream, but did not use this name in his book.

Upheaval Wash comes in from the left at mile 43.5; Upheaval Dome, about four miles up this wash, is a circular feature of uncertain origin in the Mesozoic strata. Geologists debate whether this feature is the result of a salt diapir or is a meteorite impact crater.[53] A fortress-like structure appears on a low hill on the inside of the bend beginning at about mile 40. Appropriately, the left side is called Fort Bottom, and a short hike from the left bank leads to an old cabin as well as the fortress. Abruptly, the Buttes of the Cross appear (Figure 4-5) at about mile 34. The recently formed Millard Canyon Rapid (mile 33.8) creates the only obstacle for canoeists, and then only at low water.

Passing Bonita Bend, the river begins its slow but steady descent beneath the White Rim Sandstone and into the Paleozoic strata that characterize Stillwater Canyon. Many interesting rock formations with creative names can be seen in this reach. The Sphinx is an odd-looking column just above the river at mile 26.6; Candlestick Tower can be seen in the distance at about mile 22. Turks Head at mile 21 is an eroded bedrock point that resembles a Middle Eastern fez. Many potential hiking stops are in this reach, if one can find the way from bank to bedrock. Many Ancestral Puebloan sites are also found in this reach, and Jasper Canyon (mile 9.3, river right) is closed to visitors above the main waterfall owing to its status as a *relict area* (never had livestock grazing or any other disturbance).[54]

Many visitors stop at the mouth of Jasper Canyon to see some granaries just above the river terrace. Once this was a prime camping site in this reach, but in 2001 much of the vegetation in the canyon mouth was reduced to ash and charcoal. It is not surprising that the dense riparian vegetation in Canyonlands burns intensely when ignited. Although lightning strikes can start fires, the most common fires result from carelessness; flying sparks from campfires set the thickets ablaze. The ecological effects of a fire like the one at the mouth of Jasper Canyon will be discussed in Chapter 6. Fire scars are apparent all along the Green River, from Trin Alcove to near the Confluence, and boaters are well advised to exercise extreme caution with open flame. Some have had their camps reduced to charred heaps as a result of their inattention.

Two of the most significant landmarks on the Green River become visible at mile 0.9. On river right, a steep side canyon informally called "Powell Canyon" provides a scrambling access to the rim. Members of the Powell expedition hiked to the top here in both 1869 and 1871, and they hauled their heavy camera up there on the latter trip for photographs in the Doll House. A downstream glance from the mouth of Powell Canyon reveals that the strata, mostly horizontal upstream, are now tilted. The Confluence and the Meander anticline are nearby. Canoeists begin thinking about their jet boat extraction up the Colorado River. For those going through Cataract Canyon, the nature of their trip will change significantly once they pass this historical spot.

THE COLORADO SIDE

The Daily

We arbitrarily chose the Dewey Bridge at the upstream end of Professor Valley as the start of our discussion of the Colorado River approach to Cataract Canyon. Certainly one could go from points upstream, particularly the start of Westwater Canyon, and go all the way to Hite, and several well-developed put-ins used heavily by commercial river companies are downstream. But Dewey Bridge marks both the mouth of the Dolores River and the location of the gaging station that is most relevant to flow past Moab and into Cataract Canyon. Just as arbitrarily, we chose to end our discussion of the Daily at the Potash boat ramp in Meander Canyon.

From Dewey Bridge down to where the Fisher Towers can be seen from the river, boaters pass between the ubiquitous wall of riparian vegetation. However, unlike the approach on the Green side, the strip of riparian vegetation is often thin or discontinuous. Channel narrowing has occurred at points in Professor Valley and Meander Canyon, although the magnitude of narrowing is generally not as large as along the Green River. Unlike the Green River, which has narrowed over much of its length, narrowing along the Colorado River in Canyon Country has mostly occurred on the inside of bends and at the mouths of tributaries. An exception is the river corridor near Grand Junction, Colorado; there the Colorado River narrowed ten to fifteen percent between 1937 and 1993.[55]

Ranches and newer resorts and developments can be seen along this stretch of the Colorado River in places where the rock walls recede from the river's edge. Agriculture in Canyon Country began when the Mormons settled there in the middle of the nineteenth century. The Elk Mountain Mission built on the banks of the Colorado River north of Moab was the beginning of American settlement in Spanish Valley.[56] The mission began and ended quickly in 1855 as a result of hostile interactions between the Mormons and Utes, the original inhabitants of the valley. More aborted settlement attempts occurred in the 1870s until 1877, when several ranchers settled in Spanish Valley. In 1880, a post office was established in the growing settlement of Moab, named in biblical references to the arid Moab Mountains of Jordan. With settlement came farming in the rich alluvial soils of the Colorado River and Pack and Mill creeks.

Farming continues today where broad bottomlands, transportation, and the Colorado River intersect. The area around Grand Junction, Colorado, is now the largest urban population on the Colorado Plateau and is world-renowned for its fruit-tree production, and most notably for its peaches. Green River, Utah, is similarly known for its melon crops irrigated with Green River water. Unlike Moab, these communities were linked to the outside world by railroad. Moab was also famous for tree fruits such as apricots and apples, but its citizens lacked an affordable way to get the produce to market. This prompted several attempts at freighting fruit with river boats. Moab had ferry service in the canyon just upstream from the modern bridge; the ferry was replaced with the first Colorado River bridge in 1912.[57] Highways and bridges eventually brought Moab closer to commodity markets.

Both upstream and downstream from Moab, agriculture has declined and is being replaced by tourist facilities. Decrepit siphons, as well as active ones, can be seen leading to bottomlands on the Colorado River in Professor Valley and in the reach twenty to thirty miles downstream from the Portal. Agriculture remains somewhat viable in the region, but many of the orchards have since been converted into vineyards or alfalfa fields and others into various development projects to satisfy our growing, restless society.

Hittle Bottom, at mile 87 on river left, is a common put-in site for river runners who want to run the Daily reach. Downstream from this point, the river is sluggish as it moves around a large island, but Onion

Figure 5-5. Ida Gulch Rapid (mile 80.8, Professor Valley)

A. June 24, 1905. Whitman Cross, a geologist with the U.S. Geological Survey, photographed the Colorado River in Professor and Castle valleys in the 1900s. His photograph of the Colorado River in flood shows the inundation of extensive groves of cottonwood trees on both sides of the rapid. The foreground bench appears to have been overgrazed at about this time. (Cross 806, courtesy of the U.S. Geological Survey Photographic Library)

Creek Rapid offers a splashy ride. In all, there are five significant rapids in Professor Valley. Ida Gulch Rapid, where the Colorado River is forced northwards by a tributary (Ida Gulch) coming in from the south, has some large, fun waves to play in (Figure 5-5). New Rapid, too new to appear in some river guides,[58] increased from a riffle to a sizeable rapid in 1975 after an undercut cliff face fell into its head. The star of the reach is Castle Creek, or Whites Rapid, where boat-flipping holes appear right of center at many water levels. The size of the whitewater in the Daily increases with discharge; twenty-foot waves have been observed at high water in New Rapid.

The Daily run can end at a number of points, but few boaters continue downstream below Big Bend (mile 71). Downstream, the flatwater moves slowly towards the bridge and developments at Moab. Spanish Valley opens up, revealing the strong contrast of the Atlas uranium tailings piles on river right and the Matheson Wetlands on river left. Here, Russian olive is as dense as it gets, and tamarisk forms the typical thicket; but cottonwood trees provide several layers of structure that attract birds. Although a keen eye is required for dodging the numerous sandbars that can

trap the unwary, the reach between Big Bend and Potash provides a good time for that time-honored outdoor sport of birdwatching.

In contrast to insects, amphibians, and aquatic mammals that are virtually restricted to a riparian or aquatic habitat, other residents of the canyon seem to flaunt their ability to approach and depart the river at will. White-throated Swifts (*Aeronautes saxatalis*) are the birds that zing by the cliffs all day long, catching gnats and mosquitoes on the wing. They have short tails, saber-shaped wings ideally suited for speed and maneuverability, and feet that cling to vertical walls. Swifts only land when necessary and spend almost all their waking hours in the air eating, courting, and copulating. Copulating pairs can be seen locked together, tumbling through the air for 500 feet or more. Swifts can exceed 200 miles per hour in flight, and as a group are considered among the world's fastest birds.[59]

These birds nest in small colonies found on cliff faces under alcoves, returning to the same spot continuously for many years. Their nests are made of grass and feathers, glued together with saliva. The swifts' high-pitched chattering can be heard throughout the day as they zoom low along the water or high

B. October 7, 1999. The river is at a lower stage, and the decrease in cottonwoods is dramatic. Despite the difference in water level, there is no indication that the rapid—a favorite on the daily run—has changed. Shrub cover on the foreground benches has increased, possibly because of reduced grazing pressure and favorable rainfall in the last two decades of the twentieth century. (Dominic Oldershaw, Stake 3902)

up near the canyon walls. They are tiny and when temperatures or prey items are low, swifts often go into *torpor* (a reduced-activity state, similar to estivation) to save energy.

In the well-developed riparian areas of the approaches to Cataract Canyon, Yellow Chats (*Icteria virens*) are very common. These are highly noisy, yellow-breasted birds that chatter and move about endlessly. Ravens squawk from their roosts in the cliffs and swoop down in the morning to clean campsites or steal lunches. Mockingbirds (*Mimus polyglottos*) can be seen at Spanish Bottom along the river's edge. These birds are *polyglottos* ("many languages") and have a huge repertoire of songs (up to 150), as they imitate just about everything they hear. Studies have found that the males with the largest number of songs also have the largest territory and the best chance of mating. Mockingbirds are very territorial, and they use songs to deter other species and flash their white wing patches as warning to other birds.

Great Blue Herons (*Ardea herodias*) are seen all along the river, standing and watching for lunch to swim or crawl by their waiting beaks. Distinctive in flight as well as in their standing posture, great blues are the largest herons in the United States. They eat mostly fish, amphibians, crayfish, insects, rodents, and sometimes other birds. After spearing their prey, they swallow it whole. Herons will travel twenty to thirty miles from their nests in search of food. The male chooses the nest site, which is often twenty to sixty feet above water in a rookery tree with other breeding herons, although they sometimes nest in shrubs. The three to five eggs are incubated in large stick nests, which the young fly from after two months.[60]

Cowbirds (*Molothrus ater*) are also common in this area. Cowbirds look like starlings, but are *molobros* ("greedy beggar" in Greek) and have a much more insidious side to them. They originally developed a lifestyle centered on eating insects stirred up by moving herds of bison. However, the fact that the herds were moving posed a problem when it came to nesting. Cowbirds solved this by becoming parasites: they lay their eggs in the nests of over 200 species of other birds. The cowbirds throw out one or two of the eggs of the other species, and lay their own, which are often very cleverly disguised to match the eggs of their victim. Most victimized parents, unable to tell the cowbird eggs from their own, then raise the cowbird chick as one of their own. Unfortunately, the cowbird chick soon outgrows its nest mates, and pushes them out of the nest to starve. Some birds fight back: the Yellow Warbler, for instance, builds a new nest on top of the old one once it discovers cowbird eggs in its nest. This can go on until there is a stack of four nests! In the case of the endangered Southwestern Willow Flycatcher, over fifty percent of nests in the Grand Canyon are affected.[61]

Potash

The main boat ramp for Cataract Canyon river trips—particularly motorized ones—is twenty road miles and seventeen river miles downstream from Moab on river right and just downstream from the Potash mines. The pavement ends just upstream at the mine complex; the road becomes the White Rim Trail

RAVENS

Steven Anderson

When we see an eagle, we experience a thrill, and the word "magnificent" often pops into our minds. But we barely notice ravens (*Corvis corax*), the most common bird seen in Cataract Canyon. Ravens belong to the Corvid family, which includes crows, magpies, jays, and nutcrackers. At twenty-four inches high, the raven is the largest songbird in North America. Ravens can make an amazing variety of different sounds; aside from their songs they are capable of imitating human speech, other birds, and other animals.

In Western society, ravens get a mixed review, but they are most infamous because Edgar Allen Poe and others have used them to personify dread or the presence of evil. Ravens' troubled reputation extends back to antiquity when these scavenging birds pecked out the eyes of corpses. Given that eyelessness adds considerably to the gruesomeness of a corpse, ravens did alienate people. However, they also have had their share of admirers. The Norse god Odin had a pair of ravens named Huginn (thought) and Muninn (memory), who gave him advice. In one of the interleaved Noah stories, a trusted raven is sent out to see if dry land had appeared. To the Alaskan Inuit, the raven is both a creator and trickster god.

Their habit of scavenging is probably the main contributor to their unsavory standing, and scavenge they do, but only part of the time. Ravens will eat almost anything, including garbage, road kill and the babies of other animals. The dominant birds ordinarily have first dibs on food, but when food appears suspicious, birds of lower dominance are encouraged to eat first. In times of plenty, food is cached to be eaten later, but the caching has to be done with some stealth, since other ravens are happy to raid what has been stored away.

Raven society is organized into two classes. The younger birds often gather in groups of up to forty birds that roost in the same area and show a loose cooperation. These "teenagers" often behave like human adolescents: mobbing established pairs, showing off flying skills, and selecting mates from the group. Because the lining of the raven's mouth darkens with age, the younger birds can sometimes be identified by their pink mouths. In contrast to the community spirit of their young, the mature birds pair off, excluding other ravens from their territory. Pairing is long term, often for life, but "divorce" is not unknown, and sexual exclusivity is not a part of the bargain.

The raven's primary wing feathers are highly flexible, and because of this ravens are among the most agile flyers of the larger birds. They have a marvelous sense of recreation: they play "catch" with a twig as they fly along, repeatedly slide down a snowy roof or stream bank, tease wolves or coyotes (sometimes to their sudden demise), mimic other birds, fly upside down and a host of other activities that appear to have no purpose other than pure enjoyment.

The feathers of the head and body are used for communication of dominance, courting, threat, or again, for fun. The feathers just behind the eyes can be raised as a pair of "horns," or else they can raise all of their head feathers together for the fuzzy head look. Other body feathers can be extended down over the legs and wings held more horizontal than usual. Swaggering around this way gives a clear statement, "Look at me, I'm fantastic!"

Although some people argue that it is not possible to attribute intelligence to animal behavior, it appears that ravens are smart. Their genius caught the attention of the ancients creating the rich mythology of raven intelligence. Stories of cooperation between pairs of birds to obtain food are legendary. One bird serves as the distracter of an animal with food while the other bird gets the food. There are even reports of ravens alerting wolves and humans to the location of potential prey, presumably so the ravens could share in the kill. Reports of using tools such as twigs to get at otherwise unattainable food, or dropping hard-shelled animals or eggs on rocks to break them open, are likewise numerous. The raven, rather than an evil omen, is one of the smartest, most fun-loving, and most talented flyers of the bird world.

if one continues on to the west. The red rocks that dominate the view at Potash are part of the Undifferentiated Cutler Formation. This ramp is on the outside of a bend and roughly marks the brief rise and fall of Paleozoic strata, in the form of the Hermosa Group, in Meander Canyon. Across the river, Jackson Bottom, a large *rincon* (or abandoned river meander) opens in the cliffs.

Potash—potassium salts associated with anhydrite domes—has long been of economic interest on the Colorado Plateau. The salts are primarily turned into fertilizers; but other uses for the salts include synthetic rubber and matches. The first attempts at potash mining in the region began during World War I and the 1920s in what is now Arches National Park.[62] Although much of the initial potash mined from the region came from sites well north of Moab, a discovery downstream about fifteen miles along the Colorado River soon placed Moab in the upper echelon of the potash industry. The Texas Gulf Sulfur Company (later known as Texasgulf) mines potash here, using Colorado River water to dissolve subsurface deposits of the Paradox Formation.[63] The company built a railroad spur to Moab in the mid-1960s, exclusively to service the salt and potash produced at this operation. The Potash boat ramp, the most common put-in for Cataract Canyon on the Colorado River side, is just downstream from the mine headquarters.

Down the Lazy River

On those hot summer days when the water is low the approaches seem to involve more swimming than boating. The last significant rapid on the Colorado River upstream is in Professor Valley. It is no accident that most river trips in Canyonlands depend on motors to push boats across the flat waters to the rapids, and the sluggish pace and hot air encourage frequent stops for playing in the water. Like the Green, the Colorado River seems to move too slowly upstream from the Confluence. As the spring flood subsides, the river creates navigational obstacles that frustrate summer boaters, as shifting sandbars disguise the deepwater channel.

Some subtle changes occur further downstream on the Colorado River. At Dewey Bridge, seven river gravel terraces appear to loom high above the river. Some of these terraces were mined from the time of their discovery through 1942 and yielded the second highest total amount of placer gold (terraces along the Green River in northern Utah were higher).[64] Downstream from Moab, several terrace levels were also mined, and the bulldozer trenches can be seen from the river and roads. The last place that they are really obvious from the river is in Jackson Bottom across from Potash. As the river meanders downstream, the cobble terraces gradually disappear behind the riparian zone. These Pleistocene gravels go underwater as one progresses down both approaches to Cataract Canyon.

Continuing downstream, the floodplains of both rivers widen out, with some notable exceptions. On the Green River, extensive bottomlands appear in certain sections where either erosive bedrock (*e.g.*, the Chinle Formation) or abandoned river meanders (*e.g.*, Anderson Bottom) occur at river level. Tributaries with significant drainage areas such as Salt Creek on the Colorado and Upheaval Wash on the Green appear to have their mouths choked with sediment, as if the mainstem rivers are backing sediment up into the tributaries.

The slopes above the river offer one clue as to why there are no rapids here, particularly in Meander Canyon. In segments lined with sandstone walls, little talus appears on the slopes, which is one reason they are called "slickrock." Even in reaches with more heterogeneous bedrock, such as interbedded limestones and sandstones, the amount of talus on the canyon walls is minimal. As the Confluence is approached from either direction, however, a lithologic change occurs high on the walls. What is mapped as Elephant Canyon Formation upstream is segregating into discrete sandstone and shale formations that have important ramifications for the river.

The Colorado River between the Confluence and Moab has a slope of 1.15 feet per mile, and the Green River between the Confluence and Mineral Bottom has a slope of 1.28 feet per mile. In Glen Canyon, the former free-flowing Colorado River had a slope of 2.01 feet per mile and the river was considered to be sluggish by those who had the privilege of running it

Figure 5-6. Below Little Bridge in Meander Canyon (mile 28.7)

A. September 16, 1914. Eugene C. LaRue, hydrologist for the U.S. Geological Survey, photographed this upstream view of the Colorado River while on a surveying trip. LaRue had been down to the U.S. Reclamation Service drill rig at the Confluence and was returning to Moab. This view shows a lunchtime stop on a sandbar, formed because the prominent rock upstream creates an eddy at higher discharges. (E.C. LaRue 1349, courtesy of the U.S. Geological Survey Photograph Library)

B. August 28, 2000. The rock has split into pieces. The sandbar is noticeably smaller, both because sand has been eroded and because riparian vegetation—mostly non-native tamarisk—has encroached from the bank onto the bar. (Steven Young, Stake 2226).

before Glen Canyon Dam turned it into a reservoir. The slope of both the Green and Colorado rivers increases with distance away from Cataract Canyon. The slope in Desolation and Gray Canyons is 6.17 feet per mile and the slope in Professor Valley is 5.02 feet per mile.[65] The reason is Cataract Canyon: its tremendous rapids and boulder-strewn margins are backing up the river and decreasing its slopes.

The low slopes of the approaches affect their uses and ecology. The Colorado River, which carries extensive motorized boat traffic, has numerous sandbars that trap unwary boaters at low water. Curiously enough, boaters do not have to worry about rocks that might damage propellers or knock off lower units on motors. The riparian communities that thrive at river's edge (Figure 5-6) attract rich, faunal assemblages. The situation changes dramatically as the approaches at the Confluence are left behind, with the notable exception of one prominent wide spot: Spanish Bottom (Chapter 6).

Aquatic Mammals

Otters, beavers, and muskrats are more or less restricted to the river corridors in Canyon Country. All three species were largely extirpated by fur trappers around the turn of the century, but reintroductions and reentry from other parts of the Colorado River drainage have aided their comeback. In large river systems, beavers (*Castor canadensis*) do not build dams that span the rivers but instead build lodges on thickly vegetated banks or dig burrows into the banks.[66] Because beavers prefer well-developed riparian vegetation, they are found mostly above Cataract Canyon, especially along the slower-moving Green River. Beavers are diurnal and although they are seldom seen while floating the river, careful inspection of the banks will yield numerous lodges and/or burrows, especially when water levels are low. The openings to the lodges or burrows are below the average high-water line and the tunnel from the burrow to the beaver's den then leads upward above the high water line. However, water that rises unexpectedly or rapidly can drown both adults and their young.

Beavers prefer willow (especially coyote willow) and cottonwood seedlings for food, although there is evidence that they will eat tamarisk and tuberous roots as well. Despite limited trapping these days, population numbers still remain much lower than was previously recorded. The reason for this is not known, although it may be related to changes in the distribution of native vegetation and the large increase in tamarisk, or it just might be that reestablishment of this species is particularly slow.

Otters (*Lutra canadensis*) have been sporadically sighted along the Green and Colorado rivers since the late 1880s.[67] John Sumner of Powell's 1869 expedition spotted otter tracks at the Big Drops. Otters once occurred on most of the major rivers in Utah, but were either trapped out or their preferred habitat—dense riparian vegetation and permanent water—was lost or altered. While otters themselves are seldom seen, their tracks, distinctive slide marks, and scat can be seen on the river banks. They are excellent swimmers, and are able to detect prey in the murky water by using their whiskers. Prey consists of almost anything they can find in water including fish, crayfish, toads, muskrats, and small beavers. However, fish is their preferred diet and so otters are generally found where fish congregate. On the Colorado and Green rivers, fish concentrate where macroinvertebrate populations are the highest: that is, stretches of river with rocky bottoms. As with beaver, otter populations are much lower than historic levels, despite the fact that it has not been legal to trap them for many years.

Muskrats (*Ondatra zibethicus*) are also found along the river and are seen fairly often, appearing as a small nose followed by a gentle wake. They prefer more stable river environments and so are found mostly above Cataract Canyon. As with beaver and otters, thick riparian vegetation is their favored environment. Muskrats eat vegetable matter, including grasses and cattails.

Macroinvertebrates

Life in the Colorado River is unlike that found in most rivers and streams. In clear water, high light levels throughout the water column result in large quantities of algae and cyanobacteria, which then support a bustling food chain. In contrast, the thick, muddy waters of the Colorado River let in little or no light, and thus support very few *autotrophic* (organisms that make their own food) life forms.[68] One of the few algae able to survive in this environment is the bright green, filamentous algae *Cladophora glomerata*. At low water, this species can be seen coating rocks. It is *Cladophora* that covers "Big Mossy," a rock often used as a marker by river guides finding their way through Big Drop 3 (see Chapter 8).

A second reason the Colorado River is different from most rivers and streams is the lack of rocky bottoms that provide secure anchorage and minimal fouling for both algae and macroinvertebrates. Instead, the bottom of the Colorado River is mostly constantly-moving sand and mud. Thus, in spite of adequate nutrients, the smaller life in this river is limited by lack of light, food, and suitable attachment sites. Limited production at the lower ends of the food chain means limited production of higher-end species such as fish.

Most of the macroinvertebrates found in the river are the larval stages of land-based insects. Examples include mayflies, dragonflies, damselflies, caddisflies, and *dipteran* (*e.g.*, house) flies. Populations are not evenly distributed along the length of the river. Most insect larvae need places to attach that will not be covered with sediment. Such places are found on vegetation that hangs down into the water, in backwater areas where water input is limited to certain times of the year, and where the river has a rocky bottom. During flood times, tributaries can also be important contributors of organic matter and macroinvertebrates.

The story of algae and macroinvertebrates is very different in the side canyons that feed into the Colorado River. Here, clear water and rocky bottoms are evident, and they provide for high growth rates for both algae and macroinvertebrates. The flora and fauna of these pools and streams are also diverse: one survey recorded fifty-two species of algae in side canyons.[69] Nine taxonomic (classification) orders and over thirty families of insects can be expected in these aquatic environments.[70] These insects include the examples listed above, as well as many beetles, water boatmen, backswimmers, water striders, and midges. Many of these species can complete five to ten generations in one year while some, like mayflies, complete up to thirty-five generations.[71] This is very unusual for most ecosystems, which may partially explain why birds are so attracted to desert water sources.

Aquatic insects have two basic life styles: either they have a pupal stage, or they do not. Mayflies, dragonflies, damselflies, stoneflies and the *Hemiptera* (butterflies) go through successive molts, gradually developing mature body parts. The others (caddisflies, moths, Diptera, and most beetles) live in aquatic environments as larvae; upon pupation, they emerge as adults for a brief terrestrial fling at reproduction. Most aquatic organisms in desert environments must learn to cope with periodic flooding and drought. One way that these organisms adapt is by completing unsynchronized life cycles so that there are always enough flying adults alive to recolonize a stretch of stream that has been depopulated. Some winged adults also leave during high flows, returning once the water has subsided. Water striders are able to detect the vibrations of oncoming flood waters, and leave the water surface, sitting out the floods in streamside vegetation. Most species lay prodigious amounts of eggs in multiple batches as insurance against unfavorable conditions.

Aquatic insects have fascinating ways of making a living. Water striders walk on the water's surface, while dragonfly larvae propel themselves by expelling water through their rectums. Many diving beetles carry an air bubble with them so they can breathe under water. The air bubble is collected under a wing-cover or in dense hairs.[72] These insects feed in every way imaginable: some (*Gomphidae*, dragonfly larvae, and damselflies) hide under the sandy bottom or are camouflaged, waiting for prey to swim by them; others (backswimmers and waterboatmen) actively pursue their prey in the water or, like damselflies, may crawl along vegetation, looking for lunch. Adult dragonflies capture their prey while flying, and can often be seen mating in flight as well. Damselflies also copulate while flying; the male holds on even while the female is laying eggs.

Sounds in the Night

Finding a brush-free place to camp is a problem on both approaches, but it seems particularly acute on the Colorado River side. An occasional sandy island offers its comfort, but more often boaters must find the paths through the tamarisk and camp on one of the numerous bottomlands and sediment-flooded tributary mouths in this reach. After filling meals and refreshing beverages the relaxed campers can lean back, look up at the starry sky, and listen for the telltale sounds of amphibians.

Of the eight species of amphibians in Canyonlands National Park,[73] there are three amphibians frequently seen in the approaches to Cataract Canyon. These species are the red-spotted toad (*Bufo punctatus*), Woodhouse's toad (*Bufo woodhousii*), and the non-native bullfrog (*Rana catesbeiana*). Another common but seldom seen species is the spadefoot toad (*Spea* sp.).[74] The mating call of Woodhouse's toad is short (one to three seconds) and drops in pitch at the end, while the call of the red-spotted toad is long (ten seconds) and sounds like a cricket. The bullfrog's call is unmistakable; it sounds like a large bull in pain. Male frogs and toads spend up to twenty-five percent of their time singing in a desperate attempt to attract females. Females have good reason to be choosy: in Woodhouse's toad, bigger males have larger offspring at metamorphosis, which have a better chance of survival. Bigger males call the most and are the most successful at reproduction. However, the correlation between larger males and more calls does not always hold for other species.

Red-spotted and Woodhouse's toads are normally nocturnal and are found near permanent and intermittent water. Red-spotted toads breed after the summer rains and then lay eggs which are able to hatch in only a few hours. Tadpoles become adults in one or two months, enabling the small (one to three inch-long) toads to live in the temporarily filled potholes that dot the landscape. The color of the adults is different when habitats differ: they are whitish in white soils, light tan in volcanic soils, and brown in reddish soils. The flattened body of the red-spotted toad enables it to squeeze into rock crevices. It is nocturnal during summer, but active in morning and evening during spring and fall, catching and eating insect prey.

The canyon treefrog (*Hyla arenicolor*)[75] can be found on rocks and trees near water during the day; at night, they venture forth and can be found far from water. They are very tolerant of high body temperatures and desiccation, which helps them to control parasitic invasion, increase digestion rates, and protect against infection. Even though they can live at cooler temperatures than many frogs, they are often found basking in the sun on vertical rock faces, which is very unusual for an amphibian. Canyon treefrogs are fairly good at restricting water loss, and have an enlarged bladder that stores up to twenty-five percent of their body mass in dilute urine which can be used for evaporative cooling. This frog eats many kinds of insects, and breeds in July and August during summer rains. Eggs are laid in large masses that float on the water surface.

The large (three to eight-inch long) non-native bullfrog was introduced west of the Rocky Mountains sometime in the early 1900s. Since then, this species has spread throughout western river systems, gobbling up eggs and tadpoles of native species. Bullfrogs seldom leave riparian corridors, unless to inhabit someone's watered lawn, and can lay up to 20,000 eggs annually.[76] They sometimes remain as huge tadpoles for up to two years, and the adult lifespan lasts four to five years.

Spadefoots, although often incorrectly called spadefoot toads, are classified into their own family and are not true toads. They dig two to three-foot burrows with the "spade" on their hind foot, going as deep as necessary to find the water table, and spend most of their lives deeply buried in sand. While buried, these animals conserve water in several ways, including encasing themselves in a dry, hard covering composed of several layers of skin; filling their very large bladders before burrowing (this bladder can represent thirty percent of body weight); and storing nitrogenous wastes in their body tissues at levels that are toxic to most animals.[77] Because this body waste storage creates a more concentrated solution in the spadefoot than the surrounding soil water, additional water from the soil is drawn into the animal.

Spadefoots can lose up to fifty percent of their body weight during their time in the soil, which may be as long as two years. The cue for emergence from their burrows is not moisture, but the low frequency sound created by thunder and/or rainfall. Once they emerge,

they immediately begin to eat, drink, and mate, as time is short. Spadefoots eat beetles, grasshoppers, ants, spiders, and termites, and can eat up to fifty-five percent of their body weight in one day.[78] Like toads, they also have a "pelvic patch" on their lower abdomen, which is a very thin-skinned area that readily absorbs water from soils or free water.

Spadefoots do not have a defined breeding season, but rely on water availability as they must reproduce in water. Their breeding calls can be heard for miles and most breeding occurs within one or two days of emergence. A single adult can lay up to 3,000 eggs that hatch in twelve to twenty-four hours, with the tadpoles transforming in seven to fifteen days.[78] The first hatchlings often secrete a growth inhibitor to prevent later eggs from hatching. The tadpoles are omnivores or even cannibalistic and can endure high water temperatures (100°F). If the pond water gets too low before the tadpoles are fully developed, they can leave the water even if their tails are still attached.

Tiger salamanders (*Ambystoma tigrinum*) are the only salamanders that regularly occur in the North American deserts, and are the world's largest land-dwelling salamanders.[80] They eat invertebrates, tadpoles, and other salamander larvae. This salamander is seldom seen, as it lives in burrows and only emerges when there is enough free surface water available for reproduction. Generally, dozens of salamanders emerge together, migrating to the nearest water to mate and feed. Tiger salamanders lay eggs once or twice annually, with eggs hatching in nine days (at water temperatures of 77°F).[81] Unlike the tadpoles of frogs and toads, salamander tadpoles have four spindly legs and bushy external gills that remain throughout their larval life. After one to three years as aquatic larvae, salamanders depart their ephemeral pool home to become terrestrial adults, leaving the pool before it dries out.

Salamanders that live in a year-round water source may either adopt the terrestrial form or stay aquatic. Those adopting the terrestrial habit lose their gills and fins, develop fatter legs, and gain a more impermeable skin. Those that stay aquatic actually reproduce as larvae. Even in year-round water sources, however, all salamanders leave during some years at seemingly unpredictable intervals. This tendency toward desertion may have developed in order to escape predation, as leaving in a random fashion makes them an unreliable food source for predators.

Bears along the River?

Some of the best camping spots in Meander Canyon are in the sandy flats at the mouths of tributaries on river left. Some of these side canyons are quite large, including Indian (mile 16) and Salt (mile 3.5) creeks. In the summer of 2001, river runners were quite surprised to see bear tracks at the mouths of these canyons. One party of canoes actually saw a black bear next to the river.

Black bears (*Ursus americanus*) are uncommon along the river, but they are occasionally seen during drought years. Males come down the major drainages from the Abajo Mountains, so if you are going to see bears, you will most likely find them on river left of the Colorado. These animals are omnivores, eating mostly plants and insects. In drought years, they have been seen eating prickly pear cactus, probably for both food and water.[82] Because bears prefer areas with more moisture and vegetation, they are generally restricted to mountains. However, young males range widely in search of new territories, and have been reported to cross hundreds of miles of desert to reach a new home. While appearing clumsy, these animals can travel at a good speed, with the ability to sprint at thirty miles an hour.[83] Bear populations in this region do not appear to be in good health: recent surveys in the Abajos have found very few males, while surveys in the Book Cliffs just north of Moab show almost no females.[83]

The Long Approach Ends

The lower reaches of Meander Canyon can be monotonous, with a sound track of a droning motor, squeaking oarlocks, or the splish-splash of paddles entering and exiting the water. The telltale openings in the riparian vegetation lead to interesting hikes, including the short one to petrified wood weathering from the Undifferentiated Cutler Formation on river

right at mile 36.9 and Ancestral Puebloan structures on river left at miles 23.5, 20.2, and 16.5 in the canyon of Indian Creek. Hikers should know that lower Salt Creek and Elephant Canyon (river left, miles 3 to 3.5) are closed from May 1 to September 1 owing to bighorn sheep lambing. The cool river water beckons swimmers on a hot summer day; and when the water is low, swimmers can bob and walk downstream, feeling the sand dunes on the channel bed rise and fall under them.

Signs appear in the bedrock walls that the Confluence is approaching. A prominent white band appears on the cliff at river left at mile 18.5; and although some jokingly call this a "high-water mark," it actually is a sandstone band made *gypsiferous* (containing the mineral gypsum) by the evaporation of groundwater discharge (see section on Sapping, Chapter 3). The Meander Anticline, which causes the strata on both sides to dip away from the river, gradually assumes prominence around mile 17. For those wanting a strenuous hike, the Loop, which begins at mile 12, offers and up-and-over hike through a saddle that eliminates about four miles of sitting on boats. The Slide, a riffle only 1.5 miles upstream from the Confluence, signals the proximity of Cataract Canyon.

THE INCREASE IN RIPARIAN VEGETATION

Repeat photography of the Green and Colorado rivers shows a large increase in both native and non-native vegetation along the banks. We have matched fifty-four photographs in Labyrinth and Stillwater canyons on the Green River and thirty-nine photographs in Professor Valley and Meander Canyon on the Colorado River. All of these camera stations now have tamarisk, compared to roughly forty percent of the original photographs, which span the period from 1871 through 1968. The earliest photographs with a tamarisk in them were taken by E.C. LaRue in 1914, and whether the trees in the photograph are in fact tamarisk is debatable but cannot be ruled out (these particular trees are now long gone).

Overlooked in the concern over non-native species are the changes in most native species. If one looks carefully, desert olive clumps still mark the line of the old channel banks, particularly along the Green River. Gambel's oaks remain common, and many have persisted in dense thickets over the last century upstream from Mineral Bottom. Seepwillow appears in the old views as well; they are just much less numerous than now. Only cottonwoods have decreased significantly along the approaches to Cataract Canyon. The decrease in cottonwoods will be discussed in Chapter 7.

Notes

1. John Macomb, *Report of the Exploring Expedition from Santa Fe, New Mexico, to the Junction of the Grand and Green Rivers of the Great Colorado of the West, in 1859, under the Command of Capt. J. N. Macomb; with Geological Report by Prof. J. S. Newberry* (Washington, D.C.: Government Printing Office, 1876).

2. K.R. Thompson, *Annual Suspended-Sediment Loads in the Colorado River near Cisco, Utah, 1930–82* (Salt Lake City, Utah: U.S. Geological Survey Water-Resources Investigations Report 85–4011, 1984); K.R. Thompson, *Annual Suspended-Sediment Loads in the Green River at Green River, Utah, 1930–82* (Salt Lake City, Utah: U.S. Geological Survey Water-Resources Investigations Report 84–4169, 1984).

3. G.A. Hayden, *Benthic Ecology of the Colorado River System through the Colorado Plateau Region* (Flagstaff: Northern Arizona University, unpublished M.S. thesis, 1997).

4. W.L. Graf, "Late Holocene Sediment Storage in Canyons of the Colorado Plateau," *Geological Society of America Bulletin* 99 (1987): 261–271.

5. Thompson, *Annual Loads in the Colorado River*, 10; Thompson, *Annual Loads in the Green River*, 8; Allen Gellis, Richard Hereford, S.A. Schumm, and B.R. Hayes, "Channel Evolution and Hydrologic Variations in the Colorado River Basin: Factors Influencing Sediment and Salt Loads," *Journal of Hydrology* 124 (1991): 317–344.

6. J.B. Graf, R.H. Webb, and Richard Hereford, "Relation of Sediment Load and Flood-plain Formation to Climatic Variability, Paria River Drainage Basin, Utah and Arizona," *Geological Society of America Bulletin* 103 (1991): 1405–1415.

7. M.M. Van Steeter and John Pitlick, "Geomorphology and Endangered Fish Habitats of the Upper Colorado River. 1. Historic Changes in Streamflow, Sediment Load, and Channel Morphology," *Water Resources Research* 34 (1998): 287–302.

8. E.D. Andrews, "Downstream Effects of Flaming Gorge Reservoir on the Green River, Colorado and Utah," *Geological Society of America Bulletin* 97 (1986): 1012–1023.

9. J.C. Schmidt and J.B. Graf, *Aggradation and Degradation of Alluvial Sand Deposits, 1965–1986, Colorado River, Grand Canyon National Park, Arizona* (Washington, D.C.: U.S. Government Printing Office, U.S. Geological Survey Professional Paper 1493, 1990).

10. R.A. Firmage, *A History of Grand County* (Salt Lake City: Utah State Historical Society, 1996), 69.

11. W.L. Graf, "Fluvial Adjustments to the Spread of Tamarisk in the Colorado Plateau Region," *Geological Society of America Bulletin* 89 (1978): 1491–1501; T.M. Allred and J.C. Schmidt, "Channel Narrowing by Vertical Accretion along the Green River near Green River, Utah," *Geological Society of America Bulletin* 111 (1999): 1757–1772.

12. H.G. Stephens and E.M. Shoemaker, *In the Footsteps of John Wesley Powell: An Album of Comparative Photographs of the Green and Colorado Rivers, 1871–72 and 1968* (Boulder, Colorado: Johnson Books, 1987), 164–165; Graf, "Fluvial Adjustments to the Spread of Tamarisk," 1497.

13. Graf, "Fluvial Adjustments to the Spread of Tamarisk."

14. Andrews, "Downstream Effects of Flaming Gorge Reservoir," 1012.

15. Allred and Schmidt, "Channel Narrowing by Vertical Accretion."

16. W.L. Stokes, *Geology of Utah* (Salt Lake City: Utah Museum of Natural History, Occasional Paper Number 6, 1986), 92.

17. Firmage, *History of Grand County*, 251. Elgin was resettled after abandonment in the 1920s.

18. *Ibid.*, 252.

19. *Ibid.*, 288.

20. M.R. Kelsey, *River Guide to Canyonlands National Park and Vicinity* (Provo, Utah: Kelsey Publishing, 1991), 38–61.

21. John Weisheit, *The Diary of the Seven Who Took Too Much* (Moab, Utah: unpublished diary, Dan O'Laurie Canyon Country Museum, 1996–1997).

22. Firmage, *History of Grand County*, 249–250.

23. The authors thank Steve Young of the National Park Service for details of ferry sites and history.

24. Dusty Simmons, "Uranium Mining History of Canyonlands," *The Confluence* 7 (2000): 8–11.

25. Raye Ringholtz, *Uranium Frenzy: Boom and Bust on the Colorado Plateau* (Albuquerque: University of New Mexico Press, 1991).

26. Simmons, "Uranium Mining History," 8.

27. Ringholtz, *Uranium Frenzy*, 78–83.

28. *Ibid.*, 10.

29. George Simmons, "Diary: July 1956 Cataract Canyon Expedition," *The Canyon Legacy* 32 (1998): 7–15.

30. W.L. Chenoweth, "The Hite Uranium Mill," in

Cataract Canyon, ed. J.A. Campbell (Durango, Colorado: Four Corners Geological Society, 1987), 159.

31. Simmons, "Uranium Mining History," 10–11.

32. *Moab Site Project, Preliminary Plan for Remediation* (Grand Junction, Colorado: Department of Energy, Project Number MOA-999-0003-00-000, Document Number X0000402, 2001).

33. "Final Environmental Impact Statement Related to Reclamation of the Uranium Mill Tailings Site, Moab, Utah," U.S. Nuclear Regulatory Commission, Office of Nuclear Material Safety and Safeguards, NUREG-1531, Vol. 1 (Washington, D.C.: 1999).

34. J.H. Knipmeyer, *Butch Cassidy Was Here, Historic Inscriptions of the Colorado Plateau* (Salt Lake City: University of Utah Press, 2002); James Knipmeyer, "The Denis Julien Inscriptions," *Utah Historical Quarterly* 64 (1996): 52–69; James Knipmeyer, "Inscriptions in a Graveyard," *Canyon Legacy* 32 (1998): 2–6.

35. David Quammen, "Sympathy for the Devil," in *Insect Lives*, eds. Erich Hoyt and Ted Schultz (New York: John Wiley and Sons, 1999), 79–82.

36. *Ibid.*

37. John Cooley, *The Great Unknown* (Flagstaff, Arizona: Northland Publishing, 1988), 80.

38. Personal communication, Bill Bates, Utah State Natural Resources Division, Salt Lake City.

39. T.W. Fleischner, *Singing Stone: A Natural History of the Escalante Canyons* (Salt Lake City: University of Utah Press, 1999), 56.

40. Williams, *A Naturalist's Guide to Canyon Country*, 33.

41. Albee *et al.*, *Atlas of the Vascular Plants of Utah*, 129.

42. *Ibid.*, 57.

43. Fleischner, *Singing Stone*, 61.

44. R.D. Dorn, "A Synopsis of American *Salix*," *Canadian Journal of Botany* 54 (1976): 2769–2789; S.L. Welsh, N.D. Atwood, S. Goodrich, and L.C. Higgins, eds., *A Utah Flora* (Provo, Utah: Brigham Young University, 1993), 623–633.

45. B.J. Albee, L.M. Shultz, and Sherel Goodrich, *Atlas of the Vascular Plants of Utah* (Salt Lake City: Utah Museum of Natural History, Occasional Publication No. 7, 1988), 552; Lyman Benson and R.A. Darrow, *Trees and Shrubs of the Southwestern Deserts* (Tucson: University of Arizona Press, 1981), 364–366; Fleischner, *Singing Stone*, 59.

46. R.H. Webb, *Late Holocene Flooding on the Escalante River, South-Central Utah* (Tucson: University of Arizona, unpublished Ph.D. dissertation, 1985); Susanmarie Clark, *Potential For Use of Cottonwoods in Dendrogeomorphology and Paleohydrology* (Tucson: University of Arizona, unpublished M.S. thesis, 1987).

47. R.M. Lanner, *Trees of the Great Basin* (Reno: University of Nevada Press 1984), 144–146.

48. Lanner, *Trees of the Great Basin*, 195–197.

49. T.E. Dawson, J.R. Ehleringer, and J.D. Marshall, "Sex Ratio and Reproductive Variation in the Mistletoe *Phoradendron juniperinum*," *American Journal of Botany* 77 (1990), 584–589.

50. W. Larcher, *Physiological Plant Ecology* (Berlin: Springer-Verlag, 1980).

51. J.R. Ehleringer, S.L. Phillips, W.S.F. Schuster, and D.R. Sandquist, "Differential Utilization of Summer Rains by Desert Plants," *Oecologia* 88(1991): 430–434.

52. Lanner, *Trees of the Great Basin*, 147–150.

53. P.W. Huntoon, "Upheaval Dome, Canyonlands, Utah: Strain Indicators that Reveal an Impact Origin," in *Geology of Utah's Parks and Monuments*, eds. D.A. Sprinkel, T.C. Chidsey, Jr., and P.B. Anderson (Salt Lake City: Utah Geological Association Publication 28, 2000), 619–628.

54. Nick Van Pelt, C.D. Schelz, and D.W. Johnson, *Relict Vegetation Site Descriptions, Colorado Plant Reserve, Canyonlands National Park, Colorado National Monument, and Natural Bridges National Monument* (Salt Lake City, Utah: Nature Conservancy, Great Basin Field Office, 1992).

55. Van Steeter and Pitlick, "Geomorphology and Endangered Fish Habitats of the Upper Colorado River," 301.

56. R.A. Firmage, *A History of Grand County* (Salt Lake City: Utah State Historical Society, 1996), 73.

57. *Ibid.*, 226.

58. New Rapid is not depicted on the maps in the Belknap river guide.

59. Fleischner, *Singing Stone*, 45–47; Karen Krebbs, Ken Kaufman, and Desert Museum staff, "Bird Accounts," in *A Natural History of the Sonoran Desert*, 402–403; Chris Elphick, J.B. Dunning Jr., and D.A. Sibley, eds., *The Sibley Guide to Bird Life & Behavior* (New York: Alfred A. Knopf, 2001), 353–355.

60. Krebbs *et al.*, "Bird Accounts," in *A Natural History of the Sonoran Desert*, 373–458; Elphick *et al.*, *The Sibley Guide*, 73, 170–176.

61. Williams, *A Naturalist's Guide to Canyon Country*, 118; B.T. Brown, "Rates of Brood Parasitism by Brown-headed Cowbirds on Riparian Passerines in Arizona," *Journal of Field Ornithology* 65 (1994): 160–168.

62. *Ibid.*, 249.

63. Stokes, *Geology of Utah*, 91–92.

64. M.G. Johnson, *Placer Gold Deposits of Utah* (Washington, D.C.: U.S. Government Printing Office, U.S. Geological Survey Bulletin 1357, reprinted by Del Oeste Press, Tarzana, California, 1980), 6–7.

65. These slopes are based on profiles measured by the

U.S. Geological Survey expeditions in 1921 and 1922; see Chapter 1.

66. Williams, *A Naturalist's Guide to Canyon Country,* 88 and 97.

67. One of the author's saw a river otter above Rapid 13 in October 2003, one of the few recent sightings of this aquatic mammals in Cataract Canyon.

68. Carothers and Brown, *The Colorado River,* 63–80; Hayden, *Benthic Ecology of the Colorado River;* D.W. Blinn and G.A. Cole, "Algal and Invertebrate Biota in the Colorado River: Comparison of Pre- and Post-Dam Conditions," in *Colorado River Ecology and Dam Management,* ed. G.R. Marzolf (Washington, D.C.: National Academy Press, 1991), 102–123.

69. Seville Flowers, "Algae Collected in Glen Canyon," in *Anthropological Papers: Ecological Studies of Flora and Fauna in Glen Canyon (Glen Canyon Series Number 7),* eds. C.E. Dibble and A.M. Woodbury (Salt Lake City: University of Utah Press, 1959), 203–205.

70. Carothers and Brown, *The Colorado River,* 76–78.

71. Tom Dudley, "Aquatic Insects of the Sonoran Desert," in *A Natural History of the Sonoran Desert,* eds. S.J. Phillips and P.W. Comus (Tucson: Arizona-Sonora Desert Museum/University of California Press, 2000), 357–364.

72. *Ibid.*

73. National Park Service records, Canyonlands National Park, Moab, Utah, 2002. These records are continually being updated, and supercede those published in Charlie Schelz, comp., "Species Numbers for Vertebrates," *The Confluence* 7 (2000): cover.

74. Craig Ivanyi, Janice Perry, T.R. Van Devender, and Howard Lawler, "Reptile and Amphibian Accounts," in *A Natural History of the Sonoran Desert,* 535–542; Williams, *A Naturalist's Guide to Canyon Country,* 158–162.

75. The occurrence of the canyon treefrog in Canyonlands National Park is not well documented. It does not appear on the current National Park Service species list for the park; however, G.A. Hammerson, in *Amphibians and Reptiles in Colorado* (Niwot, Colorado: University Press of Colorado, 1999), lists this species as occurring in Canyonlands, and it has been documented in nearby areas (Natural Bridges National Monument and Capitol Reef National Park). Both National Park Service biologists and USGS scientists conducting present-day field investigations postulate that the species occurs in Canyonlands. Due to the high likelihood that this species does indeed inhabit Canyonlands National Park, we have chosen to include it in our species list and description.

76. Ivanyi *et al.,* "Reptiles and Amphibians," in *A Natural History of the Sonoran Desert,* 535–542; Williams, *A Naturalist's Guide to Canyon Country,* 160.

77. Ivanyi *et al.,* "Reptiles and Amphibians;" Williams, *A Naturalist's Guide to Canyon Country,* 159.

78. Williams, *A Naturalist's Guide to Canyon Country,* 159.

79. Ivanyi *et al.,* "Reptiles and Amphibians;" Williams, *A Naturalist's Guide to Canyon Country,* 159.

80. S.J. Tweit, *The Great Southwest Nature Factbook* (Anchorage: Alaska Northwest Publishing, 1992), 73–74; Williams, *A Naturalist's Guide to Canyon Country,* 162; J.A. MacMahon, *Deserts* (New York: National Audubon Society Nature Guide, Alfred A. Knopf, 1985), 474.

81. Tweit, *The Great Southwest Nature Factbook,* 73–74; MacMahon, *Deserts.*

82. Tom Clark, Capitol Reef National Park Resource Management, personal observation, 1999.

83. Tweit, *The Great Southwest Nature Fact Book,* 19–20.

84. M.G. Hengesbaugh, *Creatures of Habit* (Logan: Utah State University Press, 2001), 126–131.

6

THE CENTER OF THE UNIVERSE

The Confluence of the Green and the Grand and Vicinity

Off again early and commenced the real work of exploration . . .

John C. Sumner, July 21, 1869.[1]

Many people have places they think of as the center of the universe, and for lovers of the southwestern United States, these spots are often found in the region surrounding Moab. One group of Cataract Canyon boaters holds that the epicenter is at the beach between Big Drops 2 and 3 on river right or the beach on river left above Big Drop 1. Some people think it is Standing Rock in the Maze District; still others think it is at one of the prominent over-looks such as Dead Horse or Grand View points. We have a different opinion: the real center of the universe is the Confluence of the Green and Grand (now Colorado) rivers. Whether you agree or not, you have to admit that this is a very powerful place, created by the combined forces of two great rivers (Figure 6-1).

The setting has a powerful feel. From the perspective of looking down the Colorado, the first downstream view is of what appears to be a triangular peak. That triangular peak is really the tip of a bedrock peninsula crowned with brightly colored red, orange, and white rocks. The Green River, because of its meandering, appears on the right to be flowing towards the viewer, and the joined rivers move downstream to the left. The color of the waters usually are different shades ranging from green to red, and the flow is calm enough that the two do not fully mix until well around the corner downstream. Broad terraces line all the channel banks, and the first large beaches one sees on either approach are here. Tamarisk dominates, but peachleaf willow, sandbar

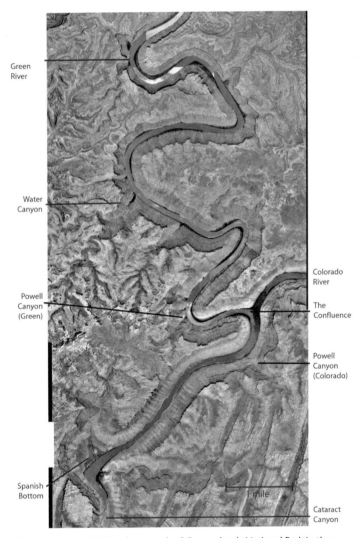

Figure 6-1. Aerial Orthophotograph of Canyonlands National Park in the Vicinity of the Confluence.

Figure 6-2. The Confluence from the Maze District (mile 216.3)

A. May 31, 1889. The Confluence of the Green and the Colorado rivers is the site of many colorful episodes in western history. Denis Julien was the first known explorer of European origin to pass here in the 1830s. The Powell Expedition paused here in 1869 and 1871. In 1889, when the Brown-Stanton Expedition reached the Confluence, their cooks found two plates left by one of the Powell expeditions. Many inscriptions are found on the rocks in the vicinity of the Confluence. The Green (left) and Grand (center) rivers combine to form the Colorado River (exiting right) in this upstream view. The rivers are at flood stage, and the riparian species appear to be mostly native willows with scattered cottonwood trees. A few boxelder trees may be present on river left (right center). (F.A. Nims 35, courtesy of the National Archives)

B. March 24, 1997. The riparian vegetation is greatly increased on both sides of the river. Most of this development is due to invasion of non-native tamarisk trees, although native riparian species have increased also. Desert vegetation in the foreground is a saltbush community. Resolution of the old photo was not sufficient to identify persistent plants. (R.H. Webb, Stake 2429)

willow, cottonwood, netleaf hackberry, and boxelder are all here in abundance as well (Figure 6-2).

Occasionally people who know the significance of the place stop at the Confluence. They doggedly hike up the sand banks and crash through the tamarisk to search for a bit of history. Will they find the kitchen paraphernalia that the Powell Expedition allegedly lost here? Do they know where the Kendrick inscription is? How about the Kolb inscription, or the ones that the sheepherder left? Will they find rotting lumber and rusty old drill casings left from U.S. Reclamation Service days? The Confluence *is* history: the stories of those who came here, some to discover and others to make a living. All were attracted, much as all of us are, to the center of the universe.

This chapter offers a respite from river travel to explore the region's history and biology in detail. Here, we discuss the Confluence itself, the corridor of the combined rivers downstream to Spanish Bottom, and

the uplands of the Maze District that are commonly accessed from the river by well-marked trails. Canoeists coming down the Green River often find themselves with time on their hands here, waiting for their jetboat pickup. River rafters commonly prefer to spend a day in this spot to take extended hikes to the uplands. Whatever your situation, the Confluence and Spanish Bottom offer a place for the contemplation of the larger history and ecology through which this river flows.

TRAVELERS BY LAND AND WATER

The Confluence was a much sought-after place during the exploration of the Southwest. The Domínguez-Escalante expedition of 1776 was the first group of Europeans to realize its existence, as they circled the watershed, crossing two major rivers in the north but only one in the south. Denis Julien found it but either

126　　CATARACT CANYON

he did not think to put his signature at the Confluence or time has removed or hidden his inscription.[2] The Johns—Macomb and Newberry—sought it but did not reach it in 1859. But another John, the determined Major Powell, finally established its location and in so doing established himself in American history.

Since the days of Powell, many adventurers have come and gone from the Confluence. The early arrivals carved their names in rocks for those that followed; these explorers included surveyors measuring for a railroad, photographers hoping to augment their fame and income, wishful herdsmen thinking there was enough forage to sustain grazing, engineers attempting to build a dam, a geologist examining gypsum domes, and miners marking their uranium claims. Nowadays jetboats furiously rush past searching for canoeists who paddled down the Green or Colorado rivers and need a ride back to Moab. On Memorial Day weekend, a group of powerboat operators and their families speed by en route from Green River to Moab. Whitewater boaters seeking the thrills of Cataract Canyon occasionally float past to take pictures and ponder a story or two about Powell's exploits, but mostly they also are intent on signing the register box downstream and getting to the whitewater.

The Regional Problem of Topography

Travel routes on the Colorado Plateau are determined by the Colorado River and its tributaries. Where there are hard rocks, the river is entrenched in deep gorges, and where there are soft rocks like shale, the river passes through a broad valley or extensive badlands (for example Interstate-70 north of Canyonlands). Consequently, river crossings always occur where the soft rocks meet the river. For the Grand Junction and town of Green River crossings, the soft rock is Mancos Shale; for Moab and Lee's Ferry, the Chinle Shale; and for Hite, the Organ Rock Shale. When the rock becomes harder, the landscape is carved with deep canyons that impede travel.

The direction of water flow has always been an important consideration when determining regional travel routes. The Green and Colorado rivers generally flow south and southwest, and the lateral drainages generally flow east and west toward the two rivers. Therefore travel south and north is much more time consuming due to the sheer numbers of lateral drainages that must be crossed in the process. This is why Macomb and Newberry experienced such difficulty trying to locate the Confluence, as they came overland from the nearest civilization, which at that time was well southeast of Canyonlands. Julien and Powell reached the Confluence more easily because they traveled downstream on the Green River. The north/south railroad route following the Colorado River, as Brown and Stanton had proposed in 1889, was never built primarily because of the perceived problems with construction in a landscape that seems more vertical than horizontal. To this day, there still is no north-south railroad route on the Colorado Plateau.

The topography of the Colorado Plateau has effectively discouraged development and encouraged preservation. Lt. Joseph Ives and Macomb reported this landscape to be totally unproductive, prophesying that it would remain forever unvisited. However, the great deterrent of rugged topography has also been a great attractor, as it creates superlative scenery for tourist snapshots as well as the quiet of true wilderness. Communities, though sparse and generally small (San Juan County has a population density of 1.5 people per square mile), dot the landscape. But take a moment and imagine the population density and development that would have occurred if the Green and Colorado rivers had proven to be navigable like the Ohio and Mississippi rivers! Cataract Canyon might have been filled with locks and dams.

Missing the Turn

The Friendship Cruise is a family-oriented boating event that occurs almost every Memorial Day in Canyonlands. Boats launch down the Green River from the town of Green River and participants spend the night in the canyon, traditionally at Anderson Bottom. When they reach the Confluence, the powerboats turn upstream on the Colorado River, power through the Slide (mile 1.5), and take out at either the

Figure 6-3. Talus and Boulders (mile 215.8)

A. May 31, 1889. This downstream view from the left side of the Colorado River shows the proposed route of the Denver, Colorado Cañon and Pacific Railroad. Between the Confluence and Lower Red Lake Canyon in 1947, Harry Aleson looked in vain among boulders such as these for the Denis Julien inscription mentioned by Frederick Dellenbaugh in his book *A Canyon Voyage*. Aleson finally found the inscription in 1951 near Lower Red Lake Canyon. (F.A. Nims 67, courtesy of the National Archives)

Potash boat ramp or Moab. This tradition began in 1958 and has run every year since then unless the water has been too low to allow powerboats to navigate around the rocks in the rivers safely.

Occasionally, a boat "misses the turn" and goes down, instead of up, the Colorado River. Some of these compound their mistake by entering the rapids, occasionally with tragic consequences. The first of these occurred during the second Friendship Cruise in 1959, when Frank Rich drowned.[3] The most tragic was on May 29, 1993, when three people in a powerboat entered Big Drop 2 at nearly 70,000 ft³/s. The hull of the boat was sliced in half at about its waterline, two of the passengers died, and the passenger who survived surfaced on the pile of lifejackets that none of them were wearing.[4] Although it is difficult to imagine that someone could actually mistake the rapids of Cataract Canyon for the flat water between the Confluence and Potash, consider that excessive alcohol consumption was likely in at least one of these incidents.[5]

THE VEGETATION AND DISTURBANCE

The short distance between the Confluence and the beginning of the rapids in Cataract Canyon contains a good example of the long-term effects of cattle grazing and fire in ecosystems that did not evolve with either type of disturbance.[6] Along the sides of the river where cattle once wandered up from Spanish Bottom, one can see large stands of the exotic annual grass cheatgrass and tumbleweed (also called Russian thistle or *Salsola kali*) (Figure 6-3). The fine fuels produced by these plants and tamarisk support frequent fires that have swept along the banks on both sides of the river. These fires, started by careless campers, constantly knock back the nonadapted native plants and enhance the dominance of the exotic plants.

Domestic Livestock Grazing

Grazing of domestic livestock has been important in shaping many of the plant communities in the western

B. June 3, 1993. Rockfalls dominate the river terraces in much of Cataract Canyon, but this is most dramatic just above Spanish Bottom. Nims appeared enamored with the large boulder in the foreground, and thus captured one of the few places that has remained relatively rock-fall free in the last century. However, notice the huge house-sized rock in the midground center that has rolled down since the original photo. Seven persistent shadscale individuals can be seen on the left side of the photograph. A newly established hackberry bush appears in the right foreground. The register box for Cataract Canyon river trips is across the river from this camera station. (R.H. Webb, Stake 3064)

United States. Before the advent of drilled wells and portable stock tanks, there was little free surface water in many of the low-elevation lands during most of the year and only a few areas were available for grazing by large herbivores. What grazing did occur in Canyonlands was mostly during the winter season when dormant plants and frozen soils were less susceptible to damage and near perennial water sources. Although much of the region was essentially untouched, the focusing of grazing around perennial water caused locally heavy impacts.

Many ecosystem characteristics currently found in Canyonlands indicate that these communities did not evolve with more than occasional light grazing, as shown by three pieces of evidence. First, the native bunchgrasses found here lack most mechanisms found in grasses to prevent them from grazing damage; when heavily grazed, the local bunchgrasses die and are replaced by shrubs. In contrast, grasses in regions that evolved with large herds of grazing animals—like the Great Plains of the Midwest or the Serengeti

Plains of eastern Africa—have adapted ways to protect them from grazing damage.[7] These include points of growth (*meristems*) that are located close to or below the soil surface, out of the way of injury from biting teeth; high amounts of silica to make the plant tissue less palatable and thus less attractive to herbivores; and the ability to grow new leaves from underground stems called *rhizomes*. Second, Colorado Plateau ecosystems rely on biological soil crusts for many ecosystem services; in the types of soils found here, well-developed crusts can only form when heavy trampling is absent. Finally, dung beetles are universally present where herds of hooved mammals have been present over evolutionary time, and are completely lacking in this ecosystem.[8]

Enter the western stockman. Cattle first arrived in North America around 1550 and were driven through Utah with the Domínguez-Escalante party in 1776.[9] Large herds entered Utah with the Mormons in 1847. By the mid-1800s, huge herds roamed the West, and the area just east of Cataract Canyon was a favored

Figure 6-4. The fire at Lower Red Lake Canyon (mile 213.4)

A. May 31, 1889. This upstream view is on river left and shows the flanks of the anhydrite diapir at Lower Red Lake Canyon. This diapir is called the Prommel Dome, named after a petroleum geologist who visited the area in the 1920s. River crossings have also occurred nearby as the drainage provides a route out of this Colorado River gorge. One such river crossing occurred in the 1890s to ford cattle stolen by Butch Cassidy and the Robber's Roost gang. (F.A. Nims 32, courtesy of the National Archives)

B. July 22, 1992. In July 1989, hikers from Lower Red Lake Canyon accidentally set fire to a tamarisk thicket. The fire spread upstream on the left bank of the Colorado River—shown here in the foreground—before jumping across the river and then burning downstream through the dense riparian vegetation of Spanish Bottom. Fires due to human negligence along the Green and Colorado rivers have decimated cottonwood stands. Seepweed appears in the center foreground with non-native cheatgrass, tumbleweeds, and tamarisk. (Steve Tharnstrom, Stake 2622)

drive for cattle headed to new ranges or to the railroad. Mormons first built ranches in the Moab area in 1855, but this effort failed because of poor relations with the nomadic Utes.[10] The continuous history of livestock grazing in Canyon Country actually began in the mid-1870s with the appearance of stockmen from two directions: non-Mormon herders entered westward from Colorado, and Mormon herders entered eastward from central Utah. These men and their livestock were to have significant and widespread effects on perennial vegetation throughout this region.

One of the first livestock ventures near Moab started when Crispin Taylor arrived from Juab County, Utah, in 1874.[11] Taylor was part of the first wave of an expanding livestock industry that serviced the growing demand for meat from the precious-metal mining districts of Colorado, particularly in the San Juan Mountains. Taylor's herd was taken by the Utes but ranchers returned, some to be killed by Utes and others to prosper. The Mormons raised livestock for personal consumption as well as for a church-owned

herd maintained to help members in need. Few Mormon ranchers raised stock on a scale large enough for export. Nonetheless, in 1870, the ratio of cows to people in this region exceeded any other Utah county.

These family ranchers were soon dominated by large stock operations attracted by grass that always appeared to be at least a foot high. By 1880, Utah had 278,000 cattle on its landscape—a little more than the number of people in the state—and Grand and San Juan counties had about 23,700 of that total.[12] The combination of hard winters and summer droughts in 1885-1886 began the decimation of herds along the Utah-Colorado border.[13] The drought lingered, and the drought of 1896—ironically also an El Niño year—killed fifty percent or more of the cattle herds in southern Utah. Over the decade of the 1890s, cattle numbers remained constant in Utah[14] owing to the severe losses of this drought.

By the 1890s, productivity of the land decreased rapidly due to overgrazing and drought, and the large operations pulled out, leaving the resident ranchers to wrest a living from the rapidly degrading landscape.

One of the strategies in the mid-1890s to get more productivity from the land was to introduce sheep, who browse shrubs.[15] Sheep withstood the drought effects much better than cattle, and so after the drought, sheep numbers increased until four million of these animals were grazing annually in Utah. Looking for forage, ranchers pushed their livestock further into the wilderness of rocks, including the bottomlands along the Green and Colorado rivers. In 1914, Otho Murphy grazed cattle along the river near the Confluence.[16] In the grassy valleys hidden in the cliffs above the river, sheep grazed, coming down to the river for water at Spanish Bottom. Transportation to market as well as just getting across the river were perennial problems, and extended overland travel through the maze of rocks and canyons offered the only reliable transportation of animals to market. Historically, local stockmen used the shallow water at Spanish Bottom to ford their cattle across the Colorado River, using trails in the Doll House and Red Lake Canyon for getting into and out of the canyon.[17] Grazing near the Confluence was desperate at best and economically infeasible at worst.

For the first twenty years of the twentieth century, rainfall was mostly above average in Utah, and overstocking resumed. But the uncertainty of the region's climate, combined with overstocking of the ranges, continued to take their toll. The ranges were drought-stricken in the early 1930s during the Dust Bowl, and the federal government acted to regulate grazing on public lands. This resulted in the Taylor Grazing Act and the formation of the Bureau of Land Management, which subsequently greatly reduced the numbers of livestock in this region.[18]

Grazing was reduced or eliminated in the area with the establishment of Canyonlands National Park in 1964. The remains of cattle grazing can still be seen in many places throughout Canyonlands, including Spanish Bottom and the alluvial terraces lining the Colorado River. Exotic plants, especially cheatgrass and Russian thistle, invaded many of the areas heavily utilized by livestock. Due to the slow decomposition rates in the ecosystem, livestock dung can still be found as well. At Spanish Bottom, old fences remain. The broad bottomland is dominated by a shrubland,

not the grassland that most likely was present before the cattle came.

The Ecology of Fire

When walking downstream along the left bank of the Colorado River, or look across at it from Spanish Bottom, it is possible to see that an ecological disaster happened here not long ago. A fire roared through here in July 1988,[19] leaving the charred tree stumps and barren ground (Figure 6-4). Ignited by a camper burning toilet paper in Lower Red Lake Canyon on river left, the fire raced quickly upstream, consuming tamarisk, boxelders, cottonwoods, native willows, and cheatgrass. It then jumped to river right and burned downstream into Spanish Bottom. The fire did not stop until it had burned through the riparian vegetation on both sides of the river, as well as adjacent cheatgrass and greasewood communities well into the interior of Spanish Bottom.

This was a very hot fire, and it left little but several inches of ash, fire-hardened mud dauber nests, and the bones of trapped deer. The next spring, Spanish Bottom was covered with a carpet of two species of beautiful yellow-flowered annual plants that often follow fire: golden corydalis (*Corydalis aurea*) and beeplant (*Cleome serrulata*). After persisting for several years, both species disappeared. Instead, cheatgrass steadily reinvaded areas where it had been and now again dominates much of the ground cover. Along the river's edge, many of the cottonwoods and willow trees died. Some sandbar willow resprouted, but tamarisk now dominates yet more of the river corridor vegetation than it did before the fire.

Some communities thrive with fire while others respond poorly. Which do what depends on whether the community that burned evolved with periodic fire, the types of plant and animal species that are present to recolonize the burned area (including exotics), and how current environmental conditions compare to conditions before the fire and when the native community was established. Whereas many ecosystems in the western United States depend on recurrent fire to maintain their natural integrity,[20] this is not true for the plant communities at lower elevations on the

Colorado Plateau. In this region, we find almost no evidence of fire until extensive European settlement.

Before the invasion of cheatgrass and tamarisk, vegetation communities had large interspaces between plants, low productivity, and the minimal biomass available for burning. Therefore, fires started by lightning were quickly starved by lack of fuel. Now, the interspaces between plants are full of fine fuels from exotics, and visitors to the area light fires to burn trash and toilet paper or just to have a fire. As a result of occasional carelessness, high winds, or just plain bad luck, fires now sweep wholesale through landscapes that seldom, if ever, experienced fire. Once these communities burn, exotic plants—particularly tamarisk and cheatgrass—are optimally poised to take over. This is a large part of the ecosystem history at Spanish Bottom.

SPANISH BOTTOM

As river runners move downstream from the Confluence, wearing lifejackets fully clipped on and snugged up, the first real landmark they see is a large, prominent sign on river right that declares "Dangerous Rapids Ahead." A register box can be found lying on the sand. It is not attached to anything, and it may beneath the sign alongside the well-beaten trail, or on the top of the bank, depending on water levels. The large annual stage change here makes a fixed object like this problematic.

After signing up for camps in Cataract Canyon and reembarking for the journey downstream, a visitor might turn the bend and see several peculiar sights on the downstream skyline. On river left, a grayish-white dome appears next to the river. The right side looks incongruous with its near-vertical cliff capped by weird, whitish pinnacles that tower above a strangely flat bottomland. It seems that every color in the spectrum is on display here. At the Confluence, the Honaker Trail Formation, with its dull grayish sheen, dominates the rocks at river level. In the middle of the cliffs above, the predominately red rocks of the Elephant Canyon Formation are prominent. Higher on the cliffs, one catches distant glimpses of a red-stained white sandstone called the Cedar Mesa Sandstone, which occurs as a consistent formation.

Welcome to Spanish Bottom, with its striking scenery, expansive hiking, and impressive ecology. You are unlikely to pass this place without pausing for some off-river recreation before literally plunging over the brink at Rapid 1 just downstream. Spanish Bottom is the portal to many places including the Maze via the Doll House trail, with its fantastic canyons, spires, and seemingly endless expanses of slickrock; to the Needles area, via the Red Lake Canyon trail on the other side of the river; and to Cataract Canyon.

Were the Spaniards at Spanish Bottom?

The Spaniards entered the Colorado Plateau in A.D. 1540 with hopes to satiate their quest for gold. They established ranches, mines, military posts, and missions in the Mexican-border states. In 1680, the progeny of the Ancestral Puebloans were successful in driving the Spaniards from New Mexico during the Pueblo Revolt, but in 1692 the Spaniards returned for their second conquest. In the 1770s, Spanish merchants and clergy explored the Colorado Plateau for resources and travel routes but again returned to Santa Fe, thwarted by a truly rugged and remote landscape. In 1821, the Mexicans gained independence from colonial Spain, and Mexican merchants entered the Colorado Plateau, successfully forging a route from New Mexico to California for trade with their countrymen. The commerce typically was in textiles, horses, and illegal Indian slaves.[21]

The route they took from New Mexico to California crossed the Colorado Plateau because the more direct route through Arizona had three disadvantages: lack of water, lack of pasturage for beasts of burden, and too many hostile natives. The trail is known today as the Old Spanish Trail, even though the nationality of its users was Mexican and the route was used more recently than some previously thought: from the 1820s to the 1840s.[22] It was not a trail for wagons pulled by stock animals, but instead was used by pack trains. The trail from Santa Fe to Los Angeles crossed the San Juan River near present-day Farmington, New Mexico, the Colorado River near Moab, and the Green River near Green River, Utah. Once the territory was ceded from Mexico to the United States in 1848, wagons began to use the trail, and Orville Pratt led a party through Spanish Valley in that year. Few followed because it was a very unpopular trail for wagon trains, owing to the rough terrain.

Discussions of alternate routes to the Old Spanish Trail have generated a controversy among modern-day historians. We know that one route crossed the Colorado River at Grand Junction. The presence of an alternate route at Spanish Bottom is seriously questioned despite plenty of circumstantial and questionable evidence.[23] The questionable evidence includes a folk legend that some Spaniards or Mexicans used illegal Indian slave labor to mine secretly in the mountains of the Great Basin near present-day Provo and Salt Lake City. No one has found such diggings in these mountains; however, legend claims that the Indians hid the mine sites to discourage intervention in their lifestyle.

If it dates to the early 1800s, the route through Spanish Bottom likely was part of the larger trail system to California and was used for several reasons. Its use saved time by eliminating the crossings of both the Green and Colorado rivers, which was required on the routes further east. Fewer Utes inhabited Canyonlands than in the mountains to the east, and adequate forage and springs for the pack animals were present in the isolated Maze District. The latter reason is why some older residents of southeastern Utah believe in this route's antiquity.[24]

Other historical evidence indicates that the alternate route was real, or at least that a well-used route had been established by the mid-1800s. In 1871, Frederick Dellenbaugh observed a heavily used trail leading down Lower Red Lake Canyon;[25] this is the same trail along which the well-traveled Denis Julien made one of his inscriptions. To find this inscription, and a few prehistoric Indian petroglyphs as well, land on river left near the mouth of Lower Red Lake Canyon (opposite Spanish Bottom), work your way through the tamarisk, avoid the biological soil crusts by using the trails, and climb to the ridge on the downstream side of the canyon mouth. Ascend this ridge to a subtle sandstone layer, stained reddish brown with age, and a close inspection of the nearby boulders will yield some faint writing.

The Doll House Trail has a series of very heavy, flat stones that serve as stair steps over a limestone ledge as the trail on river right rises from the river. These stones, called the Spanish Stairs by local ranchers and oil prospectors in the 1920s,[26] were not placed by river runners or backpackers.[27] Regardless of who first built it, other legendary people have used it. Supposedly the Wild Bunch—including Butch Cassidy and the Sundance Kid—used the trail through Spanish Bottom as a reasonably anonymous way to get from Colorado to their hideout near Robber's Roost to the west.[28] It most certainly was used by herdsmen or rustlers moving livestock through Canyonlands. Until proven otherwise, the legend of the Spanish Trail at Spanish Bottom is certainly entertaining as possible truth.

The Doll House Hike and the Ecology of Canyonlands

At the downstream end of Spanish Bottom, the river turns abruptly to the left. On river right, a rather tortured cottonwood tree beckons as a convenient place to tie off your boat in the shade. Up the bank and through the cheatgrass, a trail leads to the base of a steep, boulder-strewn slope. Overhead, the Doll House's pinnacles and oddly shaped outcrops beckon. The Doll House, formed by differential erosion of the Cedar Mesa Sandstone, attracts hikers and off-road enthusiasts alike, since both a four-wheel-drive dirt road and the Doll House trail converge above Spanish Bottom. The trail switchbacks ever upwards from Spanish Bottom, first crossing the Honaker Trail Formation, then into Elephant Canyon Formation, and finally into the Cedar Mesa Sandstone after a short stretch of hiking over slopes of reddish-looking soil that turns to incredibly sticky mud when it rains.

As you catch your breath for the ascent ahead, you might see little animals on or adjacent to the trail, tempting you to stray from the trail. In addition, friends are that-a-way, but the trail goes this-a-way, and you will want to cut across the bottomland or the islands of soil in the Doll House. Your proposed path would pass through odd-looking, bumpy, black soil, which seems uninteresting and useless. But hopefully you resist the trackless terrain, saving biological soil

Figure 6-5. The Land of Standing Rocks

A. September 16, 1871. John Wesley Powell and his men climbed up to the peninsula of rock between the Green River and the downstream leg of the Colorado River. At a cleft overlooking the Colorado River about a half mile downstream from the Confluence, they took several photographs of rock formations in the Cedar Mesa Sandstone. "It was a marvellous [sic], mighty desert of bare rock, chiseled by the ages out of the foundations of the globe; fantastic, extraordinary, antediluvian, labyrinthian, and slashed in all directions by crevices . . . ". The desert was not entirely bare: many plants grow in the cracks in the rocks and islands of soil that punctuate what Powell named the Land of Standing Rocks. (E.O. Beaman 747, courtesy of the National Archives)

B. August 23, 1968. In 1968, Hal Stephens and Gene Shoemaker retraced the Powell Expedition, and Stephens matched Beaman's view (A). They noted that several junipers had persisted since 1871 and that a dead snag was still present in exactly the same shape. (Stephens and Shoemaker, 1987, p. 174–175) (H.G. Stephens Z-3)

crusts. One rule of thumb applies: if you have to go off trail, step on rocks and not on the fragile soil among them.

Common Insects

On hot summer days, insects are commonly seen along the Doll House Trail. Although velvet ants (*Dasymutilla* sp.) look cute and cuddly, with their orange or red, velvet-covered backs, they are actually wasps that can give a very painful sting.[29] The wingless individuals are females, and only females have stingers. Females scurry about on the ground, looking for the nests of ground-nesting bees or wasps. Once she locates one, the female enters the nest, opens a cell where there is a host larva present, and lays an egg

C. March 30, 1998. On the tip of the spur of rock just above the foreground ledge, a little juniper tree has not changed in size for 127 years. Beside the rock nearby and to the right, a squawbush is still alive. Several blackbrush and green Mormon tea individuals appear about the same size since 1871. As they have in most of the western United States, juniper trees have increased in density. A dead snag of a juniper tree, which is readily identifiable in the 1871 view near the closest juniper, is still present and looks remarkably similar, showing that decomposition in this arid environment is slow. The distribution of biological soil crusts in the midground and background is the same. (Steve Tharnstrom, Stake 3578)

near or on the host. After the velvet ant larva hatches, it will feed upon the host bee or wasp larvae.

Antlions (*Brachynemurus* sp.) make their living by trapping ants. These insects hollow out pit traps in the sand by backing around in an ever-tightening circle while pushing sand out with their jaws. The hope is to catch a passing ant or other insect. Once the ant falls into the hole, it is unable to climb out due to the loose sand. At the bottom of the pit, the antlion larva waits, pinchers ready. The unfortunate ant is paralyzed by injected venom, and the antlion proceeds to suck its insides out. Adult antlions do not live in the pits, but instead are active on the soil surface at night. They only live about one month.

Darkling beetles (tenebrionids) are a very common sight in deserts throughout the world, with more than 1,300 species.[30] They are all small (about one inch long), wingless and black. They eat dead plants and fungi, and as such, are very important recyclers of plant material. Some have a foul spray that they squirt from their anal area, giving them the nickname "stinkbugs." Most, however, do not have this spray, and none are poisonous. During hot days, they generally stay buried in the sand. These beetles are avoided by predators that fear they will get sprayed. This does not stop grasshopper mice; they just grab the beetles and shove their abdomens down in the sand, and then bite their heads off.

Telebrionid beetles are very well-adapted to desert living and they can live for years without food. They have thickened covers over their exoskeletons that protect them from abrasion by sharp sand grains. They also have a space below their forewings that insulates their main bodies from heat and thus reduces water loss. The outside wing cover can be up to 140°F while the body temperatures are much lower; this temperature differential may also set up cooling convective air currents. These beetles are able to tolerate body temperatures of 104°F for short periods. Because they have a relatively high body temperature, they are able to be day-active; as most of their predators are nocturnal, they may escape predation with this strategy. When the angle of the sun is low during mornings, afternoons, and in winter, the wing covers of these beetles transmit warming infrared rays through to the beetle's body. When the sun angle is high in the middle of a summer day, these same wing covers absorb ultraviolet and visible light, preventing their passage through to the body. Black may also warn away would-be predators or assist in faster warming in the morning or cooler seasons. In addition, these animals are not always black: when humidity is low, they can turn a pale blue and reduce their heat gain.

Figure 6-6. The Land of Standing Rocks

A. October 24, 1911. The Kolb brothers used Powell's 1875 account as their river guide, and they decided to match as many as they could of Beaman's 1871 photographs that appeared in Powell's account. This led them to climb up to the Land of Standing Rocks and stand in a position near to where Beaman had stood. "We had found neither bird, nor rabbit; not even a lizard in the Land of Standing Rocks." (Kolb, 1914, p. 125) The vegetation is desert scrub on Cedar Mesa sandstone. (Kolb 5754, courtesy of the Cline Library, Northern Arizona University)

Upland Conifers

Climbing up the seemingly vertical trail, the Doll House trail approaches the Spanish Stairs. Looking above, you can see the domes of the Doll House, as well as some rather inviting-looking shade under some scrawny trees. Most of the trees along the cliffs and in the uplands of Canyonlands are the coniferous pinyon pine and juniper trees. Pinyons and junipers are related as Gymnosperms, although they are in different families and are the most common trees seen on the Colorado Plateau and in the Great Basin; together, they dominate over 75,000 square miles of the western United States.[31] Junipers tend to dominate drier sites at lower elevations, and pinyons dominate the wetter, higher elevation sites. These trees grow together in habitats where conditions are intermediate.

Juniper. Utah juniper (*J. osteosperma*) occurs throughout the Colorado Plateau, where it commonly co-occurs with Colorado pinyon. Both species can live for more than 127 years (Figures 6-5 and 6-6) on the cliffs above the river. Utah juniper is a multi-stemmed tree with a trunk that twists easily in the wind, creating very odd shapes. This species is able to shut off water to whole branches in times of drought, sacrificing the branches so that the whole plant may live.

Juniper can grow very slowly if limited by nutrients or water. A six-inch tree can be over fifty years old, while the same tree on a fertile site can reach fifteen to

twenty feet. The modified wax-covered, berry-like cones are blue, small, and fleshy and are on the trees year-round. Birds, coyotes, and jackrabbits all feed on these cones, dispersing the seeds in their feces. Utah juniper has few pests other than mistletoe. Gnats, also called "no-see-ums," can be found living in juniper bark.

Junipers have been used in many ways by humans. Roof beams found at prehistoric ruins in Chaco Canyon have been dated at 500 A.D.[32] Berries were used as food by Indians and have long been a source of flavor for gin. Shredded bark was smoked, woven into sandals, and used for rope. Juniper wood, which is hard and long-lasting when burned, was used for cooking, bows, and carved utensils. In the more re-cent past, ranchers found that juniper logs make excellent fence poles, as the wood resists rot.

Pinyon. Pinyon pine has been the subject of much literature and lore, and they are an important source for food and shelter to both humans and animals in this region. Colorado pinyon, which has two to three needles per cluster, is found in deserts where summer rain is an important source of moisture, like Canyon Country. Many organisms, including humans, depend heavily on pinyon trees for food and shelter.[33] Mule deer, rock squirrels, white-tailed antelope squirrels, Hopi chipmunks, mice (especially pinyon mice), ravens, jays, woodrats (packrats), black bears, humans, and even desert bighorn sheep all love pinyon nuts. Porcupines eat the inner tissue of pinyon bark. Bark beetle and engraver beetle larvae are commonly found under the bark. The parasitic pinyon dwarf mistletoe (*Arceuthobium divaricatum*) is commonly found attached to branches, tapping into the lifeblood of the tree. Another parasite is the pinyon blister rust, which alternates between gooseberry and other currants and the pinyon tree. Exuded pitch attracts pitch midges, which also eat the exposed tissue.

Other animals use pine pitch for more unusual purposes. Some bees build hives exclusively of pine pitch. Sawfly larvae eat the pine pitch and store it in their gut, using it to squirt at predators. Some sawfly species are only found on particular pine species. These tiny insects are born in the cones of pinyon trees, and subsist on pine pollen until pupation; thus the timing of their emergence from eggs must be synchronous with pollen production. Colorado pinyons are also hosts to the pinyon spindle gall midge (*Pinyonia edulicola*). Adults lay their orange eggs on the pine needle; once the larvae hatch, they migrate down to where the needles attach to the branch and begin feeding. This stimulates a growth response in the pinyon, and a gall is formed at the base of the needles. Inside these galls, up to fifty larvae will spend the winter, well protected and well fed, as the gall tissue is much more nutritious than normal pinyon needle tissue. In spring, the larvae metamorphose into adults, and the cycle repeats. Although the infested needles die, overall injury to the tree is minimal. However, the midge eggs laid on the pinyon needle surface are at risk, since a tiny wasp (*Platygaster* sp.) searches for them. If the eggs are found, the female wasp oviposits eggs within the midge eggs. As the midge larvae grows, the wasp larvae grows inside it, slowly eating it from the inside out. Finally, the wasp larvae kills the midge larvae and emerges.

Seeds of the pinyon tree fly outwards explosively from the cones in the fall, spraying sticky seeds up to fifty feet away. Seeds also stick to the legs and feet of birds, and are transported from tree to tree. When pinyon trees produce a seed crop, typically every three to seven years, most trees in a local area produce prodigious amounts of seeds at the same time, a phenomenon called *masting*.[34] Other plants on the Col-

orado Plateau mast, including blackbrush and oaks. Masting occurs in many plant species in many habitats throughout the world, especially the tropics. Species that mast do not produce seed every year.

There are several theories as to why masting occurs. Because it is often a very local occurrence (for instance, while one group of pinyon trees may have a huge seed crop, a stand less than five miles away may not have any seeds at all), it is unlikely that favorable environmental conditions are the only explanation. Masting also ensures that predator swamping (lots of seed produced all at once ensures that some will escape being eaten) will occur, that trees will save up energy to take advantage of good seed production years, and that wind-pollinated species will enjoy some success.

Masting implies that the surrounding plants somehow "know" all the neighbors are planning on making seeds. How might trees communicate to attain this synchronous reproduction? There are many possibilities. Chemical signals may travel along roots which then secrete the chemical "message" into the soil. Unusual environmental events such as very wet years or specific precipitation timing may be responsible. These conditions may be combined with photoperiod signals. There also may be some airborne chemical signal released by trees ready to reproduce. This last scenario has been demonstrated in ripening fruit trees: maturing fruit gives off ethylene which hastens ripening in nearby fruit and thus adjacent fruit tends to ripen and drop all at once. Ethylene has also been shown to induce flowering and the dropping of leaves and fruit. Therefore, a similar chemical could be used to induce such synchronicity in pinyon.

Pinyons and Pinyon Jays. Unlike the seeds of most pine trees, pinyon seeds lack membranous wings, which aid in wind dispersal. Instead, pinyon trees mostly depend on birds for seed dispersal. Pinyon jays are the most involved in this, but Western Scrub Jays help as well. Pinyon Jays are loud, highly social jays that nest in pinyon or juniper trees. While these jays eat things other than pinyon nuts (such as insects, seeds, and berries), they depend heavily on pinyon trees. The trees, in turn, depend heavily on the Pinyon Jays.[35]

Late in summer, the pinyon seeds ripen within the green, sealed cones. At the same time, the jay yearlings are ready to fly. Flocks of adults and yearlings pick pinyon cones and peck them apart, storing the seeds in their esophagi. Not all seeds are used: tan seeds usually contain only aborted embryos, and the jays ignore these. Instead, they concentrate on the dark brown seeds that are almost all fully developed. But even these seeds are not taken indiscriminately. Picking up a seed, Pinyon Jays will both weigh and tap the seed, much like we do to watermelons, to see if it contains a normal *endosperm*. If so, they will stuff it in their mouths. Once full, they fly back to their nesting grounds and cache the seeds in the ground. During fall, the cached seeds are used for courtship: the males dig up the seeds and feed the seeds to the females.

Incubating female jays live almost exclusively on pinyon nuts, as do hatchlings. Forgotten cached seeds germinate when conditions are favorable, creating the next generation of pinyon trees. In years when seeds are not produced, the birds know not to breed because green pinyon cones not only feed the birds; they also stimulate testis development in the male jays for late summer breeding. This appears to be a visual stimulus: when jays cannot see those green cones, the birds do not mate.

So who gets what out of this relationship? The birds receive a stimulus to breed during a time when food is available, obtain good nesting sites, and enjoy a high-fat/high-protein food source that is easily obtained over many months. The trees oblige the birds by keeping membrane-covered seeds from falling out of the cone onto the ground. The cones open widely giving the jays easy access, and the seeds are color-coded for their nutritional quality. The tree, in exchange, gets its seeds dispersed and planted widely across the landscape into high-quality sites, a critical benefit to a species that produces large seeds that cannot be windblown. Large seeds represent a big investment for plants, and it is important that they end up in habitats favorable for growth. In addition, birds that carry seeds long distances facilitate the exchange of genetic material among and between populations, so that a given stand of trees represents a mix of populations from the surrounding area.

Upland Flowering Trees

Most upland flowering trees grow in the side canyons. These include boxelder, netleaf hackberry, oaks (mostly *Quercus gambelii*), western hophornbeam (*Ostrya knowltonii*), birchleaf buckthorn (*Rhamnus betulifolia*), and cottonwood. The singleleaf ash, however, grows elsewhere.

When hiking in the uplands around slickrock you can almost always find this tree. This is a puzzling plant. It is one of the few large-leafed plants found in this desert. Touch the leaves: they are always very cool relative to the hot surrounding air because of the high transpiration rates of this plant. It grows in what appears on the surface to be an extraordinarily inhospitable place: cracks in the slickrock, with little or no visible soil. Some adaptations do help to reduce water loss: there is only one leaf on each petiole, and these leaves are thick and waxy. But how is it able to live in a slickrock crack?

Living in cracks can be advantageous to a plant. First, these cracks are actually a relatively water-rich environment, as they concentrate water from the surrounding rock into a small area. Second, not many plants can live in such a nutrient-poor environment, so competition from neighbors is minimal. However, the plant needs to have woody roots that can transport water over long distances (*i.e.*, shrubs or trees), since the water that flows down a crack may go a long distance before it stops and is available for root uptake. Living in a rock crack with minimal soil also requires slow growth and the ability to handle a very low nutrient supply. Singleleaf ash, along with a few other shrubs that exist in slickrock cracks, employ all the above mechanisms. They are some of the slowest-growing plants around and subsist on little because of their very low metabolic rates.

Crack-inhabiting shrubs of this region also need thick roots. If you look at roots growing in cracks, most often the roots will be the size of the crack, and appear to be pushing against both sides of the crack. It was long thought that roots made cracks by sending in small roots that gradually expanded and pushed the rock apart. While this probably occurs, what happens more frequently is that the root fills the crack so that they are as closely appressed to the rock surface as possible. This contact enables the plant to absorb both the water and nutrients that wash down the crack and the nutrients weathering out of the rock. Thus, the walls of the crack become the "soil" that supports the plant.

Like the boxelder trees along the river, singleleaf ash is one of the first plants to leaf out in spring, and it flowers earlier than most plants as well. It is commonly believed that the winged appendages of this plant's seeds help the seeds to land away from the mother plant, thus lessening competition with the parent and enhancing genetic exchange within the surrounding community. However, appendages on seeds can also inhibit dispersal. When seeds from crack-inhabiting shrubs are placed in a wind tunnel to test for their dispersal ability, appendages that generally increase dispersal instead inhibit travel. For instance, the wings of singleleaf ash seeds catch in cracks. This also happens with the long, thin tails attached to mountain mahogany seeds. The tails are covered with short stiff hairs that catch on the first rough spot encountered. Even though the appendages may enhance travel while the seed is falling, once it hits the ground, the same appendages can restrict movement. This may be the best strategy for a plants adapted to a habitat that is small and patchy across the landscape. Instead of wide dispersal, staying close to home may be a better answer.

Reptiles

As one spends more and more time in Cataract Canyon, the lack of animal life becomes ever more apparent. Reptiles are usually the most commonly encountered vertebrates, but even they may seem scarce. For example, H.E. Gregory, one of the geologists who followed Powell into the region, wrote:

> Of the reptiles, some half dozen varieties of lizards, also garter snakes, bull snakes, and rattlesnakes and one box turtle were noted on sand flats and among rocks. But lizards are much less common than in regions south of the San Juan River, and harmful snakes are surprisingly rare. On long traverses during four field seasons only six rattlesnakes were seen.[36]

There is more animal life at Spanish Bottom—where the riparian, river bottom, and upland vegetation meet—than at most other places along the river. Despite the common perception, there is a surprising diversity of reptilian life found in and around this bottomland; a total of twenty species of reptiles are found in Canyonlands National Park.[37]

Lizards. Lizards in the Canyonlands region are day-active and have two types of activity patterns.[38] Sit-and-wait predators are intermittently active and include sagebrush lizards (*Sceloporus graciosus*), side-blotched lizards (*Uta stansburiana*), and horned lizards (*Phrynosoma platyrhinos*). Pursuit predators like the whiptail lizard (*Cnemidophorus tigris*) run continuously. While the latter strategy results in a greater food reward and thus faster growth rates, whiptails have metabolic rates twice those of the other lizards, lose much more water, and are more exposed to predation owing to strategy of continuous pursuit as opposed to a "sit-and-wait" strategy.

Many lizards are famous for losing their tails when you try to catch them. This often prevents capture by predators; in addition, the tail keeps moving about even when detached to further distract the pursuer. Tail dropping is not a trivial affair, as they are important for moving about, especially when used as a counterbalance when running fast. Lizards with tails are better at territory acquisition, which may explain why females who do not establish territories drop their tails more easily than males. Tails are also used to store fat for use when food is low.[39]

Three types of lizards are most commonly seen in Cataract Canyon. These include collared lizards (*Crotaphytus collaris*), whiptails (*Cnemidophorus* sp.), and side-blotched lizards (*Uta stansburiana*). Collared lizards are large (ten inches long), with black and fluorescent blue collars around their necks. These are beautiful lizards, brightly colored in orange, yellow, and/or green. They prefer areas of open vegetation and boulders, and are often seen sitting on tall boulders for better views of their prey (and maybe the scenery, too!). They are sit-and-wait predators: rather than chase their prey, they generally wait until it comes within reach. Long legs hold their bodies well off the ground at a forty-five degree angle with the tail and forelimbs raised. These lizards can run very fast and have a long stride. Unlike many lizards that drop their tails to distract predators, collared lizards retain theirs for balance when they run fast. This species primarily eats grasshoppers, but will also eat other lizards and insects. They have a simple daily schedule: morning, bask and search for prey; midday, retreat from heat; afternoon, bask and eat until dark. Females lay one to thirteen eggs and can reproduce more than once each year. The males are highly territorial, and are sexually active in their second summer; reproduction is then possible over the next several years.

Whiptails are the big, slender lizards you see running about during the day, whipping their extremely long tails from side to side while probing the air with their tongues up to 450 times per hour. Unlike collard lizards, they chase their prey, which includes a variety of invertebrates and smaller lizards, and they eat on the run. Foraging often occurs in brief spurts when ambient air temperatures are high. Six of the twelve species of whiptails reproduce sexually and lay one to six eggs late in spring. However, another six species (including the plateau whiptail) are *parthenogenic*, which means all individuals are female and all can produce viable, although unfertilized, eggs.[40] Parthenogenesis is believed to occur when two separate species mate. In whiptails, females will mount and psuedocopulate with other females, apparently triggering a hormonal change needed for ovulation. Because all individuals can reproduce, these species can reproduce much faster than other species. But because each individual is a clone, this species has less genetic variability to help adapt to changing conditions.

Side-blotched lizards are the most common lizard in this area. These are very small lizards, with a blotch of color under their front legs. The life span is usually only five months, although some have been known to live up to two years. During their short lives, they produce several clutches of eggs when resources are abundant. Territory size and quality are based on the aggressiveness of the male.[41] Because of their small size, these lizards are active year-round, coming out of hibernation on warm winter days. They feed and bask in morning and evening, living mostly on insects, and

in turn form the prey base of many larger species in the Canyonlands region. Side-blotched lizards are active during the day only as long as is necessary, as they are highly susceptible to predation, water loss, and heat stress.

Snakes. After reading western novels and watching western movies, many people come to the desert convinced there are snakes behind every bush, waiting to bite the unwary visitor. Actually, while there are some snakes in Cataract Canyon, their numbers are few, and most try desperately to avoid detection when in the presence of large animals (including, and perhaps especially, humans). Of the nine snake species recorded in this area, only rattlesnakes pose any danger to humans. Three subspecies of rattlesnakes (*Crotalus viridis*) occur in Canyon Country: the midget faded (*C. v. concolor*), prairie (*C. v. viridis*), and Great Basin (*C. v. lutosus*) rattlesnakes.

An inordinately large number of myths and legends concern the rattlesnake's behavior. Most stories, unfortunately, exaggerate the danger of these snakes. As with the other snakes, rattlesnakes are mostly out at night when their prey (mostly mice) are active. *Loreal pits* on the sides of their heads give them an extremely accurate (within a few tenths of a degree), three-dimensional picture of the "temperature landscape" around them: that is, where warm temperatures are concentrated relative to the surrounding air. This technique works best at night when the temperature difference between a warm-blooded small mammal and the cool night air is greatest. Differential heat output also enables rattlesnakes to distinguish large animals that they want to avoid from small, edible animals. This ability to "scope" appropriate prey combined with better night vision enables snakes to do most of their hunting in the dark. There is some daytime activity when air temperatures are cooler. In general, desert species are more nocturnal than montane species.

Six other species of snakes are commonly found in this region.[42] The gopher (or bull) snake (*Pituophis catenifer deserticola*) is the most common snake encountered and is often mistaken for a rattlesnake, which it imitates well. They have a similarly shaped head and when threatened, they will coil and rise to a striking position, spin their tail in dry leaves (sounding quite like a rattle), and hiss. These snakes are active throughout the day except in extreme heat. Gopher snakes live mostly on small rodents such as squirrels and mice, some birds, and bird eggs. They kill their prey through constriction and then engulf the prey whole. Males engage in ritual combat, but rarely bite each other. This species lives in most habitats found in Canyon Country, and are one of the most widespread snakes nationwide.

Other snakes in Canyonlands include garter (*Thamnophis* sp.), racer (*Coluber* sp.), night (*Hypsiglena torquata*), rat (*Elaphe guttata emoryi*), southwestern blackheaded (*Tantilla hobartsmithi*), and whip (*Masticophis taeniatus*) snakes. Garter snakes here are the same genus as those in your garden and are found mostly in wet places. Racers are fast snakes and are often seen climbing trees. The night snake is seldom seen as it ventures out only at night to prey on lizards, small snakes, frogs, salamanders, and small mice. It subdues these with a mild venom that has no effect on humans. The rat snake also is strictly nocturnal and preys on small mammals. Black-headed snakes are probably the most unusual snakes found here. They are small and burrow under vegetation, living on soil animals such as worms, millipedes, and insect larvae. Whipsnakes are extremely fast, and eat lizards, other snakes and small rodents. They are often seen up in the foliage of shrubs.

Mammals

A total of fifty-one mammals are found in Canyonlands National Park (Appendix 2).[43] There are many mammals commonly found in the upland habitats around Spanish Bottom and throughout Cataract Canyon that could be viewed while hiking the Doll House Trail.[44] Chances are you will not see many of them during the typical hot summer day as they are active in the evening or nighttime hours to conserve moisture in this arid environment.

Mice and Kangaroo Rats. About half of the species of mammals in this region are rodents.[45] Rodents are a very important part of desert fauna as they are the preferred food of most of the larger predators. The most common rodents in this region are mice in the genus *Peromyscus*, which includes deer, pinyon, brush, and canyon mice.[46] All of these species prefer upland habitats, including human houses. Deer mice (*P. maniculatus*) often use burrows made by other animals, and eat seeds, larvae, and insects. Females breed year-round, have four young per litter, and can have up to five litters per year. Deer mice are skilled climbers of cacti, trees, and cliffs in search of food. They are also the primary vector for hantavirus.

The brush mouse (*P. boylii*) lives in shrub habitats, including pinyon-juniper stands and oak groves. It also is an avid climber and often runs up shrubs or trees for protection. This species eats pine nuts, acorns, insects, and cactus fruits; forages throughout the year; and does not store food. The pinyon mouse (*P. truei*) is probably the cutest mouse of this group: it has huge ears and big innocent eyes that watch you while it crosses your campsite at night looking for dropped morsels. These mice prefer pinyon-juniper woodlands, which provide them with shelter in the form of juniper bark, food from pinyon nuts and juniper berries, and nesting sites in tree bases or limb crotches. The canyon mouse (*P. crinitus*) prefers rocky hillslopes and is seldom found in flat areas. They are remarkably agile and appear to run up sheer rock faces. Because of this talent, this species is often found in areas inaccessible to other mammals. These mice have very long tails, which helps distinguish them from the other species of *Peromyscus*.

Unlike most other mice, the grasshopper mouse (*Onychomys leucogaster*) eats other mice in addition to scorpions, grasshoppers, and other insects. Grasshopper mice prefer to live in grasslands, where there is a plentiful supply of rodents to eat. Occasionally they eat some plant material. Though it seems unlikely, these mice actually imitate wolves in several ways. They form family packs and the parents teach the young how to hunt. They aggressively defend their territories and will kill intruders. In addition, they stand on their hind legs and make howling noises, just like tiny wolves. They use sand for dust bathing, although their incredibly foul odor and huge flea infestations belie the idea they ever bathe at all.

Ord's kangaroo rat (*Dipodomys ordii*) is not a rat at all and, in fact, kangaroo rats in general are not related to any other North American rodent. They are bipedal with very long tails for balance and are swift runners. They prefer very sandy soils with open vegetation. Along with pocket mice, they have enlarged middle-ear chambers so they can hear low-frequency sounds created by nighttime predators. Kangaroo rats take great pains to reduce water loss: during the day, they plug their burrows to conserve moisture and cool temperatures. They are strictly nocturnal and very picky eaters. They avoid seeds with too much fat, because digestion of fats produces too much excess heat that must be dissipated, or too much protein, which creates toxic waste that requires water to excrete.[47]

It was long thought that kangaroo rats were so effective at reducing water loss that they could obtain all the water they needed from seeds. This is true during the cooler seasons; however, in times of high water stress, such as summer, they are heavily dependent on insects as a source of water. Like many small mammals, kangaroo rats only breed when green plants are present. This species is heavily dependent on the seeds of the blackbrush plant, and populations rise and fall with seed production of this shrub. Kangaroo rats are solitary, joining together only long enough to reproduce. Like grasshopper mice, they often take sand baths to keep their fur smooth and unmatted. Unlike grasshopper mice, they do not stink or support copious flea populations.

Ground Squirrels, Chipmunks, and Packrats. White-tailed antelope ground squirrels (*Ammospermophilus leucurus*) are easy to identify, as they hold their tails high over their backs when running, exposing their white undersides. Such tail-waving may be a way of providing shade for this day-active species. These ground squirrels live in burrows or rock crevices. They usually forage for fruits and seeds on the ground or in yucca and cactus. They also eat insects such as Jerusalem crickets, grasshoppers, beetles, lizards, and rodents, including those that are already dead. This species is often seen on the tops of shrubs, surveying their kingdom. They are diurnal, rather than nocturnal, and can withstand body temperatures of 106°F.

When the temperatures climb higher than 106°F, they spread saliva on their faces and necks for some evaporative cooling or retreat to their burrows where they flatten their bodies onto the cool soil. Once they lose their excessive body heat, they go back to the surface to resume their foraging.

Hopi chipmunks (*Eutamias rufus*) are commonly seen running about during the day across rocks and through vegetation. They are identified by their small, striped faces, although they are often confused with the antelope ground squirrel. Unlike the antelope ground squirrel, these chipmunks do not carry their tails over their backs while running. The Hopi chipmunk eats seeds of various plants as they become available, especially Indian ricegrass, juniper, pinyon, oaks, and cliffrose. They also eat fruits, berries, fungi, invertebrates, and small vertebrates; drink water; and are found nesting on rocky hillslopes where shallow depressions collect water after rainstorms.

The common packrat (woodrat) species in Cataract Canyon include the white-throated, desert, bushy-tailed, and Mexican packrat.[48] White-throated packrats are closely associated with pricklypear cactus. They both eat and build their nests around the cacti, using the spines for protection. Bushy-tailed packrats are the most sedentary of the packrats, as they use the same rocky-crevice sites year after year. Bushy-tailed packrats are not as good as other packrat species at bringing home goodies they have discovered, as they will often drop an object they are carrying if they come across something more interesting on the way. The desert packrat likes to build its nest in rocks and in juniper trees. The Mexican packrat, while not particular about where it builds its nest, prefers to eat foliage over other plant parts.

Rabbits. Although mice and rodents are the most numerous mammals in the region, rabbits are the most commonly seen.[49] Rabbits generally are nocturnal and *crepuscular* (active evening and mornings); however, on cool days they will be active as well. They do not need to drink water as they obtain adequate moisture from the plants they eat. Rabbits excrete two kinds of feces: one is soft, and is often immediately reingested for further digestion and more efficient extraction of nutrients; the other type is hard and is not eaten. Though this sounds sort of disgusting, many (if not most) animals eat feces. The process of digestion is fairly inefficient, and feces contain many nutrients yet to be mined by the consuming animal; we humans are the exception in not taking advantage of this easy source of nutrition!

Desert cottontails (*Sylvilagus audubonii*), like mice, seem to be eaten by everything. They have only a few effective defenses: good eyesight, good hearing, and speedy legs. However, they are seldom a match for their pursuers, and when approached they often leave their hiding places, making them easy prey for their faster-moving predators. They make up for this high mortality with a tremendous reproductive rate. They are capable of breeding at three months of age and can have multiple litters in a year. The nest is shallow and lined with grass and fur. The mothers leave the nest for the entire day, covering the babies with additional grass and fur and returning to nurse only a few times at night. The young stay at the nest for a mere two weeks before venturing forth into the world.

Cottontails are small animals, weighing about two pounds. They prefer thick, brushy habitat with lots of hiding places. The ears of desert cottontails are larger than nondesert species, and are used both for better hearing and as a way to dump excess body heat. Unlike most cottontails, the desert species seldom spend the hot part of the day in shallow depressions but will more commonly climb sloping trees or hide in the burrows of other animals. Desert cottontails will eat almost anything that is green, although they prefer grass and cactus. They are not wanderers and are most often found within 400 yards of home.

Black-tailed jack rabbits (*Lepus californicus*) are also common in this region. They are much larger than cottontails and can weigh up to ten pounds. They are not actually rabbits but are hares, and their young are born with lots of fur and open eyes. Jacks depend on speed, zigzagging, and leaping to escape predation. They run up to thirty-five miles per hour and can leap twenty feet high. They are most active in late afternoon and at night, foraging on a wide variety of plants. Open vegetation is preferred, where predators are visible and where there is minimum vegetation to dodge; thus, populations of jackrabbits will increase in areas where intense livestock grazing reduces vegetation cover.

You can tell what plants a jack rabbit has been eating: they leave a very clean cut line, like a knife might make. Cottontails leave a rough, nibbled edge, and twigs eaten by deer look pinched off. Jackrabbits can go several miles a day for food but return home to their burrow every night. Like cottontails, they seldom drink water. When very thirsty, cottontails, packrats, and jacks can be seen clipping off stems of perennials shrubs like yuccas and sucking plant juices from the cut edge.

Jackrabbits usually do not burrow to escape heat but instead rest in the shade of plants. However, if it is very hot they will dig a hole and climb into it. They have large, thin-skinned, highly vascular ears capable of eliminating up to one-third of their body heat. Excess body heat can also be reduced by panting through the nose. Jackrabbits breed throughout the year, incorporating elaborate courtships rituals that include leaps and dances. They are also very social animals, sometimes collecting in groups of twenty-five or more on moonlit nights just to socialize. Like cottontails, jackrabbits are a popular meal for coyotes, foxes, raptors, and large snakes.

Large Mammals. Larger mammals live in this region as well, although low amounts of food and water limit their numbers (see Chapter 4).[50] The Powell Expedition, hoping to supplement their diet with fresh meat, had a difficult time finding large game to shoot.[51] Large mammals here—except for the kit fox and badger—do not burrow; instead, they utilize their large body mass, reduced surface-to-volume ratio, and shade to keep cool. In addition, they are more mobile and can travel to water. They also utilize panting to cool down, which moves air over moist surfaces of the tongue, mouth, and throat and dissipates body heat.

Mule deer (*Odocoileus hemionus*) are widespread in this region, but are infrequently seen along the river corridor. The exception is Spanish Bottom, where deer are a fairly common sight in the early morning and at dusk. Unlike other North American deer, mule deer often *stott* (jump using all four feet at once) rather than run. The rut begins in fall, and one male may mate with several females. Gestation for the female is about 200 days. Fawns are born in the summer, and then stay with their mother for a year or so. If there are mountains nearby, mule deer will often migrate to higher elevations in the summers. Current deer populations are at much higher elevations than in the past. Development of water sources for livestock has increased the amount of range available for foraging, the conversion of grass-dominated rangeland to shrubs due to cattle grazing has increased their food supply, and reduction of predator populations has reduced mortality. Early journals of travelers throughout Utah reported that deer were scarce, and many parties traveling through this country stayed hungry as a result.

Desert bighorn sheep (*Ovis Canadensis nelsoni*) were hunted by the Ancestral Puebloans in the Canyonlands National Park area. They are often depicted in petroglyph and pictograph images on canyon walls. The Puebloans used the sheep for food and used the horns for utensils and sickles for cutting food plants. Uranium miners in the 1950s killed them for food and brought out their horns for trophies. Desert bighorn sheep are now protected, and their numbers are increasing yearly, so that a few once-in-a-lifetime hunting permts are now issued. Current estimates indicate that there are more than 3,000 desert bighorns in Utah.

Badgers (*Taxidea taxus*) are seldom seen, but their large burrows with mounds of dirt in front are common in the deep soils found between the Confluence and Spanish Bottom. Badgers are *mustelids* with musk glands, and are closely related to weasels and minks. They are flat-footed, which gives them a very comic gait, but these animals are so mean no one ever makes fun of them. When they live near humans, they are nocturnal; however, in more remote locations, such as in Cataract Canyon, they are active by day. Their favorite snacks are small mammals, especially ground squirrels, gophers, rats, and mice. Because most prey animals are sleeping in their burrows during the day, they are an easy catch for the incredibly effective and specialized dirt-digging badger.

Badgers have huge front claws, and a membrane that slides over their eyes so they can see while digging.[52] They have tiny ears that are full of fur to keep out dirt while tunneling. Upon discovering a burrow of their small and helpless prey, the dirt flies and the badger generally has a meal within a few minutes. Few animals will attack badgers, as they are fierce. They prefer living in places with deep, sandy, open soils where digging is good. They are solitary and have a large home range. They tend to use a different den every day, so places with badgers also have lots of holes. Many animals inhabit old badger burrows, and the badgers often go back to their old burrows to eat the new residents. They mate in July, but the females delay implantation of the babies until late winter. Two to five young are born in February, and stay with their mothers for about three months.

Coyotes (*Canis latrans*) are highly intelligent and adaptable animals, and are one of the few species to benefit from human settlements, in spite of concerted efforts by humans to kill them.[53] Coyotes live in many varied habitats that range from deserts to city margins. They have keen senses of hearing, vision, and smell. Coyotes are always wiry, weighing only fifteen to twenty-five pounds. Just about anything is a food item to the coyote: they feast regularly on carrion, cactus fruits, seeds, plants, rabbits, rodents, snakes, and insects. They will dig up burrows as well as chase prey down. Kit foxes are also eaten, as these two species compete for similar prey. If hungry, coyotes will also kill bighorns, deer, pronghorn, and domesticated animals, including your pets if they are left out at night. Coyotes can leap as high as fourteen feet, and run twenty-five to thirty miles per hour over long distances. Unlike wolves, coyotes run with their tails down.[54] Coyotes have been known to cover over 400 miles while in search of food or new territories.

Coyotes are social and live in small family groups, in dens centrally located in their hunting area. Like other canines, coyotes have scent glands in their paws. They mark their territories by scraping areas of soil and leaving scents from these glands, or with urine and scat. Young coyotes are born in April and May, with fewer pups born in years when prey numbers are low. They are very secretive about the location of their den sites and will move readily if they feel threatened. Some yearling pups will stay a full year with their parents and help with the next brood. Coyotes, like wolves, sing to communicate, to keep in touch, and apparently for fun. Yipping and barks are especially noticeable at dusk and dawn.

Wolves (*Canis lupus*) once roamed Canyon Country. George Bradley of the 1869 Powell Expedition said after being on the Green River for just over a month, "Now and then a wolf is seen, and after dark they make the air resound with their howling."[55] They are now extirpated from the Colorado Plateau; in 1939, Rusty Musselman trapped the last known wolf east of Monticello, Utah.[56] The last known wolf seen in Grand County was probably in the 1950s.

Bobcats (*Felis rufus*) are solitary, nocturnal, and secretive animals that live on cottontails, rodents, snakes, squirrels, porcupines, birds, bats, and, occasionally, deer. Bobcats are much more common than mountain lions, as they can utilize smaller prey and thus can live in more marginal habitats. Like mountain lions, they are mostly ambush killers who need to eat daily; unlike mountain lions, they seldom leave their kill. They are good climbers, but prefer to hunt on the ground. Bobcats weigh fifteen to twenty pounds, although their long legs often make them look larger. The young stay with mother from late spring until fall, at which point they leave to find their own territories. Bobcats range a few square miles, cover their scat, and retract their claws when walking.

Mountain lions (*Puma [Felis] concolor*) are solitary and strongly territorial animals, except when they are breeding. Males can be over six feet long and weigh about 145 lbs; females are much smaller, weighing about 75 lbs. Mountain lions are active in the day, foraging for deer, coyotes, bighorns, livestock, pronghorns, porcupines, squirrels, mice, raccoons, birds, and grasshoppers. They easily kill animals larger than themselves with their huge, powerful jaws which snap the neck or slash the jugular vein of their victim. Mountain lions have quite small hearts and lungs for their size and so are limited to chases of less than 300 ft. Consequently, they usually hunt by sneaking up and then forcefully leaping (up to 23 ft) onto the prey, knocking it down. After feeding, mountain lions hide the remaining food under leaves or soil, and will return each day to feed on it. Mountain lions need to kill every 6 to 10 days for sufficient nutrition, and they hide their kill and return for daily feedings. During the day and/or after feeding, mountain lions rest in thickets and on rocky outcrops. Mountain lions have home ranges of up to 25 mi^2, and male territories overlap those of several females. They have no set breeding season. When breeding, pairs will stay together for a few days. Once born, kittens remain with the mother for 18 months. Some siblings may stay even longer, helping raise the next few litters.

Upland Birds

Upland birds are also common along the rocky slopes between the Confluence and Spanish Bottom. Probably the most easily recognized (by sound) are the Canyon Wrens (*Catherpes mexicanus*) and Rock Wrens (*Salpinctes obsoletus*).[57] They are hard to see, being small, rather plain, and solitary, but they are heard frequently throughout the day. Canyon Wrens have the most distinctive call, starting at a high pitch and sliding downwards, like a waterfall of sound. Both wrens nest in rock crevices or rock piles. The males build several dummy nests of twigs, grasses, and leaves before the female chooses one. Rock Wrens often make a path of small stones leading to their nest—they may do this so they can easily relocate their nest in piles of similar-looking rock—and they sometimes line their nests with small rocks. Both these birds bounce about the rocks during the day, looking for spiders and insects to eat.

Black-billed Magpies (*Pica pica*) are very distinctive and common birds found only west of the Rocky Mountains. They have long black tails, white chest bands, black heads, white wing patches, and are conspicuously noisy. Magpies mate for life, and build a new nest every year. These nests are huge, being two to four feet tall with a roof, door, and floor. Once abandoned, many other birds use magpie nests. Magpies eat mostly insects, but will also eat carrion, other birds' eggs, and young animals.

Western Scrub Jays (*Aphelocoma coerulescens*) are also a common upland bird, preferring habitats domi-

Figure 6-7. The Junction Dam Site (mile 216.1) September 17, 1914. In the autumn of 1914, the U. S. Reclamation Service floated a barge with a drill rig to the Confluence. They drilled in the river to ascertain depth to bedrock as part of their evaluation of the Junction Dam Site, which was a quarter-mile downstream from the Confluence. Crews drilled to a depth of 124.5 feet, never reaching bedrock. During the drilling, USGS hydrologist Eugene C. LaRue took this photograph of the drilling barge. A flash flood caused an eight-foot rise in river level, and the accumulation of driftwood on the drill rig snapped the cables and broke the rods and casings and ended the drilling. The Reclamation Service eventually determined that this site was unsuitable for dam construction. Had this dam been built, the Moab Valley would have been flooded. The town of Green River, which is higher in elevation, was to be spared from flooding because of its importance to railroad commerce. (E.C. LaRue 50, courtesy of the U.S. Geological Survey Photographic Library, Stake 3573)

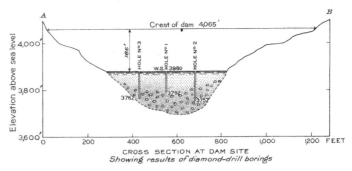

Figure 6-8. Schematic Diagram Showing the Deposits beneath the Colorado River and Exposed in the Holes Drilled in 1914 Downstream from the Confluence.

nated by shrubs and scattered pinyon-juniper trees. They eat a variety of foods that include bird eggs, young birds, spiders, scorpions, nuts, acorns, and ticks from the backs of deer. Both Western Scrub and Pinyon Jays are noisy, but Western Scrub Jays tend to be solitary, whereas Pinyon Jays often travel in large groups. Western Scrub Jays have a very distinctive, undulating flight pattern. These birds appear blue in color, with a grayish-white bib under their throat. Interestingly, only a few birds, such as parrots, have feathers that are truly blue. None of the birds on the Colorado Plateau have blue feathers; those that look blue are actually grey. Only when sunlight hits the feathers in a certain way do you see blue, which is why the color of these birds appears to change as they fly by you.

Hummingbirds are also a frequent summer sight. In the Canyonlands region, Black-chinned (*Archilochus alexandri*), Rufous (*Selasphorus rufus*) and Broad-tailed (*Selasphorus platycercus*) Hum-

mingbirds are most common.[58] In all these species, the females build the nests of grass and leaves, using spider webs for strength. The nests are camouflaged by adding leaves, sticks, moss, lichens, and plants to the outer edge. The insides are lined with hair and feathers. Hummingbirds are all highly territorial and are promiscuous breeders. Females may mate with more than one male, and males almost always mate with more than one female. The tiny eggs incubate for two weeks; after hatching, the young are fed a mixture of nectar and insects and fledge in three weeks.

Rufous Hummingbirds do not spend much time on the Colorado Plateau, as they breed in the northwest United States and Canada and winter in Mexico, a 2,000-mile trip. Their time in Canyon Country is limited to passing through twice a year. They are very aggressive birds, and will take over feeders and flowers from Black-chinned and Broad-tailed Hummingbirds. Rufous Hummingbirds, as their name implies, are bright orange and have a distinctive low chip, chip, chip call. These hummingbirds (as well as Anna's and Allen's) often carry hummingbird flower mites on their bills. Flower mites are tiny arachnids that live within flowers and need to move when the flower dies. The mites crawl onto the hummingbird's bill while it is feeding and enter its nostrils for the trip to the next flower, where they get off and stay until that flower begins to die.

Black-chinned Hummingbirds are seen for the longest span of the year in the Canyonlands region, as they nest here. These birds eat plant nectar and a lot of small flying insects, including gnats, and consume

Figure 6-9. Biological Soil Crusts Downstream from Lower Red Lake Canyon (mile 214.3)

A. May 31, 1889. In this downstream view at Rapid 1, a crew member of the Brown-Stanton Expedition holds a survey rod marked in one-foot increments. He is sitting on a flank of the evaporite diapir at Lower Red Lake Canyon covered with gypsic soils. Biological crusts thrive on gypsic soils, and the flats in the foreground and midground are black with the dense crusts. (F.A. Nims 39, courtesy of the National Archives)

nectar. During courtship, the males fly up to one hundred feet into the air and then drop suddenly in a characteristic pendulum-shaped dive that is accompanied by a whirring sound. In addition, males and females both fan and pump their tails rapidly while hovering.

Broad-tailed Hummingbirds are medium-sized and prefer pinyon and juniper trees. Very territorial, they can often be seen surveying their kingdoms from high perches. Broad-tailed Hummingbirds nest beneath branches or clumps of leaves, and feed on penstemon, yucca, gooseberry, ants, aphids, and other small insects. Their courtship flight is similar to that of the Black-chinned Hummingbird, except that the dive is U-shaped and they hover before diving. They have a high pitched chirp, but the most diagnostic characteristic of this species is the loud metallic humming noise of their wings during normal flight and hovering. Black-chinned Hummingbirds will occasionally hybridize with Broad-tailed Hummingbirds.

THE DEEPEST PART OF CATARACT CANYON

At Spanish Bottom, river trips are treated to the spectacle of weird, colorful pinnacles lining the rim downstream. From either the top of the Doll House Trail, with its panoramic views upstream and downstream, or from the river, staring up at the imposing cliffs, the logical question is: Is this the deepest place in the canyon? Well, that depends on how you define "deep" and what you call the river bottom.

River guides are often plagued with "how much" questions like "How much does the river flow?" The answers are often pat ones, but sometimes a trick answer might offer itself. To the question "Where is the deepest point in Cataract Canyon?" there are actually three answers. One is a point downstream near Palmer Canyon, where the walls tower 2,000 feet above the reservoir.[59] A more perceptive guide might answer that the river is deepest below Rapid 12, where water depth has occasionally been measured at more than ninety feet. But few know our trick answer, which is that the fill of rock and sediment under Spanish Bottom is at

B. March 28, 1994. Many trails are apparent through the soil crusts on this flat. No trails are visible in 1889, indicating that the modern trails are a result of people, not animals. Destruction of ancient soil crusts is harmful to the ecosystem in Cataract Canyon. To protect this resource, hikers must stay on trails. Much of the native riparian vegetation has been replaced by tamarisk along the river corridor. The tamarisk trees are taller than native willow, and the tamarisk now blocks the view of most of the river. In the foreground are seepweed plants that appear persistent. The midground is dominated by shadscale and Mormon tea, and two new pricklypear are present. (Steve Tharnstrom, Stake 2790)

least 125 feet thick; and probably thicker in the area overlying the bedrock down there somewhere.

Spanish Bottom is similar to the bottomlands upstream, and it is the last bottomland on the Colorado River along its historic course until just upstream from Needles, California. The fact that it is just upstream from Rapid 1 is no coincidence. The gradient of the river changes from 1.41 feet per mile from the Confluence to Rapid 1 to an astonishing 13.6 feet per mile from Rapid 1 to Tilted Park. If it feels somewhat like going over the spillway of a dam, you are right. Taking this further, Spanish Bottom is sort of like the deposition that would occur just upstream of the dam in a silted-in reservoir. Many feet of fine-grained sediment, typical of what the Colorado River transports in suspension, overlie coarse talus and bedrock.

In August 1914, a crew from the U.S. Reclamation Service, the predecessor of the Bureau of Reclamation, boated downstream with supplies from Green River, Utah, to where the last dirt access road met the Green River near the mouth of the San Rafael River. At this location, other crew members had finished building a

big, wooden, box-like floating platform with a steam-powered drill rig mounted at its center. The entourage then continued downstream with the drilling platform to its destination, the Confluence. Tom Wimmer and Harry T. Yokey piloted the supply boats. The entire party was impressed with the Confluence as a proposed dam site, because a dam built at that location would flood two canyons and double the total storage. Had this dam been built, the town of Moab would have been flooded. The hydraulic engineer for the project, Eugene C. LaRue, recommended that the townspeople of Moab relocate into the Mill Creek drainage. He also recommended that the height of the dam not exceed the elevation of Green River, Utah, so as to preserve the existing railroad.[60]

Anchoring the scow-like platform a quarter mile downstream from the Confluence, the party drilled four holes into the bed of the river (Figure 6-7). In their report, they stated:

On August 29 [1914] the first hole had reached a depth of 90 feet, encountering nothing but river sand...on September 16 [in hole No. 2] a depth of 124.5 feet had been reached, 50 feet of which was river sand and the remainder sand and sandstone boulders. On September 30 hole No. 3, about 325 feet downstream, had reached a depth of 120 feet in boulders and sand...On October 3 [in hole No. 4] rock, probably a boulder, was encountered at 101.5 feet depth.[61]

The bed of the river was sand or a mixture of sand and boulders, with no bedrock encountered for at least 125 feet (Figure 6-8). The boulders they encountered were red, suggesting that they had fallen into the river from the canyon heights. Disappointed, the crew concluded that this site was not suitable for a dam.

In the vicinity of the Confluence, talus cones missing from the walls upstream mantle the lower slopes of the canyon walls. With the exception of The Slide, about a mile and a half upstream, only small debris flows occur above Cataract Canyon. Downstream within the Canyon and beginning at Rapid 1, debris flows become frequent, issuing from nearly all tributaries, gullies, and steep chutes. The sand beneath the bed of the river is evidence of what these debris flows have done—the sand is stored behind the only dam in Cataract Canyon: a natural low-head dam created by debris flows dropping boulders into the Colorado River, constricting the passage of water and backing it up to the Confluence.

RAPIDS AHEAD!

For all who stop and hike at Spanish Bottom, invariably the time comes to pack up the gear and go downstream. Hikers must be gathered from the innumerable hiking trails in the region; hopefully those hikers have stayed on the trail and not strayed into the biological soil crusts that are so ubiquitous here (Figure 6-9). Life jackets are required for downstream travel from the Confluence; now it is time to cinch down all the straps.

When the boats are finally shoved off from the banks, some river runners will go a short distance—the beach below Rapid 1 is one of the most enticing campsites in all of Cataract Canyon—while others

may experience most or all of the whitewater that remains upstream of Lake Powell. It is just a short distance downstream to the main attraction: the whitewater of Cataract Canyon. After a hot, dusty hike to the inscriptions, a lunch under the tamarisks, or a long hike to the Doll House, most people are eager to move downstream, either to the more-inviting camps or the splash-cooling rapids of Cataract Canyon. To some, the history of the Confluence and Spanish Bottom—as well as their significance as major geographic features in the Colorado River drainage—lingers long after the trip is over.

Notes

1. John Cooley, *The Great Unknown* (Flagstaff: Northland Publishing, 1988), 116.

2. Lloyd Holyoak, the first river ranger in Canyonlands National Park, remembers seeing a Denis Julien inscription at the Confluence in the 1960s. He has since returned repeatedly and cannot relocate the inscription. Lloyd Holyoak, interview, June 2002.

3. P.T. Reilly, "How Deadly is Big Red?" *Utah Historical Quarterly* 37 (1969): 252.

4. National Park Service Incident Report Number 937010; see *www.nps.gov/cany/river/reports.htm*.

5. National Park Service Incident Report Number 820165; see *www.nps.gov/cany/river/reports.htm*.

6. R.N. Mack and J.N. Thompson, "Evolution in Steppe with Few Large, Hooved Mammals," *The American Naturalist* 119 (1982): 757–773.

7. *Ibid.*; G.L. Stebbins, "Coevolution of Grasses and Herbivores," *Annals of the Missouri Botanical Garden* 68 (1981): 75–86.

8. Mack and Thompson, "Evolution in Steppe;" Stebbins, "Coevolution of Grasses and Herbivores."

9. D.D. Walker, "The Cattle Industry of Utah, 1850–1900: An Historical Profile," *Utah Historical Quarterly* 32 (1964): 182–197.

10. F.M. Tanner, *The Far Country: A Regional History of Moab and La Sal, Utah* (Salt Lake City: Olympus Press, 1976).

11. Maxine Newell, "Modern History of Canyonlands," *Naturalist* 21 (1970): 40–47; R.A. Firmage, *A History of Grand County* (Salt Lake City: Utah State Historical Society, 1996), 103–104. George and Silas Green may have arrived in Moab with cattle before Taylor, but the facts are in dispute.

12. Walker, "The Cattle Industry of Utah," 189–191.

13. V.N. Price and J.T. Darby, "Preston Nutter: Utah Cattleman, 1886–1936," *Utah Historical Quarterly* 32 (1964): 232–252.

14. Walker, "The Cattle Industry of Utah," 189.

15. Firmage, *A History of Grand County*, 174–175.

16. Scheire, *Cattle Raising in the Canyons*, 24.

17. R.F. Negri, ed., *Tales of Canyonlands Cowboys* (Logan: Utah State University Press, 1997).

18. D.L. Donaghue, *The Western Range Revisited* (Norman: University of Oklahoma Press, 1999).

19. Another fire, which affected a smaller area, burned across from Spanish Bottom in 2002.

20. S.G. Whisenant, "Changing Fire Frequencies on Idaho's Snake River Plains: Ecological and Management Implications," in *Proceedings: Symposium on Cheatgrass Invasion, Shrub Die-off, and Other Aspects of Shrub Biology and Management,* eds. E.D. McArthur, E.M. Romney, S.D. Smith, and P.T. Tueller (Washington, D.C.: U.S. Department of Agriculture, Report GTR-INT-276, 1990), 4–10.

21. David Lavender, *Colorado River Country* (Albuquerque: University of New Mexico Press, 1988).

22. C.G. Crampton and S.K. Madsen, *In Search of the Spanish Trail: Santa Fe to Los Angeles, 1829–1848* (Layton, Utah: Gibbs Smith, 1994).

23. C.G. Crampton, *Standing Up Country: The Canyon Lands of Utah and Arizona* (New York: Alfred A. Knopf, 1965), 48.

24. Interview, Kent Frost, Monticello, Utah, May 2000; Benjamin Silliman, quoted in R.S. McPherson, *A History of San Juan County: In the Palm of Time* (Salt Lake City: Utah State Historical Society, 1995), 79 and note 18.

25. F.S. Dellenbaugh, *A Canyon Voyage: The Narrative of the Second Powell Expedition* (New York: Putnam, 1908), 118.

26. Pearl Baker, *The Wild Bunch at Robbers Roost* (Lincoln: University of Nebraska Press, 1989).

27. McPherson, *A History of San Juan County*, 79.

28. McPherson, *A History of San Juan County*, 326.

29. Floyd Werner and Carl Olson, *Learning About & Living With Insects of the Southwest* (Tucson, Arizona: Fisher Books, 1994), 127–128; David Williams, *A Naturalist's Guide to Canyon Country* (Helena, Montana: Falcon Press/Canyonlands Natural History Association, 2000), 171.

30. J.L. Cloudsley-Thompson, *Ecophysiology of Desert Arthropods and Reptiles* (Berlin: Springer-Verlag, 1991), 25–140; Sowell, *Desert Ecology*, 84.

31. R.M. Lanner, *The Piñon Pine: A Natural and Cultural History* (Reno: University of Nevada Press, 1981), 1–11.

32. Lanner, *The Piñon Pine*, 174.

33. *Ibid.*, 35–44.

34. Heinrich, *The Trees in My Forest*, 26–28.

35. Lanner, *The Piñon Pine*, 45–55.

36. H.E. Gregory, *The San Juan Country* (Washington, DC: U.S. Geological Survey Professional Paper 188, Government Printing Office, 1938), 27.

37. National Park Service records, Canyonlands National Park, Moab, Utah, 2002. These records are continually updated, and supercede those published in Charlie Schelz, comp., "Species Numbers for Vertebrates," *The Confluence* 7 (2000): cover.

38. Cloudsley-Thompson, *Ecophysiology of Desert Arthropods and Reptiles*, 154–155.

39. David Williams, *A Naturalist's Guide to Canyon Country* (Helena, Montana: Falcon Press/Canyonlands Natural History Association, 2000), 143.

40. Sowell, *Desert Ecology*, 110–112; Williams, *A Naturalist's Guide to Canyon Country*, 149; R.B. Huey, E.R. Pianka, and T.W. Schoener, *Lizard Ecology* (Cambridge: Harvard University Press, 1983), 205–231.

41. Huey *et al.*, *Lizard Ecology,* 149–168.

42. Williams, *A Naturalist's Guide to Canyon Country,* 151–155.

43. National Park Service species lists, Canyonlands National Park, Moab, Utah, 2002. These records are continually updated and supercede those published in Charlie Schelz, comp., "Species Numbers for Vertebrates," *The Confluence* 7 (2000): cover.

44. Williams, *A Naturalist's Guide to Canyon Country,* 82–105; David Armstrong, *Mammals of Canyonlands* (Moab, Utah: Canyonlands Natural History Association, 1982).

45. Armstrong, *Mammals of Canyonlands*, 80; Williams, *A Naturalist's Guide to Canyon Country*, 82–105.

46. Armstrong, *Mammals of the Canyon Country*, 124–133; Williams, *A Naturalist's Guide to Canyon Country*, 82–105.

47. Sowell, *Desert Ecology*, 85–87.

48. T.A. Vaughan, "Ecology of Living Packrats," in *Packrat Middens*, 14–27; Williams, *A Naturalist's Guide to Canyon Country*, 92–93.

49. Pinau Merlin, "Rabbits and Hares," in *A Natural History of the Sonoran Desert*, eds. S.J. Phillips and P.W. Comus (Tucson: Arizona-Sonora Desert Museum/University of California Press, 2000), 493–495.

50. Schmidt-Nielsen, *Scaling*; Schmidt-Nielsen, *Animal Physiology*; Armstrong, *Mammals of the Canyon Country*; and Williams, *A Naturalist's Guide to Canyon Country*, 82–105.

51. John Wesley Powell, *The Exploration of the Colorado River and Its Tributaries* (New York: Dover Publications, 1961).

52. Pinau Merlin and Peter Siminski, "Mustelids," in *A Natural History of the Sonoran Desert*, 480–482.

53. S.P. Young and H.H.T. Jackson, *The Clever Coyote* (Lincoln: University of Nebraska Press, 1978); Pinau Merlin and Peter Siminski, "Coyote and Fox," in *A Natural History of the Sonoran Desert*, 473–475.

54. Young and Jackson, *The Clever Coyote*; Susan Tweit, *The Great Southwest Nature Fact Book* (Seattle: Alaska Northwest Books, 1994), 31–32.

55. John Cooley, *The Great Unknown* (Flagstaff, Arizona: Northland Publishing, 1988), 80.

56. A.C. Cashin and Janet Wilcox, "The Phantom Wolf of Westwater and Other Wolflore of San Juan County," *Blue Mountain Shadows* 5 (Blanding, Utah: Journal of the San Juan Historical Commission, 1989), 13.

57. F.A. Ryser Jr., *Birds of the Great Basin: a Natural History* (Reno: University of Nevada Press, 1985), 363–365, 378–386, 411–412; Williams, *A Naturalist's Guide to Canyon Country*, 107–132.

58. Williams, *A Naturalist's Guide to Canyon Country*, 111–112; Fleischner, *Singing Stone*, 47–50.

59. F.E. Mutschler, *River Runners' Guide to Canyonlands National Park and Vicinity, with Emphasis on Geologic Features* (Denver: Powell Society, 1977), 64.

60. E.C. LaRue, *Water Power and Flood Control of Colorado River below Green River, Utah* (Washington, DC: Water Supply Paper 556, Government Printing Office, 1925), 48.

61. U.S. Reclamation Service, *Fifteenth Annual Report* (Washington, DC: U.S. Government Printing Office, 1916), 515. Quoted in LaRue, *Water Power and Flood Control*, 49.

7

SLIDING SLOPES AND RUNNING RAPIDS

The First Ten Rapids and Tilted Park

On starting, we come at once to difficult rapids and falls, in many places they are more abrupt than in any of the canyons through which we have passed, and we decide to name this Cataract Canyon.[1] . . . While we are eating supper, we very naturally speak of better fare, as musty bread and spoiled bacon are not palatable. Soon I see Hawkins down by the boat, taking up the sextant—rather a strange proceeding for him—and I question him concerning it. He replies that he is trying to find the latitude and longitude of the nearest pie.[2]
— John Wesley Powell, 1869

It usually takes time for boats going downstream to leave Spanish Bottom, particularly if the water is high. Loads are checked, and extra straps added, just in case, just in case. Oar locks are tested, and motors are warmed up and gunned, just to be sure that they will not quit at the head of one of the rapids downstream. No gear is allowed to ride in the boat without being attached, usually to the frame; these boats are "rigged to flip." When all the fiddling with straps has ceased, and all fidgeting has ended, the boats head down to the next bend. An ominous sound wafts over the water, and a horizon line appears in the river. The rapids of Cataract Canyon are ahead, and the white-water comes quickly and furiously (Figure 7-1). Check your lifejacket once more and get a firm handhold because it is time to run rapids.

Downstream from Spanish Bottom everything changes, and the origin of the change lies in those colorful walls that tower above the river. A new formation—the Halgaito Shale—comes into view quickly around the corner, and its effects on the canyon are striking. The reddish-looking slope, which geologists consider too thin and variable to be declared a unique formation at Spanish Bottom, is part of the reason why Cataract Canyon exists. The canyon changes form immediately. The walls are broken and covered with talus, unlike the nearly solid bedrock that appears along the approaches. Unlike upstream, distinct beaches appear, offering a change to those tired of crashing through the thick brush looking for a flat place to sleep. The biology changes as well: gone are the omnipresent tamarisk thickets seen upstream, replaced by scattered tamarisk and another tree—netleaf hackberry—that was not as apparent upstream. Life in the river is different also, with one endangered fish replacing another and each fighting for dear life against competition with a number of non-native fishes.

SOUND

As you leave Spanish Bottom and drift towards the entrance to Cataract Canyon, take a minute to notice the sounds (or the lack thereof) around you. If you motored down to Spanish Bottom, the contrast is striking once the motors are turned off; if you floated to this point, you may have already noticed one of the most extraordinary features of this desert: the lack of sound. Listening carefully, you won't hear much other than an occasional peep from one of the inhabitants: a Canyon Wren's cascading song, a bullfrog bellowing like a stuck cow, a nighthawk's whooshing sounds in the evening, the not-quite-right call of a mockingbird or chat, the metallic zinging of a hummingbird, or the croak of a raven. It is so silent here that in fact, when the ambient sound level of the region was monitored,

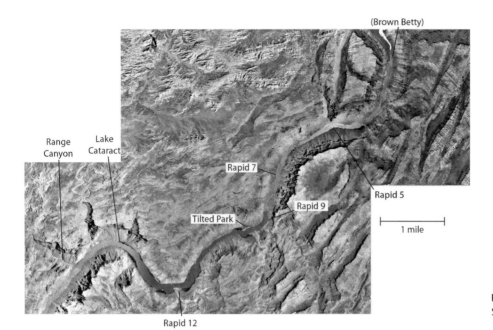

Range Canyon

Lake Cataract

Rapid 7

Tilted Park

Rapid 9

Rapid 5

(Brown Betty)

1 mile

Rapid 12

Figure 7-1. Map of the Colorado River between Spanish Bottom and Range Canyon.

it was found to be quieter than a recording studio.[3]

Quiet is a resource that is easily lost (*e.g.*, excessive aircraft overflights in Grand Canyon National Park). In Cataract Canyon, motors are the biggest threat to silence, whether they are attached to vehicles, boats, or planes. Although you may feel like you are in a remote place, there are many roads crisscrossing the land, providing vehicle access. Scenic tours by boats, helicopters, and airplanes are ever-increasing. Boats are regulated by the National Park Service, the Bureau of Land Management, and/or the State of Utah. Airspace, on the other hand, is controlled by the Federal Aviation Administration. There has been little response from this agency to the concerns of those landlocked souls who resent the intrusion of low-flying aircraft. Few places in our human world still offer the gift of silence. An intangible asset, the quiet is something you do not miss until it is gone, and even then, you often cannot figure out what you lost.

THE RAPIDS

Some Definitions

Water moving through rapids has a distinct terminology. The unfortunate thing is that some words mean different things to the river-running community. At the risk of starting an argument, here are some brief definitions of the terms we use to refer to water movement in Cataract Canyon. A *rapid* is a drop in the water surface that presents at least some obstacle to downstream navigation; a *riffle*, in contrast, has no significant obstacle. Both rapids and riffles typically have air-entrained surfaces, and are thereby defined as types of *whitewater*. *Eddies* are recirculation zones (see section on "Where to Camp") where water moves upstream in a circular fashion; *whirlpools* are essentially violent eddies with a significant downward vector of velocity. An *eddy fence* is the border between fast-moving downstream flow and a particularly strong eddy; these features are carefully scrutinized by river runners because they can flip boats, particularly small ones, unexpectedly.

There are many terms used to describe the hazards in rapids. Some of these enjoy a modicum of widespread usage. A *wave* is a water-surface rise that can come from any number or combination of features in a rapid; a *crashing wave* breaks upstream periodically. The *amplitude*, or height, of waves typically is measured from upstream trough to peak, and as a result wave height is not constant and may not be apparent from the banks. A *ledge wave* appears to fall over a bedrock ledge, but more commonly it crests over a squared-off boulder or group of boulders. *Lateral waves* are spawned from either the constriction that forms the rapid or by an obstacle, such as an emergent large boulder, on or near the bank. *Tailwaves* develop at the bottom of the rapid when fast-moving water interacts with slower-moving water in downstream pools and eddies. *Compressional waves* are somewhat of a misnomer (water is essentially incompressible in this setting), but this term is used to describe very large tailwaves.

Crashing waves become *holes* when they break upstream continuously. Similarly, *pourovers*, which form when water flows vertically over a rock, can become holes when the discharge rises. Some holes are the most dangerous features on the river because they have significant downward and upstream vectors of velocity. While *flushing holes* may flip boats, the flotsam is quickly released; *keeper holes* may trap boaters. In some cases, the only way out of a keeper hole is for trapped persons to get out of their lifejackets and trust their fates to the river. *Corkscrewing holes* are some of the most awesome, and potentially dangerous, features on the river because swimming boaters may be *recirculated* above and below water over a long, downstream trending line. Some terms that refer to flipped boats in holes are very colorful, including *Maytagging* and *window shading* (going around and round). A word of warning: inexperienced boaters should avoid interaction with all of the terms used in this paragraph.

First Impressions

Twelve numbered rapids comprise the first segment of Cataract Canyon. John Wesley Powell's expedition of 1869 was the first to describe these rapids. Each of Powell's men reacted differently to the whitewater of Cataract Canyon. George Bradley obviously enjoyed it, commenting,

> The tide mark indicates that the water is sometimes 15 to 20 ft. higher than now and there must be fun here when it is at that height.[4] . . . [The rapids] don't interest me much unless we can run them. That I like but portage don't agree with my constitution.[5]

Powell was more cautious:

> . . . but maybe we shall come to a fall in this canyon which we cannot pass, where the walls rise from the water's edge, so that we cannot land, and where the water is so swift that we cannot return. Such places have been found, except that the falls were not so great but that we could run them with safety. How will it be in the future? So they speculate over the serious probabilities in jesting mood.[6]

Sumner's reaction was negative: ". . . driftwood 30 ft. high on the rocks. God help the poor wretch that is caught in the cañon during high water."[7]

Powell and his crew never saw the high water that they imagined, but others eventually would. In 1889, Brown and Stanton experienced Cataract Canyon at around 40,000 ft³/s, and Clyde Eddy saw 54,200 ft³/s in 1927.[8] Bert Loper and Charles Russell were the first to see the really big stuff in 1914 when the river was probably flowing around 85,000 ft³/s (Chapter 2). Georgie Clark saw the canyon at 88,600 ft³/s in 1957,[9] and Linda Witkopf, Brian Coombs, Steve Bathemas, and John Williams, along with other local river runners, ran the river at a discharge of about 114,000 ft³/s in 1984.[10] Although each of these expeditions had their share of boat flips, no one drowned or was seriously injured. But close calls were common.

Dr. Elzada Clover and her graduate student, Lois Jotter, visited Canyon Country in 1938 to botanize in the canyons from Green River, Utah, to Hoover Dam.[11] The group, led by Norman Nevills with Don Harris as one of the boatmen, had a harrowing experience at the beginning of Cataract Canyon. The party landed to scout the first two rapids from the left shore, and, as the trip occurred during the snow melt in late June, the water was raging at about 59,000 ft³/s. As the party was scouting, they saw Harris's boat, the *Mexican Hat*, hurl through the rapids unmanned; the boat had floated free from its mooring and was grabbed by the swift current.

Shaken and embarrassed, Harris and Jotter jumped in one of the other boats—the *Wen*—and chased the *Mexican Hat*, finding it upright somewhere below Rapid 5. The chase was vintage whitewater adventure, considering the stage of water, and ended with

Figure 7-2. Persistent Driftwood above Rapid 4 (mile 210.8)

A. June 4, 1889. A couple days of progress were lost for the Brown-Stanton Expedition due to camera repairs and difficulties incurred while lining and portaging the boats. Surveying for the railroad bed continued on the left side of the Colorado River. Downstream, Stanton moved the survey to the right side of the Colorado River in Marble Canyon. The black triangular area in the upper right corner is the result of Nims's shading the lens from the sun. (F.A. Nims 77, courtesy of the National Archives)

Jotter spending a sleepless though exciting night in the boat. This incident showed that the rapids could be run, but Nevills became more conservative, ordering frequent linings. This unnecessary hard work, combined with Nevills insistence on over-dramatizing the danger of the rapids, ended his relationship with Harris. Clover and Jotter succeeded in collecting many plants and together published their results,[12] which are particularly valuable for their documentation of exotic plants along the river. Nevills only ran Cataract Canyon two more times, on a trip in 1940 that included Barry Goldwater (see Chapter 8) and in 1945.

Low Versus High Water

What makes Cataract Canyon so challenging—and what separates it from other dam-controlled whitewater such as the Grand Canyon—is the incredible difference in navigation between low and high water. Where pools are present at low water, massive waves stand, one after another, when the spring flood occurs. Where the river is pool–drop–pool–drop at low

water, it is one continual reach of raging whitewater when the discharge rises. This impressive seasonal change makes memorizing the runs through rapids quite difficult. It has also spawned numerous opinions about the quality of whitewater rafting at different water levels in Cataract Canyon.

At low water, the first ten rapids of Cataract Canyon are nothing special. Clean runs require the following: miss the hole in Rapid 1 (easy), avoid the rock at the head of Rapid 2 (easy), make a well-timed pull either right or extreme left in Rapid 5, assess whether the tailwaves in Rapid 7 will flip you or not and commit, and try to find enough water in Rapid 8 to float through it.

What is Cataract Canyon like in extremely high water? Sumner's observation still holds: the canyon can be very dangerous at water levels above 50,000 ft³/s and boats frequently flip.[13] At these levels, the tailwaves of Rapid 1 flow right into the wave train of Rapid 2 and the waves are at least ten to fifteen feet high. Some, such as Rapid 5, are washed out; however, the driftwood and eddies always seem to wreak

B. June 4, 1993. The flow on this day was 60,000 ft³/s. Based on Nims's photo, Jim Braggs of the National Park Service estimated the flow of 1889 at about 40,000 ft³/s. The driftwood lodged in the center front portion of this photo is still in place. Trees and shrubs in general have increased, including singleleaf ash, hackberry, Frémont barberry, and squawbush; persistent needle-and-thread grass, and Indian ricegrass are also noted. Cheatgrass and tamarisk are now present. According to tree-ring analysis, the prominent hackberry on river right (left center) sprouted in 1802. (R.H. Webb, Stake 3067)

some havoc. But the big concern is lower Rapid 7, which has the nickname "the North Sea." Here the wave train can be as high as a two-story house and boats have been known to fall back on themselves ("doing an *endo*") in the attempt to run this rapid. It may be of comfort to know that the waves can be avoided, but just try to keep the adrenaline level down while floating past them!

Rapid 1 (Brown Betty)

In 1889, the cooks for the Brown-Stanton Expedition cut loose their float of provisions to save themselves and their boat, the *Brown Betty*, from being swept into Rapid 1. Because of this incident, river historian Dock Marston decided that Rapid 1 should be called Brown Betty in the 1960s, and Les Jones used the name on his scroll map which was published in 1962. As it turned out, the *Brown Betty* survived the accident but then was destroyed downstream in Rapid 6. Like Capsize Rock in Rapid 15, which is not the rock that the Best Expedition capsized on (see Chapter 8),

the name of Brown Betty Rapid does not coincide with where the boat sank, but in this case, where she was first imperiled.

Besides the misapplied name, there is another reason to be interested in this little rapid: Rapid 1 is the beginning of the longest sustained drop in the profile of the Colorado River downstream from Grand Junction. Upstream from this point, debris flows—if they occur at all—are small and do not significantly affect the channel. Downstream from this point, all the way to Dark Canyon, debris flows dump significant amounts of rock into the river, creating all those wonderful rapids.

Few river trips other than the Brown-Stanton Expedition have had problems in Brown Betty Rapid. Most of the early expeditions seemed to run the rapid after scouting. Despite the fact that a debris flow has entered the upper right side of the rapid, little appears to have changed in the rapid's hydraulics. A small, thrashing hole that appears at right center at 5,000 to 10,000 ft³/s is obvious in several early photographs, and a few rocks have been moved from the river banks.

Figure 7-3. The Toe of a Debris Flow at Rapid 5 (mile 210.7)

A. October 26, 1911. One of the Kolb brothers—probably Ellsworth—took this view on the left side of the Colorado River looking downstream. The other brother—probably Emery—appears in the view taking movies of the rapid. Rapid 5 occurs because debris flows come from an unnamed canyon on the right at the top of the rapid. The most recent debris flow from this canyon occurred about 500 years ago. At left center, a high bank of poorly sorted and unconsolidated sediments is the remnant of a much larger debris flow that came from river left. Holocene debris-flow deposition totally blocked the Colorado River here, and the river's overflow went across the bench on the right side until the debris-flow dam was eventually breached. Netleaf hackberry trees now grow under this remnant at about the 100,000 ft^3/s stage of the Colorado River. (Kolb 5745, courtesy of the Cline Library, Northern Arizona University)

B. March 29, 1994. Although Rapid 5 is unchanged, the amount of sand on the beach on the right has increased. This increase is typical for the big camping beaches in Cataract Canyon. Tamarisk and native willows have established themselves on both the left and right sides of the channel in eddy settings. Under the remnants of the old debris fan, netleaf hackberry trees are persistent. Many of these trees were cored to develop a tree-ring chronology of Colorado River flows (Salzer *et al.*, 1998). (Steve Tharnstrom, Stake 2913)

Rapids 2 through 4

Broad coalescing debris fans spread away from small tributaries on the left side of both Rapids 1 and 2. As remnants of past debris-flow activity, the toes of these fans are truncated, leaving a thirty- to forty-foot escarpment along the Colorado River. Although the left debris fans appear to set the gradient through these rapids, the debris fans coming from river right actually determine the locations of these rapids.

Rapid 2 begins at a constriction from a tributary on river right. This tributary had a debris flow in 1997 that left a prominent red stripe down the long slope leading from the cliffs but did not cause a significant change in the river. Rocks at the head and in the middle of Rapid 2 create a series of holes and waves, which are fun or are easily missed if desired. Rapid 2

flows into the largest pool on the river in Cataract Canyon. This pool is somewhat asymmetrical; the eddy on river left is much larger than the one on river right, in part because of the slight right-hand turn that leads into Rapid 3. On the left side, an ancient landslide deposit has been exposed along the upper part of the eddy. The presence of an eddy at the toe of a landslide deposit reinforces the fact that the current whitewater is associated with debris flows and debris fans, not other mass-wasting features.

The pool at the bottom of Rapid 2 leads to Rapid 3, which forms mostly because of the interaction of an island at the left center of the channel and a debris fan coming from river right. The tributary that feeds into this debris fan has had a debris flow in the last century, but the material deposited in the river has not changed this small rapid significantly. Larger debris

Figure 7-4. Rapid 6, Cataract's Disaster Falls (mile 209.8)

A. October 17, 1909. In the fall of 1909, Julius F. Stone took a pleasure trip with Nathaniel Galloway, Charles C. Sharp, Seymour S. Dubendorff, and Raymond A. Cogswell. Cogswell, the trip photographer, captured this view of the rapid while the others lined boats and portaged baggage. This is possibly the place where the *Emma Dean* capsized on the Powell Expedition in July 1869. This is also where the *Brown Betty* was destroyed during the Brown-Stanton Expedition of 1889. (R.A. Cogswell 486, courtesy of the Bancroft Library, University of California)

B. March 31, 1998. Rapid 6 is unchanged, despite the fact that most of the boulders in the left foreground are new. There is only one tamarisk tree in this view, as tamarisk are not prevalent in whitewater sections of Cataract Canyon. (Dominic Oldershaw, Stake 3603)

flows have occurred across the river and upstream of the rapid, but this debris fan impinges on the eddy, not whitewater. The island is overtopped at around 40,000 ft³/s, and it is possible to run the left channel around the island at about this level; below 10,000 ft³/s, a backwater that likely is significant to native fishes forms in its downstream end. Large boulders have rolled from the sides of the island in the last century, making the specifics of its surface unrecognizable in the repeat photographs.

Like Rapid 3, Rapid 4 results from flow around an island. This island is much lower than the one at Rapid 3 and is overtopped at flows of about 20,000 ft³/s or higher. The initial part of Rapid 4 does not have significant whitewater, although some larger waves develop in the lower part of the rapid. In very high water, Rapid 4 has explosion waves that occur for no apparent reason; instead, they are random and appear unpredictably. Driftwood is trapped on river left below the rapid, some of it for more than a hundred years (Figure 7-2). Although tributaries feed into the left side of Rapid 4, no debris flows have occurred here in the last century, and the whitewater results from material washed from the larger rapids upstream.

Rapid 5

Rapid 5 is merely a swift-water reach at discharges about 30,000 ft³/s. At this level, the main reason river runners know of its existence is that a reliable high-water beach occurs just downstream on river right. At low water, Rapid 5 presents the most significant navigational hazard upstream from Mile Long Rapid. A large, boat-flipping hole on river left must be avoided, either to the right by cutting right around a guard rock, or, more rarely, to the extreme left. The left run is more difficult because a large rock downstream from the hole can either cushion a raft or catch it, depending on water level. There is a right run splitting the difference between two pourovers when the river is low.

Our repeat photography shows that Rapid 5 has not changed since the photos were taken (Figure 7-3), or even longer, if some wood caught in boulders on the debris fan high above the highest water level of the river is a reliable indication. These fine twigs of native plants were transported in the last debris flow to come down the canyon here and are dated at 545 years before present.[14] This tributary, whose debris fan forms Rapid 5, is similar to other larger tributaries in Cataract

Figure 7-5. Toreva Blocks and the North Sea (mile 209.5)

A. September 17, 1921. The 1921 U.S. Geological Survey Expedition paused in the middle of Rapid 7 to take this photograph. Eugene C. LaRue used a panoramic camera to capture the tilted walls in this part of Cataract Canyon. This view is the left half of his panoramic photo. These tilted sections of bedrock are called Toreva blocks, and they result from rotation of the bedrock mass on the underlying Paradox Formation. (E.C. LaRue 82, courtesy of the U.S. Geological Survey Photographic Library)

Canyon, none of which have had historical debris flows.

Rapid 6

Rapid 6 might be renamed "Disaster Falls," since Powell's expedition (in 1869) flipped a boat and the Brown-Stanton party (in 1889) destroyed a boat here. The rapid is rather straight-forward, if one cedes to the large rocks on river right. Most river runners find these rocks easy to avoid. The rapid is created by a constriction originating from a tributary on river left. This tributary may have pushed those large boulders over to river right, but there are also plenty of other sources for boulders in this part of Cataract Canyon. The tributary has not had a debris flow in the last century (Figure 7-4).

Rapids 7 and 8

Below Rapid 6, views of the giant Toreva block at Tilted Park attain prominence (Figure 7-5). It grows to dominate the downstream view as you row to miss the waves (or go *for* the waves) in Rapid 7. At discharges above 50,000 ft³/s, Rapid 7 forms what is called the "North Sea," a series of symmetrical waves that achieve astounding proportions. In 1993, at 70,000 ft³/s, we counted eleven waves in the wave train, and the largest had trough-to-crest heights exceeding twenty feet. We would know, because we were in a twenty-two-foot motor snout that climbed and climbed and climbed from trough to crest as we passed through the North Sea. Boats this size have been known to flip on these waves, especially if a wave crashes upstream onto the boat at an unfortunate time or literally throws it end-over-end. Rapid 8 is washed out at high water, providing a little respite.

At low water, the nature of these rapids is better revealed. Rapid 7 appears to be a combination of outwash from Rapid 6 upstream and debris flows from river left. Like Rapid 3 upstream, Rapid 8 appears to be mostly a debris bar consisting of a combination of upstream outwash and debris flows entering from a tributary on river left. The two rapids are separated by a large pool at low water. A series of reddish terraces on river right suggests that the Colorado has relatively recently (in a geological sense) been at a higher level here. Both tributaries on the left at Rapids 7 and 8 have had debris flows in the last century. Sev-

B. July 23, 1992. Fourteen Mormon tea plants are still present in the left foreground. Multiple Indian ricegrass, galleta and muhly grass plants persist as well. In the foreground, the hackberry tree present in 1921 has increased in size and new trees have grown up at this site. The sandbar at lower right is still present, but changes in the constriction upstream have decreased the size of the eddy, thereby decreasing the size of the sandbar. Across the river, willows can be seen among the boulders. (Steve Tharnstrom, Stake 2629a)

eral small chutes from river left between these rapids have also had recent debris flows.

The North Sea illustrates one type of rapid that occurs at high water in Cataract Canyon. Rapids here form when water flows over piles of boulders. Most waves or hydraulic features result from water flowing through a constriction (*e.g.*, lateral waves), over a single boulder (*e.g.*, the hole in Rapid 5), or through a gap in a line of boulders (*e.g.*, the entrance to Rapid 2). Other waves result from combinations of these factors as well as changes in channel direction. At low water, the largest hazard in Rapid 7 results from laterals that build and converge owing to the combination of a constriction and a turn towards the right at the bottom of the rapid. The largest hazard at low water in Rapid 8 is getting stranded on a boulder in the wide, shallow rapid, so the run is to the far right.

At high water, the river stage greatly exceeds the sizes of these boulders, and flow and hydraulic features respond to overall changes in gradient and constriction. The low water parts of Rapids 6 and 7 essentially disappear, and the North Sea forms across what is a large pool at low water. The towering waves are best described as compressional waves since they result from fast water moving through a constriction

and hitting the slower water of the pool. Lateral waves form from both sides of the channel and converge in the center, forming pyramid-shaped waves. These waves build as they interact with the slower water recirculating in the eddies on both sides of the river. Much like water flowing into a bathtub, or the plunge pool beneath a waterfall, the energy of the fast-moving water dissipates partially in these waves. It is not a good idea to let that energy dissipate on you, and these waves can be missed partially or totally by running to the left.

Rapids 9 and 10

Below Rapid 8, the canyon widens out into the expanse of Tilted Park. Rapid 9 is a wide, shallow rapid that offers no particular navigational hazards (Figure 7-6). This rapid forms as a result of two broad, coalescing constrictions pushing out from Y and Cross canyons, which enter from river left. Historic debris flows from Y Canyon, the upstream one of these two canyons, have constricted the river more here, but changes to the rapid are not noteworthy. The main problem with Rapid 9 is breaking out of the tailwaves at the bottom to reach the enticing beaches of Tilted Park.

Figure 7-6. The Best Expedition at Rapid 9 (mile 208.7)

A. July 21, 1891. The Best Expedition, organized by James D. Best but promoted by Harry McDonald, passed through Cataract Canyon to assess mining potential and to develop sites for the proposed Denver, Colorado Cañon
and Pacific Railroad. Most of the crew members were Colorado River veterans
of previous expeditions. One crew member is shown running the rapid
standing up. The bank above the heads of the boatmen is the remnant of an
ancient debris flow. (J.A. McCormick, not numbered, courtesy of the Huntington Library)

B. March 30, 1994. McCormick's photo point could not be exactly reoccu-
pied because a debris flow has significantly altered the debris fan and rapid.
Tamarisk has invaded in the foreground and across the river. On the extreme
left and across the river, three junipers persist from 1891. (Steve Tharnstrom,
Stake 2917)

Rapid 10 washes out at high water. In low water, a
fun breaking wave develops that attracts considerable
attention from campers at the spacious beach on the
right. Some boaters repeatedly play in this rapid,
using any available means of floatation (from life
jackets to logs and boats). Boats, large and small, attempt to *surf* the wave by remaining on its upstream
face with minimal exertion. Some excellent kayakers
can stay on waves like the one in Rapid 10 for what
seem to be hours.

Rapids 11 and 12

Downstream from Rapid 10, the river slowly weaves
among cobble and sand bars. The walls narrow below
Tilted Park, then widen out again as two more unnamed tributaries enter from river left, forming a broad,
coalescing debris fan. At low water, river runners might
not pay much attention to the little riffles named Rapids
11 and 12. Neither poses a hazard at low water and
both are fast-moving water at flood stage.

Repeat photography indicates that many changes
have occurred in the reach between Tilted Park and
Rapid 12. Aside from vegetation changes, discussed in
the following section, the channel of the Colorado
River appears to have changed in several places. In
1921, the U.S. Geological Survey surveyed a three-
foot drop at mile 207.2 (Rapid 11) and a one-foot
drop a tenth of a mile downstream (Rapid 12). Now,
the drops of the two rapids appear to have reversed.
Rapid 12 has the greater fall while Rapid 11 is barely
noticeable.

When debris flows occur from tributaries, the lateral accretion of the banks as well as the bed rise from
boulders rafted into the channel raise the bed of the
Colorado River (Figure 7-7). This rise has had the
combined effect of creating a greater fall at the point
where the debris flow enters the river and a lower
slope upstream. The changes at Rapids 11 and 12
stem from a debris flow in the downstream canyon of
the pair at Rapid 12. The only thing we know about
that debris flow is that it definitely occurred after

Figure 7-7. Channel Change at Rapid 11 (mile 207.1)

A. June 6, 1889. The Brown-Stanton Expedition paused at this site to dry their gear and reload boats before rowing down a quiet stretch now informally called "Lake Cataract." This downstream view shows coyote willow on a long sandbar. (F.A. Nims 62, courtesy of the National Archives)

B. March 30, 1994. The channel of the Colorado River has shifted more than 200 feet to the right of the former camera position. Debris flows from tributaries just upstream and at Rapid 12 constricted the river upstream and downstream from this camera station and moved the river channel away from the former beach. The camera position in 1994 is too low because the surface of the former beach has lowered. The coyote willow on the former river banks has been replaced with non-native tamarisk and native rabbitbrush, four-wing saltbush, desert olive, and prince's plume. One new cottonwood is obscured behind the dense vegetation. (Steve Tharnstrom, Stake 2918).

1889 and probably after 1921, when geologist Sidney Paige photographed the canyon.

Low-Flying Aircraft and Deep Water

Generally, few aircraft are heard in Cataract Canyon. The sound of helicopters usually means bad news: someone needs to be evacuated from some part of the canyon. High overhead, small planes ferry passengers from Hite to Moab or elsewhere on the Plateau. Occasionally, someone decides to joyride through Cataract Canyon, and the results can be disastrous.

In June 1985, a trip was camping downstream of Rapid 12 where the Kolb brothers once met Charles "One-Eye" Smith (Figure 7-8). Two friends decided to deliver ice cream to the trip by dropping the ice cream, wrapped in a lifejacket, out of an airplane. The plane made three passes at altitudes of only thirty-five to fifty feet above the water, and the last pass ended when the plane hit the water, reportedly because of engine failure.[15] The two men crawled from the wreckage before it sank and were rescued by their friends. The pilot was battered, and his passenger had a broken collarbone and had to be evacuated. The plane sank within fifteen minutes.

That airplane remains in the eddy below Rapid 12. This eddy supports one of the remaining concentrations of the endangered humpback chub;[16] perhaps the plane carcass serves as artificial habitat for these fish, much like artificial reefs are created offshore for oceanic fishes. The wreckage probably is in deep water, because this eddy has the reputation of being the deepest point in the remaining river, at one time sporting a ninety-foot depth.[17] Another deep point—seventy-three feet—was just upstream of Easter Pasture Canyon at mile 193.6, and was measured in 1967 before the reservoir filled.[18] Pools in canyon rivers scour and fill, depending on flow, sediment load, and when in the year the depth is measured. In 1992, we used a depth finder and found the pool at Rapid 12 to be thirty-six-feet deep at a flow of around 5,000 ft³/s, making it the deepest point of any place we measured between Rapid 1 and the top of Big Drop 3.

Figure 7-8. The Kolb Brothers meet Charles "One-eyed" Smith (mile 206.9)

A. October 27, 1911. On a leisurely prospecting trip from Green River, Utah, Charles Smith camped in the eddy below Rapid 12. The faster-paced Kolb brothers had noticed his tracks upstream and finally caught up with him here. Note that Smith's boat does not have waterproof compartments. (Kolb 922, courtesy of the Cline Library, Northern Arizona University)

B. March 31, 1998. This site remains a popular camping beach, although it may be very rocky in some years. The water level is much higher than in 1911, but few rocks have changed. As seen along other parts of the river corridor, tamarisk have invaded and cottonwoods have perished. Many native willows are still present. (C. Schelz, Stake 3539)

THE STABILITY OF RAPIDS

Debris Flows and Rapids

The change in the canyon walls is obvious the moment you turn the bend and enter Rapid 1. Upstream, the cliffs are mostly clean of loose rock and, with the occasional exception, solid looking. The view downstream of Rapid 1 is one of broken loose rock, on both sides of the river, as far as the eyes can see. Because of the broken rocks, river runners, beginning with Powell, have associated the rapids of Cataract Canyon with rockfalls, landslides, and rotational slumps. They are partially correct.

Looking closely at the material exposed in escarpments near the river, one can see three definite landslide deposits within the first ten rapids. The first, between Rapids 2 and 3, is in an eddy. The second, upstream from Rapid 5, is at the end of the tailwaves to Rapid 4. The final one, between Rapids 7 and 8, is a slump block on river left, which is adjacent to another large eddy. All of these deposits have large angular blocks and a white appearance, indicating that all the material was generated locally in the Honaker Trail Formation.

There is no evidence in Cataract Canyon that either landslides or rockfalls have blocked the river or even transported large boulders into the river. Rocks bouncing down from the cliffs lose their considerable energy on the lower slopes; and with the exception of a rockfall at Rapid 18, no historical rockfalls have had a significant effect on the river (see Chapter 8). Rockfall deposits characteristically have a significant internal structure consisting of jumbled, angular clasts with little fine-grained material (*matrix*) between the larger particles. No large deposits with this type of structure are present in Cataract Canyon. Talus slopes consisting of abundant loose rock are common, but these slopes accumulate isolated rockfalls, not the large events that could significantly affect the river. Similarly, landslides, which move relatively slowly, do not have sufficient energy to push large particles into the river.

Several piles of reddish sediment attract attention between Rapids 1 and 9. The first are the truncated toes of the debris fans that line the right side of Rapids 1 and 2, which terminate against the landslide deposit. The second is downstream from Rapid 5. Lower

Rapid 5, a minor riffle, occurs adjacent to this deposit, which looks like an asymmetrical mound of clay and boulders. The third lines the right side of the river from the lower part of Rapid 6 through Rapid 8. Some have interpreted these piles as landslide deposits, although a better interpretation would be that they are ancient debris-flow deposits that have been truncated by river reworking. Although these deposits are adjacent to whitewater reaches, the rapids form by more recent debris fans pushing out from tributary mouths.

If you look high up in the cliffs above Rapid 1, you will see a reddish brown ledge of soft rock that is not visible in the strata upstream. This rock is the first outcrop of Halgaito Shale, inter-fingered with Elephant Canyon Formation,[19] and is one of the primary reasons why debris flows occur here. Mix one part Halgaito Shale with ten parts sand to boulders and two parts water, dump it over a cliff, and debris flows result. The red-stained gullies that scour the slopes just downstream from Rapids 1 and 2 on the right are a mute testament to the influence of Halgaito Shale on Cataract Canyon.

Debris flows from a clay-rich source would not create rapids unless a ready source of boulders was available. The fracturing of bedrock obvious in the view downstream from Rapid 1 creates abundant talus. Some of the tributary canyons, such as the ones at Rapid 4 (river left) and Rapid 5 (river right) apparently formed along fault zones that probably are related to salt deformation in the Paradox Formation beneath the canyon floor. Periodic rockfalls load the tributary floors and are readily incorporated in debris flows that sweep through the canyons. Debris flows have the ability to transport large particles into the river, which flushes away the fine-grained matrix and leaves the large particles in piles at the mouths of tributaries. Without the combination of fractured rock to produce large boulders and debris flows to transport them into the river, Cataract Canyon likely would not have its rapids.

Bottomlands Versus Debris Fans

The areas of Tilted Park and downstream at Rapid 12 may remind some of the wide reaches of the approaches to Cataract Canyon. Along the approaches to Cataract Canyon, bottomlands are most extensive in the mouths of tributaries, but they may also occur as continuous terraces that stretch for miles along the rivers. The *grade*, or bedrock channel bed, of tributaries clearly projects well below current river level, suggesting that both the Green and Colorado rivers are now higher than they once were. The area now covered by alluvial terraces is available for deposition because the beds of the two rivers have risen in response to the downstream obstruction created by the rapids of Cataract Canyon.

Bottomlands along the approaches are built from sediment deposition during overbank flooding. Two depositional models are possible: the bottomlands can grow towards the center of the river (*lateral accretion*), or narrow segments of the bottomlands can rise vertically through overbank flooding (*vertical accretion*). Although both processes may have occurred on the Green River, historical channel narrowing has mostly occurred through vertical accretion (see Chapter 5). Tributary canyons add little sediment to the bottomlands: most tributaries have cut arroyo slots through the bottomlands, seeking the grade of the river.

The broad landscape of Tilted Park is formed through a combination of the same types of processes in addition to one that is fundamentally different. Again, the bed of the Colorado River has risen owing to a downstream blockage; in this case, that blockage originates from Range Canyon, where a debris fan forms Mile Long Rapid (Chapter 8). Although one might expect to find bottomlands here similar to those found upstream, the tributaries on both sides of the river produce significant amounts of coarse-grained sediments that the river cannot easily remove. Accumulations of coarse-grained sediments from debris flows are called debris fans and occur throughout the Colorado River system. Debris-flow deposits are inter-fingered with river alluvium deposited during floods. The river deposits occur as thick beaches on the edge of both sides of the river.

Debris flows cause both vertical and lateral accretion in Tilted Park and other wide, relatively flat debris fans (Figure 7-9). Vertical accretion occurs on the apex of the debris fan—near where the channel exits

Figure 7-9. Cryptobiotic Soils on the Gypsum Dome at Rapid 12 (mile 207.0)

A. June 6, 1889. Franklin Nims often climbed to capture long views of the canyon, as exemplified by this down-stream view across from Rapid 12. To reach this camera station, Nims and his assistant had to walk up a gypsum plug through dense biological soil crusts. Their trail to the camera station appears in the foreground (F.A. Nims 63, courtesy of the National Archives).

the confining walls of the cliff—and lateral accretion occurs along the Colorado River as coarse-grained sediments push out into the river. River alluvium adds to the vertical accretion. This mixture of sediments, in addition to the width of the canyon, contributes to a near-ideal setting for cottonwood trees. Debris-flow sediments are highly permeable, allowing river water to penetrate further into the river banks than would occur in the finer-grained river deposits that line the approaches to Cataract Canyon. Finally, because the floor of Tilted Park slopes towards the river, owing to lateral accretion, floods can easily overtop the banks, allowing the overbank flooding that is necessary for cottonwood germination and establishment.

Dams and Rapids

By some calculations, dams upstream from Cataract Canyon—particularly Flaming Gorge Dam on the Green River and the Blue Mesa Complex (consisting of Crystal, Morrow Point, and Blue Mesa dams) on the Gunnison River—reduce flow in the Colorado River by perhaps ten to twenty percent (see Chapter 3). The reduced flow should mean reduced forces on the boulders that comprise rapids, and therefore rapids should be more stable in the reaches downstream from dams.[20] In the Grand Canyon, debris flows continue to occur, meaning that many rapids are getting narrower and increasing in fall as the boulders pile up and the river no longer has the power to remove them.[21]

There is no photographic evidence that channel narrowing at rapids is occurring in Cataract Canyon, except perhaps in reaches with lower slopes (*e.g.*, Tilted Park). Although debris flows have occurred at Rapids 1, 2, 7, and 8, as well as others downstream, none of these rapids appears to be significantly different than they were a century ago. The presence of only large boulders in rapids, which is one way to view stability,[22] are a combined effect of the elapsed time since the last significant debris flow and the magnitude of the largest river flow since that debris flow. The term "stable rapid" is in one sense an oxymoron because rapids change subtly, owing to dissolution

B. June 5, 1993. There are nine persistent Mormon tea plants, seven persistent shadscale, two new cottonwoods, and many non-native tamarisks in this photograph. A trail that Nims probably started is also apparent in the foreground of this view. The channel of the unnamed tributary at the base of the hill is now braided because of debris-flow activity. New debris flows from the canyon at Rapid 12 have deposited many large boulders in the lower left and center parts of this view. The island that previously was in the eddy below Rapid 12 has become attached to the bank because the eddy at lower left that appears in the 1889 view has been filled in. (R.H. Webb, Stake 3069)

and *corrasion* of rocks by suspended sand grains. New boulders plucked from debris fans can become lodged within the matrix of larger boulders on the bed of the river. With one debris flow, a stable rapid can rapidly change irrespective of river flows. Rapids are piles of boulders that the river inexorably tries to remove, and with the help of geologic time it will do so.

WHERE TO CAMP

Cataract Canyon is only sixteen miles of free-flowing river, and the choice of campsites is limited. If your group has signed up for Tilted Park, it is time to commit in your boat, particularly if you are rowing. First, whether it is windy or sand is blowing will affect that decision. Pulling right in Rapid 9 takes you to the most prized beach, a protected site under the cottonwoods and beneath the prominent Toreva block that towers over Tilted Park. Pulling left takes you toward a shallow, cobbly landing at most water levels that is bad for boat parking but provides access to lots of hiking. Staying in the center also allows you to run

Rapid 10, pulling into a large, although exposed beach adjacent to that rapid on the right. Step out of the boat and you are in another one of Cataract Canyon's unique areas.

On river trips, the words *sandbars*, *campsites*, and *beaches* are used interchangeably, although some fine campsites—particularly at high water—are on the bedrock ledges of the approaches. On both approaches to Cataract Canyon, campsites are mostly on broad alluvial terraces. Historically, most of these terraces have grown in size as the channels narrowed, but vegetation encroachment has significantly reduced the usable area of sandbars (Table 7-1). As a result, campsites are scarce if you do not want to crash through the tamarisk wall. The situation is similar from the Confluence down to Spanish Bottom, although the combined flows of the two rivers has kept the low-water channel margin relatively free of vegetation, allowing camping on small sandbars. At the lip of Rapid 1, campsites along the Colorado River abruptly change in form and abundance.

| | NUMBER OF SANDBARS | | | | | |
| | ALL | | Approaches to Cataract Canyon | | Cataract Canyon | |
Deposit Type	Number	Percent	Number	Percent	Number	Percent
Channel Margin	59	37	8	6	21	21
Separation Bars	95	59	17	29	78	76
Reattachment Bars	6	4	3	5	3	3
All Sandbars	160	100	58	100	102	100
Increased	72	45	12	21	60	59
Decreased	68	43	44	76	24	24
Unchanged	20	12	2	3	18	18

Types of Sandbars

Beginning at the bottom of Rapid 1, sandbars look similar to those found in other canyons where debris flows occur and debris fans alter the flow of the river.[23] Researchers have classified these types of sandbars in Grand Canyon, where they are commonly found.[24] *Channel-margin deposits* include the river terraces that are common along the approaches to Cataract Canyon as well as small sandbars that line the sides of the river above and below rapids (Figure 7-10). *Separation bars* form on the downstream side of debris fans or other relatively large channel obstructions, beginning where flow "separates" from the channel margin and moves downstream adjacent to the eddy fence. Separation bars typically are in the middle or are on the upstream side of eddies and are the main type of camping beach. *Reattachment bars* form on the downstream sides of eddies where current is moving downstream against the channel banks. These tend to be the most unstable type of sandbar.

Separation bars are the most common type of sandbar we observe in Cataract Canyon (seventy-six percent), whereas channel-margin deposits are the most common along the approaches (sixty-six percent). This is totally expected, because few debris fans are found on the approaches to Cataract Canyon and broad floodplains do not occur downstream of Rapid 1. Of the 160 interpretations we have made of sandbars in Cataract Canyon, sixty-one percent are ex-posed at stages of less than 30,000 ft³/s, thirty-four percent are exposed between 30,000 and 70,000 ft³/s, and five percent are exposed at stages of greater than 70,000 ft³/s. Therefore, most of our interpretations are on sandbars exposed at low to intermediate discharges. Camping at flood stage in Cataract Canyon generally means coping with rocky slopes, therefore; there is not a lot of emergent sand around when the annual flood is occurring.

Changes in the Beaches of Cataract Canyon

Interpretation of changes in sandbars is risky since sandbars change relatively frequently. Most sandbars are small at the beginning of the year. Depending on the size of the spring flood, sandbars may be built to enormous size or they may only increase by a small amount. As the flood recedes and the newly deposited sand emerges, its streamside margin is quickly eroded as new flow patterns develop in eddies, leaving a vertical or near vertical wall at the river's edge. During July and August, particularly after a big spring flood, the sound of sandbars calving into the river is common, and some people, unaware of the hazard, have been injured by collapses. As the summer turns to fall, the vertical cliffs of sand turn to steep slopes, as a result of camper footprints, wind, and gravity. Floods build sandbars; gravity, low river flows, and human usage inevitably erode them.

Not all spring floods create similar sandbars. The

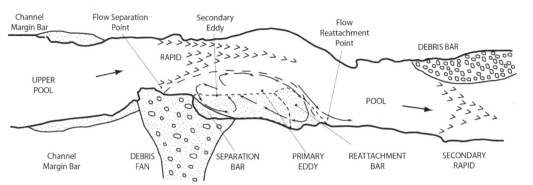

Figure 7-10. Schematic Diagram of a Rapid and Sandbars in Cataract Canyon. (Showing the terminology of a rapid-eddy system, this diagram is loosely based on Rapid 5.)

1993 flood, which peaked at 71,400 ft³/s, left enormous sandbars through Cataract Canyon. The 1995 flood had a peak of 81,000 ft³/s but was sustained over several weeks, and the sandbars were smaller than those deposited in 1993. Some beaches created in 1993 were temporary: a very nice beach was created on river left above Big Drop 2, but this beach gradually eroded away. The same thing happened above Big Drop 3 on river right. One of the most important findings from repeat photography, however, is that some sandbars always form in certain places—such as downstream from debris fans[25]—and these places are the sites for relatively reliable campsites.

With these things in mind, sandbars are doing well in Cataract Canyon but not so well on its approaches. In Cataract Canyon, fifty-nine percent of the sandbars shown in our photography had increased in size and eighteen percent appear to be of similar size. Some sandbars, most notably the beach downstream of Brown Betty Rapid, consistently look larger in photographs taken after the 1950s. In contrast, seventy-four percent of the sandbars on the approaches appear to be smaller, which is not surprising considering the large amount of channel narrowing that has occurred in the twentieth century (see Chapter 5); also, thirty-seven percent of sandbars on the approaches have vegetation encroachment, decreasing their usefulness as campsites.

Our observation that sandbars are doing well in Cataract Canyon is difficult to explain in the face of several hydrological changes. First, peak discharges have decreased, owing at least in part to flood control operations of dams upstream (see Chapter 3). Second, the sediment loads of both rivers have decreased historically (see Chapter 5), indicating that less sand is moving through Cataract Canyon. These changes might be expected to create smaller sandbars in Cataract Canyon, but, fortunately for river runners, that has not been the case.

TRASH FISH

Many of the historical river trips through Cataract Canyon stopped, at least briefly, at the Confluence to fish. Fishing was one way these trips could supplement their meager, and sometimes rotting, provisions, and fish were plentiful. Franklin Nims, photographer for the Brown-Stanton Expedition, photographed a whole stringer of what appear to be now-endangered Colorado pikeminnow (*Ptychocheilus lucius*) at the Confluence in 1889. Settlers in the Upper Basin referred to these fish as Colorado River salmon and frequently caught them as well.[26]

About three-quarters of the native fishes of the Colorado River are endemic, making this fishery unique in the United States.[27] The most notable native species in Cataract Canyon are Colorado pikeminnow, which prefer the flatter slopes and slower waters of the approaches, and humpback chub (*Gila cypha*), which prefer the whitewater of Cataract Canyon.[28] Unfortunately for these species, they were not considered to be "sport fish" worthy of a recreational fishery, and the history of fishes in the Colorado River basin in the twentieth century is dominated by attempted reductions in natives and stocking of non-native fishes. Of the thirty-one fish species currently found in Cataract Canyon,[29] only ten are native. Four of these are federally listed endangered species.[30] In 1986, intensive investigations in the canyon yielded a catch of only 17.5 percent natives and 82.5 percent non-natives.[31] The fishery as a whole could be categorized as a combination of natives and naturalized exotics,[32] but the fate of the natives is uncertain at best.

Channel catfish (*Ictalurus punctatus*) are one of the native fishes' main competitors. Catfish occur throughout Cataract Canyon and are valued regionally as a sport fishery. The story of how catfish arrived in the Colorado River is similar to how other economically valuable fishes came to compete with or displace native fishes.[33] Because of its warm water and high sediment load, the Colorado River was recognized in the nineteenth century for its potential for catfish.[34] Horace Rutledge, the mayor of Moab in the

1910s, ran on a platform of the improvement of local sport fisheries in the Colorado River. In 1919, he had a shipment of channel catfish delivered by rail to Thompson, Utah, and he released some near Matrimony Springs and some near Grand Junction. They expanded so quickly that the river became known for its catfish by the late 1920s.[35] With a similar motive, carp were introduced to the Colorado in the 1880s.[36] The natives became *trash fish*, undesirable to anglers accustomed to the sport fishes.

Humpback chub primarily use habitat in reaches that have debris flows, debris fans and bars, and large eddies. They are closely associated with boulders, talus, and eddies in swiftly-flowing reaches,[37] which pretty well describes the free-flowing river in Cataract

---

SPECIAL FISH IN A BIG MUDDY RIVER

Richard A. Valdez

Cataract Canyon hardly seems a fit place for man, beast, or fish. The Colorado River through the canyon is a violent, reddish-brown stream of water where life for all but the most specialized forms of fish is impossible. Eight species of fish have successfully evolved and thrived in this muddiest and swiftest of North American rivers for nearly three million years; Colorado pikeminnow (*Ptychocheilus lucius*), humpback chub (*Gila cypha*), bonytail (*Gila elegans*), roundtail chub (*Gila robusta*), speckled dace (*Rhinichthys osculus*), razorback sucker (*Xyrauchen texanus*), flannelmouth sucker (*Catostomus latippinis*), and bluehead sucker (*Catostomus discobolus*). The first five species are minnows, ranging in size as adults from a mere four inches to over three feet in length. The Colorado pikeminnow has the distinction of being North America's largest minnow at once-reported weights of over a hundred pounds, and was once marketed commercially as the "white salmon" of the Colorado River. The last three species are suckers that range in size from one to two-and-a-half feet in length and weigh up to about twelve pounds.

The success of these fish species in the Colorado River is not mere chance. Each is equipped with specialized physical and physiological features that enable it to thrive in water temperature ranges of nearly 100°F, high salinity levels, high turbidity, and high water velocity. The skin of each species is thick and their scales are small and deeply embedded to resist the abrasive forces of roughened sand particles rushing by as underwater sand storms. The eyes of all eight species are

small and underdeveloped, leaving the fish to rely on a highly developed neuromast system, which is a network of chemoreceptors on the head that enable these fish to locate minute odors and food at great distances. A highly developed lateral line system complements their high-tech locator apparatus by enabling the fish to sense underwater sounds through specialized scales that transmit and amplify these vibrations in the air bladder, sending messages to the inner ear. Locating a struggling insect on the surface of the muddy river is routine for these fish during a feeding foray.

The humpback chub and razorback sucker, as their names suggest, have specialized dorsal humps that serve as hydrodynamic stabilizers in swift water and keep the fish upright or pressed to the river bottom in high velocities. The humpback chub also has large fan-like fins that enable it to soar and glide in the variable river currents, much like an eagle maneuvers wind currents with hardly a flap of the wings. The dorso-ventrally compressed body of the bluehead sucker is well adapted to a bottom existence in high-velocity cobble riffles. This species also has a hardened cartilagenous ridge on the inside of its lower jaw used as a scraper for dislodging algae, diatoms, and small insects from rocks. In contrast, the Colorado pikeminnow is a long cylindrical fish that migrates many hundreds of miles, once moving most of the length of the Colorado River from the Gulf of Lower California to tributaries in Colorado and Wyoming. Although none of the eight Colorado River fish species is considered a strong swimmer, each has developed its own survival strategy in a river where swiftness and power have given way to thick skin, small eyes, dorsal humps, and elaborate locator systems.

Canyon. Humpback chub probably spawn on debris bars within the canyon, making Cataract one of the remaining five reaches upstream of the reservoir where this species has a significant population. "Significant" translates to small: only twenty-two adult humpback chub were caught in a four-year period.[38]

Overall in the Colorado River drainage, competition from exotics for food is the most detrimental factor for the continued existence of native fishes.[39] Locally, conversion of fisheries from natives to sport fishes has had dramatic effects. In 1962, just prior to closure of Flaming Gorge Dam on the Green River, the poison rotenone was released to kill nongame fishes (read: trash fish).[40] It was effective, too effective: dead fish floated up downstream in Dinosaur National Monument despite an intensive detoxification program. Although native fishes reclaimed their habitat downstream from the unregulated Yampa River within four years, rainbow trout (*Salmo gairdneri*) dominated the reach immediately below the dam. Rainbow trout also dominates the waters just downstream from Glen Canyon Dam. This species do not threaten native fish in Cataract Canyon because they cannot tolerate the combination of seasonally warm water and high sediment load.

Flow regulation has important consequences for native fisheries. If cold water is released from the bottom of the reservoir, most fish species—especially natives—cannot reproduce.[41] Flood control may cause filling in of gravels and backwater habitat that are important for egg laying and larva and young-of-the-year survival.[42] Reduction of turbidity, and particularly the introduction of non-native organisms, may completely change the food base of the river.[43] These problems are only partially felt in Cataract Canyon, which is too far downstream from the reservoirs to see significant changes in either temperature or turbidity. The native fishes here appear to be primarily threatened by introduced species.

TILTED PARK

Tilted Park is named for the strongly dipping strata in the Honaker Trail Formation that surrounds a broad reach of the Colorado River in Cataract Canyon.

Most of the more strongly skewed rocks are Toreva blocks, or rotational slumps; the one on river right is conspicuous from several miles upstream. At Tilted Park, the Colorado River is placid, and Rapids 9 and 10 are not composed of significant whitewater, although Rapid 10 has a punch to it when the river is low. River rafters call the reach beginning at the bottom of Rapid 12 "Lake Cataract," which is in deference to Mile Long Rapid downstream. This reach of Cataract Canyon is always a pleasant one, for there are no major rapids to worry about and there are many camps with good hikes; this is also where cottonwood galleries provide welcome respite from the blazing sun of summer. These are the last significant cottonwood stands along the Colorado River until upstream of Needles, California. Most people find this a pleasant place to spend the night or even layover among the tilted rocks of Cataract Canyon.

Anhydrite Domes and Tilted Rocks

Upstream, at the mouth of Red Lake Canyon, jumbled-looking, whitish rocks form a dome-like structure on the left side of the Colorado River. These rocks are the remains of an anhydrite dome extruded upwards from the underlying Paradox Formation (see Chapter 3). Two more of these rock formations are less conspicuous and are snug between the mouths of Cross and Y canyons and between the unnamed canyons at Rapid 12. These domes reveal aspects of subterranean geologic structure important to petroleum exploration, and are of direct economic interest for their salts, particularly potash. They also give us clues as to why Tilted Park deserves its name.

In 1921, geologists H.W.C. Prommel and H.E. Crum, working as consulting geologists for the oil industry, worked in Canyon Country investigating salt domes.[44] They identified, described, and named several domes in Cataract Canyon, including ones at the Confluence and at the mouth of Red Lake Canyon. Most of the names these scientists gave the domes have been ignored, and new names have since been created, ironically, to honor Prommel and Crum. The significance of these geologists' work and some of their ideas are discussed in Chapter 7.

The anhydrite dome between the two unnamed canyons at Rapid 12 is named the Crum Dome, although Crum never described it. The lower Red Lake Canyon dome became the Prommel Dome. And, in Tilted Park, the anhydrite dome between Cross and Y canyons, originally called the South Dome,[45] is now called the Harrison Dome, named after one of the original researchers on salt domes on the Colorado Plateau.[46] Interestingly, all of these domes—as well as another prominent dome downstream at Gypsum Canyon—are near large rotational landslides or slumps in the walls of Cataract Canyon. The relation between domes and slumps is simple: salt occurs in the subsurface geology, and the overlying bedrock is sliding on it.

Toreva Blocks

As you may recall from Chapter 3, geologists call large movements of rock and soil *mass wasting*, and the means by which mass wasting occurs are collectively known as *colluvial processes*. Familiar examples of colluvial processes include rockfalls, avalanches, and landslides. Mass wasting typically occurs when rock and soil are wet but not completely saturated; instead, a *failure plane* is present beneath the surface that provides a slippery slope for the overlying material to slide on. Failure planes may or may not be lubricated by water or other slippery media (*e.g.*, salt). If the overlying soil and rock are sufficiently saturated, the slide may turn into a debris flow, which is more properly termed a *fluvial process* because of its dependence on saturated media for movement.

As discussed in Chapter 3, large cliff faces have a lot of forces concentrated at or beneath their base. If a potential failure surface develops, either along a joint in the bedrock or a bedding plane, the stresses in the cliff may cause the base to rotate outward into the free space of the canyon, and Toreva blocks form. The movement may be relatively slow or fast, although the faster the movement, the more chances of the block disintegrating into rubble. This may be the difference between the relatively intact Toreva blocks in Tilted Park, which moved slowly, and the large landslide de-

posit opposite the mouth of Gypsum Canyon. Because they form in bedrock, Toreva blocks generally are large in scale, like the ones in Tilted Park.

Some geologists who have been through Cataract Canyon speculate that the presence of the tilted rocks is the reason for its rapids.[47] The reasoning goes like this: the unloading phenomena on the cliffs pushes large blocks of bedrock into the river, and the river forms rapids in its attempt to cut through the obstruction. The problem with this idea is that rapids are associated with tributary canyons in Cataract Canyon, and no significant rapids form at either Toreva blocks or landslide deposits except by coincidence. An example of the latter occurs at the now-gone (due to Lake Powell inundation) Gypsum Canyon Rapid. This rapid formed from a large debris fan from Gypsum Canyon—a significant debris-flow producer—that pushed the river into the opposite wall, which happened to be a landslide deposit.

Otherwise, the placid waters of Tilted Park speak volumes: the current river gradient has little to do with past movements of the canyon walls. The one big exception is that the movements that created the Toreva blocks and landslides produced abundant sediment for debris-flow transport from tributaries that have developed within them or along their failure planes.

Vegetation in the Canyon

The sudden narrowing of the canyon walls at the entrance of Cataract Canyon means many things to the plants and animals that live there. Air temperatures are very different within the canyon: in the winter it is colder, as the canyon is shaded most of the day, and in the summer, temperatures are often hotter, as heat gets trapped within the canyon walls. New substrates appear—including clays and gypsum—but most dramatic is the effect of increasing water speed: rather than sediments being deposited along the river's edge, they are being swept away. This means that the wide flat banks covered by riparian vegetation found above Cataract Canyon are absent within the canyon. Instead, one finds upland vegetation communities extending to the water's edge.

Tamarisk. Unlike the walls of tamarisk that line the river channels upstream, tamarisk is relatively sparse in Cataract Canyon. Of the 226 photographs we have matched in Cataract Canyon, 180 are downstream from Rapid 1. Tamarisk appears in seventy-four percent of our repeat photographs—compared with 100 percent of the photographs between the Confluence and Rapid 1—and the distribution of tamarisk is more restricted in the whitewater reach. Most of the individuals are small and likely post-date the last large flood in Cataract Canyon (1984), although some individual plants depicted in 1956 photographs at Rapid 5 are still alive. The larger individuals are confined to the quieter shorelines of eddies; these plants tend to grow in the stage range corresponding to about 50,000 to 80,000 ft³/s. As discussed in Chapters 4 and 5, tamarisk probably arrived in Cataract Canyon as early as the 1910s. Within the canyon, on river right at Rapid 3, large tamarisk individuals germinated in 1941,[48] likely following a major flood of that year.

Netleaf Hackberry Trees. Within Cataract Canyon, upland shrubs dominate the slopes, and species not readily apparent upstream appear, including netleaf hackberry trees. Hackberry trees are wavy-barked deciduous trees in the elm family that live to be several hundred years old.[49] The oldest one we know of is near Rapid 4; it germinated in 1802.[50] Regionally, they are widely distributed, being found from 600- to 6,000-feet elevation along streams and rivers from central Washington to northern Mexico and east to Kansas.[51]

Hackberry leaves are toothed, feel like sandpaper, and are commonly covered with little bumps caused by insect galls. They are also frequently infected by mites, causing the branches to form small "witches' brooms." These trees are also infected by mistletoe and powdery mildew. Hackberry trees are a favorite spot for the small orange-brown empress butterfly, whose larvae and pupae are found only on this plant.[52] The pupae, which look just like hackberry leaves, stay quiet and disguised as such until a few hours before emergence, which generally occurs just before dawn. Darkness masks the vulnerable emerging adult. After their wings harden, the new adults fly away, leaving the tree in mid-morning.

This is also the time one is most likely to see male empress butterflies perched on the ground, defending a specific tree from other males. As females lay eggs only on hackberry leaves, it is tempting to assume that males defend trees to get access to females looking for a place to lay eggs. A nice story, but it appears to be untrue. Females only mate once, and by the time they are looking for a place to lay eggs, the eggs have already been fertilized. But where there are eggs, there are soon to be larvae, and where there are larvae, there will be virgin females to mate with, and that appears to be why empress males defend a specific tree.

Hackberry is most often found in clumps on the steep rocky slopes above the river. These trees have very inconspicuous greenish flowers, and the fruit is thick skinned and single seeded. The common belief is that the seeds are eaten and dispersed by birds and mammals. However, hackberry seedlings are seldom seen, and the fact that the trees occur in clumps has led researchers to believe that they also reproduce vegetatively from roots that sprout suckers. Hackberry most often forms a line along the slopes that appears to mark high water lines of pre-dam years. This may mean that while these trees generally reproduce vegetatively, recruitment by seeds can occur in very wet years (and thus during high water). It is also possible that the original trees took root during a climate regime that was more favorable to establishment by seed. These trees are clearly long-lived, as many persist in our repeat photos.[53]

Hackberry trees lay down conspicuous annual rings with widths that vary consistent with water availability and air temperature. Comparisons of Hackberry tree rings, which are seldom missing, above and below Glen Canyon Dam (Cataract and Grand canyons, respectively), and of rings laid down before and after the construction of the dam show several things.[54] First, they indicate that the response of hackberry trees to water flow and air temperature in Cataract Canyon has not changed with the construction of the dam. In contrast, tree rings below Glen Canyon Dam in Grand Canyon indicate that riparian temperatures have cooled considerably since the dam was constructed, probably because much colder water now flows out from the dam. The tree rings also record the lack of high water flows since dam construction. As high water once provided a significant source of summer water before the dams were constructed, the effect on hackberry populations has been in question. Overall, however, the trees in Grand Canyon seem to profit, not suffer, from the presence of the dam, probably owing to a more consistent water supply. It may be that this species is able to compensate for lack of early summer floods by adjusting its root architecture or root activity times.

In Cataract Canyon, the tree-ring series for hackberry reflects the volume of the annual flood, which is related to peak discharge. High growth in hackberry occurred in several high-water years in Cataract Canyon, including as recently as 1983 and 1984, but also in receding years 1958, 1921, and 1911; for reasons potentially related to tree damage, growth was not high during 1884.[55] However, the year of highest growth in hackberry was back in 1869, the year of the first Powell Expedition. The year that an extremely large flood left evidence in one of the photographs taken on the second Powell Expedition in 1871 might have also been that year (see Figure 7-13).

Upland Shrubs. Most of the upland shrubs in Cataract Canyon are plants that are long-lived, deeply rooted, drought resistant, and have the ability to grow in very rocky, low-nutrient soils. One of the most common shrubs is Mormon tea.[56] This plant is very different from the other shrubs in this habitat, as it is not a flowering plant; instead, like conifers, it is a *gymnosperm*. Instead of flowers, Mormon tea has tiny cones that occur on joints along the stem. In the absence of leaves, it uses the green stem for photosynthesis. There are three species of this dioecious plant in the area. Most of the plants you can see from the river are either *Ephedra torreyana* or (rarely) *E. viridis*; *E. cutleri* is mostly found on very sandy soil that blows about like small dunes and is not visible along the river corridor.

Mormon tea can reproduce either by stem sprouts or by seed, depending on the substrate. In very unstable, sandy soils, stem reproduction is favored, whereas reproduction by seed is more common in rocky or very stable soils. Mormon tea is commonly

identified as a species whose individuals persist over 100 years,[57] and some individuals in Canyonlands appear to be the same size after 130 years. It is widely believed that early settlers drank Mormon tea as a stimulant. However, chemical analysis shows that these species have very little of the stimulant ephedrine in them (in contrast to the Chinese *Ephedra*, which is packed with ephedrine). The settlers may have chosen to drink Mormon tea for its high levels of vitamin C, and most likely not for its very bitter taste.

Several species of cacti are also common along these slopes. Like Mormon tea, most cacti produce tiny leaves in the spring. These are seldom seen, as they are dropped after a few days or weeks, and cacti depend on their green stems (which we call pads or the body of the cactus) for photosynthesis. Pricklypear cactus is the most often encountered cactus species along the slopes of Cataract Canyon.[58] Individual pricklypear plants living over 100 years are commonly found in Grand Canyon,[59] but no persistent prickly pear have been found in Cataract Canyon.

Pricklypear cactus grow by initiating new joints in the spring, which then elongate until the onset of the dry season (mid-May). New pads are put on every ten years or so, but in drought years the pads are shed to keep the plant from dying. Pads that are shed or that are knocked off by passing animals can lie on the soil surface for months and then may reroot when it rains. This makes pricklypear a tenacious plant that is difficult to remove. Pricklypear provides an important source of shelter for many animals, including mice, packrats, rabbits, and rattlesnakes. All but the rattlesnake are ungrateful guests, as the same mammals that use the plant as shelter also eat their pricklypear homes. These plants are pollinated by ground-nesting bees and are home to many other insects, with the most famous being cochineal, a scale insect. When crushed, these insects give off a brilliant crimson liquid that is used to make crimson dye. For many years, only royalty could wear this color, and these insects were an extremely valuable and jealously guarded crop.

Snakeweed has increased both its density and its range in both Cataract and Grand Canyons over the past 100 years, according to the repeat photography of this species (Chapter 10). This same increase has been seen throughout the West, and snakeweed is now a common component of most low-elevation western landscapes.[60] Local increases in this plant have been ascribed to livestock grazing, as cattle avoid snakeweed, choosing to eat palatable plants instead. However, as snakeweed is not common in the Holocene or Pleistocene fossil record, it is likely that the region-wide increase of this plant is also partially due to climate change. This short bush, with bright green foliage and bright yellow flowers, appears to be short-lived because it has not been identified as persistent in any of our repeat photography. Snakeweed mostly uses winter rain, and its flowers are insect-pollinated while the seeds are wind-dispersed.

Blackbrush, another plant that commonly lives over 100 years, is restricted to the area around the southern borders of Utah and Nevada, stretching between Colorado and California.[61] It is ubiquitous throughout the Colorado Plateau and at higher elevations in the Mojave and Great Basin deserts. Blackbrush, being restricted to the north by cold and to the south by drought, grows along the river corridor of the approaches and on or near the tops of the cliffs in Cataract Canyon. It is generally considered to be a relict member of the rose family, and climatic conditions that favored establishment of the huge stands we see today are no longer present. However, blackbrush appears to be very responsive to shifting climate regimes, indicating that rather than being a relict it is just extremely slow to colonize and/or grow to adult size.[62]

Blackbrush produces what appear to be yellow flowers following very wet winters. Close examination shows the "petals" of these flowers are actually colored *sepals* (modified leaves next to flower petals), although occasionally one can find up to four real petals.[63] These short shrubs are wind pollinated; this makes sense, as the plants often occur as monocultures covering many square miles of shallow sandy soils. As seen with pinyon pines, blackbrush plants mast, producing huge numbers of seeds when conditions are favorable. However, masting requires so much energy that if favorable conditions occur two years in a row, the plants will not produce seeds in the second year.

Blackbrush seeds are large and cached by rodents, especially kangaroo rats. Very few seedlings, however, are ever produced. The cached seeds are eaten throughout the winter, and the young seedlings mowed down by hungry rodents in the spring. In addition, the young plants require successive wet seasons to survive, which is not a common occurrence in deserts. Researchers in the Mojave Desert and the Colorado Plateau report only one successful (and lasting) *recruitment event* in the last fifteen years, that being in 1993.[64] Reciprocal transplants have demonstrated that the seeds "know" where they came from: regardless of where they are planted, they germinate at the same time as seeds growing at their place of origin. Unlike many desert plants, blackbrush plants in poor habitat can grow very slowly, even in favorable years; a six-inch plant can easily be fifteen to twenty years old. While few things appear to kill or eat blackbrush, it is easily killed by fire. Because of the extremely low recruitment rate, once a stand is burned it is essentially gone for centuries.[65]

Four-wing saltbush has one of the most flexible life-history strategies in this landscape.[66] It grows on a wide variety of soil textures, chemistries, and depths. It grows in all community types, including deep-soiled grasslands and river bottoms, and shallow-soiled pinyon-juniper stands and mixed shrub communities. Individuals are commonly found to persist for at least 108 years in Canyonlands. This plant is dioecious, and, as with many dioecious plants, males occur in drier, less-fertile areas while females occur in wetter and more fertile areas. Sex of the plant can shift if conditions change. Seeds are held on the stem over the winter and well into the spring, making four-wing a favorite dining spot for seed-eating birds. The leaves and stems are also an important forage plant for wildlife.

Shadscale is another generalist plant that grows under a wide range of soil conditions.[67] It is found on shales, gypsum, and shallow sandy soils. But unlike most plants, shadscale seeds require infection by a fungus in order to germinate. Because this fungus only grows under warm, moist conditions, its presence may assist the seeds in determining optimal conditions for germination. When growing on very salty soils, shadscale excretes large amounts of salt onto the surface of its leaves. The process of excretion serves several functions: it protects the plant from salt overload, it enables it to utilize very salty water, and the salt it excretes reflects the sun. This keeps leaf temperatures and thus water loss down, and also protects the leaf from radiation damage. Shadscale individuals commonly show up in the repeat photos and can also, like four-wing saltbush, live at least 108 years based on our repeat photography. They are important browse plants for wildlife.

Skunkbush, or lemonade bush, is also common on the slopes of Cataract Canyon and can live at least 130 years. Although not poisonous, this shrub is a close relative of poison oak and poison ivy, and has very similar-looking leaves.[68] Skunkbush occurs in many habitats, although it does prefer a bit of shade. It is found in shadowy canyons, under overhangs, or in the shade of large trees or shrubs. It can grow on both coarse and fine-textured soils. Berries from this plant provide food throughout the winter for birds, and also provide copious amounts of saliva for the thirsty hiker who can tolerate their sour taste.

Common Upland Herbs. If you watch the upland vegetation as you float down the river, you will notice many tall stalks dotting the steep rocky slopes. These stalks—green in spring, yellow with flowers in summer, and tan in fall—belong to prince's plume (*Stanleya pinnata*). Locoweeds (*Astragalus* sp.) are low-lying plants in the pea family that provide most of the purple flowers on these slopes.

Another common plant is wild buckwheat, whose several species range from diminutive herbs to large shrubs.[69] They are readily identified by their colored stems and their inverted pyramid-shaped flower heads. In spring, the main plant stems are a light, bright green, while the stems that form the flower heads are red. In fall and winter, these red stems make a colorful addition to a mostly-brown plant community. The most easily identified buckwheat species is the desert trumpet (*Eriogonum inflatum*), an herbaceous plant six- to twenty-four-inches high. It is called the desert trumpet because the main stem of the plant is generally swollen beneath each node.[70] This swelling

is caused by a moth larva that lives inside the stem, and stems that lack the moth larvae are not inflated. As testament to the success of this, one seldom sees this plant without an inflated stem.

Jimsonweed, or sacred datura (*Datura wrightii*), is also common along the river corridor, typically in more shaded areas.[71] The leaves of this plant are large, very dark green, and form a spreading open canopy that can be up to three feet across. The leaves, fruits, and seeds of this plant contain numerous toxic alkaloids, making it a plant that most animals avoid. Humans sometimes ingest this plant for its hallucinogenic properties; however, toxin levels vary widely among plant parts, among individual plants, and throughout the year, making it very difficult to judge how much to take without risking severe poisoning. Consequently, many folks who eat jimsonweed end their adventure in the hospital in great pain.

Jimsonweed has large, white, trumpet-shaped flowers that open at dusk throughout the late summer (July-September) and are pollinated by huge hawkmoths (also called sphinx or hummingbird moths).[72] The tongues of these hawkmoths bend in a special way so that only they can reach the pollen and nectar. Hawkmoths both pollinate jimsonweed and lay their eggs on its leaves. After hatching, the larvae spend their whole lives on a single plant. In the process of eating the alkaloid-containing leaves, the larvae incorporate these poisons into their body tissue and become highly inedible themselves. In the late summer, the fertilized flowers form spiny, golf-ball-sized fruit. When cold temperatures arrive, this perennial plant dies back to the ground.

Being a Desert Plant. Is the life of a desert plant a rapid rush from germination to adult, or is it a slow, steady slog through the different life stages? Though one might be tempted to bet that desert plants live the slow life, most desert plants adopt both lifestyles, depending on the situation.[73] When water and nutrients are limited, which is most of the time, the plants expend only minimal energy to stay alive, and thus grow very slowly, if at all. However, the unpredictable desert climate can also deliver water and nutrients at high rates for a short time and most desert plants are

Figure 7-11. Tilted Park (mile 208.6)

A. June 6, 1889. After their arduous portages in the rapids upstream, the Brown-Stanton Expedition decided to spend most of the day in the cottonwood grove on river left at Tilted Park. They needed to dry their equipment after the wreck of the *Brown Betty*. The crew members began to question Frank Brown's leadership at this point in their expedition, and it was here that they decided to split the expedition in half. In this upstream view, Franklin Nims captures a beach devoid of vegetation except for scattered cottonwood seedlings. (F.A. Nims 58, courtesy of the National Archives)

B. July 24, 1992. Tamarisk has invaded the formerly barren sandbars at Tilted Park. Some of Nims's other photographs from this site are totally blocked by tamarisk thickets. The cottonwood seedlings in photograph A apparently did not persist as they were established at a site vulnerable to flooding. Coyote willow and scattered tamarisk trees line the left side of the view. Hackberry in the background on river left have increased, but junipers appear to be in the same positions on the slopes above. (G.B. Bolton, Stake 2630)

able to take quick advantage of plentiful resources. This ability to switch strategies helps resolve some apparent contradictions when analyzing the dynamics of desert communities.

Most of the repeat photos show communities that are basically unchanged, with the species composition static and many of the individual plants appearing to be about the same size as they were over 100 years ago. In contrast, several of the photos show areas disturbed since the first photo, yet the new plants are the same size as the plants in the old photos. When areas are artificially revegetated, seedlings grow slowly in dry years.[74] However, a few wet years in succession will take most species from a seed to full adult size. In addition, plants that grow in slickrock cracks where water and nutrients are limiting grow very slowly, whereas individuals of the same species in nearby soils where water and nutrients are more abundant grow much more quickly. Clearly, desert plants have very flexible life-history strategies and are able to take advantage of wet conditions and put on huge growth spurts.

The Decline of the Cottonwoods

Pulling up to the prominent beach on the right side of Tilted Park, your eyes are pulled to the cottonwood trees standing behind the wall of tamarisk (Figure 7-11). These cottonwoods beckon silently in this hot, sunny environment, and if you watch river parties disembark here, most people beeline for the shade they offer. We are not alone in this behavior: birds and many other beasts, including insects, also seek out the cottonwood. All welcome the shade, protection and food offered by these lovely trees.

Sadly, while cottonwoods are thriving along the many small streams in the southwestern United States, they appear to be declining along the major rivers, especially the Colorado (Figure 7-12).[75] This decline has been noted in many alluvial reaches along large rivers throughout the western US.[76] Some observers believe that ninety percent of the original cottonwood stands in the Southwest have been destroyed by a variety of human activities.[77] This is very clearly the case in Tilted Park and downstream at Rapid 12. As you float

Figure 7-12. Rapid 10 (mile 208.1)

A. June 6, 1889. As the Brown-Stanton Expedition continued downstream, Franklin Nims made another upstream view of Tilted Park. John Wesley Powell named Tilted Park for the prominent rotated Toreva blocks. The view is across Rapid 10, which has no discernible waves at this high discharge of about 40,000 ft³/s. (F.A. Nims 60, courtesy of the National Archives)

the river, leafless skeletons are starkly outlined against red cliffs and blue sky; some are the victims of human-caused fires and some have died for reasons about which we can only speculate.

A little knowledge of the life history of cottonwood trees is necessary before addressing the reasons for such decline. As discussed in Chap. 5, fire is now sweeping through these corridors at an accelerated rate, and cottonwoods do not fare well once severely burned. Seed development in cottonwoods is synchronized with late-spring floods generated by melting snows in the mountains. Receding flood waters once left behind fertile and moist silt beds, creating perfect conditions for seed germination. Dams, however, now prevent major floods and trap some of the sediment that once moved downstream. This means that seedbeds that were once annually renewed now have to wait for floods that somehow manage to thwart the dams. In addition, floodwaters once reduced populations of small mammals that eat cottonwood seedlings, including deer mice, kangaroo rats and especially the vole (*Microtus montanus*).[78]

Flow of water in and out of banks during the annual flood plays a crucial role in keeping cottonwoods healthy. In some places, downcutting, channel meandering, and trapped sediment has stranded mature trees far from water, both horizontally (as seen at Tilted Park) and vertically (as seen at Spanish Bottom). These conditions may or may not be fine for the adult trees, but they definitely signal death for the seedlings. Channel narrowing, which has occurred in the Tilted Park area, could be part of the reason that mature cottonwood trees are dying back: the trees are farther away from dependable water. Lack of soil moisture was found to be the dominant source of seedling mortality along the upper Green River.[79]

Tamarisks now crowd the river bank, contributing to channel narrowing.[80] Shade and salty soils from tamarisk also inhibit cottonwood germination, so even if the seeds make it to the beach there is often no space, light, or favorable soils to allow the establishment of young cottonwoods. The old trees may simply be dying without replacement. Further compounding the problem is the increase in the beaver population. This animal's favorite foods are cottonwood and willow. Remember Denis Julien? Beavers

B. July 24, 1992. In the foreground, eight individuals of Mormon tea persist while five have died. Well-developed biological soil crusts appear in both the 1889 and 1992 views. Across on river right, tamarisk forms a dense thicket with cottonwood trees appearing behind. Frémont cottonwoods have died on both sides of the river at Tilted Park. The camping beaches at Tilted Park are larger, possibly because tamarisk has stabilized the banks on the right side of Rapid 10. (G.B. Bolton, Stake 2716)

were once trapped out of most of the Colorado River drainage, and now they are making a comeback. A lesser problem is that seedlings are eaten by livestock, elk, moose, and deer, while beavers cut down the adult trees for food and lodging material.[81]

Given that dams and tamarisk are human-caused impacts that have altered the edology of the river, some creative solutions may be required if cottonwoods are to remain in places like Tilted Park. Planting *poles* (de-limbed trunks of young trees) in places where water is too swift for tamarisk and beavers is one possibility. Preventing fires will certainly prevent further losses. Selectively removing tamarisk from areas where cottonwoods are declining may help. Operating dams to mimic natural flow regimes is another potential solution.

THE LARGEST FLOOD?

In hydrology, one learns that there are floods, then there are *floods*, and then there are FLOODS. Cataract Canyon has had its share of all of these. The largest flood of the twentieth century occurred in 1921, when about 147,000 ft³/s roared through the canyon in late June. This barely exceeded the second largest flood—145,000 ft³/s in 1917—and was much larger than the 114,000 ft³/s experienced in 1984. The legendary 1884 flood, which was not actually measured anywhere but instead was estimated after the fact, supposedly was 225,000 ft³/s in Cataract Canyon. Well before that, reportedly about 4,000 years ago, about a half-million cubic feet of water per second entered Grand Canyon,[82] and presumably most of that came through Cataract Canyon.

Really big floods have a significant impact on the landscape, and flood evidence may be preserved for a long time in an arid environment.[83] Large floods leave deposits that are similar to beaches, only perched well away from the river. These flood deposits, also called *slackwater deposits*, have not been found in Cataract Canyon except as overbank sediments in wide areas such as Tilted Park. However, driftwood piles also provide excellent evidence of past floods; their only drawback is that the wood decomposes with time, leaving little or no recognizable flood evidence. The age of driftwood piles may be determined by

Figure 7-13. Tilted Park (mile 208.6)

A. September 19, 1871. The second Powell Expedition camped on river left at Tilted Park. E.O. Beaman captured this upstream view of a cottonwood tree with driftwood wrapped around it near the channel of Cross Canyon. The presence of this driftwood rack suggests that a large Colorado River flood occurred prior to the Powell Expedition arrival. The most likely years for such a flood would be either 1862 or 1869, when large floods were documented in the settled regions downstream in Arizona. (E.O. Beaman 750, courtesy of the U.S. Geological Survey Photographic Library)

B. October 16, 1999. Although the cottonwood that is the subject of Beaman's photograph has died, more cottonwoods are now in the view. Many of these cottonwoods appear to be dying, however. The driftwood that was wrapped around the now-dead tree has disintegrated into small fragments that still litter the ground. A line of mature tamarisks now lines the left side of Tilted Park, giving way to dense stands of native willows along the left side of Rapid 9. The previously denuded foreground has been colonized with twelve plant species and several non-native annuals. The exposed soil now has a healthy coverage of biological soil crusts. (Sam Walton, Stake 3921)

examining the trash they contain, whether there is sawn wood or not, or by radiocarbon dating. For example, the 1884 flood deposits in Cataract Canyon contain sawn wood, which means the flood occurred after settlement of the drainage basin upstream.[84]

In 1871, well before the 1884 flood, E.O. Beaman of the second Powell Expedition took a photograph of a cottonwood tree on river left in Tilted Park (Figure 7-13). Fresh-looking driftwood was wrapped around this tree and was lying around on the sandy soil in the foreground. This particular tree, which has since died, is several hundred yards away from the current bank of the Colorado River, and the driftwood pile has been reduced to indiscernible wood fragments. Terraces created by the 1884 flood are closer to the Colorado River. Clearly, Cataract Canyon experienced a very large flood shortly before Powell first explored the canyon. Our knowledge of flow in the Colorado River in the mid-1800s is dim, however—there were no gaging records or even people to witness floods— but several pieces of evidence point to a large flood occurring in the 1860s. First, the driftwood around the tree appears fresh looking in an 1871 photograph, not 4,000 years old. Second, a legendary flood occurred in the Southwest just before Powell's expedition.

The most famous flood in Utah history is the forty-day and forty-night rainfall flood of the winter of 1861-1862. Beginning on Christmas Day, 1861, the storm actually lasted forty-three days.[85] Floods generated by this storm are the largest known in parts of Oregon and California.[86] Based on scant depositional evidence near Needles, California, this flood had a discharge estimated to be *in excess of* 400,000 ft³/s.[87] Although flooding was extensive in the Virgin River, no one knows exactly how much of this water passed through Cataract Canyon. But that now-deteriorated driftwood, vivid in an old photograph, demonstrates that the Colorado River has had much larger floods than we have experienced in our recorded history of Canyonlands.

INSECTS ALONG THE RIVER

Now we have arrived at the halfway point of what is left of the free-flowing Colorado River through Cataract Canyon, and most of the animals seen here have been crawling or flying invertebrates: animals without backbones. Invertebrates make up eighty-five percent of all animals on Earth, however, while vertebrates only make up the rest.[88] Paraphrasing Thomas Eisner, we do not need to worry about insects inheriting the earth because they already own it. There are somewhere between one and thirty million species of insects on this planet, representing at least two-thirds of all species on Earth.[89] There are more species of insects than the rest of the animal kingdom combined.

Insect Species of the Colorado Plateau

Insects found on the Colorado Plateau are most closely related to those of the Rocky Mountains, although the Colorado Plateau contains many endemics. While this region has never had a complete insect inventory, it is estimated that there are probably about 14,000 to 26,000 insect species on the Colorado Plateau and in the Great Basin combined.[90] There is very high diversity among some groups. Most notably, this region supports sixteen percent of all robber fly species known for the United States, seventeen percent of all stonefly species, twenty percent of

all butterfly species, and thirty percent of all ant species. It is estimated that there are over 6,000 insect species associated just with shrubs.[91] In addition, we know that many insect species in this vicinity are yet to be described, as evidenced by a recent survey of ground-dwelling bees in the nearby San Rafael Swell; scientists there found a total of 333 species in one survey, of which 200 were new to science.[92]

This region is rich in Orthoptera (grasshoppers and crickets), including the famous Mormon crickets, and is host to sixty-one species of grasshoppers alone.[93] Heteroptera (plant bugs) are commonly found on juniper, pinyon, sagebrush, shadscale and four-wing saltbush. The Homoptera (leafhoppers, aphids, and scale insects with plant juice-sucking mouthparts) are especially fond of big sage; there are up to forty-six aphid species and 112 leafhopper species that specialize just on this plant species. There are forty-four species of grass-feeding leafhoppers in this region, including those that specialize on warm-season grasses such as blue grama and muhly (*Muhlenbergia* sp.) grass and those that specialize on cool-season grasses such as Indian ricegrass and sand dropseed. Some leafhoppers are found only on one species of grass. Grasses in this region that support these specialists include grama, galleta, sand dropseed, and saltgrass. Grama grass alone has eight leafhopper species that are found on no other plants. However, not all eight leafhopper species occur on all grama grass plants: shifts in leafhopper composition can be seen with very subtle changes in climate or soils. There are also endemic leafhopper species in this region.

Many different types of flies (Diptera) can be found here as well. These include Nematocera (craneflies, gall midges, and mosquitoes) and Brachycera (robber flies, blowflies, horseflies, deerflies, and houseflies). Craneflies are the largest family in Diptera, with 14,000 species worldwide and 1,600 in North America. They are often called "mosquito eaters" even though they do not eat mosquitoes. In fact, most adults do not feed at all. Many species of cranefly lay their eggs and spend their larval lives in aquatic or semiaquatic habitats. In deserts, however, many spend their larval lives underground feeding on leaf litter and roots of desert shrubs, especially sagebrush and saltbushes. Most cranefly species found in the Mojave, Great Basin, and Colorado Plateau deserts are endemics. It is thought that most cranefly lineages began their evolution in low-elevation, highly xeric deserts since they have a high diversity and constant presence of sagebrush, saltbushes, and other shrubs. Only recently in evolutionary time have craneflies moved to higher elevations or more mesic habitats. Interestingly, though, there are no species endemic to the Chihuahuan or Sonoran deserts; it may be because sagebrush and saltbush are much less common in these deserts.

Robberflies inhabit all life zones. There are 158 species in Utah, sixty-eight of which are widespread and seventeen occur only in the drainages of the Colorado River. There are several species endemic to the Colorado Plateau. Robberflies are distinguished by their extremely large eyes, and are found mostly in shrub-dominated habitats. There they sit on rocks or low shrubs, waiting for their insect prey to fly by them. They kill their prey by injecting a fast-acting toxin into flying insects on the wing.

Moths and butterflies are a common sight in this region. It is not easy to tell them apart, but butterflies generally hold their wings vertically when they land, while moths hold their wings horizontally. Butterflies have delicate slender bodies with little hair, while moths tend to be fat-bodied and hairy. Butterflies have thin antennae with a knob at the tip, while moths often have antennae that are feathery, and that lack any knob. At night, you are more likely to encounter moths, while during the day, you are more likely to encounter butterflies. During the day, butterflies tend to congregate at the tops of hills or mountains. While butterflies tend to be more brightly colored, there are still plenty of moths with similar gaiety expressed on their wings. Many butterflies are associated with specific types of riparian areas, and changes in water levels that alter vegetation are likely to affect these species.[94]

Bees are a common inhabitant of this region, and are very important pollinators of many rare plants. Most are ground-nesting solitary bees, unlike the imported social European honeybee. A solitary lifestyle may have been favored in deserts because long-term food supplies are inadequate for a large colony. Despite this limitation, imported honeybees are doing well in many desert environments. This can be a problem for the often highly specialized native bee species. While the exotic generalist honeybees can take nectar and pollen from many plants, the natives are often limited to one or several species. If a honeybee colony is established nearby, the exotic bees can quickly deplete the nectar and pollen of the plants required by the natives, resulting in starvation of the natives.

BATS

Bats are a commonly seen small mammal in this region. If you are camped on river right at Tilted Park and it is evening, bats are probably swooping around you. Bats fly at night or in the early evening, scooping up insects in flight, and are one of the most diverse orders of mammals on Earth. With over 1,000 species, they make up almost one-fourth of all known mammal species.[95] Fossil bats have been found that are over fifty million years old, yet appear similar to bats seen today. Bats are found on every continent except Antarctica and in every habitat except the most extreme cold or hot ones. They come in a wide variety of sizes and lifestyles: some are tiny, while others have huge six-foot wingspans; some are herbivorous, some insectivorous, and some are true carnivores that live on lizards, frogs, rodents, and fish. Three species are parasitic and live off of other animals' blood. Bats are important pollinators of many common and rare plants. Sadly, over half of the North American species are either rare or endangered.[96]

Bats have a large surface-to-volume ratio. This, combined with their skin-covered wings, means they have difficulty maintaining adequate body heat, especially when flying at night. During the day, they conserve heat by folding their wings over their small bodies. However, night flying can be a precarious balance between gaining energy by eating and losing heat through flight. Bats divide foraging times by air temperature: some species fly when air temperatures are cooler while others fly at warmer air temperatures. Different species of insectivorous bats often feed at different heights and/or on different prey sizes to reduce competition for food. During cold weather, bats can lower their body metabolism and enter torpor.

Bats use a unique device called *echolocation* for navigation and finding their prey. By emitting ultra-sonic sounds and then timing the returned signal, they can determine the size, shape, direction of travel, and texture of their prey. This echolocation "radar" is so sensitive it can detect something as narrow as a human hair.[97] Some of the bats' prey have found ways to fight back. Moths can mimic echoes of a bat at close range, confusing them and making the bat think it is about to collide with another bat, causing it to veer off course and miss. However, bats find clever ways to fool the moths: some bats have big ears and quiet voices so the moths do not hear them, and some bats emit signals below what moths can detect, thus enabling the bats to sneak up and catch the moths.

Bats mate during the fall or right before hibernation. The females store the sperm until spring and bear usually just one baby in late June. The females and babies live in maternity colonies that can number up to 15,000 individuals. Many bodies keep the colony warm. Males roost separately in cooler colonies and often enter torpor daily to conserve energy.

Vesper bats are probably the most commonly encountered mammal in Cataract Canyon.[98] This bat family includes the western pipistrelle (*Pipistrellus hesperus*), big brown (*Eptesicus fuscus*), and pallid (*Antrozous pallidus*) bats.[99] These bats are largely insectivorous and consume small insects such as mosquitoes, leafhoppers, and moths. Vesper bats are tiny bats, and are sometimes seen during the day. Big brown bats are very common throughout the West and consume many insects, especially beetles. They fly in straight lines twenty to thirty feet off the ground. Pallid bats forage primarily on the ground, eating lizards, insects, scorpions, mice, seeds and cactus fruits. Free-tailed bats are occasionally seen and are identified by their tails, which extend more than one-third beyond their tail membranes. They are strong long-distance fliers, and may range up to fifty miles a night to forage. This region does not support any of the huge colonies of bats such as are seen in southern New Mexico in places like Carlsbad Caverns.[100]

THE RESPITE ENDS

Once again, it is time to proceed downstream. A long row across Lake Cataract ends at the top of a thundering series of rapids known collectively as Mile Long. From here to Lake Powell the rapids will be continuous, particularly at high water, when the ability to reach the river's bank in a row boat can only be achieved after a great deal of exertion. It is worth remembering that what is behind—the wide canyon and flat river of Tilted Park—owes its existence to the rapids ahead and the tributary canyons that create them. Also, bid those cottonwoods goodbye, because no more of this species will be seen downstream.

Notes

1. John Wesley Powell, *The Exploration of the Colorado River and Its Tributaries* (New York: Dover Publications, 1961), 216.

2. John Cooley, *The Great Unknown* (Flagstaff: Northland Press, 1988), 114. Powell claimed Hawkins made this statement on July 19, 1869 at the Confluence, but according to Powell's journal Hawkins actually made the remark on July 22 at Tilted Park; see W.C. Darrah, "Major Powell's Journal: July 2–August 28, 1869," *Utah Historical Quarterly* 15 (194): 125–131 and note 8.

3. E. Gdula and M. Gudorf, "Southeast Utah Group Sound Monitoring Program, 1994–1996, Final Report," (Moab, Utah: Southeast Utah Group, National Park Service, unpublished, 1998), 1–17.

4. John Cooley, *The Great Unknown* (Flagstaff, Arizona: Northland Publishing, 1988), 118.

5. *Ibid.*, 119.

6. Powell, *The Exploration of the Colorado River*, 218.

7. Cooley, *The Great Unknown*, 118–120.

8. Clyde Eddy, *Down the World's Most Dangerous River* (New York: Frederick A. Stokes Company, 1929), 63–120.

9. R.E. Westwood, *Woman of the River: Georgie White Clark, White-Water Pioneer* (Logan: Utah State University Press, 1997), 91–95.

10. Discharges for some historical river trips are given in John Weisheit, "Response from John Weisheit," *The Confluence* 3 (1996): 22–23. Details of high-water runs in the early 1980s come from John Weisheit, "High Water Remembered," *The Confluence* 2 (1995): 23; John Weisheit, personal communications with the 1984 participants of high water in Cataract Canyon, circa 1990.

11. Nancy Nelson, *Any Time, Any Place, Any River: the Nevills of Mexican Hat* (Flagstaff, Arizona: Red Lake Books, 1991), 8.

12. E.U. Clover and Lois Jotter, "Floristic Studies in the Canyon of the Colorado and Tributaries," *American Midland Naturalist* 32 (1944): 591–642.

13. John Weisheit, personal communication with the National Park Service, 1997, when emergency funds for swiftwater rescue were initiated.

14. Radiocarbon date of 545Å75 years before present, sample number GX-19927, Geochron Laboratories, Cambridge, Massachusetts.

15. National Park Service, Incident Report 850181; http://www.nps.gov/cany/river/report11.htm

16. R.A. Valdez, *The Endangered Fish of Cataract Canyon* (Salt Lake City, Utah: Bureau of Reclamation, Fisheries Biology and Rafting Contract No. 6-CS-40-03980, 1990), 56.

17. Steve Young, National Park Service, personal communication, 2000.

18. L.B. Leopold, *A View of the River* (Cambridge, Massachusetts: Harvard University Press, 1994), 27.

19. P.W. Huntoon, G.H. Billingsley, Jr., and W.J. Breed, *Geologic Map of Canyonlands National Park and Vicinity, Utah* (Moab, Utah: Canyonlands Natural History Association, 1983).

20. W.L. Graf, "The Effect of Dam Closure on Downstream Rapids," *Water Resources Research* 16 (1980): 129–136.

21. R.H. Webb, *Grand Canyon, A Century of Change* (Tucson: University of Arizona Press, 1996), 145–161; R.H. Webb, P.G. Griffiths, T.S. Melis, J.G. Elliott, and J.E. Pizzuto, "Reworking of Debris Fans by the 1996 Controlled Flood in Grand Canyon," in *The 1996 Flood in Grand Canyon: Scientific Experiment and Management Demonstration*, eds. R.H. Webb, J.C. Schmidt, R.A. Valdez, and G.R. Marzolf (Washington, D.C.: American Geophysical Union, Geophysical Monograph 110, 1999), 37–51; R.H. Webb, P.G. Griffiths, T.S. Melis, and D.R. Hartley, *Sediment Delivery by Ungaged Tributaries of the Colorado River in Grand Canyon* (Tucson, Arizona: U.S. Geological Survey Water Resources Investigations Report 00-4055, 2000).

22. Graf, "The Effect of Dam Closure," 129.

23. J.C. Schmidt and D.M. Rubin, "Regulated Streamflow, Fine-Grained Deposits, and Effective Discharge in Canyons with Abundant Debris Fans," in *Natural and Anthropogenic Influences in Fluvial Geomorphology: The Wolman Volume*, eds. J.E. Costa, A.J. Miller, K.W. Potter, and P.R. Wilcock (Washington, D.C.: American Geophysical Union, Geophysical Monograph 89, 1995), 178–195.

24. J.C. Schmidt and J.B. Graf, *Aggradation and Degradation of Alluvial Sand Deposits, 1965–1986, Colorado River, Grand Canyon National Park, Arizona* (Washington, D.C.: U.S. Government Printing Office, U.S. Geological Survey Professional Paper 1493, 1990).

25. J.C. Schmidt, P.E. Grams, and R.H. Webb, "Comparison of the Magnitude of Erosion along Two Large Regulated Rivers," *Water Resources Bulletin* 31 (1995): 618–631.

26. Fred Quartarone, *Historical Accounts of Upper Colorado River Basin Endangered Fish*, ed. Connie Young (Golden, Colorado: U.S. Government Printing Office, U.S. Fish and Wildlife Service, Committee of the Recovery Program for Endangered Fish of the Upper Colorado River Basin, 1995).

27. R.R. Miller, "Origin and Affinities of the Freshwater Fish Fauna of Western North America," in *Zoogeography*, ed. C.L. Hubbs (Washington, D.C.: American Association for the Advancement of Sciences 51, 1958), 188–222.

28. R.A. Valdez and R.D. Williams, "Endangered Fishes of Cataract Canyon," *Proceedings of the Desert Fishes Council* 18 (1986): 212–219; R.A. Valdez, *The Endangered Fish of Cataract Canyon* (Salt Lake City, Utah: Bureau of Reclamation, Fisheries Biology and Rafting Contract No. 6-CS-40-03980, 1990), 33–36.

29. National Park Service records, Canyonlands National Park, Moab, Utah, 2002. These records are continually updated, and supercede those published in Charlie Schelz, comp., "Species Numbers for Vertebrates," *The Confluence* 7 (2000): cover.

30. U.S. Fish and Wildlife Service, *Upper Colorado River Endangered Fish Recovery Program* (Denver, Colorado: www.r6.fws.gov/coloradoriver, 2000).

31. Valdez, *The Endangered Fish of Cataract Canyon*, 212.

32. S.W. Carothers and B.T. Brown, *The Colorado River through Grand Canyon* (Tucson: University of Arizona Press, 1991), 82–88; W.L. Minckley, "Native Fishes of the Grand Canyon Region: An Obituary?" in *Colorado River Ecology and Dam Management*, ed. G.R. Marzolf (Washington, D.C.: National Academy Press, 1991), 124–177.

33. The authors thank Richard A. Valdez for this detailed account of catfish introduction.

34. D.S. Jordan, "Report of Explorations in Colorado and Utah during the Summer of 1889, With an Account of the Fishes Found in Each of the River Basins Examined," *U.S. Fisheries Commission Bulletin* 9 (1891): 1–40.

35. R.A. Firmage, *A History of Grand County* (Salt Lake City: Utah State Historical Society, 1996), 33.

36. P.B. Holden and C.B. Stalnaker, "Distribution and Abundance of Mainstream Fishes of the Middle and Upper Colorado River Basins, 1968–1973," *Transactions of the American Fisheries Society* (1975): 218–231.

37. Valdez, *The Endangered Fish of Cataract Canyon*, viii.

38. *Ibid.*, vii.

39. Holden and Stalnaker, "Distribution and Abun-

dance of Mainstream Fishes;" J.N. Rinne and W.L. Minck-ley, *Native Fishes of Arid Lands: A Dwindling Resource of the Desert Southwest* (Fort Collins, Colorado: U.S. Department of Agriculture, Forest Service General Technical Report RM-206, 1991), 41.

40. C.D. Vanicek, R.H. Kramer, and D.R. Franklin, "Distribution of Green River Fishes in Utah and Colorado Following Closure of Flaming Gorge Dam," *The Southwestern Naturalist* 14 (1970): 298–315; P.B. Holden, "Ghost of the Green River: Impacts of Green River Poisoning on Management of Native Fishes," in *Battle Against Extinction: Native Fish Management in the American West,* eds. W.L. Minckley and J.E. Deacon (Tucson: University of Arizona Press, 1991), 43–54.

41. Vanicek *et al.*, "Distribution of Green River Fishes," 297.

42. M.M. Van Steeter and John Pitlick, "Geomorphology and Endangered Fish Habitats of the Upper Colorado River. 1. Historic Changes in Streamflow, Sediment Load, and Channel Morphology," *Water Resources Research* 34 (1998): 288–302.

43. D.W. Blinn and G.A. Cole, "Algal and Invertebrate Biota in the Colorado River: Comparison of Pre- and Post-Dam Conditions," in *Colorado River Ecology and Dam Management*, ed. G.R. Marzolf (Washington, D.C.: National Academy Press, 1991), 102–123.

44. H.W.C. Prommel and H.E. Crum, "Salt Domes of Permian and Pennsylvanian Age in Southeastern Utah and Their Influence on Oil Accumulation," *Bulletin of the American Association of Petroleum Geologists* 11 (1927): 373–393.

45. *Ibid.*, 374.

46. T.S. Harrison, "Colorado-Utah Salt Domes," *Bulletin of the American Association of Petroleum Geologists* 11 (1927): 111–133.

47. One publication describes debris fans and the relations among tributaries, rapids, and debris fans, yet concludes that the large rapids are all caused by slumps; J.K. Rigby, W.K. Hamblin, Ray Matheny, and S.L. Welsh, *Guidebook to the Colorado River, Part 3: Moab to Hite, Utah through Canyonlands National Park* (Provo, Utah: Brigham Young University Geology Studies 18, Part 2, Studies for Students No. 6, 1971), 15–17.

48. The year 1941 was determined from ring counts on thirty-six individuals harvested at Rapid 3 and was obtained on the largest trees; smaller trees germinated afterwards. Alex McCord, Laboratory of Tree-Ring Research, personal communication, 1995.

49. David Williams, *A Naturalist's Guide to Canyon Country* (Helena, Montana: Falcon Press/Canyonlands Natural History Association, 2000), 34; Damian Fagan, *Canyon Country Wildflowers* ((Helena, Montana: Falcon Press/Canyonlands Natural History Association, 1998), 125.

50. M.W. Salzer, V.A.S. McCord, L.E. Stevens, and R.H. Webb, "The Dendrochronology of *Celtis reticulata* in the Grand Canyon: Assessing the Impact of Regulated River Flow on Tree Growth," in *Tree Rings, Environment, and Humanity*, eds. J.S. Dean, D.M. Meko, and T.W. Swetnam (Tucson, Arizona: Radiocarbon Publishing, 1996), 273–281.

51. A.M. DeBolt, *The Ecology of* Celtis reticulata *Torr (Netleaf Hackberry) in Idaho* (Corvallis: Oregon State University, unpublished M.S. thesis, 1992), 1–13; B.J. Albee, L.M. Shultz, and Sherel Goodrich, *Atlas of the Vascular Plants of Utah* (Salt Lake City: Utah Museum of Natural History, Occasional Publication No. 7, 1988), 601.

52. John Alcock, *Sonoran Desert Summer* (Tucson: University of Arizona Press, 1990), 18–23.

53. Albee *et al.*, *Atlas of the Vascular Plants of Utah*, 257.

54. Salzer *et al.*, "Dendrochronology of *Celtis reticulata*."

55. *Ibid.*, 278.

56. Williams, *A Naturalist's Guide to Canyon Country*, 29; J.A. MacMahon, *Deserts* (New York: Alfred A. Knopf, 1985), 508; Stanley Welsh, N. D. Atwood, Sherel Goodrich, and L. C. Higgins, eds., *A Utah Flora* (Provo, Utah: Brigham Young University Press, 1987), 29–31; Fagan, *Canyon Country Wildflowers*, 118; Albee *et al.*, *Atlas of the Vascular Plants of Utah*, 257; Lyman Benson and R.A. Darrow, *Trees and Shrubs of the Southwestern Deserts* (Tucson: University of Arizona Press, 1981), 380.

57. J.E. Bowers, R.H. Webb, and R.J. Rondeau, 1995, "Longevity, Recruitment, and Mortality of Desert Plants in Grand Canyon, Arizona, U.S.A.," *Journal of Vegetation Science* 6 (1995): 551–564; Webb, *Grand Canyon, A Century of Change*, 50–52.

58. M.A. Dimmitt, "Plant Ecology of the Sonoran Desert Region," in *A Natural History of the Sonoran Desert*, eds. S.J. Phillips and P.W. Comus (Tucson, Arizona: Arizona-Sonora Desert Museum/University of California Press, 2000), 209–212; Williams, *A Naturalist's Guide to Canyon Country,* 57; Webb, *Grand Canyon, A Century of Change,* 50–52.

59. Webb, *Grand Canyon, A Century of Change,* 53–54.

60. Williams, *A Naturalist's Guide to Canyon Country,* 32; Webb, *Grand Canyon, A Century of Change,* 45–50 and 79–80; MacMahon, *Deserts,* 498.

61. J.E. Bowns and N.E. West, *Blackbrush (*Coleogyne ramosissima *Torr.) in Southwestern Utah Rangelands* (Logan, Utah: Utah Agricultural Experiment Station Research Report 27, 1976); S.A. Lei, "Spatial Distribution of Blackbrush (*Coleogyne ramosissima* Torr.) Populations in the Mojave Desert," *Bulletin of the Southern California Academy of Sciences* 100 (2001): 96–99; Albee *et al.*, *Atlas of the Vascular Plants of Utah*, 534; Benson and Darrow, *Trees and Shrubs of the Southwestern Deserts*, 275–276.

62. Ken Cole and R.H. Webb, "Late Holocene Vegetation Changes in Greenwater Valley, Mojave Desert, California," *Quaternary Research* 23 (1985): 228–235; K.L. Hunter, *Impacts of the Little Ice Age on the Vegetation of Southern Nevada* (Las Vegas: University of Nevada, unpublished M.S. thesis, 1991).

63. Fagan, *Canyon Country Wildflowers*, 95.

64. Todd Esque, personal communication (Mojave Desert); Susan Meyer and Tim Graham (Colorado Plateau).

65. R.A. Minnich, "Wildland Fire and Early Postfire Succession in Joshua Tree Woodland and Blackbrush Scrub of the Mojave Desert of California," in *Ancient Surfaces of the East Mojave Desert*, eds. R.E. Reynolds and J. Reynolds (Redlands, California: San Bernardino County Museum, 1995), 99–106; S.A. Lei, "Postfire Seed Bank and Soil Conditions in a Blackbrush (*Coleogyne ramosissima* Torr.) Shrubland," *Bulletin of the Southern California Academy of Sciences* 100 (2001): 100–108.

66. Williams, *A Naturalist's Guide to Canyon Country*, 30; Fagan, *Canyon Country Wildflowers*, 88.

67. Williams, *A Naturalist's Guide to Canyon Country*, 31; John Sowell, *Desert Ecology* (Salt Lake City: University of Utah Press, 2001), 47; S.D. Smith, R.K. Monson, and J.E. Anderson, *Physiological Ecology of North American Desert Plants* (Berlin: Springer, 1997), 47.

68. Williams, *A Naturalist's Guide to Canyon Country*, 39.

69. Fagan, *Canyon Country Wildflowers*, 86, 94, and 105.

70. Dimmitt, "Plant Ecology of the Sonoran Desert Region," 251–252.

71. *Ibid.*, 143, 298–259, and 339; Williams, *A Naturalist' Guide to Canyon Country*, 63.

72. Dimmitt, "Plant Ecology of the Sonoran Desert Region," 339; S.L. Buchmann and G.P. Nabhan, *The Forgotten Pollinators* (Washington, D.C.: Island Press, 1996), 104.

73. Smith *et al.*, *Physiological Ecology of North American Desert Plants*, 60.

74. Jayne Belnap, personal observation.

75. Webb *et al.*, *Changes in Riparian Vegetation in the Southwestern United States*; R.H Webb, personal observation of more than 2,000 repeat photographs in the region; Cooper *et al.*, "Factors Controlling the Establishment of Cottonwoods."

76. D.J. Cooper, D.M. Merritt, D.C. Andersen and R.A. Chimner, "Factors Controlling the Establishment of Fremont Cottonwood Seedlings on the Upper Green River, USA," *Regulated Rivers: Research and Management* 15 (1999), 419–440.

77. S.J. Tweit, *The Great Southwest Nature Factbook* (Bothell, Washington: Alaska Northwest Books, 1992).

78. D.C. Andersen and D.J. Cooper, "Plant-Herbivore-Hydroperiod Interactions: Effects of Native Mammals on Floodplain Tree Recruitment," *Ecological Applications* 10 (2000), 1384–1399; D.C. Andersen, K.R. Wilson, M.S. Miller, and M. Falck, "Movement Patterns of Riparian Small Mammals During Predictable Floodplain Inundation," *Journal of Mammalogy* 81 (2000), 1087–1099.

79. D.M. Merritt and D.J. Cooper, "Riparian Vegetation and Channel Change in Response to River Regulation: A Comparative Study of Regulated and Unregulated Streams in the Green River Basin, Utah," Regulated Rivers: Research and Management 16 (2000), 543–564; Cooper *et al.*, "Factors Controlling the Establishment of Cottonwoods."

80. W.L. Graf, "Fluvial Adjustments to the Spread of Tamarisk in the Colorado Plateau Region," *Geological Society of America Bulletin* 89 (1978): 1491–1501; T.M. Allred and J.C. Schmidt, "Channel Narrowing by Vertical Accretion along the Green River near Green River, Utah," *GSA Bulletin* 111 (1999) 1757–1772.

81. Andersen and Cooper, "Plant-Herbivore-Hydroperiod Interactions."

82. J.E. O'Connor, L.L. Ely, E.E. Wohl, L.E. Stevens, T.S. Melis, V.S. Kale, and V.R. Baker, "A 4,500 Year Record of Large Floods on the Colorado River in the Grand Canyon, Arizona," *Journal of Geology* 102(1994): 1–9.

83. R.C. Kochel and V.R. Baker, "Paleoflood Hydrology," *Science* 215 (1982): 353–361.

84. R.H. Webb, D.E. Boyer, K.L. Orchard, and V.R. Baker, *Changes in Riparian Vegetation in the Southwestern United States: Floods and Riparian Vegetation on the San Juan River, Southeastern Utah* (Tucson, Arizona: U.S. Geological Survey Open-File Report OF 01-314, 2001), 1 sheet; K.S. Thompson and A.R. Potochnik, eds., *Development of a Geomorphic Model to Predict Erosion of Pre-Dam Colorado River Terraces Containing Archaeological Resources* (Flagstaff, Arizona: SWCA Environmental Consultants, Cultural Resources Report No. 99–257, 2000).

85. R.H. Webb, *Late Holocene Flooding on the Escalante River, South-Central Utah* (Tucson: University of Arizona, unpublished Ph.D. dissertation, 1985), 4–5.

86. W.N. Engstrom, "The California Storm of January 1862," *Quaternary Research* 46 (1996): 141–148.

87. J.L. Patterson and W.P. Somers, *Magnitude and Frequency of Floods in the United States: Part 9. Colorado River Basin* (Washington, D.C.: U.S. Government Printing Office, U.S. Geological Survey Water-Supply Paper 1683, 1966), 384.

88. Barbara Terkanian, "A Vertebrate Looks at Arthropods," in *A Natural History of the Sonoran Desert*, eds. S.J. Phillips and P.W. Comus (Tucson: Arizona-Sonora Desert Museum/University of California Press, 2000), 287.

89. C.R. Nelson, "Insects of the Great Basin and Colorado Plateau," in *Natural History of the Colorado Plateau and Great Basin*, eds. K.T. Harper, L.L. St. Clair, K.H.

Thorne, and W.M. Hess (Niwot, Colorado: University Press of Colorado, 1994), 211–237; Terkanian, "A Vertebrate Looks at Arthropods," in *A Natural History of the Sonoran Desert*, 285.

90. Nelson, "Insects of the Great Basin and Colorado Plateau," in *Natural History of the Colorado Plateau and Great Basin*, 211–237.

91. *Ibid.*

92. Griswold, F.D. Parker, and V.J. Tepedino, "The Bees of the San Rafael Desert: Implications for the Bee Fauna of the Grand Staircase-Escalante National Monument," in *Learning from the Land: Grand Staircase-Escalante National Monument Science Symposium Proceedings*, eds. L.H. Hill and J.J. Koselak (Salt Lake City, Utah: Bureau of Land Management, GI-98/006+1220, 1997), 175–186.

93. Nelson, "Insects of the Great Basin and Colorado Plateau," in *Natural History of the Colorado Plateau and Great Basin.*

94. S.M. Nelson, "Study of Butterfly Assemblages at a Variety of Riparian Sites" (Denver: Bureau of Reclamation, Technical Memorandum 8220-01-16, 2001).

95. Janet Tyburec, "Bats," in *A Natural History of the Sonoran Desert*, 461.

96. *Ibid.*, 462.

97. *Ibid.*, 469.

98. Williams, *A Naturalist's Guide to Canyon Country*, 81–82.

99. Tyburec, "Bats," in *A Natural History of the Sonoran Desert*, 467–470.

100. Tweit, *The Great Southwest Nature Factbook*, 19.

8

HELL TO PAY

Mile Long Rapid and the Big Drops

Down we go among the rapids. Huge rocks have fallen from the walls, great angular blocks scattered down the talus and stream along the channel. The walls too are very craggy. . . . The west wall is very bold and grand, nearly vertical. The waters make roaring music at the foot of the cliffs, plunging over falls and whirling and foaming among the rocks. The men work with a will that seems wonderful. Here we have cataracts.

–John Wesley Powell, September 21, 1871[1]

There is quiet water behind and quiet water ahead, but in order to get there you have to go through some of the biggest whitewater commonly run in North America (Figure 8-1). This water is not for the novice boater: at certain water levels, more oar boats flip than make it through upright in Cataract Canyon. Occasionally, even those seemingly invincible twenty-two- and thirty-three-foot motorboats go over, spilling their passengers into freezing cold, spring runoff water. At low water, the lion becomes a lamb, and relatively tame rapids make the uninitiated wonder about the veracity of all those stories about the Big Drops. An adrenaline rush lies ahead, just before the massive letdown of the quiet waters of a reservoir. It is time to snug up the lifejackets, recheck the duffle, and run some whitewater. Rapid after rapid is ahead, culminating in two of the most threatening reaches in the Southwest: Big Drops 2 and 3.

RAPTORS

Many river runners plan their descent through Mile Long Rapid by scouting, usually from the broad debris fan at the mouth of Range Canyon. The long walk down to Rapid 15 and its inscriptions allows plenty of time for birdwatchers to scan the cliffs, looking for those large birds of prey known as raptors.

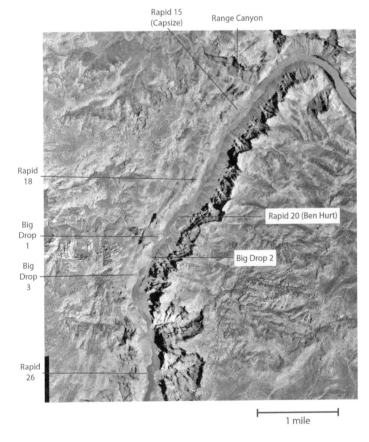

Figure 8-1. Orthophotograph of the Colorado River between Range and Imperial Canyons.

Many raptors love the steep-walled cliffs of Cataract Canyon, and these birds are often seen soaring over the cliffs and rivers during the day.[2] They are common from here through the Big Drops and onto the upper reaches of the reservoir.

The most frequently seen raptor is the carrion-eating Turkey Vulture (*Cathartes aura*). They are easily distinguished by the v-shape and light coloring under their wings as well as the upward angle of their wings while soaring; in contrast, eagles hold their wings flat.[3] Like eagles, Turkey Vultures hardly ever flap while soaring, and can ride rising air currents for hours. They have keen eyesight and an acute sense of smell (unlike other birds), that help them find dead prey. Up close, they appear quite ugly with their bright red, naked heads, but their nakedness is useful for easy cleaning after their consumption of rotting carcasses. Turkey Vultures nest on cliff faces, tree stumps, caves, and even on the ground. They lay one to three eggs, usually in a cliff or rock-face nest, and fledging takes about three or four months. Although vultures have similar appearances worldwide, the North American vultures are related to storks, while those in Europe, Asia, and Africa are related to hawks and eagles.

Golden Eagles (*Aquila chrysaetos*) also commonly soar during the day, looking for rabbits, small mammals, lizards, chicks of other birds, and carrion. They will also eat fish if given the chance.[4] Golden Eagles form long-term or lifetime bonds with their mates, and return to the same nests every year. Nests consist of huge piles of sticks, five feet tall and four-to-six feet across, on cliff ledges. The males feed the females during incubation and chick rearing. Two eggs are laid, although the larger chick eventually kills the smaller one.

Red-tailed Hawks (*Buteo jamaicensis*) are the most widespread raptor in North America, and the most frequently seen in this region.[5] These large hawks have broad, rounded wings and short, broad tails which are a rusty red underneath, hence their name. They are solitary birds, and their females return to the same nesting territory each year. Nests are made of sticks located in tall trees or sometime cliff ledges. In deserts, most Red-tailed Hawks live in riparian areas or by human habitations where large trees abound. You will often see these birds sitting on high perches (including power lines as well as cliffs), watching for prey, which are mostly rodents but occasionally also snakes. Once caught, the food is brought back to the perch for consumption.

Peregrine Falcons (*Falco peregrinus*) are found where high cliffs are abundant. They eat mostly birds, including swifts, swallows, doves, and smaller riparian birds. Both peregrines and eagles defecate over the edge of their eyries, often hitting the cliff face below. While peregrine droppings forms long, smooth white streaks down the cliff face, eagle feces are clumpy and the streaks are shorter. Peregrines lay eggs directly on the rock ledge. These birds mate for life but before they do that partake in an elaborate courtship ritual: the male and the female find a smaller bird in flight and begin flying on either side of it. At some point, the male snatches the smaller bird out of the air and hands it to his mate while still in flight. Peregrines have dive speeds of 180 miles per hour, which makes them one of the fastest birds on Earth. Their prey is often killed by the blow delivered when the falcon hits at high speed or when the falcon severs the spinal cord with a sharp bite.

Peregrine populations were once devastated by dichloro-diphenyl trichloroethane, otherwise known as the agricultural insecticide DDT. This chemical thinned their eggshells such that the eggs could not tolerate the weight of a sitting adult bird. Once DDT use in the United States was banned, peregrine populations made a dramatic comeback, and the population in Glen Canyon National Recreation Area now appears to be the second largest in the continental United States.[6] However, Mexico is now using ever-expanding amounts of DDT. Many migratory birds winter in Mexico and are then eaten by the peregrines, who bioaccumulate DDT in their body fat. Sadly, there is new evidence that peregrine eggshells may be thinning again.

Bald Eagles (*Haliaeetus leucocephalus*) are not a common sight in Cataract Canyon. However, a few birds do winter there every year, coming south from the Pacific Northwest and Canada. They prefer fish but will eat most anything, dead or alive. One study

TABLE 8-1. Changes to the Rapids of Cataract Canyon and Its Approaches.

Rapid name	Changes	Notes
Millard Rapid (Green River)	New rapid	Debris flow and/or a flash flood from Millard Canyon
Murphy Rapid (Green River)	Little change	
Salt Wash (Colorado River)	Little change	
The Slide	Unchanged	Supposedly changed in 1907 on basis of steamboat records
Rapid 1 (Brown Betty)	Slight changes on right	Debris flows on river right, top of the rapid, date unknown
Rapid 2	No apparent changes	Debris flow in 1997 below rapid on river right
Rapid 3	Changes in gravel bar	Large debris flow in 1997 on river left did not affect rapid
Rapid 4	No apparent changes	
Rapid 5	No changes	Last debris flow occurred about 500 years ago
Lower Rapid 5	No changes	
Rapid 6	No changes	No debris flows
Rapid 7	Changes not completely known	Debris flow from canyon on river left
Rapid 8	Left side more constricted	Debris flow from canyon on river left
Rapid 9	Left side more constricted	Debris flow from canyon on river left
Rapid 10	No changes	
Rapid 11	Decreased fall	Drowned out by increased constriction at Rapid 12
Rapid 12	Increased constriction	Debris flow from canyon on river left
Rapid 13	No changes	No debris flows from Range Canyon
Rapid 14	More constricted on left	Debris flow from canyon on river left
Rapid 15 (Best Rapid)	Left side more constricted, Main rocks in channel are unchanged	Debris flows from canyon on river left
Rapid 16	No changes	
Rapid 17	No changes	
Rapid 18	Button Hole may be historic rockfall	Rockfall on river left
Rapid 19	No data	
Rapid 20 (Ben Hurt Rapid)	No data	
Rapid 21 (Big Drop 1)	Changes on river left at high water	No historic debris flows from Calf Canyon; debris flow from left chute, 1871-1928
Rapid 22 (Big Drop 2)	Several large rocks moved	Debris flows from canyon on river left
Rapid 23 (Big Drop 3)	Left side completely changed	Debris flows from canyon on river left
Lower Rapid 23	No changes	
Rapid 24	No changes	No debris flows from canyon on river right
Rapid 25	No changes	
Rapid 26	Gravel bar rearranged, no other changes	No debris flows from canyon on river left
Rapid 27 (Imperial Canyon Rapid)	No known changes but partially submerged by Lake Powell	No debris flows from Imperial Canyon

showed their diet to be 86.6 percent live prey, 7.7 percent scavenged dead and 5.7 percent food stolen from other animals.[7] Bald Eagles are now more numerous and stay longer in this area because of the clear water and easily obtained fish in Lake Powell. However, they tend to avoid areas where they will encounter people.[8]

One thing most of the raptors have in common is that they will eat carrion. In this way, they help clean up the canyon walls and shorelines. If birds do not get there fast enough, other creatures will take care of most dead animals. Some of these decomposers also help recycle plant material into reusable nutrients.

THE SCALE OF THESE RAPIDS

Conventional wisdom holds that the rapids of Mile Long and the Big Drops are created by slump blocks.[9] Beginning with John Wesley Powell, observers have remarked on the large slump blocks and slopes littered with massive blocks in Cataract Canyon. As noted in Chapter 7, however, the river is wide where many of the actual landslide deposits are, indicating that the Colorado has had little difficulty dealing with the obstructions created by landslides and Toreva blocks. In addition, no significant slumps or landslides are present in either Mile Long Rapid or the Big Drops. Instead, the drops begin at tributary mouths, although in some cases those tributaries are very small and the debris fans are only noticeable at low water. In the late 1990s, the real reason for Cataract's rapids became apparent in this reach. Debris flows reached the Colorado River at Rapids 14, 15, 22, and 23, with some changes to the whitewater. Repeat photography shows that at least one large debris flow that occurred before 1940 significantly altered Big Drop 3 and other changes to rapids in Cataract Canyon (Table 8-1).

TABLE 8-2. Rockfalls Observed in Cataract Canyon.

Location	River mile - Side	Effects on river
The Slide	1.5-R	None
Obscure location	216.0-L	None
Obscure location	215.9-L	None
Obscure location	214.5-L	None
Rim on trail to Spanish Bottom	213.0-L	None
Obscure location	212.5-R	None
Tilted Park	208.2-L	None
Rapid 12	207.0-L	None
Rapid 18	204.1-L	May have created the Button Hole
Big Drop 2	202.2-L	New rocks on debris fan
Big Drop 3	202.2-R	None
Big Drop 3	202.1-R	None
Below Big Drop 3	202.0-L	None
Gypsum Canyon	196.6-L	Dammed side canyon about three miles upstream of the reservoir

ROCKFALLS

Although the rapids of Cataract Canyon are created by debris flows, rockfalls contribute considerable colluvium to the river corridor. Rockfalls are particularly prominent along both banks through Mile Long Rapid and the Big Drops (Table 8-2). Some hydraulic features in these rapids, such as the Button Hole in Rapid 18, may be the result of recent rockfalls (Figure 8-2). Our repeat photography shows that rockfalls have occurred historically throughout Cataract Canyon. Although most rockfalls are very local, originating from ledges in the Honaker Trail Formation, others may have come from high on the cliffs, moving large blocks of Cedar Mesa Sandstone near or into the Colorado River.

THE RAPIDS OF MILE LONG

For several miles through Tilted Park and Lake Cataract, the Colorado River flows peacefully between sculptured walls of limestone and sandstone and its banks are lined with small trees. The river abruptly changes from placid to raging at the mouth of Range Canyon (mile 205.0, river right). Mile Long Rapid, the collective name for eight rapids that become one long rapid at high water, is at hand. There is

a knob on the right-hand cliffs, called "The Button" (for obvious descriptive reasons) that reminds river runners of where they are and what they are approaching. It towers over one of the most significant whitewater obstacles in this reach: the Button Hole.

The name "Mile Long Rapid" is traditionally attributed to the Brown-Stanton Expedition, who arduously portaged their boats down the left side of this rapid in 1889. However, Stanton never uses that name in his accounts. Whoever first named it Mile Long Rapid is debatable, but this name appears in Clyde Eddy's description of Cataract Canyon from 1927.[10] The single name for this complex of whitewater is insightful, because the rapids of Mile Long have one thing in common: most of the sediment in the river here appears to have come in from Range Canyon, and each low-water drop is controlled by debris flows from distinct tributaries, most of which come from river left.

The Preliminaries: Rapids 13 and 14

Some rapids seem to be merely nuisances. Rapids 13 and 14 are in this category: they precede the first significant threat in the group collectively known as Mile Long, and form around the debris fan at Range

Figure 8-2. Rolling Boulders at Rapid 18—the "Button Hole" (mile 204.1)

A. June 8, 1889. The Brown-Stanton Expedition portaged their boats down the left side through most of Mile Long Rapid (Rapid 13 to 19). Rapid 18 is at the downstream end of Mile Long and forms a substantial navigation hazard. For example, in 1909 Seymour Dubendorff of the Stone Expedition flipped his boat at the top, probably on or near the rocks and waves shown in this downstream view. At its lower end, the Button Hole flips many unwary boatmen in medium flows. (F.A. Nims 68, courtesy of the National Archives)

B. March 31, 1994. The large boulder that now blocks the view came from an isolated rockfall, which is common throughout Cataract Canyon. Although our photographic evidence is not conclusive, we believe that the Button Hole formed in the twentieth century as a result of one of these isolated rockfalls. (Steve Tharnstrom, Stake 2920)

Canyon, the largest debris fan in Cataract Canyon. Range Canyon has not had a twentieth-century debris flow, and Rapid 13 probably has been stable historically. Rapid 13 can be considered a riffle, drowned out by its larger relatives downstream.

Rapid 14 begins at a little debris fan produced by a tributary on river left. This tributary and several chutes upstream and downstream from it produced small debris flows in the late 1990s. Rapid 14 offers more of a challenge than Rapid 13 as its tailwaves lead directly to a part of Rapid 15 into which one usually does not want to take a boat. Even worse, at about 5,000 ft³/s, a sneaky little flat rock lies just beneath the surface in the tailwaves of Rapid 14 and well above Rapid 15. While intently looking at the line of rocks that mark the entry to Rapid 15, river runners can find their boat perched on this rock to the enjoyment of any other spectators who happen to be watching from the rocks on river right, pausing in their search for the famous inscriptions at Rapid 15.

Rapid 15 (Best Rapid)

Rapid 15 offers the first technical challenge to river runners in Cataract Canyon (Figure 8-3). This rapid today is affectionately known by several names: "Capsize" and "Hell to Pay" are the most commonly used despite the fact that the Western River Guides Association endorsed the name "Best Rapid" in the 1960s.[11] At discharges below about 40,000 ft³/s—in other words, discharges that are most commonly run—the tailwaves from Rapid 14 sweep towards the left side of this rapid, which is a sieve of rocks on a debris fan. A half-hearted pull to the right might land you in a ledge wave or, at lower water, on a rock that spawns a rooster-tail wave; a stronger pull might earn you the right to wrap on what is called Capsize Rock, which protrudes from the center of the river and the rapid. A very strong pull, plus some maneuvering to dodge other rocks, puts you in the promised land of the right-hand run, which sweeps around in an S-turn through this rock-strewn channel. Going left of Capsize Rock is okay and even wise at certain water levels.

Figure 8-3. "Hell to Pay—Boat No. 1 Sunk and Down" (mile 204.7)

A. July 22, 1891. The Best Expedition miscalculated the strength of the eddy fence at the entrance to Rapid 15 and pinned one of their two boats in this rapid. The A-frame attached a rope from shore to the boulder and the drift-wood logs were used in a failed attempt to pry the pinned boat off the rock. Because of this accident, the crew made a classic inscription in a large boulder to the right of the camera station, and the rapid is now called Capsize Rapid. However, a different boulder (more midstream), which is barely visible on the right edge of this view, is erroneously called Capsize Rock. (J.A. Mc-Cormick, not numbered, courtesy of the Huntington Library)

B. March 31, 1994. Capsize Rapid is created by debris flows from both sides of the Colorado River. The larger of the two tributaries, which enters on river left (on the opposite side from the camera station), had a large debris flow in the last century. Using a number of photographs of the rapid, we have determined that the date of this debris flow is contained between 1927 and 1964. Hackberry trees are now larger, but no new clumps have become established. Tamarisk trees have become established in the foreground. (Mike Taylor, Stake 2847)

Capsize Rock has repeatedly earned its name because it traps the unaware. One summer in the 1990s an aluminum dory wrapped on its upstream face and hung there as a monument for an entire winter as a reminder that one should take this rapid seriously. In a way, it is surprising that an entire mound of boat parts does not protrude from the low-water wave here, because Capsize Rock has trapped a large number of boats in recent Cataract Canyon history.

To avoid becoming one of the statistics, some guides use little tools to help them remember the run. Some people think of the low-water run as a baseball game with the massive rocks protruding from the current as the bases, to be avoided or rounded instead of touched. Visualizing the rapid at 5,000 ft³/s, the tail-waves of Rapid 14 lead towards a somewhat flat rock protruding from the head of the rapid. This rock is called "Second Base," which is strange since the game of baseball begins with the batter at home plate. A large, rectangular rock sticks well out of the flow on the right side; this is called "Third Base." Capsize

Rock is therefore "Home Plate." So the river guide "batter" begins by going to second plate, heading for third, and then rounding home. This does not make baseball sense to a true fan but it can get you through the rapid.

One thing that Capsize Rock—or Home Plate, if you prefer—did not trap was boat number 1 of the Best Expedition of 1891. They wrapped their boat, a well-documented, epic boat wreck, on Third Base, not Capsize Rock. Hopefully you will never have as much time here as they did, but if you ever do, you might want to inspect the boulders on river right carefully for their inscriptions. Most inscriptions, from the Best Expedition and others who followed their example, are pretty obvious: the most famous of these reads "Camp #7, Hell to Pay, No. 1, Sunk & Down." At some point, a vandal changed "Sunk" to "Drunk." Another inscription by James Best can no longer be seen as the boulder rolled over in 1983 during a heavy rainstorm. Other inscriptions, including an isolated "1891" on the trail leading downstream, are a bit

Figure 8-4. Capsize Rapid (mile 204.5)

A. September 19, 1921. Rapid 15 has posed a navigation problem for boatmen throughout the twentieth century. However, in 1921 the U.S. Geological Survey Expedition had little problem running the rapid at low water. In this photograph, one of the USGS boatmen successfully navigates the rapid. (E.C. LaRue 99, courtesy of the U.S. Geological Survey Photographic Library)

B. July 24, 1992. A large pile of boulders fills the former eddy. The new rocks came from the debris flow that occurred between 1927 and 1964 and show the extent of channel narrowing on the left side of the rapid. (Tom Wise, Stake 2582)

more obscure. One near river level simply says "HMc," apparently an unfinished reference to Harry McDonald, the head boatman of the Best Expedition.

We have matched thirteen historical photographs of Rapid 15 over the last decade, and most of the original photographs were taken between 1891 and 1921. They reveal a rapid that has changed considerably since the Best Expedition's unfortunate visit to "Third Base." Rapid 15 still has most of the features seen by the Best Expedition, but there also have been some significant changes. The right side of the rapid has not changed very much; all the big rocks in the rapid were there in July 1891, although several rocks have rolled over or split in half. The rocks on the right side are related to occasional rockfalls from the cliffs on river right, reworking of boulders from a large pile of sediment that looms over the downstream part of the rapid, and boulders washed down from Range Canyon.

The left side is a completely different story because of debris-flow deposition. Rocks there have been pushed into the river from a small canyon that is not much larger than it appears from river level (Figure 8-4). That canyon has flashed slurries of debris several times in the last century, including a relatively large event between 1921 and 1964 and smaller debris flows in September 1997 and 1999. As a result, the

little debris fan on river left has risen as much as six feet and the rapid is a little narrower than it used to be, particularly at high water. All of the low-water obstacles in the rapid have been there since Best's expedition, although some appear a little more rounded now. All the changes to the rapid are to the left of Capsize Rock.

Rapids 16 through 19

Walking down the river bank on either side of Mile Long Rapid is a challenge. The boulders are large and loose, and scrambling on the banks is required (Figure 8-5). Interesting river history can be seen in this walk, though, if one looks carefully at some large boulders on either side of the river at Rapid 16. This rapid, formed by outwash from a left tributary overlain on the outwash from Range Canyon, is mostly memorable for the large, midstream boulder at its head that one must miss at low water. At high water, it is difficult to separate the waves of Rapid 16 from those created upstream and downstream.

A series of inscriptions here, in silver paint, tells what little is known of the story of Bill Davis's Cataract Canyon career. According to the inscriptions, Davis boated Cataract in 1952, 1953, 1954, and

Figure 8-5. Desert Vegetation at Rapid 16 (mile 204.4)

A. June 8, 1889. Franklin Nims took this upstream view at Rapid 16 to show the proposed railroad route. His view shows one of the numerous tributary channels that enter the Colorado River in Mile Long Rapid. (F.A. Nims 42, courtesy of the National Archives)

1964; some of these trips were solo. One rock tells a cryptic story of a typical Cataract disaster:

> JULY 7 1952 BILL & FERN DAVIS WENT OVER
> UPSIDE DOWN CARRIED 300 FT. UNDER
> WATER UPSET HERE

The discharge on July 7, 1952 was 29,100 ft³/s, and it is likely that the Davises flipped in Rapid 15, although it is possible they went over that midstream rock at the head of Rapid 16.

Rapid 17 forms at a constriction created by a Range Canyon outwash and a tributary entering from the left. Rapid 18 is similar, although this rapid has a major feature near the bottom center that catches unprepared river runners. The Button Hole forms at intermediate discharges, with a crescendo in the 30,000 ft³/s range, and it is a really good idea to miss this hole on either side. We speak from personal experience: one of the authors lost most of her clothes one fine summer day while recirculating in this hole. Rapid 19, the last in this closely spaced group, is somewhat similar to Rapid 8 upstream, as the lower section is shallow at low water and requires picking a careful route to avoid hitting submerged rocks. Rapids 16 through 19 are continuous at high water and are called the "South Seas" in reference to the irregular, choppy nature of the waves.

Rapid 20 (Ben Hurt)

The tailwaves of Rapid 19 spread into a broad pool, and eddy circulation on the right side captures both sand for a beach and driftwood. The downstream limit of this pool is constrained by a large island in the center of the river. Depending on the water level, the river runs left, right, and even over the center of the island. In recent years, the island has not been fully covered, and a few straggling tamarisks are now becoming established on its highest points. A rapid forms around this island, particularly on its right side.

The rapid gained its name for something else found on the highest point of this island. In the late 1950s, Joe Baker and A.C. Ekker were traveling down the Green River during the Friendship Cruise. On a lark,

B. March 31, 1994. The most striking feature of this photo pair is the lack of change in desert vegetation. Eighteen Mormon tea plants are still present from the time that Nims took his photo and only two new ones were found. The number of netleaf hackberry trees has increased from two to five, a typical increase in the fast-water section of Cataract Canyon. Most of the rocks in the view are unchanged. (Steve Tharnstrom, Stake 2919)

they decided to run the rapids of Cataract Canyon with Baker's motorized speed boat. While scouting Rapids 1 and 2, the improperly tied rope on their boat loosened and the boat bobbed down the rapids right before their very eyes. The boat was called the *Ben Hurt*, and the section of boat that had the name emblazoned on its side came to rest on the island at Rapid 20.[12] The hull reportedly was washed from the island in 1973. Over the years, the name has been twisted into Been Hurt or even Ben Hur, the title of a book and movie about Roman gladiators. Another name applied to this whitewater is "Island Rapid," which is seldom used.

At high water, Rapid 20 is wet and nonthreatening. At low water, most river traffic passes right of the island, passing through some small waves that do not represent the size of what is below. The island is anchored in place by a pile of large boulders that likely originated from Range Canyon. Some of these boulders create formidable holes at the bottom of the island, creating a hazard to the uninitiated boaters of Cataract Canyon.

The Significance of Mile Long Rapid

In summary, Mile Long is one continuous rapid that starts from debris-flow outwash at Range Canyon (Rapid 13) and extends down to the island at Rapid 20. The low-water rapids (Rapids 13 through 19) are created by the combination of the outwash from Range Canyon, which sets the overall gradient, and debris flows from smaller tributaries on river left. Much of the debris on the island at Ben Hurt likely came from Range Canyon and was pushed into place and shaped into the island by an ancient Colorado River flood.

Range Canyon, then, is one of the most significant producers of coarse-grained sediment (*e.g.*, boulders) in what remains of the free-flowing sections of Cataract Canyon. One would not come to this conclusion merely by looking at docile Rapid 13. But consider the following on your next Cataract trip: that rapid's debris fan, and the canyon that created it, are the reason for Lake Cataract, which extends back upstream, drowning out Rapids 11 and 12. Just picture what kind of flood, or series of floods, it would take to push all that sediment out of the canyon and flush it downstream to Ben Hurt.

There is evidence that the drop through Mile Long Rapid was bigger at one time. River-polished gravels over on the left side above Rapid 13 suggest that the level of the Colorado River was as much as twenty to thirty feet higher than the current river level at some time in the last few thousand years. The next time you visit those inscriptions at Capsize Rapid, look up at the pile of red dirt just downstream on the right side. That sediment came from the little tributary on river left, and the subtle topography to the right of this pile (towards the right cliffs) hints that the river may have been flowing over what is now dry land and fifty feet or so above current river level. Most of the rapids in Mile Long are the same as they were more than a century ago, but a century is just a little blip in geologic time. Mile Long Rapid and its little part now known as Rapid 15 are far from being stable over the long run.

Desert Varnish

The thundering of water as it pours through Mile Long Rapid, and the thought that you and your small boat are soon to plunge into the madness below, can make it difficult to focus on the surrounding scenery. It is easier below Rapid 20, floating in the relatively calm water above Big Drop 1. The huge cliffs that tower over the water in this narrow part of Cataract Canyon are difficult to ignore. These walls have black stripes running down their faces: the black color, and the compounds that comprise it, are called *desert varnish*. Desert varnish tends to accumulate where water gathers on slopes, and as a result, the faces below ephemeral waterfalls tend to have the darkest varnish.

Interestingly, the reason desert varnish is black is similar to the reason that biological soil crusts are dark. The black coloration of the stripes is mostly due to the combination of microbes and manganese and iron oxides.[13] These metals are attached to fine silt and clay particles that are blown about by the wind. Cyanobacteria, microfungi, and bacteria similar to those found in biological soil crusts live both on and

in the cliff faces. When the cliff face is wet, the metal-bearing particles stick. If microorganisms are present, they accumulate and concentrate the metals in their body tissue. In addition, the organisms themselves also manufacture dark pigments for protection from solar radiation.[14]

Desert rock varnish is often very thin; in some places it is merely 0.0004 inches thick. It only forms on relatively stable rock faces; limestone, for instance, rarely accumulates varnish, which is why the prominent cliffs in the Honaker Trail are mostly white. Desert varnish can take thousands of years to form. Ancient peoples loved desert varnish as a canvas for their pictures, which is why most petroglyphs that have survived the test of time are on varnished sandstone blocks. The pink sandstone of the rock contrasts sharply and beautifully with the dark brown of the varnish.

THE BIG DROPS AND BEYOND

A short but swift section of river begins at the bottom of Rapid 20 and heads towards a rapid that curves around a debris fan on the right side. Upstream of this debris fan on river left is a prominent, large beach littered with driftwood logs. This sandbar is a commonly used camp that has a line of hackberry trees that separates it from the talus slopes behind. Clearly visible beyond those trees is a greyish slope, formed in an outcrop of Paradox Formation. A closer inspection of this slope reveals paths lined with stones, and flat campsites carved into the slope, reinforced with rock walls. Someone had time on his hands here. At really big water, such as the floods of greater than 100,000 ft³/s in 1983 and 1984, the Big Drops can make time move very slowly.

The Big Drops refer to the rapids that begin at the mouth of a prominent canyon on river right. Downstream from the debris fan at the mouth of this canyon are three rapids that the U.S. Geological Survey referred to as Rapids 21, 22, and 23. Today these rapids are more commonly called Big Drop 1, Big Drop 2 and Big Drop 3, or collectively the Big Drops. The three have also been combined into one rapid called the Big Drop or Little Niagara.[15]

Where the Big Drops got all these names is debatable, but John Wesley Powell was the first to note the large fall in the river at this point. As was his tendency, Powell exaggerated the drop, calling it seventy-five feet in three quarters of a mile.[16] The actual drop through this reach is thirty-two feet in less than a mile, which is still an astounding slope of 37 ft/mi. It is desirable to consider this group collectively because as with the case of Mile Long Rapid the three individual rapids are linked to the canyon on river right at mile 202.8.

Particularly in the last decade, the Big Drops have become the most dangerous place on the Colorado River through all of its whitewater reaches on the Colorado Plateau. Of the fourteen deaths recorded in the river history of Canyonlands National Park, eleven occurred in the Big Drops and most were the result of boat flips.[17] Unless one is a highly experienced guide who has recently seen the river, or is a river runner with suicidal tendencies, scouting is mandatory for at least Big Drops 2 and 3.

Big Drop 1

Big Drop 1 forms around the debris fan issuing from a canyon variously known as Calf or Teapot. The reason for the confusion has to do with whether the person referring to the canyon is looking for lost cows up on the rim or looks up from the river and sees a unique rock formation on the cliffs at the canyon mouth that resembles a teapot. The rapid is also known in some guidebooks as Kolb Rapid,[18] although the Kolb brothers had no problems running this rapid and camped downstream between Big Drops 2 and 3, painting their name on a wall under an overhanging limestone block.

Appearing as an overgrown version of Rapid 13, Big Drop 1 is not as threatening as its cousins just downstream. Like Rapid 14, one of its biggest issues is that its tailwaves lead directly into Big Drop 2, which creates maneuvering problems for oar boats trying to enter the more dangerous rapid. At low water, a large pool separates these rapids. It is a mistake to underestimate Big Drop 1, because a sizeable hole on its left side midway through can catch and flip

boats at certain water levels. Big Drop 1 has changed historically, although no debris flows have come from the mouth of Calf or Teapot canyon since 1871. Instead, a debris flow from a river-left chute in the middle of the rapid dropped some very large boulders onto a small debris fan (Figure 8-6). One of these boulders forms a hole that is easily missed to the right at high discharges.

Big Drop 2

A well-worn path leads downstream from the beach above Big Drop 1 to the left scout point for Big Drop 2. Trails are prominent and well maintained here. Winding among the boulders, just upslope of the hackberry trees, the trail follows the river as it wends through Big Drop 1 and then ascends a slope leading to a prominent boulder. Climb to the top, and this spot affords a commanding view downstream. This boulder is referred to as "Poop Rock," not for animal droppings but for the visceral reaction that river runners can have to that downstream view.

At 70,000 ft³/s, Big Drop 2 is a terrifying maelstrom that defies description. As with other large rapids, most of its features have names. The most famous is Little Niagara Hole, formed on the downstream of Little Niagara Rock, which is a large boulder at right center that becomes emergent at about 25,000 ft³/s. As the discharge climbs above this level, Little Niagara Hole metamorphoses from a pourover to a keeper-hole to the most thrashing, vicious hole regularly seen on any river. At its most awesome level, the large wave on the downstream side of the hole crashes upstream from a height of about twenty vertical feet.

Some boats have entered Little Niagara Hole and miraculously escaped flipping, which is just as likely a feat as winning the lottery. Most go over, and occasionally frames are broken or ripped from the rubber tubes. One eighteen-foot boat reportedly submerged in Little Niagara Hole, floated downstream underwater for about 100 yards, and then slowly surfaced to the amazement of onlookers. Most of the recent deaths and serious injuries in Cataract Canyon have resulted from swimmers or boats entering Little Niagara Hole

Figure 8-6. Big Drop 1 (mile 202.5)

A. September 22, 1871. John Wesley Powell found the Big Drops to be one of the most significant obstacles for his 1869 river trip. In his famous account of this trip, he refers to the Big Drops as "a 75-foot drop." His photographer, E. O. Beaman, took this striking upstream view of the first rapid, Big Drop 1, and a remarkably clear line of hackberry trees that line the left bank at the high-water line. (E.O. Beaman 749, courtesy of the National Archives)

B. July 15, 1940. River runners who came to the Big Drops found that Powell's seventy-five-foot drop was an exaggeration, but that Powell had not under-stated the severity of the rapids. One river runner was Barry Goldwater, who later became a U.S. senator and a presidential candidate. Goldwater also had a penchant for history and he approximately matched Hillers's view of Big Drop 1 in 1940. Comparing his photo with Beaman's indicates that the hack-berries have increased in size and number. No tamarisks are present in 1940. Otherwise, the rapid is unchanged. (B.M. Goldwater Collection, not num-bered, courtesy of the Center for Creative Photography, University of Arizona)

and either getting trapped in the recirculating flow or being pounded by floating equipment.

At the top of the rapid, a massive boulder called the Marker Rock requires a choice among various runs based on flow and boater skills (Figure 8-7). Some go left, some go right, and some go down the middle. On the left side, a symmetrical lateral wave forms at most discharges and is called the Ledge Wave. At 60,000 ft³/s and above, flow between the Ledge Wave and Little Niagara is forced into a wave known as the Red Wall, which blocks the center of the channel. The Red Wall gets taller with every addi-

tional 10,000 ft³/s. Finally, at certain discrete dis-charges, a miraculous feature called "The Window" forms between the Red Wall and Little Niagara. From Poop Rock, guides describe the high-water run in terms of what percent of the time The Window is open; translated, this is essentially the probability of an upright run in an eighteen-foot oar boat. A number of hydraulic features downstream also command at-tention, dictating how one should approach the run of this rapid.

There are way too many runs at Big Drop 2 to de-scribe them all. Possible routes change with water

C. August 25, 1968. To commemorate Powell's Expedition, Hal Stephens and Gene Shoemaker retraced the route of Powell's Expedition, matching the photographs taken by Powell's photographers in 1871. At Big Drop 1, Stephens's view shows hackberry trees have dramatically increased in size and number. Tamarisk has invaded on the Calf Canyon debris fan, obscuring the prominent sandbar of 1871. The rapid is unchanged. (H.G. Stephens AA-4)

D. July 25, 1992. The striking increase in hackberry trees continued between 1968 and 1992. Comparing just the foregrounds, the number of hackberry trees has increased from four to thirteen individuals. Tamarisk has continued to increase on the Calf Canyon debris fan. Also comparing all four views, the sandbars have become noticeably larger in the last century. Sandbars are ephemeral features, however, and fluctuations in sandbars in the Big Drops occur on an annual basis. These photographs, which span 121 years, show that no debris flows have come from Calf Canyon and the rapid has not changed. (Steve Tharnstrom, Stake 2636)

level, and all runs have a potential for disaster if things do not go well. The possibilities at high water pretty much sum up some of the choices and consequences there. You can go for the center run, aiming for The Window and hoping that it opens; or if you miss to the right, maybe Little Niagara opens in front of you. Motorboats climb the Red Wall at full power, sometimes catching air over its top; but if they miss to the left the Ledge Wave can flip large boats in its corkscrew-like waves. High-powered sport boats occasionally jump the center of the Ledge Wave, landing in highly aerated water downstream and risking *cavi-*

tation, which is what happens when propeller blades lose their bite in the aerated water. Finally, the real test of nerves is the run to the right of Little Niagara Hole, which carries with it the very disastrous consequences for a failed entry.

An upright passage of Little Niagara Hole and the other features at the top of the rapid do not in any way guarantee that the run is successful. The left and center runs lead to very large tailwaves, some capable of flipping motorboats. We know this from personal experience, as one of the authors flipped his sport boat here in 1993. The far right entry leads towards a

Figure 8-7. The overall view of Big Drop 2 (mile 202.3)

A. October 29, 1937. The core of Big Drop 2 is a series of large boulders that have remained in place through the twentieth century. The Marker Rock is most upstream of these; Little Niagara Rock is the larger of the two boulders near the right bank and nearest the camera station. We call the two sharp rocks to the lower right of the Marker Rock the "Fang Rocks." The cubic boulder photographed by the Kolb Brothers (see Figure 8-8) is gone by 1937. All of these boulders probably have accumulated here as outwash from the Calf Canyon debris fan upstream. At any water level, but particularly at high water when the boulders are covered, Big Drop 2 is a serious obstacle to navigation. Buzz Holmstrom, one of the finest boatmen ever to run the Colorado River, had no problems with rapids in Cataract Canyon. On his solo trip in 1937, he took this late afternoon photograph that is one of the best overall views of this famous rapid. (Haldane "Buzz' Holmstrom, 3710 CTCN 202.6, courtesy of the Marston Collection, Huntington Library)

B. April 1, 1994. The "Fang Rocks" are not obvious, but from the disruptions of the water surface they appear to have been tilted downstream and are now mostly submerged. Most of the other boulders visible in 1937 are still present, although a debris flow has entered the rapid from the left. The new boulders are visible at right center on the debris fan. (Steve Tharnstrom, Stake 2922)

curling wave and hole spawned off rocks downstream from Little Niagara; these waves can either flip a boat or push it sideways into the tailwaves. Finally, the tail-waves lead to Satan's Gut in Big Drop 3, meaning that boats either move towards the right or catch the large, turbulent eddies on either side of the river.

At 7,000 ft³/s, Big Drop 2 is fairly docile, offering several routes for passage around or among the large rocks in midstream. Little Niagara Rock is emergent, revealing its massive size. The most common entry is left of the Marker Rock, which protrudes well above this water level, with a move back to the right to avoid the Ledge Wave. In 2003, the river reached what many believe to be its historical low (~1,600 ft³/s), and Big Drop 2 caused eighteen-foot boats to flip at discharges lower than 2,000 ft³/s. The run began right of the Marker Rock, and the strategy was to slowly butt into Little Niagara Rock, pivoting off to the left with the deep water. Another one of those

sneaky little rocks caught some boat tubes, and the river's force pushed these unlucky boats over.

Thirteen historical photographs of Big Drop 2, combined with their matches, provide information on historical changes in this rapid. Many changes have occurred, but it is uncertain if any of these have made any real difference in terms of navigation. The Kolb brothers took the first revealing photographs of this rapid in 1911. One of these photographs shows a cubic block, apparently fifteen-feet wide, resting on smaller rocks just to the right of Niagara Rock (Figure 8-8). This boulder, which would have blocked any right run of the Little Niagara Hole, was moved downstream before 1964 and now rests in the right channel of the rapid. Two pointed rocks, which we call the Fang Rocks, protruded from the water up-stream from Niagara Rock in 1911. These rocks also rolled over before 1964 and now create a little glassy hump in the water surface just upstream from Little

Figure 8-8. Big Drop 2 (mile 202.4)

A. October 27, 1911. Most river runners scout Big Drop 2, the most significant rapid at most water levels in Cataract Canyon. The Kolb brothers were no exception. Here Ellsworth poses next to a large boulder as Emery captured the scene. Ellsworth later ran both boats through the rapid because Emery was ill from drinking Colorado River water. (Kolb Brothers 1001, courtesy of the Cline Library, Northern Arizona University)

B. October 15, 1993. The large boulder is gone, swept downstream by a flood sometime in the twentieth century. Because we have many photographs of this rapid, we determined that the boulder disappeared between 1921 and 1937. We do not know where this boulder went; it probably is underwater a short distance downstream in the pool between Big Drops 2 and 3. Removal of this boulder allows a high-water right run through the rapid that avoids substantial waves that form in the center. In addition, two triangular-shaped boulders, visible at right center in the 1911 photograph, also rolled and only a small dome-shaped wave remains. (Steve Tharnstrom, Stake 3074)

Niagara Rock. Some river runners prefer a low-water run through a slot between Little Niagara Rock and another emergent rock just upstream; the Fang Rocks, if they still were upright, would have made such a run difficult if not dangerous.

Debris flows have occurred on both sides of the river in the last century, but the primary changes have been on river left. At least two debris flows, the last of which occurred in 1997, have added boulders to the debris fan and the river. The debris flows originated at the level of the Halgaito Shale and must have flowed extremely fast through what can only be described as a high-angle chute to the Colorado River. The boulders were about three to six feet in diameter, but re-working by the Colorado River has moved most of that material downstream into the rapid or even further downstream. The debris fan formed by prehistoric debris flows is essentially the same, although rockfalls have contributed isolated boulders. Several blocks twelve to fifteen feet across have been rolled from another gully on river left at the head of the pool above the rapid, probably by the debris flows.

Beginning with Powell, observers have attributed the presence of the Big Drops to rockfalls. Rockfalls certainly occur, and a ready source is nearby in the loose colluvium that mantles the slopes on both sides of the river. A few boulders three to six feet in diameter have rolled to the edge of the low-water rapid, but there is no evidence that any large rockfall capable of blocking the river or even adding its biggest boulders has occurred in the recent past. Like the now-missing boulder that the Kolb brothers photographed, most boulders here appear to be moving downstream with the current, not falling in from above and accumulating in the channel.

Big Drop 3

One could argue that the biggest problem with Big Drop 3 is that it is just downstream from Big Drop 2. This is sort of the equivalent of having Crystal Rapid lead directly into Lava Falls Rapid in Grand Canyon: the danger of the combination is much greater than if the two rapids were well separated. The positions of

Figure 8-9. The First Photograph of Big Drop 3 (mile 202.0)

A. September 24, 1871. Big Drop 3 is the final in the series of imposing rapids that makes Cataract Canyon a classic whitewater run. John Wesley Powell refers to this as "Ross Falls" in his 1871 diary. When the Powell Expedition encountered Big Drop 3 in 1869 and then again in 1871, they portaged their boats on the left side. As this view shows, the left side was choked with large boulders while the right side was very shallow. The rocks were a considerable navigational hazard to Powell's wooden boats while portaging. (E.O. Beaman 752, courtesy of the National Archives)

B. August 25, 1968. Hal Stephens matched Beaman's photograph, but his camera station is not very close to the original. Rocks in the center of the rapid have changed considerably, and new ones have replaced ones that were probably swept downstream. The stage-discharge relations of the rapid are completely changed, with more water forced to the right. These changes are discussed in one of the first river guides to Cataract Canyon (Mutschler, 1979, 60-61), by a participant in the 1968 reenactment of the Powell Expedition, but are not mentioned in Stephens and Shoemaker (1987). (H.G. Stephens AA-7)

Big Drops 2 and 3 are not accidental. Big Drop 3 is the termination of the collective rapid known as the Big Drops, and the rapid itself is essentially a large debris bar comprised of outwash boulders from Teapot or Calf canyon. In this way, Big Drop 3 is like Rapid 20 just upstream, and Rapid 8 above that, and Rapid 3 beyond that; all are formed around debris bars at the base of a complex of rapids. The only real difference here is that the "debris" of Big Drops 2 and 3 consists of extremely large boulders, some twenty to thirty feet across.

Besides Big Drop 3, two other names have been applied to this rapid. During a trip in 1952, a passenger remarked that they had just passed through Satan's Gut.[19] This name appears on Les Jones's scroll map,[20] but for some reason the first river guide in book form refers to the rapid as "Satan's Seat."[21] Most river runners now use the name Big Drop 3 and use Satan's Gut to refer to a large, corkscrewing pourover that forms on the left side of the rapid.

Satan's Gut is always there, no matter what the flow. As the water rises, the Gut typically moves to the left. This hole has considerable power in high water and can easily bend or break metal boat frames. The river is deep in this hole; we know from personal experience because one of the authors probed its depths

C. July 25, 1992. Big Drop 3 has changed more than any other rapid remaining in Cataract Canyon. Because of the debris flow from river left, many new boulders appear at the extreme right of the view. The left side now has a definite, runnable slot that is used by most river runners at discharges less than about 8,000 ft^3/s. Despite the clearing of this slot a large boulder, called "Big Mossy" by modern river runners, is new. Rocks in the center of the rapid have changed considerably, with new ones replacing ones that were probably swept downstream. The stage-discharge relations of the rapid are completely changed, with more water forced to the right. (G.B. Bolton, Stake 2585)

in 1993. The high-water tailwaves from Big Drop 2 typically just miss the pourover into the Gut, but the river has the upper hand and does not always cooperate with the best of intentions. In high or low water, this run is a leap of faith.

In order to describe runs, or just because humans like to apply names to everything interesting that they see, most of the rocks and hydraulic features of Big Drop 3 have names. Three are significant. At low water, a large rock covered with green algae, Big Mossy, protrudes from the left side of the channel and serves as one of the guides to the low-water left run (Figure 8-9). That run goes over the Table Rock, a

large flat rock that never protrudes from the current but forms a chute that river runners enter to run left at low water. This same rock is probably what anchors the position of Satan's Gut at high water.

A drop-off just right of the center of Big Drop 3 is called Frogg's Hole, named after Frogg Stewart, a boatman for Holiday Expeditions who ran triple rigs. Triple rigs, invented by Georgie Clark, consist of three row boats tied together and operated by two rowers, one on the upstream and one on the downstream side of the boat. Each oarsman uses a single oar. In high water, triple rigs run with the river and take the big hits in the Big Drops with remarkable stability. Frogg's Hole was the reward for a successful run of Big Drop 2; these cumbersome boats could not avoid it.

Finally, on the far right entry is a huge lateral wave, which has various popular names such as Big Bertha and Brahma, and which emerges during the early summer higher water to the delight of boaters. Be careful: motorboats have been thrown upside down here. As the water drops, the cleanest runs are found right of center. The right run is the way to go down to at least 10,000 ft^3/s, and some adventuresome boaters go there at even lower water levels (Figure 8-10).

There are so many runs of Big Drop 3 that it is essentially futile to describe all of them. On one August day, we watched a large, private trip make six distinct runs through Big Drop 3 at 6,000 ft^3/s, with entries on the right, center, left, and extreme left. The center run is the least desirable; Del Reid, a boatman for Norm Nevills, stuck his boat in the center of Big Drop 3 at low water in August 1940. Barry Goldwater, then an adventuresome entrepreneur before he discovered national politics, sat on the left side and photographed the extraction, drawing a detailed map of the maneuvers in his diary.[22]

At very high water, the options are less limited owing to the fact that Big Drop 3 begins to wash out except for the far left side, which becomes a near waterfall over tall rocks that are normally part of the shoreline. If you decide to stay in the wave train, you will most likely just miss this gaping hole. In lower water, many boaters have successfully fought their way left of Satan's Gut, running the narrow chute that

Figure 8-10. The First Run of Big Drop 3 (mile 202.1)

A. About August 1, 1891. After leaving their pinned boat at Rapid 15, the Best Expedition proceeded downstream in only one boat. Their loss did not deter their willingness to run rapids. In this remarkable upstream view from river right, the crew makes the first documented run of Big Drop 3. (J.A. McCormick, not numbered, courtesy of the Huntington Library)

B. April 1, 1994. The debris fan on river right has changed little in the last century, while the fan on the opposite side has changed considerably. Although some rocks in the foreground are new and some have been rotated, the larger particles are easily identified in both views. These boulders are part of the sutured network on this debris fan. On river left, large boulders have been added to the debris fan, changing the appearance of that side of the river. More water is forced to the right side because of the additional constriction, making the right run feasible at medium and high discharges. (G.B. Bolton, Stake 3084)

drops their boats into relatively quiet water below the frothing hole.

The right and center parts of Big Drop 3 have not changed historically, as indicated both by Goldwater's 1940 map and photographs taken by E.O. Beaman of the second Powell Expedition. Some smaller boulders have rolled around, but the large ones that Del Reid stuck his boat on, as well as the big ones on the right shore, are the same. The boulders in the center and on the right appear to be the remnants of a debris bar, like a smaller version of the island at Rapid 20, only with all but the very largest particles removed. The debris bar on river right has no tributary source, further indicating that these boulders were washed in from upstream. At times in its photographic history, an emergent gravel bar is present in the river just above the rapid and across the top of the entry to the right run. Sediment washing down the Colorado River has a habit of accumulating at this point, which is precisely what should happen at a rapid controlled by a debris bar.

Unlike Rapid 20, Big Drop 3 has a high-angle chute that contributes debris flows to river left. This source of very large boulders causes a constriction on the left side that adds to the ferocity of Satan's Gut and is the impetus for change in the rapid. Unlike most of the rapids in Cataract Canyon, Big Drop 3 has changed significantly, although the biggest changes occurred before 1940. At least two debris flows moved more boulders into the river or onto the debris fan after 1956. Eighteen historic photographs spanning 129 years document these changes.

The left channel of the rapid has been very dynamic. At least seven boulders, up to nine feet in diameter and visible in 1871 photographs, were rolled to lower positions in the left channel by 1940. Big Mossy rolled over into its current position sometime between 1911, when the Kolbs camped here, and 1933, when Harold Leich lost his boat. A debris flow from the left side is the apparent reason for this change: many of the large rocks that one must scramble over and among to view the rapid from river left were deposited during this debris flow.

Another debris flow occurred sometime in the second half of the twentieth century. One flat-top rock nine to twelve feet across was in the river at the head of the left channel; this rock was displaced after 1956. Also since 1956, another boulder of similar size was transported to water's edge at the head of the left channel, accompanied by many other boulders three to six feet in diameter. The river undoubtedly removed many more boulders during its annual floods, but the net effect is that the left-side debris fan has aggraded with boulders, narrowing the channel at high discharges. Downstream from the debris fan, the channel margin below the rapid has been scoured extensively, probably as a result of the increase in current along the left shore.

Debris flows have shifted rocks such that the rapid is now completely different from what Powell viewed in 1869 and 1871, despite the fact that only minor changes have occurred in either the right side or the center. In 1871, the left side must have resembled a waterfall spanning about two-thirds of the river's width, and this may have been the inspiration for the name Little Niagara, not Big Drop 2 upstream. The removal of those boulders shifted the deepest part of the river from the right to the left side. As a result, the flow pattern through the right side of the rapid is different. For a given discharge now, the stage along the right shore is lower; from a different perspective, this means that the discharge required before the right side can be safely run has increased compared with conditions in 1871. Similar changes have been observed at Lava Falls Rapid in Grand Canyon following debris flows there.[23]

Rockfalls have occurred on both sides of the river at Big Drop 3, which is similar to the history of Big Drop 2. One of Beaman's 1871 photographs shows several new rockfall stripes on the large river right talus cone above the rapid. Rolling rocks are common here: one large cubic boulder that Beaman took a photograph from, below the rapid on the left, has rolled into the river.

Driftwood

Driftwood accumulates in specific places along the Colorado River in Cataract Canyon, and no more so than in the pools that separate the individual drops in Mile Long Rapid and the Big Drops. Our repeat pho-

tography consistently shows driftwood in the same places; some of the photographs show the same pieces of driftwood in the same place, whereas most simply show a new pile (Figure 8-6). The pool on river right between Big Drops 2 and 3 is one of the areas along this stretch of river where driftwood collects. Driftwood piles are an important source of food for termites and fish. From the perspective of termites, the driftwood pile is home and food all in one package. From the fishes' viewpoint, things are a bit more complicated.

In murky rivers such as the Green and Colorado, in-stream algal growth is limited. Thus, unlike the cases of many other rivers and streams, the basis of the food chain in these rivers is not aquatic plants. Instead, land-derived materials, including plants, bugs, and anything else edible that falls into the water, provides much of the carbon. This input of plants and bugs can happen locally, from overhanging vegetation falling in or bugs falling off the vegetation into the water (especially at high water), or vegetation that has washed down from upstream. Macroinvertebrates, such as caddisfly larvae, live on this debris. Fish, in turn, eat the macroinvertebrates, occasionally supplementing this diet with bugs that fall into the water.

Fish or macroinvertebrates use some of the material floating by immediately, but much accumulates in driftwood piles as well. During floods, these piles can reenter the water, giving the macroinvertebrates and fish another opportunity to obtain its nutrients. In this sense, driftwood piles are a food "savings account." In addition, driftwood piles support lots of land invertebrates, including termites and ants. When floods occur, these invertebrates become fish food as well.

One effect of dams is that they stop upstream organic materials from reaching downstream organisms. Worse yet, people delight in burning the driftwood: most of the piles in the Grand Canyon were torched long ago.[24] This is not a problem for fish that live just below the dam, as the clear waters there support large algal populations. But the effects on fish upstream of Lake Powell, where waters remain murky, are not known. We do not understand the aquatic food chain well enough to know exactly how, and how much, driftwood contributes to the diet of native fishes.

The Remaining Rapids (Rapids 24 through 27)

When the level of the reservoir is low, four more rapids are present in Cataract Canyon. The first of these, Rapid 24, is often called "Powell's Pocket Watch" in honor of the incident in which William Dunn dunked the Major's timepiece, precipitating an armed confrontation. As with many names, we believe this one is applied to the wrong site: this incident was more likely to have occurred in the middle of the arduous portage through the Big Drops, not at the relatively benign Rapid 24.[25] This rapid has some of the largest waves at most water levels in Cataract Canyon, providing a nonthreatening roller coaster ride for boaters willing to take the center run.

Rapid 25 is a straight-forward rapid with large eddies on either side of the tailwaves. This rapid is commonly known as "Repeat" or "Rerun" because many river trips with outboard motors can up-run the eddy and make multiple passes through this rapid to the delight of the passengers. Rapid 26 forms around an island, likely the combination of outwash from Rapids 24 and 25 upstream and a debris fan from a canyon on river left. Like Rapid 25, Rapid 26 is also called "Repeat" or "Rerun," adding to the confusion of repetitious names. The repeated runs could earn the chagrin of any party that might be having lunch at the lovely beach on the river left at Rapid 25, so consideration should be paramount.

If the reservoir level is quite low, Rapid 27 becomes a very long rapid with many large, fun waves. Rapid 27 forms around the large debris fan issuing from Imperial Canyon on the left side of the river. Rapid 28 is outwash from Waterhole Canyon, which comes in from river right, but it has never reappeared since the reservoir first submerged it. None of the remaining rapids downstream from Big Drop 3 have been affected by debris flows, as far as we can tell from our photographic records.

Regrouping

Boat flips create big messes. River gear scatters over the surface of the river; some of it catching in nearby eddies, some floating far downstream. A river guide's first priority is to assure the safety of passengers, who are threatened by injury during the flip, injury during the downstream swim, and hypothermia in the cold water of the spring runoff. People thrown from boats regularly make the two-mile swim to the reservoir and beyond at high water. If several people are in the water at once, river trips may be split over a considerable distance. Safety requires knowing where the trip can safely regroup.

To enhance boating safety, the National Park Service initiated its "catch-and-release" program in the early 1990s to rescue swimming river runners downstream from Big Drop 2. The triggering discharge that starts this action is 50,000 ft³/s. Depending on the water level, park rangers ascend Big Drop 3 in powerful motorboats to take a watchful stance in the pool below Big Drop 2. If an accident occurs, rangers can quickly retrieve swimmers and afterwards help collect floating gear. Because propellers can potentially kill swimmers in unfortunate accidents, Canyonlands National Park switched to powerful jetboats in the late 1990s.

At high water, few beaches emerge from the muddy water, but an excellent one—Ten Cent Camp—is present on river left just downstream from Rapid 26. Traditionally, the name of this camp is attributed to Don Harris, who stopped here in 1952 and found two nickels lying on the sand. At low water, this camp is occupied for much of the summer by river runners who want to spend another night next to the noise of whitewater instead of the silence of the reservoir.

Caught in the Canyon

Through most of Cataract Canyon, talus slopes rise steeply away from the river, confining the river's flow to the channel. Increases in discharge cause larger changes in the water surface than would occur on the approaches, where water spreads out over broad floodplains. Water-surface changes are something else to consider when choosing campsites in Cataract Canyon, particularly in Mile Long Rapid and the Big Drops.

Clyde Eddy found this out firsthand when he camped at the beach that comes and goes along river right between Big Drops 2 and 3.[26] Eddy camped here from sheer exhaustion; bucking innovation, he had constructed Powell-style boats for his 1927 trip and then had to portage them through Mile Long and the Big Drops.[27] To add to the misery of the trip, rain fell periodically, particularly during the night of July 4th. On the evening of the 5th, Eddy found himself sleeping next to the rapid, listening in horror as it started to rise, sweeping away parts of the kitchen and gear. The rest of the night was spent gathering men and equipment and pulling the boats to a point thirty feet higher on the rocky slope than they had been the evening before.[28] The river can catch the unaware or unprepared in many ways.

SUTURED ROCKS AND STABLE RAPIDS

Of the many observations noted by the crew members of the second Powell Expedition, one of the most interesting involved the process we call *suturing*. This occurs in the canyons of the Colorado River but is especially active in Cataract Canyon when, on the margins of rapids during floods, some rocks will vibrate against each other and erode in such a manner as to appear as joined pieces of a picture puzzle. Frederick S. Dellenbaugh described the suturing of boulders at the Big Drops:

> An interesting feature of this canyon was the manner in which huge masses of rock lying in the river had been ground into each other by the force of the current. One block of sandstone, weighing not less than six hundred tons, being thirty or forty feet long by twenty feet square, had been oscillated till the limestone boulders on which it rested had ground into it at slowly and regular rocking as the furious current beat upon it, and one could feel the movement distinctly.[29]

Once a debris flow creates a rapid, the river works constantly to eliminate it. The first job is to entrain individual particles and move each of them downstream. It may be difficult to imagine, but large boulders are bounced downstream, forced along by the power of river water at flood stage. Boulders accumulate in an orderly fashion in piles downstream, creating secondary rapids, such as Rapid 15 and Big Drop 3. Once

dropped in place, these boulders then sit and are subject to the other forces in the river's bag of tricks.

In the process of entraining boulders, the force of river flow causes boulders to vibrate in place. Vibration affects the rock and its supports on the bed of the river in two ways. At contact points, each boulder rubs its neighbors, removing material on each particle. If a soft particle (such as a sandstone) rubs against a harder particle (such as a solid limestone), then the softer rock loses more mass in the process. Because of their weight, particles apply forces to their neighbors, but in the act of vibrating, these forces increase. Dissolution of minerals, particularly calcium carbonate, increases under pressure and leads to the second mechanism of suturing.

The sediment load of the Colorado River contains considerable sand and gravel, particularly at flood stage. These particles collide with boulders, in a process termed corrasion, pitting them much like what happens to a windshield in a sandstorm. Gradually, this pitting reduces the mass of the boulder. Because most of the rocks of Cataract Canyon contain soluble calcium carbonate or other salts, the rocks also dissolve, albeit slowly, as water circulates among them. It is difficult to determine how effective these processes are or how quickly they operate, but they may be the only means by which the river ultimately rids itself of the plague of boulders.

INSCRIPTIONS

People no longer survey the shores of Cataract Canyon for dams or railroads. River runners no longer line or portage rapids because their boating skills have improved right along with the equipment. Gold flakes remain in the sands of the Colorado River because the area is protected by law. Travelers through the region today do not spend as much time on the shorelines as our predecessors did, but if we did then we would discover and appreciate what they saw and did in greater detail. We might even be tempted to add our little signatures to those inscriptions that decorate many rocks near the river.

Inscriptions are one of the things river runners always find throughout Cataract Canyon. In the past, it was not illegal to carve your name on stone but, even then, most travelers respectfully chose not to do so. When they did, their carving was usually done in good taste. Inscriptions made in our modern times, given the context of our lives—ease of access and ease of life in general—most often reflect vandalism. Please restrain yourself: defacing rocks is illegal.

Most of the inscriptions to be found in Cataract Canyon are where the more difficult rapids are located, and so Mile Long and the Big Drops have many inscriptions. A few of the inscriptions here are gone or going fast, but some yet in excellent shape can be found on the right shore of Rapid 15. These inscriptions are from the Best Expedition of 1891, the miners Wright and Faatz in 1892, and the Aleson/White Expedition of 1947. Between Rapid 19 and 20 on the right, the Eddy inscription of 1927 is painted on a large block. The Kolb inscription is on the right cliff between Big Drop 2 and 3, and Nevills left an inscription on the left at Big Drop 3 after Del Reid's accident.

Walking the shores of Mile Long and the Big Drops is difficult because of the boulders placed hither and thither among piles of driftwood, but it is worth the effort. You can see interesting rocks that have been polished clean by the river, revealing wonderful fossils within. If you are really lucky, you may find survey marks from the engineers who preceded your visit. The authors found some previously unknown survey benchmarks on a trip in 1998. You will also see large white masses of gypsum buried in the talus, along with an incredible amount of human trash in the form of rubber tires, glass and plastic bottles, and cans of steel and aluminum. The driftwood piles are the most fascinating, for one can roughly estimate when the piles formed by looking at the kinds of milled lumber mixed into the pile. When gathering wood for campfires, pick the driftwood piles near the water's edge rather than from these high, historic driftwood piles.

THE ABRUPT TRANSITION

At low water, Big Drop 3 is pretty steep, but a few bumpy waves later the run ends. Pulling into the eddies downstream just below the rapid is a good idea, just in case any other boats running the rapid have problems. Floating in those eddies, your boat joins

---

THE VALUE OF INSCRIPTIONS

James Knipmeyer

Ever since the first fur trappers descended portions of the Green and Colorado river canyons in the early decades of the nineteenth century and until well into the twentieth century, visitors have left a record of their passing. Names, dates, and occasionally other information have been carved into and painted on rocks, talus boulders, and the canyon walls themselves. Sometimes they have been placed in small, out-of-the-way places away from the river banks, and sometimes in almost billboard-like fashion so that they are clearly visible from the water itself.

These inscriptions, at least up until the mid-1900s, make up a valuable historical record of Green and Colorado river travelers. Mountain men, explorers, scientists, prospectors, miners, cattlemen, and farmers—all have left their names and accompanying dates. Other than an occasional brief item in a local newspaper, many of these records are the only accounts modern historians have of a particular individual's or group's presence in the river canyons.

Because they are an historic resource, these inscriptions are very significant and should be preserved. Unfortunately, many of them have already been lost to posterity. Names and dates from the Glen Canyon gold rush of the 1880s and 1890s—formerly located in the Hite area, Narrow Canyon, and lower Cataract—were covered in the 1960s by the rising waters of Lake Powell. So, too, were many inscriptions of early-day river runners. Several names and dates, especially along the Green River and above Spanish Bottom on the Colorado, have recently been purposely obliterated by otherwise well-intentioned individuals who mistakenly believed they were eradicating offensive "graffiti."

Education and knowledge is the key to preservation of historical inscriptions. At the location of at least two such "river registers" along the Green River, the Bureau of Land Management has erected signs informing visitors of the historical significance of the inscriptions and the need for their protection. The National Park Service could, and should, do the same along its stretches of the Green and Colorado rivers. We have a new take on an old saying: "Take only pictures; don't even leave footprints."

another fleet under the water surface: carp that desperately want to run the rapid in reverse. Sometimes the carp are so dense in the eddies that it is difficult to dip an oar without striking a fish.

Up-running Cataract Canyon is illegal, but no one told the carp. Sediment, food, and chemicals floating downstream tell these non-natives that habitat could be occupied, if only they could join other members of their species who floated into Cataract Canyon from above. Carp flourish in the reservoir, but their plans to join their brethren upstream and occupy more aquatic habitat are thwarted by their inability to swim against the current of Cataract's largest rapids, at least at some water levels. Although the river tries to tell these non-native fish that they do not belong upstream, the fish collect nevertheless, just looking for a chance.

Just downstream, at Imperial Canyon, another barrier exists, this one for some humans. Downstream traffic passes from wild river to reservoir; upstream traffic from the reservoir is stopped by regulation from proceeding farther upstream. River trips are faced with a dilemma: stop and camp on the abundant sandy beaches just downstream from Big Drop 3 or take a chance on finding a dry, accessible place on the reservoir mud. Once the corner is turned at Imperial Canyon and the sound of running water is muted by the silence of the reservoir, a sudden feeling of loneliness often overcomes everyone. It is a psychological hurdle that must be surpassed in order to exit Cataract Canyon.

Notes

1. D.D. Fowler and C.S. Fowler, "John Wesley Powell's Journal: Colorado River Expedition 1871–1872," *Canyon Legacy* 5 (1990): 2–12.

2. F.A. Ryser Jr., *Birds of the Great Basin: A Natural History* (Reno: University of Nevada Press, 1985), 211–256.

3. David Williams, *A Naturalist's Guide to Canyon Country* (Helena, Montana: Falcon Press/Canyonlands Natural History Association, 2000), 125.

4. B.T. Brown, "Golden Eagles Feeding on Fish," *Journal of Raptor Research* 26 (1992): 36–37.

5. Ryser, *Birds of the Great Basin*, 231–234.

6. J.H. Enderson, *Survey of Peregrine Falcons at Zion and Canyonlands National Park and Glen Canyon National Recreation Area, 1985* (Denver, Colorado: National Park Service Reports, CS-1200-5-A034, 1987), 1–27.

7. B.T. Brown, "Winter Foraging Ecology of Bald Eagles in Arizona," *The Condor* 95 (1993): 132–138; B.T. Brown, L.E. Stevens, and T.A. Yates, "Influences of Fluctuating River Flows on Bald Eagle Foraging Behavior," *The Condor* 100 (1998): 745–748.

8. B.T. Brown and L.E. Stevens, "Winter Bald Eagle Distribution Is Inversely Correlated with Human Activity along the Colorado River, Arizona," *Journal of Raptor Research* 31 (1997): 7–10.

9. J.K. Rigby, W.K. Hamblin, R. Matheny, and S.L. Welch, *Guidebook to the Colorado River, Part 3: Moab to Hite, Utah through Canyonlands National Park* (Provo, Utah: Brigham Young University Geology Studies, v. 18, Part 2, 1971), 73–74; F.E. Mutschler, *River Runners' Guide to Canyonlands National Park and Vicinity, with Emphasis on Geologic Features* (Denver, Colorado: Powell Society, 1977), 58.

10. Clyde Eddy, *Down the World's Most Dangerous River* (New York: Frederick A. Stokes Company, 1929), 81.

11. Rapid 15 is popularly referred to as Capsize, Upset, or Hell To Pay. We call it Best Rapid because this name was endorsed by the Western River Guides Association in the early 1960s at the behest of river historian "Otis" R. Marston (Aleson Collection, Utah Historical Society, Salt Lake City). Recently, guides working in Cataract Canyon decided that "Hell to Pay" is the most appropriate name; see editor's note in R.H. Webb, "The Changing Rapids of the Colorado River: Capsize Rapid (Rapid 15)," *The Confluence* 24 (2001): 15.

12. A photograph in the Belknap collection, Cline Library, Northern Arizona University, Flagstaff, clearly shows the wrecked boat with the name *Ben Hurt*. Old memories are deceptive; the widow of Joe Baker thought the name of the boat was the *Ben Hur*.

13. J.T. Staley, J.B. Adams, and F.E. Palmer, "Desert Varnish: a Biological Perspective," in *Soil Biochemistry*, eds. G. Stotzky and J. Bollag (New York: Marcel Dekker, Inc., 1992), 173–194.

14. R.W. Castenholz and F. Garcia-Pichel, "Cyanobacterial Responses to UV-Radiation," in *The Ecology of Cyanobacteria: Their Diversity in Time and Space*, eds. B.A. Whitton and M. Potts (Dordrecht, The Netherlands: Kluwer Academic Publishers, 2000), 591–611.

15. Bert Loper called the entire reach the Big Drop in 1907; diary narrative, undated, Box 121, Folder 4, Marston Collection, Huntington Library, San Marino, California. The Kolb brothers apparently referred to the reach as "Little Niagara," although those words do not appear in Ellsworth's description of these rapids; E.L. Kolb, *Through the Grand Canyon from Wyoming to Mexico* (New York: The MacMillan Company, 1914), 138–146.

16. John Wesley Powell, *The Exploration of the Colorado River and Its Tributaries* (New York: Dover Publications, 1961), 218.

17. National Park Service records; see *www.nps.gov/cany/river/reports.htm*.

18. Rigby, *et al.*, *Guidebook to the Colorado River*, 74.

19. R.F. Nash, *The Big Drops: Ten Legendary Rapids of the American West* (Boulder, Colorado: Johnson Books, 1989), 79. Kenny Ross, a pioneering commercial river guide, used this name in Kenneth Ross, "Cataract Canyon," *American White Water* (Winter 1956); Marston Collection, Huntington Library, San Marino, California.

20. L.A. Jones, *Scroll Map of Cataract Canyon* (Bountiful, Utah: privately published, 1962).

21. F.E. Mutschler, *River Runners' Guide to Canyonlands National Park and Vicinity, with Emphasis on Geologic Features* (Denver, Colorado: Powell Society, 1977), 60.

22. B.M. Goldwater, *A Journey Down the Green and Colorado Rivers* (Phoenix, Arizona: H. Walker Publishing Company, 1940), 17–18.

23. R.H. Webb, T.S. Melis, P.G. Griffiths, J.G. Elliott, T.E. Cerling, R.J. Poreda, T.W. Wise, and J.E. Pizzuto, *Lava Falls Rapid in Grand Canyon: Effects of Late Holocene Debris Flows on the Colorado River* (Washington, D.C.: U.S. Government Printing Office, U.S. Geological Survey Professional Paper 1591, 1999).

24. R.H. Webb, T.S. Melis, and R.A. Valdez, *Observations of Environmental Change in Grand Canyon, Arizona* (Tucson, Arizona: U.S. Geological Survey Water-Resources Investigations Report 02-4080, 2002).

25. By coincidence, a modern-day boatman from Moab, Tom Wesson, found a pocket watch at this location. The watch did not belong to Powell, for that watch was damaged by water, not lost. However, the watch that Wesson found was quite old and how it got there remains a mystery.

26. The Kolb brothers used this same beach above Big Drop 3 to layover in 1911, allowing Emery to get over his stomach troubles.

27. Eddy, *Down the World's Most Dangerous River*, 94–99.

28. The really strange thing about this incident is that despite Eddy's story, and his claims that warnings were floated downstream from Green River, the gaging records on both the Green and Colorado rivers show no significant changes.

29. F. S. Dellenbaugh, *A Canyon Voyage* (Tucson: University of Arizona Press, 1984). It is interesting to speculate about which boulder Dellenbaugh was discussing. A leading candidate would be the large rock that once perched to the right of Little Niagara in Big Drop 3; see Figure 8-8.

9

CATHEDRALS IN MUD

An Elegy to Drowned Cataracts and Impressive Side Canyons

*I cannot conceive of a more worthless and impracticable region than the one we now found
ourselves in.*   –John Macomb, 1859[1]

The river runners of Cataract Canyon, who number about 7,000 annually, generally dislike Lake Powell. Another group, the 2.7 million people who annually run boats on its blue waters, treasures the reservoir. They love the easy entry to the difficult terrain, as well as the fast travel in powerboats. In an advertising campaign, the Sierra Club once compared the attempts to dam the Colorado River in Grand Canyon to flooding the Sistine Chapel to be closer to the ceiling. Think of this while boating the now quiescent waters around Mille Crag Bend (its crags and pinnacles prompted John Wesley Powell to give it this unique name): you are about 230 feet above where Powell had his view.

Whitewater boaters tend to feel jaded when they reach the reservoir's still waters, and many long for the return of its now-stilled rapids. As a result, many forget that they are still in an environmental and recreational wonderland, despite the stillness, blue water, and banks of sand and mud. Hiking beckons beyond the salt-encrusted mudflats and massive thickets of tamarisk, and all one needs to experience true wilderness is to find a path away from the reservoir. It usually is less difficult than it appears to explore side canyons and ponder the rocks, upland communities, and isolation in abundance.

Depending on the water level, the start of the reservoir may be at the base of Big Drop 3 or below Imperial Canyon (Figure 9-1). For the next twenty-four miles to the head of Narrow Canyon, Powell's waters are usually muddy or at least brown, while the still-

ness is deafening in contrast to the thundering water upstream. The now-drowned rapids were less continuous here, but those fortunate enough to have piloted boats through them agree that they were at least as exciting as the ones that remain. Here, travel on the reservoir in the motorized flotillas that characterize the end of most river trips is slow and boring. Perfect—take a hike and enjoy the real pleasures of lower Cataract Canyon.

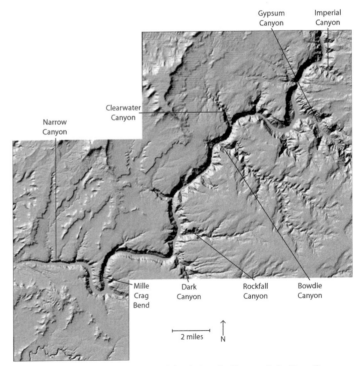

Figure 9-1. Hillshade Model Map of the Colorado River on Lake Powell between Imperial Rapid and Narrow Canyon.

GLEN CANYON DAM AND LAKE POWELL

Construction of Glen Canyon Dam began shortly after authorization of the Colorado River Storage Project in 1956. On March 13, 1963, the diversion tunnels were closed and the reservoir started filling; it reached its full pool elevation in 1980. The dam towers 583 feet above the former river level; because 127 feet of sediment were excavated from the channel, the total height of concrete is actually 710 feet above bedrock. When at its original design capacity, the depth of water behind the dam is 560 feet, creating a reservoir with a shoreline that is 1,960-miles long.[2]

Glen Canyon Dam is a multipurpose facility that controls water delivery, produces electrical power, and impounds a reservoir heavily used for recreation. Owing to its location a little more than fifteen miles upstream of "Compact Point," the division point on the river between the upper (Wyoming, Colorado, Utah, and New Mexico) and lower (Nevada, Arizona, and California) basin states, the dam regulates water delivery between the two geopolitical regions. Agreements call for an average release of 8.23 million acre-feet (ac-ft, or enough water to cover one acre to a depth of one foot) of water to the lower basin. The dam's generators can produce a maximum of 1.34 million kilowatts of electricity, which is commonly thought to be about three percent of the power needs of the Southwest. Much of this electricity is known as "peaking power," generated specifically to meet the region's needs, which generally are highest in the middle of the day. Although peak-power production (also known as "load-following production") once resulted in large daily tides released through Grand Canyon, the diurnal range in releases has been limited to attempt to minimize adverse environmental effects to sand bars and native species below the dam.

The reservoir has a maximum design capacity of 26.2 million ac-ft, and about 3.3 release years of water can be stored in Lake Powell. Evaporation from the reservoir's surface cannot be accurately measured, and estimates vary widely, but a common amount is about 2.5 percent of the reservoir's volume per year. Seepage into the porous rocks of Glen Canyon also occurs, and most estimates of the combined losses from evaporation and seepage range from 675,000 to 900,000 ac-ft/yr. According to a 1986 survey, about 0.87 million ac-ft of sediment had accumulated in the reservoir, including 52,100 ac-ft in the channels of the Colorado and San Juan rivers.[3] At this rate of accumulation (37,000 ac-ft/yr), the reservoir would fill with sediment in about 700 years. However, water storage is expected to be compromised when sediment storage exceeds twenty-five percent of the reservoir colume.[4]

WATERLOGGED HISTORY AND ARCHAEOLOGY

In Search of Dam Sites

That the Colorado River would be developed for consumptive uses was realized by even the first to explore the river. John Wesley Powell, the first person whose express intention it was to explore its canyons, was also the first to seriously propose a water-development scheme for the Colorado.[5] Powell's writings show he would have organized political entities such as states around drainage basins. To minimize water loss from evaporation and absorption, his dams would have been in the cool headwaters underlain by hard bedrock instead of in the hot deserts with soft sedimentary parent material. His completely practical plan was immediately assailed as being an anti-development agenda for the West, and he was eventually forced to resign from his job as Director of the U.S. Geological Survey.[6]

Rapid development of urban and agricultural areas in the basin—particularly in southern California—made taming the Colorado River top priority. The whole point of the 1921 U.S. Geological Survey Expedition through Cataract Canyon was to locate potential dam sites and estimate the storage capacity of reservoirs. The Reclamation Service rejected the dam site at the Confluence because of unsuitable footing beneath the channel, but the remainder of Cataract and Glen canyons was unexplored. In August and September of 1921, the U.S. Geological Survey explored Cataract Canyon, locating potential dam sites upstream from Dark Canyon and at Mille Crag Bend.

Most of the U.S. Geological Survey scientists did

their jobs and moved on to other projects, but Eugene C. LaRue had a different agenda. If Stanton was the persistent engineer,[7] stalwartly pushing his railroad, then LaRue was the relentless hydrologist, emphatically championing his dams. LaRue was zealous in his promotion of water development in the Colorado River drainage. All told, he promoted a total of thirteen primary and thirty-three alternative dam sites on the Green and Colorado rivers, mostly in Grand, Glen, and Cataract canyons.[8] According to his plan, the reservoirs would be designed to solve all the major problems of water development on the Colorado River, including maximum power development, flood control, and water storage with minimal evaporative losses and sedimentation problems. If LaRue had had his way, very little free-flowing water would be present in the river between the Utah-Colorado border and Mexico.

The most important dam in LaRue's plan would have been built four miles upstream from Lee's Ferry. His Glen Canyon No. 1 reservoir would have featured a 400-foot high dam storing more than 8 million ac-ft of water, and the reservoir would have extended to about Dark Canyon Rapid in Cataract Canyon. His monograph on water development in the Colorado River drainage shows a photograph of the old ferry upstream from the Paria River near Lee's Ferry, with the proposed powerhouse and spillway sketched in on the cliffs north of the Colorado River.[9]

Unfortunately for LaRue, larger political forces were focusing on two sites in Boulder and Black canyons, far downstream along the Arizona-Nevada border. The Reclamation Service, which had primary responsibility for recommending dam sites on the Colorado River to Congress, established four criteria for site selection: geological stability of the dam site, size (largest possible) of the reservoir, close proximity to railroads for the supply of construction materials, and minimum distance from markets that would use hydroelectric power.[10] Size mattered to the Reclamation Service; they wanted an extremely large reservoir to store as much water as possible, to store as much sediment as possible (and thereby extend the life of the reservoir), and to generate as much electricity as possible. The legislation called it the Boulder Canyon Project even though the dam eventually was built in Black Canyon.

LaRue had different ideas. He championed a basin-wide plan for water development emphasizing numerous small dams designed to create reservoirs with low surface area to minimize evaporation. He rejected the Boulder Canyon Project because it was only one dam built in isolation from the problems of the drainage as a whole. His dams were in remote sites with difficult access, making construction a daunting task. He pushed his entire plan with the Glen Canyon dam site as the lynchpin, and in so doing he crossed the line between impartial scientist and advocate. He passionately testified for his water-development plan before Congress in 1924 and 1925.

LaRue's testimony before the Senate in 1925 was followed by that of Herbert Hoover, then a prominent engineer and Secretary of Commerce. Hoover stated that Black Canyon should be the construction site because the close proximity to the power markets (namely southern California) was paramount.[11] Consequently a high, concrete, gravity/arch dam was promoted, and the choices were narrowed down to the Boulder and Black canyon sites. Congress passed the Boulder Canyon Project Act of 1928, which also included the construction of Imperial Dam and the All-American Canal near Yuma, Arizona.[12]

LaRue continued to champion his Glen Canyon dam site. In 1926, he was ordered to cease public discussion of the Boulder Dam Project by the Director of the Geological Survey, who was under orders from the Secretary of the Interior. He resigned from the U.S. Geological Survey in July 1927 under pressure for his public zealotry.[13] He became a consultant, occasionally working for the Army Corps of Engineers and other public agencies until he died in 1949.

LaRue's idea didn't die; it just remained dormant until seven years after his death. In 1956, Congress authorized the Colorado River Storage Project that included a high dam on the Colorado River fifteen miles upstream from Lee's Ferry. The Colorado River Storage Project was a refinement of LaRue's water-development plan, only with a higher dam built further upstream at a site deemed more stable. After Glen Canyon Dam was completed in 1963, Floyd

Figure 9-2. Imperial Rapid (mile 200.3)

A. September 19, 1921. During the 1921 expedition of the U.S. Geological Survey, geologist Sidney Paige photographed much of Cataract Canyon. Nearly all his photographs are blurry, perhaps because he was new to photography or perhaps because a boating accident in Dark Canyon Rapid damaged his film. In this scene at Imperial Rapid, isolated cottonwoods appear on both sides of the river, and netleaf hackberry trees appear in a broken line in the distance. (Sidney Paige 1408, courtesy of the U.S. Geological Survey Photographic Library)

B. October 17, 1999. The reservoir routinely inundates this area, depositing the silt- and clay-rich muds as appear in the foreground. The cottonwood trees are all dead, probably owing to inundation by the reservoir, and the hackberry trees are either dead or greatly reduced in size and/or prominence. (Dominic Oldershaw, Stake 3924)

Dominy bestowed the name "Lake Powell" to "honor" the explorer.[14] The reservoir filled by 1980, and during the high-water period of 1983, it stretched to the base of Big Drop 3. Since that year, the normal operating level of the reservoir has been lowered to allow for greater storage of flood waters; consequently, the reservoir retreated downstream to Imperial Rapid (Figure 9-2).

What would John Wesley Powell have thought of the reservoir that bears his name? Historians have debated this question in recent years. Based on Powell's *Report of the Arid Lands*, it appears that he would not have liked it. His dislike would not have stemmed from the inundation of Glen Canyon; Powell wanted a developed Colorado River like everyone else in his era. However, Powell knew how precious water is in the desert and he would have loathed the excessive evaporative and absorption losses from the reservoir that bears his name. In that regard, he and LaRue were in complete agreement. Both resigned from U.S. Geological Survey under the controversial cloud of Colorado River water development because they publicly advocated plans that would have developed its

waters using different strategies than what came to pass.

The Missing Rapids

Nowadays, some boaters pull off the lifejackets and start the party when they reach the bottom of what's left of Imperial Rapid (Mile 200.2). Before Glen Canyon Dam's gates were closed, the U.S. Geological Survey in 1921 recorded Imperial Rapid as the twenty-seventh rapid downstream from the Confluence. Most other rapid-counters agree with this, ±1 rapid, but downstream from Imperial Canyon the accounting of rapids diverges widely.[15] We know that at least some of these rapids were real, such as the one formerly present at or near Waterhole Canyon (Figure 9-3).

But first, before we get to the number of rapids now covered by the reservoir, what exactly is a distinct rapid? We can differentiate riffles from rapids (see Chapter 7). Using this scheme, the twenty-seven "rapids" remaining in Cataract Canyon are actually twenty-four rapids and three riffles. These twenty-four rapids vary widely in severity, leading to the issue

Figure 9-3. Upstream of Waterhole Canyon (mile 198.5)

A. June 11, 1889. The Brown-Stanton Expedition encountered a sizeable rapid upstream from Waterhole Canyon, which Franklin Nims captured in his upstream view despite the fact that it did not show the proposed railroad route. In the 1940s, Harry Aleson called this a fun rapid, and during his 1896 run George Flavell developed his call of joy here—"Whoops! Aha!" (F.A. Nims 41, courtesy of the National Archives)

B. March 27, 1997. Lake Powell began to fill in March 1963, and this rapid was covered by the still waters in 1980. Several of the large boulders are still present in the midground. Across the reservoir, at least one Mormon tea persists from 1889. Note the tamarisk and deltaic sediments that are ubiquitous in this reach (R.H. Webb, Stake 3382)

of "rapid ratings," a slippery slope if ever there was one. Comparison of the size of existing rapids with those now drowned is a lesson in subjectivity.

Further confounding this systematic classification, outwash from rapids creates secondary rapids downstream, raising the question as to whether these are sufficiently distinct. In addition, some rapids wash out or move downstream at higher discharges, adding to the confusion. At 80,000 ft³/s in Cataract Canyon one could argue that those twenty-four rapids are reduced to something closer to five sections of nearly continuous whitewater. As discussed previously, Mile Long Rapid is actually one big rapid that has been separated into seven supposedly distinct rapids. A similar situation exists for the three Big Drops.

Raymond Cogswell counted twenty-eight rapids between Imperial Canyon and Dark Canyon in 1909.[16] E.C. LaRue counted twenty-two rapids between Imperial Canyon and the head of Narrow Canyon in 1921, and considered ten fewer than Cogswell in a comparable reach. Les Jones, who boated Cataract Canyon in the 1950s and made the first scroll-type map of the river, found twenty-eight rapids. Felix Mutschler, a participant on the 1968 re-

enactment of the 1869 Powell Expedition, mapped thirty-seven rapids in 1968. So what happened? Did significant debris flows occur in lower Cataract Canyon between 1921 and 1968 creating more rapids, or was LaRue a lumper and Mutschler a splitter? Because of the Colorado River Storage Project, we will probably never know for certain what whitewater was in those twenty-four miles. We do know that several of those rapids were significant enough that river runners wrote about their severity or had boating accidents in them.

An Elegy to Dark Canyon Rapid. In remembering or commemorating, it is easy to exaggerate. Take Dark Canyon Rapid, which by one account was one of the largest rapids in the Colorado River drainage.[17] The ominous name for the canyon was coined by Mormon cattlemen in the 1880s and had nothing to do with its confluence with the Colorado River.[18] The rapid is, of course, named for the side canyon, and the name was adopted at least as early as 1907.[19] Fortunately, the name Rapid 45, which the U.S. Geological Survey assigned in 1921, never stuck. The rapid is now about 200 feet under water and sediment, so we have to take the word of historical observers and make inferences from their photographs and the 1921 survey.

Based on the combined drop of twenty-five feet in the primary and secondary rapids, Dark Canyon had the second-largest total fall in Cataract Canyon, behind the primary and secondary drops in Imperial Rapid. Dark Canyon had the quickest, sharpest drop of any Colorado Plateau rapid, which of course includes all of those in Grand Canyon. The canyon was narrow with steep walls that still mark the site today. Relatively short, the rapid curved to the right, and its center, like Big Drop 3, was littered with large boulders that became an island at low water. What stands out is that island (which is sometimes referred to as a rock garden), but did Dark Canyon Rapid really compare in severity to Big Drops 2 or 3?

It depends on the water level that river runners encountered it. The Kolb brothers would have said yes; they thought it was the worst rapid in Cataract Canyon. In 1911, they had a wild ride through it.[20] In 1921, Ellsworth Kolb, the head boatman for the USGS Expedition, lodged two boats at its head; one of them remained stuck for a day. In August 1953, Les Jones described the run:

> At 11,000 [ft³/s] very bad fall under rt. cliff—ran rt. & pulled to ctr. to miss bad rocks lower rt.[21]

Jones rated the rapid a '10' according to the Grand Canyon rating scale.[22] On the other hand, Georgie White found a washed-out Dark Canyon Rapid during her high-water run in 1957.[23] Clearly the rapid changed radically with increasing discharge and was not comparable to the three Big Drops, which are difficult to run at all water levels but rise in severity with increasing discharge.

Because it is now a memory, Dark Canyon Rapid is compared with other drowned rapids, most notably Separation and Lava Cliff rapids in Grand Canyon. A better comparison might be with the now-drowned Thirteen Foot Rapid that formerly thundered at the bottom of the San Juan Canyon. Not far from its confluence with the Colorado River in Glen Canyon, this rapid appeared to have a similar setting although in the younger bedrock of the Mesozoic. From a recreational viewpoint, at low water Dark Canyon Rapid would have had the status of Lava Falls Rapid in Grand Canyon: it was a rapid at the end of the whitewater run that guides could have used to heighten the whitewater experience of Cataract Canyon.

The Other Drowned Rapids. Other rapids in lower Cataract Canyon were noteworthy. Most river runners who experienced the full Cataract Canyon remember Rapid 28, near Waterhole Canyon at mile 198.5. Harry Aleson referred to this rapid as "a thriller."[24] Jones called this "the Chute," reporting large waves in its thirteen-foot drop. Gypsum Canyon Rapid (Mile 196.5) had a drop of only eight feet but had enough energy to flip a boat in a 1952 run down the center.[25] Several expeditions reported a significant rapid at the mouth of what is now called Rockfall Canyon (mile 187), and its drop was nine feet. Rapid 47 (mile 181.6) was not at the mouth of a tributary; historical photographs show a tongue dropping over what appears to be a ledge of Cedar Mesa Sandstone. Most observers thought it was an easy rapid to negotiate.

SOME LITTLE-KNOWN HAZARDS AND ATTRACTIONS ON THE RESERVOIR

Sometimes winter boating is the greatest pleasure in the outdoors. Even though the days are short, the winter light on the cliffs is something to behold and few people are encountered in the canyons. However, winter boating can be life threatening, owing to the high potential for hypothermia. In Cataract Canyon, boating can change from a water sport to winter survival at the head of the reservoir. During cold spells in the winter, "mush" and "sawblade" ice forms on the Colorado River and floats downstream, accumulating in quiet water. The results can be devastating to river trips.

In late December 1975, a group of experienced boaters launched from Potash, headed for a long, slow trip through Cataract Canyon.[26] There were eight people in the group in two boats, one of which was a Yampa-model raft with only two chambers. One person had noticed that the river was frozen upstream at Dewey Bridge, but given that the river was relatively ice-free at Potash, the group proceeded downstream anyway. They passed through considerable mush ice, but none of it accumulated because few eddies are present in Meander Canyon.

Three days into the trip, they came to the Slide, about one and a half miles upstream from the Confluence. At this point, a piece of sawblade ice sliced into the Yampa raft, deflating half of it and nearly dumping its passengers into the river. They patched the raft, using a lantern to heat the glue, and moved downstream to Spanish Bottom for a week of hiking and backpacking.

The run through Cataract Canyon's rapids was relatively uneventful but cold. The group rounded the corner at Imperial Canyon and saw, to their horror, that the river ran beneath a solid shelf of ice. The lead boat signaled for the second boat to stop on the right but had no time to pull his boat over before reaching the blockage. Stopped against the shelf, one of the boatmen nearly fell into an ice crevice while trying to line his boat to shore. Upon reaching the right shore, the guides faced their situation. Boating was no longer an option; travel downstream would be akin to ice skating or, worse, swimming. The only option was to stash their boats and equipment and hike out to safety.

One path lay downstream in Waterhole Canyon (mile 198.5), although no route to the rim was known to the group. Three members climbed to the rim in the late afternoon, only to have to downclimb a fifty-foot cliff and walk a couple of miles back upstream in pitch darkness. They rolled their boats up and stashed their equipment, to be recovered later. The group took a day to climb to the rim with full backpacks, using ropes to ascend the cliff during a snowstorm. Three days and forty-five hiking miles later the group had reached Hite. Like Bert Loper and Harold Leich before them, they had escaped Cataract Canyon, only they had not sunk their boats in the process; the reservoir ended their trip instead.

Most river runners ply the reservoir during the summer months, when ice is definitely not a problem. Those who go in late summer encounter the second reservoir hazard: the dreaded silt bars. Silt bars are not as significant an obstacle if the Colorado River is higher than about 20,000 ft³/s, but especially below 10,000 ft³/s they become significant impediments to downstream travel. The biggest problem occurs when the reservoir is really low, as was the case in 1992 after prolonged drought. About two miles above the highway bridge at the end of Narrow Canyon, houseboats were observed mired in a mudbath that was difficult to penetrate and even more difficult to elude. At least houseboaters exercised choice about whether to enter or not; river runners had no choice.

The third hazard of silt bars occurs when they collapse into the river. Those cracks that develop along the high silt banks suggest that failure could occur imminently, and if a boat were tied to the bank it would fill with a heavy load of dirt. This hazard was revealed to Nathaniel Galloway during his 1909 trip with Julius Stone, only on the lower Colorado River, not in Cataract Canyon. He narrowly escaped being buried in his boat while investigating a silt bank.[27]

At more normal reservoir levels, silt bars are an every-trip event for boaters in the late summer. They expect silt bars on the right near Gypsum Canyon, on the right near Palmer Canyon, and in the form of islands that occasionally are peninsulas above Rockfall Canyon and between Rockfall and Dark canyons. Mille Crag Bend is perhaps the biggest obstacle, given an extensive silt bar/peninsula on the right that requires boaters to go all the way over the bay to Sheep Canyon before they can safely turn downstream. The good news is that travel is faster during the period of low reservoir because the current can occasionally go all the way to Hite Marina. The bad news is that the distance is a bit longer in the weaving dance that boaters must perform to miss getting stuck in the mud.

Driftwood jams are a fourth hazard that affects all boats—powerboats coming upstream on the reservoir and downriver traffic—that travel the reservoir near the mouth of the Dirty Devil River. During spring runoff, and particularly in high runoff years, driftwood accumulates where the reservoir widens out and deepens. Getting through the logjam in some years is a difficult proposition, and damaging motors on logs or in tangled debris is a real possibility. Glen Canyon Dam's presence shifted this problem hundreds of miles upstream. In the 1940s and 1950s, boaters on Lake Mead reservoir encountered the same problem in the lower part of the inundated Grand Canyon. They actually encouraged burning of driftwood piles to minimize their effects on boat traffic on the reservoir.[28]

The final indignity that river runners face, particularly those in slow or nonmotorized craft, is the issue of where to camp. Some small groups "float and bloat," drifting down the reservoir while partying and then sleeping on the boats. These groups frequently awake to find themselves stuck on a silt bar a long way from Hite, making this option less preferable at low river flows. Other groups tie up and sleep on their boats. For large commercial river groups, particularly those interested in hiking the numerous side canyons, the only option is to find a dry, relatively mud-free place. These are few and far between. Exacerbating this problem is the issue of skin rashes that some people develop upon contact with the mud they must sleep on, and the multitudinous scorpions scurrying about at night. There may not be any more scorpions along the reservoir than upstream, but it sure seems that way at times.

Inscriptions and Structures

Sources of considerable history and archaeology lie beneath the surface of Lake Powell, mostly along the winding course of the Colorado River through Glen Canyon.[29] Cataract Canyon has lost important historical sites to inundation as well, particularly one of the rare Denis Julien inscriptions at mile 185.5. Robert Brewster Stanton, during his attempt to design a railroad through Cataract Canyon, found this inscription on river left at a point "where it could have only been cut . . . from a boat."[30] Bearing a date of 1836, this marking indicates Julien preceded Stanton by fifty-three years.

Other inscriptions were carved into the rocks of lower Cataract Canyon. Some of these were large panels, such as those found at Dark and Sheep canyons. Carved into the wall on the downstream side of the mouth of Dark Canyon were the names of the Kolb brothers (1911), the U.S. Geological Survey Ex-

pedition (1921), Norm Nevills (1938), Amos Burg and Buzz Holmstrom (1938), and later river runners. Other inscriptions were isolated; for example, Raymond Cogswell noted in his 1909 diary that he found the inscriptions "A.G. Turner 1907, Socialism 1912" on river right above Dark Canyon Rapid.[31] Ellsworth Kolb, passing by two years later, noted something Cogswell failed to mention: cliff dwellings and a ladder extending to them.[32] Kolb guessed that the ladder was built by "white men" (perhaps Turner?) intent on reaching the ruins. Therefore, the only truly significant archaeological site within Cataract Canyon is now beneath the reservoir.

Flora and Fauna along the Reservoir

Lake Powell has created abundant aquatic habitat where once a turbid, low-productivity river flowed, presenting an excellent opportunity for viewing wildlife. Unfortunately, very few of the native aquatic organisms remain, but their replacements do attract some native species. Particularly noteworthy is the large population of non-native fish that were stocked to increase fishing opportunities, native water birds who eat the non-native fish, and raptors who eat all the water birds. Also, scorpions and weeds thrive on the mudflats created by the lowering of the lake level from its highest level in 1983.

Because the river is frequently muddy, the most abundant non-native fishes in the inundated Cataract Canyon are bottom feeders such as carp and catfish that were planted throughout the Colorado River basin. Other common non-native reservoir fish include fathead minnows, red shiners, largemouth bass, and striped bass. It is difficult to cross the reservoir to Hite Marina without seeing large numbers of Great Blue Herons wading in the backwaters and feeding on small fishes. Similarly, Bald Eagles are now common in the winter months. Ducks and grebes are also commonly seen diving for food. Their presence, and particularly the interaction of ducks with boats, attracts a major predator, the Peregrine Falcon. These falcons follow boats and take advantage of the ducks' fear of river runners by pouncing on the distracted birds as they flee from oncoming boats. Many river runners are startled to see a duck slammed from mid-flight into the lake. Peregrines sometimes work in pairs; one bird serves as a diving decoy to get ducks into flight, while the other targets the unwary prey.

The silt bars make for a fascinating, ever-changing habitat. Subsurface decomposition can yield gases such as methane and carbon dioxide, and venting of these pressurized gases can lead to little mud volcanoes and subsidence features. At Mille Crag Bend, springs venting hydrogen sulfide were numerous along the river; these springs now vent through the silt. The weed flora is ever-changing, but usually tamarisk, Russian thistle, and non-native members of the saltbush family can be counted on to slow a hiker's movement from reservoir to desert beyond. In 2000, willow-weed (*Polygonum lapathifolium*), a weed new to Cataract Canyon, sprouted on the recently emergent silt bars. Luckily, the problems this weed might create may be restricted to the reservoir margin unless it manages to move upstream into the undisturbed tributary canyons.

HIKING IN GREAT ABUNDANCE

Hiking up the side canyons off Lake Powell is an experience in contrasts. It is difficult to miss the striking difference between the too-blue-and-too-deep-for-this-landscape reservoir and the intimate twists and turns of red, thin, slot canyons occasionally filled with rushing flood waters. It is a reminder, too, of what once was. However, there are still many secrets up the side canyons that have escaped the silent reservoir waters.

Gypsum Canyon (mile 196.5)

Gypsum Canyon offers one of the best, but least taken, hikes in the inundated Cataract Canyon (Figure 9-4). River runners may be discouraged by the wide-open valley at its mouth, which appears to offer nothing but a parched hike into the desert. Once the tamarisk is bypassed, however, the desert beyond is inviting for its wildlife and scenery, including the waterfall to which John Wesley Powell hiked on both of his expeditions. One of Powell's hikes appears to have been for the sole purpose of dragging his photographer, E.O. Beaman, to document the wonder of Gypsum Canyon.

Gypsum Canyon near its mouth is a wide valley that supports abundant wildlife. Kit foxes (*Vulpes macrotis*) are keen burrowers, and thus are found in open, dry flat areas with deep soils.[33] This preference makes them somewhat scarce in this region, as there are only a few areas with deep soils, but Gypsum Canyon is one of those places. These are incredibly cute animals, with huge ears and long tails, and are about the size of a large house cat (a foot high at the shoulder and weighing four to five pounds). They are nocturnal and eat mostly kangaroo rats, which they supplement with other mice, lizards, birds, rabbits, insects, and a bit of vegetation. Like most carnivores, they can survive without drinking water—they get enough liquid in their food.

Kit foxes are the only canine to use year-round dens, although they change dens frequently. Each den has seven to ten entrances, so, as with badgers, where you have kit foxes you have lots of holes. Kit foxes are solitary from July to September. In October, the females move into family dens and are later joined by males. Pups are born in February and March. Both parents feed the pups for about six months, at which point the pups leave the den. Kit foxes are very vocal and can be heard as much as seen.

Desert bighorn sheep (*Ovis canadensis nelsoni*) are another common, but seldom seen, animal in this region.[34] Identifying older males is easy because of their large, curling horns, which can form a full spiral and weigh forty pounds. Distinguishing females and young males apart is another matter: both have relatively straight, small horns about twelve-inches long and both have a similar body size. Bighorns prefer steep cliffs where they are safe from predators. Most foraging is done either on steep hillsides or on flat areas within reach of steep cliffs. You can sometimes hear them overhead when hiking in slot canyons, which Gypsum Canyon becomes about three miles from the reservoir. Bighorn sheep are herbivores, preferring grasses that they munch in the morning and late afternoon while moving about in small herds.

Bighorns can go several months in winter with only dew and moist plants as their sources of water. In

Figure 9-4. Gypsum Canyon (mile 196.7)

A. September 25, 1871. John Wesley Powell and Frederick Dellenbaugh climbed out Gypsum Canyon to make topographical observations during the second Powell Expedition. During this expedition, John F. Stewart named the canyon for the abundant amounts of gypsum in anhydrite deposits near the Colorado River. E.O. Beaman hiked up Gypsum Canyon but probably chose not to carry his glass plates and photographic equipment up the narrow, tortuous trail that surmounts the waterfall about four miles up Gypsum Canyon. Two of Beaman's photographs from his hike survive, both of which were views down the narrow canyon just below the waterfall. (E.O. Beaman 754, courtesy of the U.S. Geological Survey Photographic Library)

B. August 26, 1968. Hal Stephens matched both Beaman views. Stephens and Shoemaker (1968) documented a large rockfall that dammed the canyon, forming an ephemeral lake that had filled with sand by the time they reached it. The source of this rockfall is documented on the left wall of Stephens's view, altering its skyline in comparison to the photograph in Figure 9-4A. The sediments behind the lake are readily apparent in the center of this view, and fragments from the rockfall litter the talus slopes on the right side. (H.G. Stephens AC-3)

times of high water stress, their enlarged stomachs can store enough water to last several days, and they can drink up to twenty percent of their body weight in just a few minutes. When water stressed, they sometimes kick apart cactus and eat the moist internal tissue. They can withstand internal body temperatures of 107°F,[35] making them highly adapted to summer heat. When ewes are ready to give birth in February, they leave the herd and give birth to usually a single lamb, rejoining the group in a week or so. During most of the year, males and females live separately, joining to-

gether only in fall for the rut. Pregnant females prefer to give birth in the same spot where they were born.

Bighorn sheep have been residents of the canyon country for a long time, as is evident by their common occurrence in rock art[36] and in the early journals of river runners.[37] However, bighorn were extirpated throughout much of the western United States by over-hunting, and few intact herds still existed by the mid-1900s. Fortunately, the Needles and Island-in-the-Sky districts of Canyonlands National Park were two of the few places where large herds were still present. Un-

C. October 18, 1999. The rockfall dam in Gypsum Canyon was breached sometime between 1968 and 1999. The formerly impounded sediments, as well as the slopes in the foreground of this view, support long-leaf brickellbush, a short-lived colonizer of the banks of washes on the Colorado Plateau. The remnants of rockfalls that occurred after 1871 litter the talus slope in the foreground, explaining why a colonizing species of disturbed habitats would occupy more xeric slopes. (Steve Young, Stake 3599)

fortunately, the Needles herd suffered a catastrophic die-off in 1987, with herd numbers plummeting from over 200 animals to fewer than ten in one year. It is believed that they picked up a respiratory disease from nearby domestic sheep herds. Since that time, domestic sheep have been removed from the area, and herd numbers have slowly been recovering. Currently, there are about thirty animals in the Needles District, of which Gypsum Canyon is a part. Luckily, disease has not hit the Island-in-the-Sky herd. Animals from the Island herd have been transplanted to new areas

throughout the Colorado Plateau as part of the program to restore the bighorns to their former range.

Clearwater Canyon (mile 191.9)

Clearwater Canyon is another tributary that Beaman photographed in 1871 (Figure 9-5). Once this beautiful canyon had several waterfalls in its mouth; now the lowermost of these are under a thick layer of mud. Traipse around the mud and climb around the upper falls, and go on up the canyon for about two miles into a beautiful box canyon lined with hackberry trees, boxelders, and cottonwoods. As in most side canyons of the Canyonlands region, though, naked rock is the principal display.

While hiking up this canyon, or gazing upwards at the looming rock walls from the reservoir, you will be looking at many unusual houses without realizing it. Carpenter bee larvae live in yucca stalks that are carefully packed with pollen and nectar by the parent; solitary bees live in tunnels in the ground; tarantula wasp larvae live in buried spiders; other wasp larvae live in galls on plants. However, probably the most overlooked but most abundant houses are those of *endolithic* organisms. "Endolithic" means "in the rock" and that is where these organisms are found: embedded in the rock, down one or two grains from the surface. So why and how does one live in the rock?

Living in the rock has the advantage of stability. Overlying rock provides shade from the intense radiation of the sun. This means that water loss and thermal stress is reduced. Herbivory is minimal as few things eat rock, and the rock also provides protection from accidental damage. The disadvantages: endolithic organisms first have to get into the rock, which requires finding, or creating, small entry points. Second, organisms that need light as an energy source require that the rock have translucent grains like quartz that will let light in. Third, because this light is quickly extinguished with depth, organisms that need light can inhabit only a thin layer just under the rock surface and expansive growth into the rock is prevented. Finally, sexual reproduction is also difficult, unless genetic material is somehow exchanged through the rock or organisms can poke up out of the rock.

Figure 9-5. Clearwater Canyon (mile 192.1)

A. September 27, 1871. Clearwater Canyon is a ready source of potable water for river trips, particularly during the summer months when the Colorado River is filled with fine silt and clay from storm runoff. E.O. Beaman was taken by the striking scenery of this canyon and photographed a lovely waterfall and plunge pool that is partially in shadow. Cottonwoods line the bedrock channel in the midground. (E.O. Beaman 759, courtesy of the National Archives)

B. August 27, 1968. Hal Stephens matched Beaman's view in 1968. The rising waters of the reservoir had reached the mouth of Clearwater Canyon but had not entered this view. The cottonwoods had died back before Stephens took his photograph, possibly because of flooding in the side canyon. No livestock could reach this point. (H.G. Stephens AD-4)

Bacteria, cyanobacteria, and lichens have all apparently decided that living in rock is a great idea. Many species of these three groups can be found living in loosely cemented sandstones and weathered granites. These rocks have a large number of quartz grains and the acids secreted by the burrowing organisms easily create entry points. Bacteria do not need light for an energy source nor do they reproduce sexually, so they can burrow into the rock further than either cyanobacteria or lichens. Cyanobacteria and lichens need light and access to carbon dioxide for photosynthesis; thus, they are restricted to the zone just beneath the rock surface. All of these organisms can reproduce vegetatively and so never need to leave the confines of the rock. When endolithic lichens reproduce sexually, they put their spore-bearing organs

(*apothecia*) above the rock surface, which then open and release the spores when they get wet.

The cyanobacteria that inhabit rocks are bright green and can be easily seen when looked at from a broken edge of the rock. Endolithic lichens are numerous, and spotted by the apothecia protruding from the rock. Often, these appear as rings of eroded rock, with a few dots of living material inside. These were long thought to be places where lichens had once lived, eroded the rock, and then died. While this is sometimes true, these can generally be endolithic lichens, and the black dots are their apothecia. Unlike many other regions, most of the biomass of rock lichen in the Canyonlands region is found within the rock, not on top of it.

C. April 3, 1998. Lake Powell filled in 1980 and consequently, sediment has completely filled the bottom of Clearwater Canyon, covering the waterfall that was the subject of Beaman's view. Non-native tamarisk have replaced the previous riparian assemblage. (Dominic Oldershaw, Stake 3619)

Dark Canyon (mile 182.9)

Moving down the reservoir, boats pass numerous side canyons where rapids once roared (Figure 9-6). One of the most favored side canyon hikes is up Dark Canyon, famous for its year-round pools. The first problem is getting into the mouth of the canyon. This has not been a significant issue in recent years because tributary flows had carved relatively deep channels through the silt banks. In 1999, a large flood in Dark Canyon created fifteen-foot standing waves and scattered river groups camping in the canyon. No one was injured, but the channel filled with odoriferous mud, logs, and dead animals, making this choice of campsite about as desirable as sleeping near a landfill.

Camping at the mouth of Dark Canyon still occurs nearly every night of the summer, as river groups lay over to ready themselves for long hikes into its recesses. Camping on the large sandbars at the mouth is

a somber experience, particularly after a fire in 1989 destroyed the dense tamarisk thicket, leaving burnt stumps everywhere. However, most of the time hikers are able to penetrate the quicksand and tamarisk thickets and gain access to the wild canyon beyond. Dark Canyon extends for many miles and has long been sought out by backpackers in Canyonlands, who come down from trailheads near the top of the canyon.

In the clear water of the pools in Dark Canyon, it is possible to find warm water that appeals to one's sense of bathing. Swimming is fine, but bathing with soap can harm one of the canyon's most interesting residents, the water strider.[38] Water striders can walk on water because they have hairs on the ends of their legs that do not allow moisture to penetrate them, and which allow them to sit on the surface without breaking through the water tension. Tiny retractable claws at the end of their legs penetrate through the water surface, providing traction. Some tiny water striders use saliva to break through the surface film, producing a forward motion. However, if the water surface tension is lessened—and adding soap to these pools lowers surface tension—the water striders will fall in and drown. Seemingly innocuous acts in the wilderness can cause disasters for other species, especially when we add substances (shampoo, sunscreen, etc.) to isolated water sources. Water striders can detect vibrations in the water that warns them of oncoming floods, so that they leave the water before getting drowned.

Wildlife is here, attracted by all those campers and their careless tendencies with food. The animals and insects that make camping here a challenge come down from their homes in the nearby rocks, looking for a feast. Ringtails (*Bassariscus astutus*) appear to be the perfect pet: one to two pounds of fluff with a large ringed tail, big eyes, and incredibly inquisitive nature.[39] They live in side canyons, especially where there are rocky outcrops. They are omnivores, and will eat fruit, birds, snakes, lizards, small mammals, small birds, spiders, frogs, and insects, especially grasshoppers and crickets. But in places like Dark Canyon, they are more than willing to forego their natural diet to partake of any leftovers from this

Figure 9-6. Bowdie Canyon, Glen Canyon National Recreation Area (mile 190.5)

A. Summer, 1964. Canyonlands National Park was established in 1964. As part of the inventory process, national park rangers took a river trip through Cataract Canyon. They are shown here running Bowdie Canyon Rapid, which was one of the larger rapids in lower Cataract Canyon. (National Park Service 59, courtesy of Canyonlands National Park)

B. April 3, 1998. Bowdie Canyon Rapid is now inundated. Motorboats now frequently pass this site, going upstream or downstream (Dominic Oldershaw, Stake 2965)

evening's meal, should you be willing to leave it inadequately protected.

Strictly nocturnal, ringtails have the huge eyes associated with night-active mammals and also have an excellent sense of smell. They are superb climbers and leapers, using their long tails for balance, and have semi-retractable claws and the ability to rotate their hind feet 180 degrees for better purchase as they climb down cliff faces. They also climb up rock cracks like human rock climbers—pressing their feet against one wall and their backs against the other. Ringtails build dens in rock walls and piles of rock and pad them with moss, grass, and leaves. They are solitary and pair only for mating. The kits, numbering two to four, are usually born in June. Ringtails are eaten by great horned owls, bobcats, and coyotes. Many early white settlers kept ringtails as house pets, although the inquisitive nature of these animals often conflicted with the idea of an orderly house or an orderly river kitchen.

Scorpions abound in Dark Canyon. Occasionally, it is possible to hear a yelp of pain from someone who has chosen a camp in the rocks, but at Dark Canyon, you could be anywhere when a scorpion finds you. Scorpions are one of the most successful arthropods in deserts, and they are found throughout the world.[40]

However, humans seldom see them, as they prefer to hang out in dark places during the day and travel about at night. If you would like to see scorpions on a river trip, bring a battery-powered black light along and go wandering at night. Scorpions are fluorescent, and you will be astonished at all the little creatures running around on the desert floor, lit up by ultraviolet light.

Scorpions were one of the first arthropods to appear on land, and have changed little in the last 350 million years. Like all arachnids, they have four pairs of jointed legs. Sensory hairs on these legs can detect moving prey up to a foot away. Scorpions have two central eyes, and then several eyes clustered in two groups along the front edge of the carapace. They also have a pair of comb-like appendages that sweep the ground, searching for chemical signals. Female scorpions can retain sperm from the previous year and fertilize themselves in the spring. Their young are born only partially developed during the summer. The babies crawl immediately onto their mother's back, where they ride around until their first molt which occurs in seven to twenty-one days. The mother will give them water if needed. This is often a perilous journey: if the young fall off her back, their mother will regard them as prey and eat them.

Scorpions are truly adapted to a desert lifestyle. They can go months without food, withstand higher internal temperatures than those of any other arthropod, tolerate high salt concentrations in their bodily fluids when dehydrated, and their rates of water loss are some of the lowest known in the animal world. Their metabolic rates are also among the lowest of all arthropods, and they have the highest production efficiencies recorded in the animal kingdom. This means that they can function under tremendous chronic and intermittent food, water, and temperature stress. In spite of these superb adaptations to desert living, these are strictly nocturnal creatures. This indicates that their prey, mostly insects, are active at night. Avoiding predators is also a major concern. Many animals eat scorpions, including lizards, grasshopper mice, and pallid bats. To reduce competition and cannibalism, scorpions partition the night according to age: at a certain time of night, the younger scorpions will emerge, whereas the older individuals will emerge together at a different time.

Like antlions, snakes, lizards, and other predatory insects, scorpions sense their environment mostly through vibration. How long the signal is delayed between which hairs on which legs tells them the direction and distance of a vibration source. They also use chemical signals. Motionless prey are detected by *chemoreceptors*, or chemical sensors, on the tips of their appendages and the front mouthparts. Scorpions also have sensors on their bodies that respond to pheromones, carbon dioxide, the humidity of soil, and the suitability of the substrate for the placement of their *spermatophores*, little packets of sperm.[41]

Scorpions burrow during the day and move to the mouth of their burrows in response to decreasing light in the evening. However, unless they are hungry or if conditions are favorable, they may not actually leave the burrow. Being strictly nocturnal, they have very sensitive eyes. To protect their eyes in case of sudden light exposure, they have a moving, pigmented lens that automatically covers their eyes during the day, giving them "sunglasses" that retract at night.

Few scorpions have life-threatening stings, although one species in this region does: the small, brown bark scorpion (*Centruroides exilicauda*).[42] The sting of this species can be fatal to very old, very young, or very sick humans, although this is a very rare outcome to even this highly susceptible group. This species has a negative *geotaxis*; that is, they orient themselves upside down, so they often cling to the undersides of things like rocks. Scorpions can be found in large aggregations during winter hibernation. The giant hairy scorpion (*Hadrurus arizonensis*) is at its most northerly distribution here, along the shores of Lake Powell. This species burrows deep in the soil, following soil moisture, and is strikingly beautiful, with a cobalt blue body and bright yellow legs.

LIFE IN A SEA OF ROCKS

The naked outcrops of Cedar Mesa Sandstone in lower Cataract Canyon seem inhospitable, but some perennial plants thrive in this environment. For example, up the slope of one side canyon is a tiny plant, the endangered Kachina daisy (*Erigeron kachinensis*), found in only a few places in the world. It hangs on along the rocky edges of the watercourse in this canyon, somehow resisting scouring flash floods that roar through this canyon yearly. The only other known populations of this daisy are in and around Natural Bridges National Monument, an area that is many miles away and at a much higher elevation than here. So how did the daisy get here, and why is it so distant from other populations? Why is are there no pockets of it in other locations that connect it to the Natural Bridges area? It seems like there should be plenty of habitat available.

Isolated habitats and populations raise a lot of unanswered questions for biologists. For instance, consider hanging gardens, a common sight in side canyons. These moist habitats, usually found high up on canyon walls, are sometimes separated from each other by miles and miles of inhospitably dry, hot rock. Most hanging gardens have the same plants: alcove death camas, maidenhair fern, alcove bog orchid, scarlet monkeyflower, helleborine, cave primrose, and alcove columbine. How do seeds of these plants get around, and how do they manage to find each tiny wet spot, and why is the Kachina daisy, with miles of what would seem perfect habitat, unable to establish itself in more places?

Scientists have pondered these questions for a long time, and the answers vary. Much seems to depend on the specific characteristics of the plant: whether it tolerates a wide range of conditions, whether it has the ability to avoid inhospitable habitats, and of course, whether its habitats are stable or constantly changing in space and/or time. From the studies done, a few general rules can be deduced. Plants that live in these widely-spaced habitats are usually pollinated either by wind, by generalist insects, or by insects that are widespread in a given region. These plants tend to make prodigious amounts of wind-dispersed seeds. Spatially-separated habitats that are colonized by the same plant species are generally predictable in time and space, even if they are small. Hanging gardens fit these conditions perfectly: most of the plants found in these gardens have pollinators that are widespread throughout this region, most make copious amounts of wind-dispersed seeds, and the habitat, though small, is extremely reliable in both space and time.

What about the Kachina daisy? It has generalist pollinators and has wind- and water-dispersed seeds, however its habitat is tiny cracks in rocks in places that are sporadically scoured by floods. This habitat may be reliable in space but certainly not in time. How the tiny seeds end up in the rock crevices, or how they manage to stay put once they land in a suitable crack remains a mystery. We also do not know what conditions are required for the seeds to germinate. Perhaps the seeds only germinate during the few times the cracks are wet, or if the new seedlings are too little when flooded they may be easily wiped out by flood waters. Many other possibilities may explain the strange distribution of this plant as well.

THE END IS NEAR: HITE MARINA AND THE TAKEOUT

After camping at Dark Canyon and enjoying the scenery, river runners must inevitably make their way down the reservoir to the takeout. Threading their way through the mud bars in the river around Mille Crag Bend, boaters follow the reservoir as it leads through Narrow Canyon with its magnificent view of the Henry Mountains. Under the highway bridge and around the corner, a large marina beckons to river runners. Hite Marina is named for a historic river crossing that was actually about five miles downstream. Glen Canyon's legendary denizen, Cass Hite, gave Dandy Crossing its name,[43] reportedly because he thought it was a "dandy crossing." Dandy Crossing was reached from the south by way of White Canyon and from the north by way of North Wash, which originally was called Crescent Creek. To add to the confusion of name changes, the site was just downstream of the Dirty Devil River, which is the combined flow of the Fremont and Muddy rivers.

In 1883, Cass Hite, drawn to the area to avoid arrest for murder and to look for gold in Glen Canyon, established a settlement at the mouth of North Wash/Crescent Creek. Hite built a trading post and post office, which assumed his name. At one time, Hite had a school built to educate thirty students. The crossing was not a true ford as swimming was required of man and beast. Any boat available came in handy until 1946, when Arthur Chaffin built a motorized ferry boat guided by a suspended cable that crossed the river.[44] Chaffin first came to Glen Canyon around 1900 to prospect for gold and would later come back in 1932 to live at Hite with his family during the Great Depression. Chaffin was forced to move from his home one year after the Bureau of Reclamation began filling the reservoir in 1963. His ex-residence is now 258 feet under water and mud when the reservoir is full.

In 1949, a uranium processing plant went into operation at Hite. It was an experimental plant operated by the Atomic Energy Commission in conjunction with the Vanadium Corporation of America, and was closed in 1953. The plant was dismantled and some of its high-grade tailings were shipped to New Mexico for processing. The remainder of the tailings that were created now lies beneath the reservoir.[45] The Ancestral Puebloans lived here as well at a magnificent site called the "Moqui Fort," which was explored and enjoyed by early travelers. The building was a fifteen-by-twenty-two-foot stone structure, twelve feet high, and appeared to be two-storied at one time. The ruined structure became a popular place for scratching names, and many early river runners recorded their passage here.[46]

There is a surreal aura to Hite, Utah. After experiencing the awesome whitewater of Cataract Canyon, with its brown, muddy water and people few and far between, the sight of a fleet of recreational powerboats on blue water reflecting red cliffs seems like an odd wrinkle in the space-time continuum. Hite Marina is a rather sterile, dusty place inhabited by boats, campers, trailers, and the occasional park ranger. Most river runners quickly pack their vehicles, rushing to leave this place, while those who enjoy the recreational possibilities of Lake Powell busily launch their watercraft there. The two groups, who think they are from different worlds but in fact enjoy the same fantastic scenery, warily eye each other, jealous of how much ramp space each occupies. The big difference between whitewater boaters and the power boaters of Powell is their view of the value of water: free flowing or impounded. This in many ways sums up the spectrum of values in Canyon Country—whether its lands remain wild or whether they are managed for more intensive uses—and what the future will hold for this exceptional landscape.

Notes

1. John Macomb, *Report of the Exploring Expedition from Santa Fe, New Mexico, to the Junction of the Grand and Green Rivers of the Great Colorado of the West, in 1859, under the command of Capt. J.N. Macomb, with Geological Report by Prof. J.S. Newberry* (Washington, D.C.: Government Printing Office, 1876).

2. The data on Glen Canyon Dam is from a fact sheet distributed by the Carl Hayden Visitor Center, dated June 11, 1987.

3. R.L. Ferrari, *1986 Lake Powell Survey* (Denver, Colorado: Bureau of Reclamation report REC-ERC-88-6, 1988).

4. F. E. Weymouth report, U.S. Senate Documents, v. 6, 70th Congress, 2nd Sessions, December 3, 1928, to March 4, 1929. (Washington, D.C.: U.S. Gov't. Printing Office, 1929).

5. J.W. Powell, *Report on the Lands of the Arid Regions of the United States* (Washington, D.C.: U.S. Government Printing Office, 1879).

6. Donald Worster, *A River Running West* (New York: Oxford University Press, 2001).

7. David Lavender, *River Runners of the Grand Canyon* (Grand Canyon, Arizona: Grand Canyon Natural History Association, 1985), 22–32.

8. E.C. LaRue, *Water Power and Flood Control of the Colorado River Below Green River, Utah* (Washington, D.C.: U.S. Government Printing Office, U.S. Geological Survey Water-Supply Paper 556, 1925), iii–v.

9. *Ibid.*, Plate IV.

10. J.E. Stevens, *Hoover Dam: an American Adventure* (Norman: University of Oklahoma Press, 1988), 19.

11. W.B. Langbein, "L'Affaire LaRue," *WRD Bulletin, WRD Historical Note 1* (April-June 1975), 6–14.

12. Philip Fradkin, *A River No More* (Tucson, Arizona: University of Arizona Press, 1984), 272.

13. Langbein, "L'Affaire LaRue," 12.

14. Russell Martin, *A Story That Stands Like A Dam: Glen Canyon Dam and the Struggle for the Soul of the West* (New York: Henry Holt and Company, 1989), 136–137.

15. The primary sources of information on the numbers of rapids in Cataract Canyon are E.C. LaRue (unpublished data, 1921); U.S. Geological Survey, *Plan and Profile of Colorado River, Lees Ferry, Arizona, to the Mouth of Green River, Utah; San Juan River, Mouth to Chinle Creek, Utah; and Certain Tributaries* (Washington, D.C.: U.S. Government Printing Office, 1922 [1955 printing]), 22 sheets; L.A. Jones, *Cataract Canyon* (Midway, Utah: privately published, 1962), scroll map; and F.E. Mutschler, *River Runner's Guide to Canyonlands National Park and Vicinity with Emphasis on Geologic Features* (Denver, Colorado: The Powell Society, 1977). Other river guides generally follow the U.S. Geological Survey's definitions.

16. R.A. Cogswell, diary of 1909 trip, the Marston Collection, Huntington Library, San Marino, California.

17. R.F. Nash, *The Big Drops: Ten Legendary Rapids of the American West* (Boulder, Colorado: Johnson Books, 1989), 201.

18. Frank Silvey, *Early History and Settlement of Northern San Juan County, Utah* (Moab, Utah: Times-Independent Publishing Company, 1990), 15.

19. Bert Loper called it Dark Canyon Rapid in 1907; diary narrative, undated, Box 121, Folder 4, Marston Collection, Huntington Library, San Marino, California.

20. Ellsworth Kolb, *Through the Grand Canyon from Wyoming to Mexico* (New York: MacMillan, 1914), 148–150.

21. Jones, *Cataract Canyon*.

22. Grand Canyon rapids are rated according to the Deseret system. This system refers to the classification of whitewater rapids as formulated by the boaters of Utah's Wasatch Front. Deseret is a term of the Latter-day Saints (Mormons) and refers to the territory of Utah. The system is only used in the American West and is not inclusive. This system rates the rapids from one to ten, with one described as "very easy"

and ten as "extreme difficulty," according to L.A. Jones's scroll map, *Cataract Canyon*. The international system is rated by classes and in Roman numbers from I to VI. Class I is easy and Class VI means mortality is likely. The international system also takes into consideration such things as inclement weather. For more information on this topic, see http://www.americanwhitewater.org/archive/safety/safety.html#rating%20scale.

23. Georgie White, diary of 1957 trip, Utah State Historical Society, Salt Lake City.

24. John Weisheit, "Harry Aleson and Georgie Clark: The Log of the 'May Qui,'" *The Confluence* 4 (1997): 22–24.

25. G.C. Simmons, "U.S. Geological Survey Diary of the Cataract Canyon Expedition – 1956," *Canyon Legacy* 32 (1998): 7–15.

26. Peter Winn, "Icebergs in Cat," *The Confluence* 3 (1996): 20–21; and interview with Michael Collier, February 2001.

27. Julius Stone, *Canyon Country: the Romance of a Drop of Water and a Grain of Sand* (New York: MacMillan Company, 1932), 435.

28. R.H. Webb, T.S. Melis, and R.A. Valdez, *Observations of Environmental Change in Grand Canyon, Arizona* (Tucson, Arizona: U.S. Geological Survey Water-Resources Investigations Report 02-4080, 2002).

29. C.G. Crampton, *Ghosts of Glen Canyon: History Beneath Lake Powell* (St. George, Utah: Publishers Place, Inc., 1986).

30. D.L. Smith and C.G. Crampton, *The Colorado River Survey* (Salt Lake City, Utah: Howe Brothers Books, 1987), 36.

31. R.A. Cogswell, diary entry for October 21, 1909, Marston Collection, Huntington Library, San Marino, California.

32. Kolb, *Through the Grand Canyon*, 147.

33. David Williams, *The Naturalist's Guide to Canyon Country* (Helena, Montana: Falcon Press/Canyonlands Natural History Association, 2000), 95; Pinau Merlin and Peter Siminski, "Coyote and Fox," in *A Natural History of the Sonoran Desert*, eds. S.J. Phillips and P.W. Comus (Tucson:

Arizona-Sonora Desert Museum/University of California Press, 2000), 473–476.

34. Gale Monson, "Distribution and Abundance," in *The Desert Bighorn: Its Life History, Ecology, and Management*, eds. Gale Monson and Lowell Sumner (Tucson: University of Arizona Press, 1990), 40–51.

35. Pinau Merlin and Peter Siminski, "Hooved Animals," in *A Natural History of the Sonoran Desert*, 487–491; David Armstrong, *Mammals of Canyon Country* (Moab, Utah: Canyonlands Natural History Association, 1982).

36. Campbell Grant, "The Desert Bighorn and Aboriginal Man," in *The Desert Bighorn*, 7–39.

37. Webb *et al.*, *Observations of Environmental Change in Grand Canyon*.

38. Tom Dudley, "Aquatic Insects of the Sonoran Desert," in *A Natural History of the Sonoran Desert*, 357–364.

39. Merlin and Siminski, "Procyonids: Raccoons, Ringtails & Coatis," in *A Natural History of the Sonoran Desert*, 477–479; Armstrong, *Mammals of Canyon Country*, 171–176.

40. J.L. Cloudsley-Thompson, *Ecophysiology of Desert Arthropods and Reptiles* (Berlin: Springer-Verlag, 1991), 48–49 and 160–161; S.J. Prchal, "Scorpions," in *A Natural History of the Sonoran Desert*, 291–293.

41. Prchal, "Scorpions," 291.

42. Floyd Werner and Carl Olson, *Learning About and Living With Insects of the Southwest* (Tucson, Arizona: Fisher Books, 1994), 85–87.

43. C.G. Crampton, *Standing Up Country: The Canyon Lands of Utah and Arizona* (New York: Alfred A. Knopf, 1965), 124.

44. P.T. Reilly, *Lee's Ferry: From Mormon Crossing to National Park* (Logan: Utah State University Press, 1999), 425.

45. W.L. Chenoweth, "The Hite Uranium Mill," in *Cataract Canyon*, ed. J.A. Campbell (Durango, Colorado: Four Corners Geological Society, 1987), 159.

46. Crampton, *Ghosts of Glen Canyon*, 96.

10

"THE STRANGE AND IMPRESSIVE SCENERY"

Common Threads among the Canyons of the Colorado River

Remember these things lost. The native wildlife; the chance to float quietly down a calm river, to let the current carry you past a thousand years of history, through a living canyon of incredible, haunting beauty.

David Brower[1]

Once the boats are de-rigged, the gear is loaded for the return trip to Moab, and the scene at Hite is receding in the rear-view mirror, we can reflect on what we have seen in the canyons upstream. The rivers pass through flat approaches, combine to assert their mighty selves in a crescendo of whitewater, and then flatten into a huge, blue pool. Journeying through these canyons, one passes through distinctive ecosystems replete with lives whose diversity and longevity belie the wasteland appearance that some have ascribed to the region.

Ultimately, Cataract Canyon is a paradox. The whitewater is the result of geologic impoundments, yet two-thirds of the canyon is now quiescent because of water impounded behind a dam. Dams upstream on both approaches simultaneously encourage and defeat the highly valued riparian vegetation, depending on the characteristics of specific sites. Flood control can encourage the establishment and growth of some species lower on channel banks, while lowered river flows inhibit germination of some native species (*e.g.*, cottonwood) and may kill others whose roots cannot reach further for water. Tamarisk dominates riverbanks, creating the paradox of whether we should eradicate this exotic tree because it does not belong here, encourage it because it shelters an endangered bird, or discourage it to favor the native species that once lined these rivers. Millions are spent on "recovery" of endangered fishes, yet the largest threat to these species may be the exotic fishes intentionally

planted and cultivated in the reservoir below or in the flat water above Cataract Canyon. Answers to dilemmas and contrasts such as these will determine the future of Cataract Canyon and serve as touchstones for the future of wildlands in the West.

Cataract Canyon also represents values and preconceived ideas about the dual issues of whitewater and boating safety and human impact on the wilderness experience. The perception of Cataract Canyon as risky whitewater persists, and it may be well-justified at flood stage, but most of the time its rapids, while formidable, are relatively nonthreatening. The reservoir and flat approaches encourage motorized trips, to the disgust of oar purists. Because half of the canyon is inundated by Lake Powell, some consider Cataract Canyon to be lost and not worth the trip for those too-few miles of whitewater, especially compared to Grand Canyon. Inevitably, many comparisons are made between Cataract Canyon and its better-known relative downstream.

GRAND CANYON ENVY

We hear comparisons all of the time. For instance, when approaching Tilted Park on low water, a guide on a passing trip warned: "Watch out for Rapid 10! The waves are as big as Hermit!" The same has been said of Rapid 7 at 50,000 ft³/s. Hermit, a large rapid in the middle of Grand Canyon, makes Rapid 10 look like a riffle but it does not hold a candle to Rapid 7 at high water. Are Lava Falls Rapid in Grand Canyon and Big Drop 3 really comparable? Each is water flowing over and around boulders, but beyond that the comparison is meaningless. Each rapid is unique.

Whether they admit it or not, Grand Canyon envy dominates the souls of Cataract Canyon river guides. Work in the "big ditch" pays more and definitely is more glamorous; it is sort of the equivalent of being a ski patrol guide in New Hampshire versus Colorado or, closer to Moab, the difference between being a guide on the Daily versus working in Cataract Canyon. The real contrast is emotional: river runners are attracted to Grand Canyon, but they fear Cataract Canyon.[2] The Grand Canyon run is 225 or 277 miles long, depending on where you take out, while Cataract is mostly flatwater or reservoir with only sixteen miles of whitewater. The nature of the water also contributes to Grand Canyon envy: the Colorado River in Grand Canyon is usually blue and always cold, while the river in Cataract Canyon is usually muddy and changes temperature seasonally. Who wouldn't prefer boating on a river where the beer doesn't have to be in the cooler and water doesn't have to settle before it can be used in cooking?

From an environmental perspective, Cataract Canyon holds a decided edge on Grand Canyon, however. Turn off the motor, and there is silence in Cataract. Tourists flying overhead in Grand Canyon ensure few quiet moments along the river there, whereas the sound of a helicopter over Cataract Canyon is rare and portends a rescue in progress. Although stripped of perhaps ten to twenty percent of its volume, the annual flood still occurs in Cataract Canyon and the river still transports its load of sediment, lending at least the illusion that here the river is untamed. The larger tributaries in Grand Canyon have towns within their drainages; the tributaries of Cataract Canyon drain water contained in wilderness or national park lands. Parts of Grand Canyon were home to burros released by nineteenth-century prospectors; most of Cataract Canyon has not been grazed by non-native animals. Some of the most voracious predators of native fishes (trout) were stocked purposefully in Grand Canyon, but no fishes were ever deliberately and directly stocked in Cataract

Canyon. In this sense, Cataract Canyon is one of the few remaining reaches on the Colorado River that can truly be considered wilderness.

Most of the five million visitors to Grand Canyon every year see the canyon from a small number of overlooks on the South Rim. It is very amusing to some of us, seeing a tourist get out of a minivan with a camcorder glued to the eye, walking to and from the overlook while never once really looking at the view, much less appreciating its environmental attributes or meaning. While some people's experience of Canyon Country is the view from Dead Horse Point State Park, most people experience the region firsthand, if only to breathe in the dust on a dirt road. Relatively few of the visitors to either park see the landscape from the river, in part because of its expense but also because of the perceived dangers of river travel. Edward Abbey was correct: the more primitive the locomotion, the more wonder that Canyonlands reveals to the visitor.

Instead of concentrating on which canyon is "best," it is far more interesting to compare and contrast the attributes of Cataract Canyon with its geomorphic relatives on the Colorado Plateau, one of which happens to be Grand Canyon. Much is known about prehistory, paleoecology, and historical changes in Grand Canyon, so how different is Cataract Canyon from its more famous southern kindred? Other less-known canyons on the Colorado Plateau invite comparisons as well.

DEBRIS FLOWS AND RAPIDS ON THE COLORADO PLATEAU

Debris-Flow Frequency

Debris flows occur in many reaches of the Green and Colorado rivers on the Colorado Plateau, but their frequency varies considerably. Debris flows rarely occur along the San Juan River south of Canyonlands (see Figure 1-1).[3] Cataract Canyon tends to have a lower frequency of debris flows than other reaches, at least within its larger drainages, but small debris flows out of high-angle chutes are a relatively common occurrence. Debris-flow frequency is higher in Grand

Canyon, with about sixty percent of tributary canyons producing debris flows in the last century.[4] The Green River through Desolation and Gray canyons might have the highest frequency of debris flows on the Colorado Plateau; all of its rapids have changed historically, and all tributaries with a record of repeat photography have had debris flows.[5]

The common threads among these canyons are topography, directions of the river corridors, and the presence or absence of shales that are necessary for debris flows. All have sufficient cliffs and large enough tributaries to produce debris flows. In Grand Canyon, debris-flow frequency is highest in reaches that trend south-southwest;[6] the San Juan River and Cataract Canyon have mostly westerly courses, and Desolation and Gray canyons face south. Grand and Cataract canyons have the Hermit and Halgaito shales respectively; these are both terrestrial shales of Permian age and both produce debris flows. Debris flows in Desolation and Gray canyons are related to several shales of Tertiary and Cretaceous ages.

From a geological perspective, the San Juan River offers a direct comparison to Cataract Canyon. Both pass through the same bedrock at river level—the Honaker Trail and Paradox formations—yet the San Juan River has only small rapids. Powell began the idea that rapids stem from resistant bedrock at river level, yet this comparison between canyons shows the real reason for rapids. Cataract has the Halgaito Shale in its cliffs; this unit is mostly missing from San Juan Canyon, and where it does occur—well downstream of the Goosenecks—debris-flow controlled rapids are present. All of the rapids in Cataract Canyon, with the exception of the now-drowned Dark Canyon Rapid, occur where the canyon was wide, and the narrowest part of the river corridor, a place appropriately called Narrow Canyon, had no rapids to speak of. Instead of the most resistant rocks the weakest rocks in the cliffs, combined with more-resistant, boulder-producing strata, create rapids.

Rapids

Although comparisons are frequently made between rapids on *any* river and those in Grand Canyon, such comparisons are foolish. Attempts to generalize the difficulty of running rapids are made with the idea of memorizing runs and avoiding the obvious alternative choice of scouting or reading water. All rapids are different and change with water level, and disasters can befall the unwary or unlucky in any rapid. If one wants to indulge in speculative comparisons anyway, then one comparison in particular is apt: in terms of spacing of rapids, Cataract Canyon is most similar to Marble Canyon, although no rapids in this reach of Grand Canyon have the severity or technical difficulty of Cataract's rapids. From another perspective, the annual flood in Cataract Canyon makes its rapids much more difficult to river runners than the regularly scheduled dam releases in Grand Canyon, which some guides memorize and use to determine the time of day that is right to run certain rapids. In both canyons, one must read and understand water flowing around boulders to be completely functional as a guide; it is just a little more difficult in Cataract Canyon owing to the fluctuations in discharge.

From the perspective of form, the rapids of Cataract Canyon are enormous while the rapids of Grand Canyon are smaller and those in Desolation, Gray, and San Juan canyons are smaller yet. Rapids 13 through 20 are part of one large rapid that stems primarily from sediment inputs at Range Canyon. The Big Drops similarly stem from Teapot/Calf Canyon. Hance Rapid, the largest single drop in Grand Canyon, originates from Red Canyon and falls twenty-nine feet over one mile through its primary and secondary rapids. Mile Long Rapid falls forty-nine feet in 1.8 miles, and the Big Drops fall thirty-two feet in 0.8 miles. In addition to its steeper overall slope, the scale of rapids is larger in Cataract Canyon.

Longitudinal Profiles

From what can be observed at the surface, we hypothesize that the longitudinal profile of the Colorado River through Cataract Canyon developed during the Holocene (the last 11,000 years). We have presented evidence to support this throughout this book: surface deposits do not have significant soil development, suggesting that the deposition of these sediments is quite

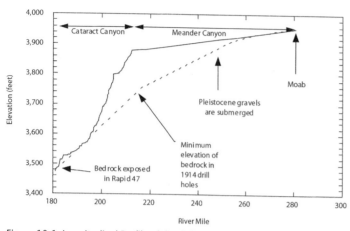

Figure 10-1. Longitudinal Profile of the Colorado River from Mille Crag Bend to Moab, Utah. The bedrock profile is reconstructed from rivers or reaches where bedrock is known to be near river level (*e.g.*, where the San Juan River flows through Honaker Trail Formation).

recent; Pleistocene gravels (more than 11,000 years old) along both approaches appear to dive beneath the surface of the rivers; tributary mouths just upstream from the Confluence appear to be choked with mainstem sediments; and drill records record more than 125 feet of sand beneath the Confluence while a bedrock-controlled rapid was present downstream of Dark Canyon. The longitudinal profile of the river shows a flat reach entering Cataract Canyon, substantial drops through Cataract to about Gypsum canyon, whereupon the profile flattens down to Dark Canyon Rapid; downstream from Dark Canyon, and at the reportedly bedrock-controlled Rapid 47, the slope of the Colorado River flattens to its "normal" slope that appears for long reaches upstream and downstream.[7]

We do not have the benefit of knowing where bedrock is beneath Cataract Canyon. If we assume that the bedrock under the river is from the Honaker Trail Formation, then a profile of the bedrock surface can be hypothesized by using another piece of information. The San Juan River flows mostly on the Honaker Trail Formation through its canyons, and its overall slope is 7.5 ft/mi. If we extend this slope upstream from Rapid 47, and modify it for other likely subsurface bedrock slopes (*e.g.*, river slopes through the Elephant Canyon Formation and Cedar Mesa Sandstone), the projected slope passes more than 120

feet beneath the Confluence, in accord with the drill-hole data, and reaches current river level at about the point where the Pleistocene gravels become submerged in Meander Canyon (Figure 10-1).

Cataract and Grand canyons have numerous similarities but more significant differences in their respective longitudinal profiles. Both canyons are bedrock-controlled—mostly by Paleozoic sedimentary rocks—although, unlike in Cataract Canyon, the Colorado River in Grand Canyon has downcut further into Proterozoic metamorphic rocks, much like it did in Westwater Canyon upstream from Cataract Canyon. The slope through Grand Canyon is 8.0 ft/mi, while the slope through the free-flowing parts of Cataract Canyon is 17.3 ft/mi.

The magnitude of sediment delivery by tributaries is one of the principal differences between Cataract and Grand canyons. As discussed above, few recent debris flows have occurred in Cataract Canyon, unlike Grand Canyon. While this indicates that debris-flow activity has been recently quiescent in Cataract Canyon, it does not minimize the importance of this process over the entire Holocene. Instead, the presence of large bottomlands upstream of Cataract Canyon, as well as wide sections of canyon such as at Tilted Park and Gypsum Canyon, indicate that large quantities of sediment have raised the bed of the Colorado by more than a hundred feet recently. No evidence in Grand Canyon indicates a similar rise, even at such legendary rapids as Lava Falls and Crystal.[8] This suggests that the Colorado River is flowing relatively close to bedrock through much of Grand Canyon. In Cataract Canyon, the river flows over boulders.

THE STABILITY OF ECOSYSTEMS

The Riparian Ecosystem

Among the major rivers on the Colorado Plateau, the riparian ecosystems of Cataract Canyon are only comparable to those on the San Juan River. Four types of riparian ecosystems have been discussed in this book. First, there are the dense riparian thickets of the approaches, typically dominated by some combination of tamarisk and coyote willow. Rarely one sees cottonwoods set back from the river; more commonly, there is desert olive marking where the banks used to be. Grand Canyon does not have the cottonwoods, Desolation and Gray canyons have more of them, and desert olive is unique to the Canyonlands region. Second, the river corridor through the whitewater of Cataract Canyon is mostly lined with scattered tamarisk and netleaf hackberry, which is most similar to the San Juan River, as only a few hackberry occur in Grand Canyon. Third, the wide canyon and low gradient reach of Tilted Park and Lake Cataract support locally dense tamarisk thickets and have declining groves of cottonwood trees. These traits are reminiscent of the reach between Desolation and Gray canyons, except that cottonwoods are not declining there.

The fourth type of vegetation occurs in the inundated part of Cataract Canyon. Here the vegetation is a mosaic of different species created by frequent fluctuations of the reservoir level. Similar conditions occur where the San Juan River meets Lake Powell and where the Colorado River in Grand Canyon meets Lake Mead. Habitat at these junction points comes and goes, and the composition and longevity of the vegetation is at the whim of climate (which controls reservoir inflows), and the politics of water development (which controls reservoir outflows). Although some endangered species—such as Southwestern Willow Flycatchers—may be attracted to these habitats when conditions are favorable, they are unstable over the long term.

Our repeat photography provides information on the stability of all types of riparian communities in Cataract Canyon and its approaches. Individual riparian trees—particularly netleaf hackberry, boxelder, and cottonwood—are readily observed and counted in photographs that span a century or greater. Clumps of other species, notably desert olive, apache plume, and sandbar willow, remain in the same spot, suggesting a long life span for the collective individual. Maximum known longevities for these species in Canyonlands range from 108 to 128 years, or essentially the entire length of our photographic record.

Desert Plants

The desert plant assemblages in Cataract Canyon and along its approaches are mostly representative of the Colorado Plateau Desert, which is considered a cool desert because it has lower winter temperatures. In contrast, the river corridor through Grand Canyon changes from cool to hot desert.[9] Nevertheless, desert plants in both canyons are extremely long-lived, and many similarities exist between closely related species. For example, Mormon tea in Grand Canyon (mostly *Ephedra nevadensis*) has a mortality rate of about seventeen percent per century[10] while Mormon tea in Cataract Canyon (mostly *E. torreyana*) has a mortality rate of between zero and fourteen percent per century, depending upon the time interval considered.[11]

Using repeat photography, individuals of all species of upland trees can be identified as persistent, including singleleaf ash, pinyon, juniper, and oak. That these species can live for at least 128 years is not a surprise; pinyon pine, for example, is known to live several thousand years. Upland shrubs that commonly live more than a century include skunkbush, blackbrush, four-wing saltbush, shadscale, rubber rabbitbrush, Bigelow sagebrush (*Artemisia bigelovii*), rough brickellbush (*Brickellia microtheca*), and birchleaf buckthorn (*Rhamnus betulifolia*). Many of these species have similar lifespans in Grand Canyon. Some plants are distinctly short-lived and are never visible in both sets of repeat photographs; these include snakeweed, buckwheat, and fluffgrass (*Erioneuron* sp).

The idea that individual grasses can live to be over a century is surprising. Although it is not possible to tell if these are the same individuals (grasses do not have distinctive stems or twigs for identification), the observed plants are growing in the same spot and are generally the same size in the matched photographs that span a century. Also, two of the long-lived grasses—Indian ricegrass and sand dropseed—reproduce by seed only. Because it is likely that new individuals would colonize slightly different spots than the parent plant, we conclude that these are persistent individuals. Galleta grass is also commonly included in the century club. Since this grass reproduces vegetatively by sending out roots that produce above-ground shoots, it is likely to be the same individual.

Climate may have played a strong role in what our photographs document. The Little Ice Age, with cold, wet winters, peaked between A.D. 1550 and 1750.[12] Very wet years were again recorded between 1609 and 1623 and 1835 through 1849. These were also years of unusually large floods and the filling of dry lake beds. Five severe freezes were recorded between 1805 and 1837—a record number for the past 400 years. Although the Little Ice Age ended sometime in the mid-1800s, rainfall remained above normal during the last half of the nineteenth century, especially between 1878 and 1891, when most southwest rivers had high rainfall and large floods. The years of 1883-1885 were unusually wet, and temperatures were extremely low. Thus, the conditions that preceded the 1898 photos were fairly wet and extremely cold.

Since the 1871 (Beaman) and 1889 (Nims) photos were taken, the climate has been highly variable, with extreme droughts followed by extremely wet periods. Overall, the intensity of summer precipitation has declined on the Colorado Plateau, resulting in less flooding of the major rivers. Until the mid-1970s, the twentieth century was quite dry and had two of the five most severe droughts of the last thousand years.[13] In the last decades of the twentieth century by contrast, precipitation increased and, although some extreme cold has been recorded, severe frost has occurred only once a decade, far less frequently than in the previous century. Thus, plants recorded in the late nineteenth century were plants that established during, or could survive, wet and very cold conditions, while the plants recorded in photographs at the end of the twentieth century were those that survived severe droughts, reduced summer precipitation, and warmer conditions.

Combined, the most obvious thing climatic information tells us is that the persistent species seen in these photos are survivors in every sense of the word, as they have made it through all the extremes: very wet and dry times, very cold and hot times, changes in rainfall timing, and now, warming temperatures. Despite organisms' preference for constancy, what we have seen over the past two centuries on the Colorado Plateau is extreme variability, yet we have a subset of vegetation that has survived these highly unpredictable conditions. This is a feat few organisms can perform.

THE FUTURE OF CATARACT CANYON: A TOMBSTONE OR A RAY OF HOPE?

Many of the changes seen in the past century or two are expected to continue in the future. Temperatures are predicted to rise, rainfall is expected to be more variable, atmospheric carbon dioxide is rising, the human population is increasing, the demand for water in the arid Southwest will increase, and dams will continue to operate. Edward Abbey struck a decidedly pessimistic note in his work (as noted in the Preface), but we are not so sure that his pessimism is fully warranted. Change is inevitable in natural ecosystems; we may lack the perspective to evaluate whether specific changes are "good" or "bad" until well after they have occurred.

Temperatures already are rising, particularly winter temperatures and daily lows.[14] We can expect this to have a large effect on the biota of Cataract Canyon, even if the increases are small. Rainfall in this region is expected to stay the same or decrease somewhat. The timing of rainfall, and particularly its inter-annual variability, is likely to change. The variability in climate is likely to be the most significant change in the future, translating into more very hot and very cold years and more very wet and very dry years. These changes are likely to have significant effects on both plant and animal communities. As we discussed in Chapter 4, organisms are able to adapt to most environments in the long run, as long as the environments are predictable. However, it appears that the already harsh environmental conditions in Canyon Country have the capacity to get even more unpredictable, making life even more difficult to handle.

Many plants and animals already live on the edge in terms of water and heat stress. Increasing temperatures alone may lead to the loss of some species. Changes in the seasonality of rainfall could alter or completely change the flora of both the vascular plant and soil biological crust communities. Even with relatively sophisticated paleoecological tools that scientists now use, no one has detected this type of change over the last 11,000 years, and thus our ability to predict what will happen is limited.

Irrespective of what increases in trace atmospheric gases might do to global temperatures, increases in carbon dioxide are widely expected to systematically affect vascular plant species. Plants using the C3 carbon pathway—the most common type for species on the Colorado Plateau—mostly use cool-season moisture and are expected to benefit from increased carbon dioxide. Insect and animal populations that use these plants would presumably benefit from the increase in plant biomass as well. Benefits could also extend, unfortunately, to non-native species (currently, all of which are C3 plants), although whether this might give exotics an added incentive to increase at the expense of native species remains to be seen. The losers would be plants using the C4 carbon pathway, which greatly benefit from summer moisture and include the saltbushes and some perennial grasses, and the insect and animal species that depend on them.

Recreational impacts are expected to increase in the future. Use of the rims and uplands may drive animals that avoid humans (*e.g.*, bighorn sheep) toward the river, while attracting those that feast on the garbage humans leave behind (*e.g.*, deer mice). On the other hand, increases in river traffic may move human-avoiding animals towards the uplands. At some point, solitude will be squeezed between the two areas. Increasing numbers of people also means increased competition for campsites both along the river and up side canyons. Often, seeing the remains of a campsite, people will push on for a more "pristine" site and thus expand the human impact zone to previously undisturbed areas.

Exotic plant and animals that are currently present in Cataract Canyon are likely to continue their increase, and we certainly can expect new species to arrive. A good example is Russian knapweed (Chapter 4), a plant that just recently arrived in Canyon Country and that continues to expand its range yearly. We found a new patch near a recently burned area opposite Spanish Bottom in 2001. Bullfrogs already occur everywhere, but there are plenty of other non-native amphibians that could survive in this country, if only

they could get here. Non-native fish are pervasive in Cataract Canyon, and striped bass—a voracious predator—has already been found within the canyon in small numbers. As fishing pressures increase, new species may be inadvertently or deliberately added to the river, making life ever more difficult for the few remaining native species in the river. Biological controls might offer a glimmer of hope for suppressing some non-native species, if only we can be reasonably assured that we are not replacing one problem species with another.

Impacts from dams are certainly going to continue in the short term, although there is a good possibility some dams may be removed in the future. Lower-elevation reservoirs—such as Lake Powell—are filling with sediment, offering the future prospect of either an extensive shallow lake or a decommissioned dam. It will be another century before a reservoir such as Lake Powell will lose its usefulness.[15] Water in the Colorado River basin was over-allocated in the Colorado River Compact, and its distribution among user groups will tighten, meaning there may be less water available in the future for riverine restoration projects, like habitat-maintenance floods from Flaming Gorge and Glen Canyon dams. Channel narrowing will continue, creating deeper channels and storing more sediment on former islands and point bars, and driftwood piles may shrink as fewer cottonwood logs are produced and annual flooding is controlled. Lowering of flood discharges probably means cottonwoods and native fish will continue to decline while tamarisk may expand its domain.

The Next Big Flood

Of all the possible changes in store for Cataract Canyon, the most intriguing involves the occurrence of an exceptionally large flood. Because most climate prognosticators call for increases in extreme events—floods and droughts—in the coming decade, the possibility exists that a flood larger than those in the twentieth century (maximum was 147,000 ft³/s) or even the nineteenth century (largest known was 225,000 ft³/s) could occur. The Bureau of Reclamation believes an even larger flood, approaching 700,000 cubic feet per second, is possible if certain extreme meteorological events coincide in time and space.[16] According to weather watchers, the probability of such a coincidence just might be increasing.

We can guess what such a flood might do to Cataract Canyon and its approaches. Riparian vegetation, particularly tamarisk, would be upended, greatly reducing its numbers. Tamarisk is brittle compared to some of the native riparian species—such as coyote willow—and flooding likely will decimate or eliminate large populations. Its abundant seedbank ensures that, without human intervention, tamarisk would return, but the possibility exists that native species might survive the flood and reduce the amount of bare substrate available for tamarisk germination and establishment. Channels may be widened on the approaches, leading to a system that resembles the river Powell boated through. Cottonwoods might get a new chance in Canyonlands, given the combination of new substrate and saturated soils that are required for its germination and establishment. All in all, extreme events could completely reverse any changes created by average climatic conditions or dam operations.

Fewer changes would occur in the geomorphology of Cataract Canyon. Large boulders may be rolled downstream out of some of the rapids. Because these rapids have already endured large floods historically, with few significant changes, a single large flood is unlikely to alter the whitewater of Cataract Canyon dramatically. Similarly, beaches come and go; if anything a large flood would replenish the high sandbars that have not been submerged since 1984.

One not-so-predictable effect of a large flood would be in the native fish populations. Some have speculated that a large flood might displace non-native species from habitat like Cataract Canyon, while native species, which evolved with extreme floods, would find a hiding place and evade detrimental impacts. Small floods in the past have temporarily displaced non-native species, only so that they return after short periods. The relation between floods and reproduction of native species is not known, meaning that native fishes are unlikely to reap any benefits from anything other than a reduction or removal of their non-native competitors.

TOWARD A GREATER UNDERSTANDING OF CANYONS

Tourists can ask the most naive questions. One frequently asked is whether the trip will end at the put-in, implying that the river will flow in a circle or that the boats will reverse course and go back upstream. Another famous question, asked at the end of a geologic discourse on bedrock geology, is: "Were the rocks here when Major Powell came through?" One of our all-time favorites, whether real or legendary, involves the woman who could not understand why those Ancestral Puebloans would have left the Glen Canyon region and its beautiful, blue reservoir.

River guides deal with questions, whether naive or informed, on a constant basis. Some questions require extreme patience, or at least the ability to suppress a smile. Some answers are hard to come by because the questions are so difficult. In this book, we have attempted to link human history, geologic processes and timescales, ecosystem attributes, and the life histories of the regions' species. Although connecting these links helps us to understand the strange and impressive scenery of Cataract Canyon, we know that our linkages are incomplete. The easy answer is to blame all changes on humans, whether it is because of our reservoirs, our livestock, or our trampling. It is much harder to understand how humans fit into a complex ecosystem that may be fragile and resilient at the same time.

Although our environmental ethic declares that we should preserve and protect our parks, change is inevitable. Separating out the relative contributions to change—human versus natural processes—may be difficult if not impossible, but separate we must if we are to chase that elusive goal called "restoration." It is our fervent hope that our portrait here of Cataract Canyon conveys the image of a dynamic landscape and ecosystem that, if anything, is in far better shape than some of its relatives elsewhere on the Colorado Plateau. Conditions here could provide realistic restoration goals for less pristine areas that warrant management for ecological improvement.

It is also our wish that this book contributes to a richer understanding of the ecosystems of Cataract

Canyon. We have barely scratched the surface of its mysteries and wonders, but hopefully our scratches will inspire others to dig deeper into its history, geology, and ecology. We would like to think that others might want to speculate as to why a certain rock is in the river, or better yet, when did it get into the river and by what means? One of the best compliments we think possible would be to hear, on a future Cataract Canyon trip, this question from a passenger: "Was that plant alive when Major Powell came through?"

Notes

1. David Brower, *The Place No One Knew: Glen Canyon on the Colorado River* (San Francisco: Sierra Club Books, 1963).

2. R.F. Nash, *The Big Drops: Ten Legendary Rapids of the American West* (Boulder, Colorado: Johnson Books, 1989), 77.

3. No significant debris flows have been observed in ninety-three repeat photographs of the San Juan Canyon; R.H. Webb, unpublished data.

4. P.G. Griffiths, R.H. Webb, and T.S. Melis, "Initiation and Frequency of Debris Flows in Grand Canyon, Arizona," *Journal of Geophysical Research*, Surface Precesses, submitted.

5. This comparison is based upon sixty-eight repeat photographs of Desolation and Gray canyons that show that all of the rapids photographed historically have changed; R.H. Webb, unpublished data.

6. Griffiths *et al.*, "Initiation and Frequency of Debris Flows."

7. Interestingly enough, geologist Hugh Miser of the 1921 U.S. Geological Survey Expedition hypothesized much the same thing, albeit without the temporal framework of Holocene creation (see Chapter 3). He never published his ideas.

8. R.H. Webb, P.T. Pringle, and G.R. Rink, *Debris Flows in Tributaries of the Colorado River in Grand Canyon National Park, Arizona* (Washington, D.C.: U.S. Government Printing Office, U.S. Geological Survey Professional Paper 1492, 1989); R.H. Webb, T.S. Melis, P.G. Griffiths, J.G., Elliott, T.E. Cerling, R.J. Poreda, T.W. Wise, and J.E. Pizzuto, *Lava Falls Rapid in Grand Canyon, Effects of Late Holocene Debris Flows on the Colorado River* (Washington, D.C.: U.S. Government Printing Office, U.S. Geological Survey Professional Paper 1591, 1999).

9. S.W. Carothers and B.T. Brown, *The Colorado River through Grand Canyon* (Tucson: University of Arizona Press, 1991); R.H. Webb, *Grand Canyon, A Century of Change* (Tucson: University of Arizona Press, 1996).

10. J.E. Bowers, R.H. Webb, and R.J. Rondeau, "Longevity, Recruitment, and Mortality of Desert Plants in Grand Canyon, Arizona, U.S.A.," *Journal of Vegetation Science* 6 (1995): 551–564; Webb, *Century of Change*, 51–52.

11. R.H. Webb and J. Belnap, unpublished data, 2003.

12. Neil Roberts, *The Holocene: An Environmental History* (New York: Basil Blackwell, Inc., 1989), 155–181; K.L. Petersen, *A Warm and Wet Little Climatic Optimum and a Cold and Dry Little Ice Age in the Southern Rocky Mountains, U.S.A.* (Richland, Washington: Westinghouse Hanford Company, 1992).

13. R.D. D'Arrigo and G.C. Jacoby, "A 1000-Year Record of Winter Precipitation from Northwestern New Mexico, USA: A Reconstruction from Tree-Rings and its Relation to El Nino and the Southern Oscillation," *The Holocene* 1,2 (1991): 95–101; Richard Hereford, R.H. Webb, and Scott Graham, *Precipitation History of the Colorado Plateau Region, 1900–2000* (Flagstaff: U.S. Geological Survey Fact Sheet 119-02, 2002).

14. R.M. Turner, R.H. Webb, J.E. Bowers, and J.R. Hastings, *The Changing Mile Revisited* (Tucson: University of Arizona Press, 2003).

15. E.R. Schultz, *Design Features of Glen Canyon* (Denver, Colorado: Bureau of Reclamation, 1961), 27, 30.

16. Morrison-Knudson Engineers, Inc., "Determination of an Upper Limit Design Rainstorm for the Colorado River Basin above Hoover Dam," (Denver, Colorado: Bureau of Reclamation, Contract No. 5-CA-30-02880, 1990); Bureau of Reclamation, *Colorado River Basin Probable Maximum Floods: Hoover and Glen Canyon Dams* (Denver, Colorado: Bureau of Reclamation, 1990).

Appendix 1

Plants of Canyonlands National Park

SCIENTIFIC NAME	COMMON NAME	SCIENTIFIC NAME	COMMON NAME
Aceraceae – Maple Family		*Asclepias latifolia*	Broadleaf Milkweed
Acer glabrum var. *glabrum*	Rocky Mountain Maple	*Asclepias macrosperma*	Dwarf Milkweed
Acer grandidentatum	Big Tooth Maple	*Asclepias rusbyi*	Rusby Milkweed[4]
Acer negundo	Boxelder	*Asclepias speciosa*	Showy Milkweed
Agavaceae – Agave Family		*Asclepias subverticillata*	Poison Milkweed;
Yucca angustissima	Narrowleaf Yucca; Fineleaf Yucca		Whorled Milkweed
Yucca baccata	Datil Yucca	*Asclepias tuberosa* ssp. *terminalis*	Butterfly Milkweed
Yucca harrimaniae	Harriman Yucca	*Sarcostemma cynanchoides*	Climbing Milkweed
Yucca toftiae	Toft's Yucca[3]	**Asteraceae – Composite Family**	
Aizoaceae – Carpetweed Family		*Ambrosia acanthicarpa*	Bur Ragweed
Sesuvium verrucosum	Sea Purslane	*Ambrosia tomentosa*	Low Ragweed
Amaranthaceae – Amaranth Family		*Antennaria parviflora*	Common Pussytoes
Amaranthus albus	Tumble Pigweed	*Artemisia bigelovii*	Bigelow Sagebrush
Amaranthus blitoides	Prostrate Pigweed	*Artemisia campestris* ssp.	Field Wormwood
Anacardiaceae – Cashew Family		borealis var. *scouleriana*	
Rhus aromatica	Squawbush; Skunkbush Sumac	*Artemisia dracunculus* var. *glauca*	Tarragon Sagebrush
Rhus aromatica var. *simplicifolia*	Squawbush; Skunkbush Sumac	*Artemisia filifolia*	Old Man Sage; Sand Sagebrush
Rhus aromatica var. *trilobata*	Squawbush; Skunkbush Sumac	*Artemisia frigida*	Fringed Sagebrush
Toxicodendron rydbergii	Poison Ivy	*Artemisia ludoviciana*	Louisiana Sagewort
Apiaceae – Carrot Family		*Artemisia ludoviciana*	Louisiana Sagewort
Cymopterus spp.	Spring-parsley	var. *ludoviciana*	
Cymopterus acaulis var. *fendleri*	Fendler Spring-parsley	*Artemisia nova*	Black Sagebrush
Cymopterus beckii	Pinnate Spring-parsley[3,5]	*Artemisia spinescens*	Budsage
Cymopterus bulbosus	Onion Spring-parsley	*Artemisia tridentata*	Big Sagebrush
Cymopterus newberryi	Newberry Spring-parsley	*Artemisia tridentata* var. *tridentata*	Big Sagebrush
Cymopterus purpureus	Purple Spring-parsley	*Aster chilensis* ssp. *adscendens*	Pacific Aster
var. *purpureus*		*Aster falcatus*	Sickle Aster
Cymopterus terebinthinus	Rock-parsley; Skeletonleaf	*Aster frondosus*	Leafy Aster
var. *petraeus*		*Aster pansus*	Elongate Aster
Lomatium parryi	Parry Biscuitroot	*Aster spinosus*	Mexican Devilweed
Apocynaceae – Dogbane Family		*Baccharis emoryi*	Waterwillow; Emory Seepwillow
Amsonia jonesii	Jones Amsonia	*Baccharis salicina*	Willow Baccharis;
Amsonia tomentosa	Woolly Amsonia		Rio Grande Seepwillow
var. *stenophylla*		*Brickellia californica*	California Brickellbush
Apocynum cannabinum	Dogbane; Indian Hemp	*Brickellia longifolia*	Longleaf Brickellbush
Apocynum sibiricum	Siberian Dogbane	*Brickellia microphylla* var. *scabra*	Rough Brickellbush
Asclepiadaceae – Milkweed Family		*Brickellia oblongifolia* var. *linifolia*	Mohave Brickellbush
Asclepias asperula var. *asperula*	Rough Milkweed; Spider Milkweed	*Carduus nutans*	Musk Thistle[1]
Asclepias fascicularis	Mexican Milkweed	*Centaurea repens*	Russian Knapweed[1]
Asclepias labriformis	Labriform Milkweed[2]	*Chaenactis stevioides*	False Yarrow; Esteve's Pincushion

SCIENTIFIC NAME	COMMON NAME
Chaetopappa ericoides	Baby White; Rose-heath
Chrysothamnus linifolius	Spreading Rabbitbrush
Chrysothamnus nauseosus	Rubber Rabbitbrush
Chrysothamnus nauseosus var. *glabratus*	Glabrate Rabbitbrush
Chrysothamnus nauseosus var. *junceus*	Rush Rabbitbrush
Chrysothamnus viscidiflorus	Low Rabbitbrush
Chrysothamnus viscidiflorus var. *stenophyllus*	Narrowleaf Rabbitbrush
Cirsium arvense var. *horridum*	Canada Thistle[1]
Cirsium calcareum	Cainville Thistle
Cirsium neomexicanum var. *neomexicanum*	New Mexico Thistle
Cirsium neomexicanum var. *utahense*	Utah Thistle
Cirsium rothrockii	Rothrock Thistle
Cirsium rydbergii	Rydberg Thistle[4]
Cirsium undulatum var. *undulatum*	Wavyleaf Thistle; Gray Thistle
Cirsium vulgare	Bull Thistle[1]
Conyza canadensis var. *glabrata*	Horseweed
Crepis runcinata var. *glauca*	Dandelion Hawksbeard
Dicoria brandegei	Desert Sandplant; Brandegee's Dicoria
Dicoria canescens ssp. *canescens*	Gray Sandplant
Dyssodia pentachaeta var. *belenidium*	Dogweed; Scale Glandweed
Encelia frutescens var. *frutescens*	Bush Encelia
Enceliopsis nudicaulis	Nakedstem; Barestem Enceliopsis
Enceliopsis nutans	Noddinghead
Erigeron argentatus	Silver Daisy
Erigeron bellidiastrum	Pretty Daisy
Erigeron divergens var. *divergens*	Spreading Daisy
Erigeron flagellaris	Trailing Daisy
Erigeron kachinensis	Kachina Dasiy
Erigeron pumilus ssp. *concinnoides*	Vernal Daisy
Erigeron utahensis	Utah Daisy
Erigeron utahensis var. *sparsifolius*	Slenderleaf Daisy
Erigeron utahensis var. *utahensis*	Utah Daisy
Gaillardia pinnatifida	Hopi Blanketflower; Reddome Blanketflower
Gaillardia spathulata	Basin Blanketflower
Glyptopleura marginata	Carveseed; Crustweed
Grindelia aphanactis	Rayless Gumweed
Grindelia fastigiata	Erect Gumweed[2]
Grindelia squarrosa var. *serrulata*	Curlycup Gumweed
Gutierrezia microcephala	Threadleaf Snakeweed
Gutierrezia sarothrae	Broom Snakeweed
Haplopappus acaulis var. *acaulis*	Stemless Goldenweed
Haplopappus armerioides var. *armerioides*	Thrifty Goldenweed
Haplopappus drummondi	Drummond's Goldenweed
Haplopappus gracilis	Slender Goldenweed
Haplopappus scopulorum var. *hirtellus*	Spindly Goldenbush[4]
Helenium autumnale var. *montanum*	Common Western Sneezeweed
Helianthella uniflora	Rocky Mountain Dwarf Sunflower
Helianthus annuus ssp. *lenticularis*	Common Sunflower
Helianthus petiolaris ssp. *fallax*	Prairie Sunflower
Heterotheca villosa var. *foliosa*	Leafy Goldenaster
Heterotheca villosa var. *hispida*	Hispid Goldenaster
Heterotheca villosa var. *villosa*	Hairy Goldenaster
Hymenopappus filifoliuss var. *hirtellus*	Fineleaf Woollywhite; Hyalineherbx
Hymenoxys acaulis	Stemless Rubberweed; Stemless Woollybase
Hymenoxys acaulis var. *arizonica*	Arizona Rubberweed
Hymenoxys acaulis var. *ivesiana*	Ive's Rubberweed
Hymenoxys richardsonii var. *floribunda*	Colorado Rubberweed
Iva axillaris	Poverty Weed; Marsh Elder
Lactuca serriola	Prickly Lettuce[1]
Lactuca tatarica var. *pulchella*	Blue Lettuce
Lygodesmia grandiflora var. *arizonica*	Skeletonweed; Showy Rush Pink
Lygodesmia juncea	Rush Skeletonweed
Machaeranthera bigelovii var. *commixta*	Sticky Spine Aster
Machaeranthera canescens	Hoary Spine Aster[2]
Machaeranthera canescens var. *aristata*	Aristate Spine Aster
Machaeranthera canescens var. *canescens*	Hoary Spine Aster
Machaeranthera grindelioides var. *grindelioides*	Rayless Spine Aster
Machaeranthera tanacetifolia	Tansyleaf Spine Aster
Malacothrix glabrata	Smooth Desert Dandelion
Malacothrix sonchoides	Sowthistle Desert Dandelion
Oxytenia acerosa	Copperweed
Perityle specuicola	Alcove Rock Daisy[2]
Petradoria pumila var. *pumila*	Rock Goldenrod
Platyschkuhria integrifolia var. *desertorum*	Desert Bahia[2]
Platyschkuhria integrifolia var. *oblongifolia*	San Juan Bahia
Pluchea sericea	Arrowweed
Prenanthella exigua	Brightwhite
Senecio douglasii var. *longilobus*	Douglas Groundsel
Senecio multilobatus	Lobeleaf Groundsel; Uinta Groundsel
Senecio spartoides var. *multicapitatus*	Manyhead Groundsel

SCIENTIFIC NAME	COMMON NAME
Senecio spartioides var. *spartioides*	Broom Groundsel
Solidago canadensis	Goldenrod
Solidago occidentalis	Western Goldenrod
Solidago sparsiflora	Alcove Goldenrod
Sonchus asper	Spiny Sow-thistle[1]
Stephanomeria exigua	Annual Wirelettuce
Stephanomeria pauciflora	Few-flower Wirelettuce
Stephanomeria tenuifolia var. *tenuifolia*	Slender Wirelettuce
Syntrichopappus frémontii	Yellowray Frémont Gold
Taraxacum officinale	Common Dandelion[1]
Tetradymia spinosa	Spiny Horsebrush
Thelesperma subnudum var. *subnudum*	Scapose Greenthread
Townsendia annua	Annual Townsend Daisy
Townsendia incana	Silvery Townsend Daisy
Tragopogon dubius	Yellow Salsify; Goatsbeard[1]
Vanclevia stylosa	Resinbush[2]
Verbesina encelioides var. *exariculata*	Crownbeard
Viquera multiflora	Showy Goldeneye
Wyethia scabra	Rough Mulesears
Xanthium strumarium var. *canadense*	Common Cocklebur[1]
Xylorhiza glabriuscula var. *linearifolia*	Smooth Woody Aster[2]
Xylorhiza tortifolia var. *imberbis*	Beardless Woody Aster[2]
Xylorhiza tortifolia	Mojave Aster; Hurtleaf Woody Aster
Xylorhiza venusta	Cisco Woody Aster[2]

Berberidaceae – Barberry Family

Berberis fendleri	Colorado Barberry[4]
Mahonia frémontii	Frémont Mahonia; Frémont Barberry

Betulaceae – Birch Family

Betula occidentalis	Water Birch
Ostrya knowltonii	Western Hophornbeam[4]

Bignoniaceae – Catalpa Family

Catalpa bignonioides	Common Catalpa[1]

Boraginaceae – Borage Family

Cryptantha confertiflora	Dense-flowered Cryptanth
Cryptantha crassisepala var. *elachantha*	Thick-sepaled Cryptanth
Cryptantha fendleri	Fendler Cryptanth
Cryptantha flava	Yellow Cryptanth
Cryptantha flavoculata	Yellow-eye Cryptanth
Cryptantha fulvocanescens	Yellow-hair Cryptanth
Cryptantha gracilis	Slender Cryptanth
Cryptantha humilis	Low Cryptanth
Cryptantha johnstonii	Johnston Cryptanth[2]

SCIENTIFIC NAME	COMMON NAME
Cryptantha kelseyana	Prickly Cryptanth
Cryptantha osterhoutii	Osterhout Cryptanth[2]
Cryptantha paradoxa	Paradox Cryptanth[2]
Cryptantha recurvata	Bentstem Cryptanth
Cryptantha tenuis	Thin Cryptanth[2]
Heliotropium convolvulaceum	Sweet-scented Heliotrope
Heliotropium curassavicum var. *obovatum*	Salt Heliotrope; Quail Plant
Lappula occidentalis var. *cupulata*	Western Stickseed
Lithospermum incisum	Showy Stoneseed; Puccoon
Tiquilia latior	Woody Tiquilia; Hairy Crinklemat[2]

Brassicaceae – Mustard Family

Alyssum alyssoides	Alyssum[1]
Arabis holboellii	Holboell Rockcress
Arabis perennans	Perennial Rockcress
Arabis pulchra var. *pallens*	Beauty Rockcress
Arabis selbyi	Selby Rockcress
Barbarea vulgaris	European Wintercress[1]
Conringia orientalis	Hares-ear Mustard[1]
Descurainia californica	Sierran Tansy-mustard
Descurainia pinnata	Western Tansy-mustard
Descurainia sophia	Flixweed[1]
Dithyrea wislizenii	Spectacle Pod
Draba cuneifolia var. *cuneifolia*	Wedgeleaf; Whitlowgrass
Erysimum asperum	Wallflower
Lepidium densiflorum	Densecress
Lepidium frémontii	Desert Peppergrass
Lepidium latifolium	Perennial Pepperweed; Broadleaf Peppergrass[1]
Lepidium montanum var. *jonesii*	Jones Pepperweed
Lepidium montanum var. *spathulatum*	Tall Pepperweed
Lepidium perfoliatum	Clasping Pepperweed[1]
Lepidium virginicum var. *pubescens*	Virginiacress
Lesquerella ludoviciana	Silver Bladderpod
Lesquerella rectipes	Dandelion Bladderpod; Colorado Bladderpod
Malcolmia africana	African Mustard[1]
Physaria acutifolia	Pointleaf Twinpod
Physaria acutifolia var. *acutifolia*	Pointleaf Twinpod
Physaria newberryi	Newberry Twinpod
Schoencrambe linifolia	Slenderleaf Plainsmustard
Sisymbrium altissimum	Tumbling Mustard[1]
Stanleya pinnata var. *pinnata*	Prince's Plume
Streptanthella longirostris	Beakpod Nippletwist
Streptanthus cordatus	Heartleaf Twist-flower
Thelypodiopsis divaricata	San Juan Tumblemustard[2]
Thelypodium integrifolium var. *gracilipes*	Tall Thelypody

Cactaceae – Cactus Family

Echinocereus engelmanni var. *variegatus*	Engelmann Hedgehog Cactus

SCIENTIFIC NAME	COMMON NAME
Echinocereus triglochidiatus var. melanacanthus	Claretcup Cactus
Opuntia basilaris var. basilaris	Beavertail Cactus[4]
Opuntia erinacea	Common Pricklypear
Opuntia littoralis var. martiniana	Littoral Pricklypear
Oputina phaeacantha	Berry Pricklypear
Opuntia phaeacantha var. major	Large Pricklypear
Opuntia polyacantha	Central Pricklypear; Plains Pricklypear
Opuntia polyacantha	Whipple Cholla
Sclerocactus whipplei var. roseus	Fishhook Cactus
Capparaceae – Caper Family	
Cleome lutea	Yellow Bee Plant
Cleome serrulata	Rocky Mountain Bee Plant
Caprifoliaceae – Honeysuckle Family	
Symphoricarpos longiflorus	Longflower Snowberry
Caryophyllaceae – Pink Family	
Arenaria congesta var. congesta	Dense Sandwort
Arenaria fendleri	Fendler Sandwort
Arenaria fendleri var. eastwoodiae	Eastwood Sandwort
Silene antirrhina	Sleepy Catchfly
Celastraceae – Stafftree Family	
Forsellesia meionandra	Greasebush; Tongue Flower
Pachystima myrsinites	Mountain Lover
Chenopodiaceae – Goosefoot Family	
Allenrolfea occidentalis	Pickleweed
Atriplex argentea	Silver Orach
Atriplex canescens var. occidentalis	Four-wing Saltbush
Atriplex confertifolia	Shadscale
Atriplex corrugata	Mat Saltbush
Atriplex gardneri	Gardner Saltbush
Atriplex gardneri var. cuneata	Gardner Saltbush
Atriplex garrettii	Garrett Saltbush[2]
Atriplex rosea	Tumbling Orach[1]
Bassia hyssopifolia	Five-hook Smotherweed[1]
Ceratoides lanata var. lanata	Winterfat
Ceratoides lanata var. ruinina	Winterfat
Chenopodium album var. album	Lambsquarter; Goosefoot[1]
Chenopodium atrovirens	Mountain Goosefoot
Chenopodium frémontii var. frémontii	Frémont Goosefoot
Chenopodium leptophyllum	Narrowleaf Goosefoot
Corispermum villosum	Tickseed
Cycloloma atriplicifolia	Winged Pigweed[1]
Grayia spinosa	Spiny Hopsage
Halogeton glomeratus	Halogeton[1]
Kochia americana	Gray Molly
Kochia scoparia	Summer-cypress
Monolepis nuttalliana	Poverty-weed
Salsola paulsenii	Barbwire Tumbleweed[1]
Salsola pestifer	Russian Thistle; Tumbleweed[1]

SCIENTIFIC NAME	COMMON NAME
Sarcobatus vermiculatus var. vermiculatus	Greasewood
Suaeda occidentalis	Western Seepweed
Suaeda torreyana var. torreyana	Torrey Seepweed
Zuckia brandegei var. brandegei	Spineless Hopsage; Siltbush
Convolvulaceae – Convolvulus Family	
Convolvulus arvensis	Field Bindweed[1]
Cornaceae – Dogwood Family	
Cornus sericea var. sericea	Red-osier Dogwood
Cucurbitaceae – Gourd Family	
Cucurbita foetidissima	Stinking Gourd[4]
Cupressaceae – Cypress Family	
Juniperus osteosperma	Utah Juniper
Cyperaceae – Sedge Family	
Carex aurea	Golden Sedge
Carex bella	Showy Sedge
Carex lanuginosa	Woolly Sedge
Carex nebrascensis	Nebraska Sedge
Carex rossii	Ross Sedge
Carex subfusca	Rusty Sedge
Cyperus acuminatus	Nutgrass
Eleocharis palustrus	Creeping Spikerush
Scirpus acutus	Hardstem Bulrush
Scirpus americanus	American Bulrush; Olney's Threesquare
Scirpus maritimus	Alkali Bulrush
Scirpus pungens var. longispicatus	Common Threesquare
Scirpus validus	Softstem Bulrush
Elaeagnaceae – Oleaster Family	
Elaeagnus angustifolia	Russian Olive[1]
Shepherdia rotundifolia	Roundleaf Buffaloberry[2]
Ephedraceae – Jointfir Family	
Ephedra torreyana	Torrey Mormon Tea
Ephedra viridis var. viridis	Green Mormon Tea
Ephedra viridis var. viscida	Cutler's Ephedra
Equisetaceae – Horsetail Family	
Equisetum arvense	Meadow Horsetail
Equisetum laevigatum	Smooth Scouringrush
Euphorbiaceae – Spurge Family	
Euphorbia brachycera	Shorthorn Spurge
Euphorbia fendleri	Fendler Spurge; Fendler Carpetweed
Euphorbia glyptosperma	Ridge-Seeded Spurge
Euphorbia parryi	Parry Spurge
Fabaceae – Pea Family	
Astragalus amphioxys var. amphioxys	Crescent Milkvetch
Astragalus ceramicus var. ceramicus	Painted Milkvetch
Astragalus chamaeleuce	Cicada Milkvetch
Astragalus coltonii var. moabensis	Moab Milkvetch[2]

SCIENTIFIC NAME	COMMON NAME
Astragalus desperatus var. *desperatus*	Rimrock Milkvetch[2]
Astragalus flavus	Yellow Milkvetch
Astragalus flexuosus	Pliant Milkvetch
Astragalus fucatus	Hopi Milkvetch
Astragalus kentrophyta var. *coloradoensis*	Prickly Milkvetch[2]
Astragalus lentiginosus var. *palans*	Freckled Milkvetch
Astragalus lonchocarpus	Great Rushy Milkvetch
Astragalus missouriensis var. *amphibolus*	Missouri Milkvetch
Astragalus moencoppensis	Moenkopi Milkvetch[3]
Astragalus mollissimus var. *thompsonae*	Woolly Locoweed
Astragalus monumentalis	Monument Milkvetch[3]
Astragalus nidularis	Bird's Nest Milkvetch[3]
Astragalus nuttallianus var. *micranthiformis*	Turkeypeas
Astragalus pattersonii	Patterson's Milkvetch
Astragalus piscator	Fisher Milkvetch
Astragalus praelongus	Stinking Milkvetch
Astragalus praelongus var. *lonchopus*	Longstipe Milkvetch[2]
Astragalus praelongus var. *praelongus*	Stinking Milkvetch
Astragalus preussii var. *preussii*	Preuss Milkvetch
Astragalus sabulonum	Gravel Milkvetch
Astragalus sesquiflorus	Sandstone Milkvetch[2]
Caesalpinia repens	Creeping Rush Pea[2]
Dalea flavescens var. *flavescens*	Kanab Prairie Clover[2]
Dalea oligophylla	Western Prairie Clover
Glycyrrhiza glabra	Licorice[1]
Glycyrrhiza lepidota	Wild Licorice
Hedysarum boreale var. *boreale*	Northern Sweetvetch
Lathyrus brachycalyx var. *zionis*	Zion Sweetpea
Lathyrus lanszwertii var. *leucanthus*	Lanszwert Sweetpea
Lotus utahensis	Utah Trefoil
Lupinus argenteus	Silvery Lupine; Tall Lupine
Lupinus pusillus	Dwarf Lupine; Rusty Lupine
Lupinus pusillus var. *pusillus*	Dwarf Lupine
Medicago sativa	Alfalfa[1]
Melilotus albus	White Sweet Clover[1]
Melilotus officinalis	Yellow Sweet Clover[1]
Pediomelum megalanthum	Large-flowered Breadroot
Peteria thompsonae	Thompson Peteria[4]
Psoralidium lanceolatum	Dune Scurf Pea
Psoralidium tenuiflorum	Prairie Scurf Pea
Psorothamnus thompsonae var. *thompsonae*	Thompson Indigo-bush
Sophora nuttalliana	Silky Necklacepod
Sophora stenophylla	Narrowleaf Necklacepod
Vicia ludoviciana	Louisiana Vetch
Fagaceae – Beech Family	
Quercus gambelii	Gambel Oak
Quercus havardii var. *tuckeri*	Sand Oak; Shinnery Oak
Quercus turbinella	Live Oak; Turbinella
Fumariaceae – Bleedingheart Family	
Corydalis aurea	Golden Corydalis
Gentianaceae – Gentian Family	
Gentiana affinis	Rocky Mountain Gentian
Swertia albomarginata	White-margined Swertia
Swertia radiata	Showy Green Gentian
Swertia utahensis	Utah Swertia
Geraniaceae – Geranium Family	
Erodium cicutarium	Storksbill[1]
Hydrophyllaceae – Waterleaf Family	
Nama densum var. *parviflorum*	Leafy Nama
Phacelia crenulata var. *corrugata*	Corrugate Phacelia
Phacelia crenulata var. *crenulata*	Scalloped Phacelia
Phacelia demissa var. *demissa*	Brittle Phacelia[2]
Phacelia howelliana	Howell Phacelia[3]
Phacelia ivesiana var. *ivesiana*	Ive's Phacelia
Juncaceae – Rush Family	
Juncus arcticus	Baltic Rush; Wire Rush
Juncus ensifolius	Rocky Mountain Rush
Juncus ensifolius var. *brunnescens*	Rocky Mountain Rush
Juncus longistylus	Longstyle Rush
Juncus tenuis	Poverty Rush
Juncus torreyi	Torrey Rush
Lamiaceae – Mint Family	
Dracocephalum parviflorum	Moleplant
Hedeoma drummondii	False Pennyroyal
Marrubium vulgare	Common Horehound[1]
Poliomintha incana	Rosemary Mint; Sand Mint; Purple Sage
Liliaceae – Lily Family	
Allium macropetalum	Large Petal Wild Onion
Allium nevadense	Nevada Wild Onion
Allium textile	Prairie Wild Onion
Androstephium breviflorum	Purple Funnel Lily
Asparagus officinalis	Asparagus[1]
Calochortus aureus	Golden Mariposa Lily[2]
Calochortus flexuosus	Winding Mariposa Lily
Calochortus nuttallii	Sego Lily
Eremocrinum albomarginatum	Desert Lily[2]
Smilicina stellata	False Solomon-seal
Zigadenus elegans	Elegant Death Camas
Zigadenus paniculatus	Foothill Death Camas
Zigadenus vaginatus	Alcove Death Camas[3]
Linaceae – Flax Family	
Linum aristatum	Broom-flax

SCIENTIFIC NAME	COMMON NAME
Linum perenne ssp. *lewisii*	Blue Flax
Linum puberulum	Puberlent Yellow-flax
Linum subterres	Utah Yellow-flax
Loasaceae – Loasa Family	
Mentzelia albicaulis	Whitestem Blazing Star
Mentzelia marginata	Cronquist Stickleaf
Mentzelia multiflora	Desert Blazing Star
Mentzelia nitens	Curvepod Stickleaf
Mentzelia pterosperma	Wingseed Stickleaf
Mentzelia pumila	Wyoming Stickleaf
Malvaceae – Mallow Family	
Malva neglecta	Umbrella Mallow[1]
Malvella leprosa	Alkali Mallow
Sphaeralcea coccinea	Scarlet Globemallow
Sphaeralcea grossulariifolia	Gooseberry-leaved Globemallow
Sphaeralcea janeae	Jane Globemallow[3]
Sphaeralcea leptophylla	Scaly Globemallow
Sphaeralcea parvifolia	Small-leaved Globemallow
Marsileaceae – Pepperwort Family	
Marsilea vestita	Water Shamrock
Moraceae – Mulberry Family	
Morus alba	White Mulberry[1]
Nyctaginaceae – Four O'clock Family	
Abronia fragrans	Snowball Sand Verbena
Alliona incarnata	Trailing Windmills
Mirabilis linearis	Narrowleaf Umbrellawort
Mirabilis linearis var. *linearis*	Narrowleaf Umbrellawort
Mirabilis multiflora	Colorado Four O'clock
Tripterocalyx carneus var. *wootonii*	Wooton Sand Verbena
Tripterocalyx micranthus	Sandpuffs; Small-flowered Sand Verbena
Oleaceae – Olive Family	
Forestiera pubescens	Desert Olive; Desert Forestiera
Fraxinus anomala	Singleleaf Ash
Onagraceae – Evening Primrose Family	
Calylophus lavandulifolius	Lavendarleaf Evening-primrose
Camissonia multijuga	Desert Day Primrose
Camissonia walkeri	Walker Primrose
Gaura parviflora	Willow Gaura; Lizardtail
Oenothera albicaulis	Whitestem Evening-primrose
Oenothera caespitosa	White Tufted Evening-primrose
Oenothera longissima	Tall Yellow Evening-primrose
Oenothera pallida var. *pallida*	Pale Evening-primrose
Oenothera pallida var. *trichocalyx*	Hairy Evening-primrose
Orchidaceae – Orchid Family	
Epipactus gigantea	Stream Orchid; Giant Epipactus
Habenaria sparsiflora var. *sparsiflora*	Sparse-flowered Bog orchid
Habenaria zothecina	Alcove Bog orchid[3]

SCIENTIFIC NAME	COMMON NAME
Orobanchaceae – Broomrape Family	
Orobanche fasciculata	Cluster Cancerroot
Orobanche ludoviciana	Louisiana Cancerroot
Orobanche multiflora	Spike Broomrape
Papaveraceae – Poppy Family	
Argemone corymbosa ssp. *arenicola*	Prickly Poppy
Pinaceae – Pine Family	
Abies concolor	White Fir
Pinus edulis	Pinyon Pine
Pinus ponderosa	Ponderosa Pine
Pseudotsuga menziesii var. *glauca*	Douglas Fir
Plantaginaceae – Plantain Family	
Plantago major	Broadleaf Plantain[1]
Plantago patagonica	Woolly Plantain
Poaceae – Grass Family	
Agropyron cristatum	Crested Wheatgrass[1]
Agrostis stolonifera	Redtop[1]
Andropogon glomeratus	Bushy Bluestem
Aristida arizonica	Arizona Threeawn
Aristida purpurea	Purple Threeawn
Bothriochloa barbinodis	Beardgrass; Cane Bluestem
Bothriochloa laguroides	Silver Bluestem
Bouteloua barbata var. *barbata*	Sixweeks Grama
Bouteloua curtipendula	Sideoats Grama
Bouteloua gracilis	Blue Grama
Bromus carinatus	Mountain Brome
Bromus inermis	Smooth Brome[1]
Bromus japonicus	Japanese Brome[1]
Bromus rubens	Red Brome[1]
Bromus tectorum	Cheatgrass[1]
Calamagrostis scopulorum	Jones Reedgrass
Distichlis spicata	Desert Saltgrass
Echinochloa crus-galli	Barnyard Grass
Elymus canadensis	Canada Wild Rye
Elymus elongatus	Tall Wheatgrass[1]
Elymus elymoides	Squirreltail
Elymus hispidus	Intermediate Wheatgrass[1]
Elymus lanceolatus	Thickspike Wheatgrass[1]
Elymus salinus	Salina Wild Rye
Elymus smithii	Western Wheatgrass
Elymus trachycaulus	Slender Wheatgrass
Elymus virginicus var. *submuticus*	Virginia Wild Rye
Enneapogon desvauxii	Spike Pappusgrass
Eragrostis pectinacea	Tufted Lovegrass
Erioneuron pilosum	Hairy Erioneuron
Erioneuron pulchellum	Fluffgrass
Festuca octoflora	Sixweeks Fescue
Hilaria jamesii	Galleta Grass
Hordeum jubatum	Foxtail Barley[1]
Hordeum murinum	Rabbit Barley[1]

SCIENTIFIC NAME	COMMON NAME	SCIENTIFIC NAME	COMMON NAME
Hordeum pusillum	Little Barley	*Gilia hutchinsifolia*	Hutchins Gilia
Leptochloa fasicularis	Sprangletop	*Gilia inconspicua*	Shy Gilia
Muhlenbergia andina	Foxtail Muhly	*Gilia latifolia* var. *imperialis*	Spiny Gilia[2]
Muhlenbergia arsenei	Navajo Muhly[5]	*Gilia leptomeria*	Great Basin Gilia
Muhlenbergia asperifolia	Scratchgrass	*Gilia longiflora*	Long-flower Gilia
Muhlenbergia pauciflora	New Mexican Muhly	*Gilia polycladon*	Spreading Gilia
Muhlenbergia porteri	Bush Muhly	*Gilia roseata*	Roseate Gilia[2]
Muhlenbergia pungens	Sandhill Muhly; Pungent Muhly	*Gilia subnuda*	Coral Gilia; Sand Gilia
Muhlenbergia thurberi	Thurber Muhly	*Leptodactylon pungens*	Sharp Prickly Phlox
Munroa squarrosa	False Buffalograss	*Leptodactylon watsonii*	Watson Prickly Phlox
Oryzopsis micrantha	Littleseed Ricegrass	*Phlox austromontana*	Desert Phlox
Panicum acuminatum	Bundle Panic	*Phlox hoodii* var. *canescens*	Hooded Phlox
Panicum capillare	Witchgrass	*Phlox longifolia*	Longleaf Phlox
Panicum obtusum var. *scribnerianum*	Vine Mesquite; Panic Grass	**Polygonaceae – Buckwheat Family**	
Panicum virgatum	Switchgrass	*Eriogonum alatum*	Winged Buckwheat
Phleum pratense	Timothy[1]	*Eriogonum bicolor*	Pretty Buckwheat[2]
Phragmites australis	Common Reed	*Eriogonum cernuum*	Nodding Buckwheat
Poa bigelovii	Bigelow Bluegrass	*Eriogonum corymbosum*	Corymed Buckwheat
Poa bulbosa	Bulbous Bluegrass[1]	*Eriogonum corymbosum* var. *corymbosum*	Corymed Buckwheat
Poa fendleriana	Mutton Grass	*Eriogonum corymbosum* var. *smithii*	Flattop Buckwheat[3]
Polypogon monspeliensis	Rabbitfoot Grass[1]	*Eriogonum deflexum* var. *deflexum*	Skeletonweed Buckwheat
Polypogon semiverticillatus	Water Bent[1]	*Eriogonum gordonii*	Gordon Buckwheat
Puccinellia nuttalliana	Nuttall Alkaligrass	*Eriogonum hookeri*	Watson Buckwheat
Schedonnardus paniculatus	Tumblegrass	*Eriogonum inflatum*	Desert Trumpet
Schizachyrium scoparium var. *neomexicanum*	Little Bluestem	*Eriogonum leptocladon*	Sand Buckwheat
Sorghum halepense	Johnson Grass[1]	*Eriogonum lonchophyllum* var. *lonchophyllum*	Longleaf Buckwheat
Spartina gracilis	Alkali Cordgrass	*Eriogonum microthecum*	Slender Buckwheat
Spartina pectinata	Prairie Cordgrass	*Eriogonum microthecum* var. *foliosum*	Slender Buckwheat
Sporobolus airoides var. *airoides*	Alkali Sacaton	*Eriogonum microthecum* var. *laxiflorum*	Slender Buckwheat
Sporobolus contractus	Spike Dropseed	*Eriogonum ovalifolium*	Cushion Buckwheat
Sporobolus cryptandrus	Sand Dropseed	*Eriogonum palmerianum*	Palmer Buckwheat
Sporobolus flexuosus	Mesa Dropseed	*Eriogonum shockleyi*	Shockley Buckwheat
Sporobolus giganteus	Giant Dropseed	*Eriogonum umbellatum* var. *subaridum*	Sulfur Buckwheat
Stipa arida	Arid Needlegrass	*Eriogonum watsonii*	Wild Buckwheat
Stipa x bloomeri	Bloomer Ricegrass	*Eriogonum wetherillii*	Maidens Hairnet
Stipa comata var. *comata*	Needle-and-thread Grass	*Rumex hymenosepalus*	Curly Dock; Canaigre; Wild Rhubarb
Stipa coronata var. *depauperata*	Crested Needlegrass	*Rumex venosus*	Veiny Dock; Large-valve Dock
Stipa coronata var. *parishii*	Crested Needlegrass	**Polypodiaceae – Fern Family**	
Stipa hymenoides	Indian Ricegrass	*Adiantum capillus-veneris*	Maidenhair Fern
Stipa lettermanii	Letterman Needlegrass	*Asplenium resiliens*	Little Ebony Spleenwort
Stipa neomexicana	New Mexico Needlegrass	*Cheilanthes feei*	Slender Lipfern
Stipa speciosa	Desert Needlegrass	*Northolaena limitanea* var. *limitanea*	Cloak-Fern
Tridens muticus	Slim Tridens	*Pellaea breweri*	Brewer's Cliff-brake
Polemoniaceae – Phlox Family		*Pellaea glabella*	Suksdorf Cliff-brake
Eriastrum diffusum	Spreading Eriastrum		
Gilia aggregata	Scarlet Gilia		
Gilia congesta	Ballhead Gilia		
Gilia congesta var. *frutescens*	Shrubby Gilia		
Gilia gunnisonii	Gunnison Gilia		

SCIENTIFIC NAME	COMMON NAME
Pellaea limitanea	Border Cloakfern
Portulaceae – Purslane Family	
Talinum brevifolium	Pygmy Flameflower[4]
Primulaceae – Primrose Family	
Primula specuicola	Easter-flower; Cave Primrose[3]
Ranuculaceae – Buttercup Family	
Aquilegia micrantha	Miniature Columbine
Clematis ligusticifolia	Western Virgins-bower; White Virgins-bower
Delphinium andersonii var. *scaposum*	Anderson Larkspur
Delphinium nuttallianum	Bilobe Larkspur
Ranunculus cymbalaria	Shore Buttercup
Ranunculus testiculatus	Bur Buttercup[1]
Rhamnaceae – Buckthorn Family	
Ceanothus greggii var. *franklinii*	Desert Ceanothus; Buckbrush
Rhamnus betulifolia	Birchleaf Buckthorn
Rosaceae – Rose Family	
Amelanchier alnifolia	Saskatoon Serviceberry
Amelanchier utahensis	Utah Serviceberry
Cercocarpus intricatus	Littleleaf Mountain Mahogany
Cercocarpus ledifolius	Curl-leaf Mountain Mahogany
Cercocarpus montanus	Mountain Mahogany
Coleogyne ramosissima	Blackbrush
Fallugia paradoxa	Apache Plume
Holodiscus dumosus	Mountain Spray; Shrubby Creambush
Petrophytum caespitosum	Rockmat
Potentilla biennis	Green Cinquefoil
Prunus persica	Peach[1]
Prunus virginiana var. *melanocarpa*	Chokecherry
Purshia mexicana var. *stansburiana*	Cliffrose
Rosa woodsii var. *ultramontana*	Wood's Wild Rose
Rubiaceae – Madder Family	
Galium aparine var. *echinospermum*	Catchwad Bedstraw
Galium multiflorum var. *coloradoense*	Shrubby Bedstraw
Salicaceae – Willow Family	
Populus x *acuminata*	Lanceleaf Cottonwood
Populus alba	White Poplar[1]
Populus x *canadensis*	Carolina Poplar[1]
Populus frémontii	Frémont Cottonwood
Populus tremuloides	Quaking Aspen
Salix amygdaloides	Peachleaf Willow
Salix exigua ssp. *exigua* var. *stenophylla*	Sandbar Willow; Coyote Willow
Salix gooddingii	Black Willow
Salix lucida ssp. *caudata*	Whiplash Willow
Salix lutea var. *watsonii*	Yellow Willow

SCIENTIFIC NAME	COMMON NAME
Santalaceae – Sandalwood Family	
Comandra umbellata var. *pallida*	Bastard Toadflax
Saxifragaceae – Saxifrage Family	
Fendlera rupicola	Cliff Fendlerbush; False Mockorange
Philadelphus microphyllus	Littleleaf Mockorange
Ribes aureum	Golden Currant
Ribes cereum	Wax Currant
Scrophulariaceae – Figwort Family	
Castilleja chromosa	Early Paintbrush
Castilleja flava var. *flava*	Yellow Paintbrush
Castilleja linariifolia	Linearleaf Paintbrush
Castilleja miniata	Scarlet Paintbrush
Castilleja scabrida var. *scabrida*	Eastwood Paintbrush
Cordylanthus parviflorus	Small-flower Birdbeak
Cordylanthus wrightii	Wright's Birdbeak
Mimulus eastwoodiae	Scarlet Monkeyflower
Mimulus guttatus	Yellow Monkeyflower
Pedicularis centranthera	Pinyon-Juniper Lousewort
Penstemon barbatus	Scarlet Bugler
Penstemon comarrhenus	Dusty Penstemon
Penstemon cyanocaulis	Bluestem Penstemon
Penstemon eatonii	Eaton Penstemon
Penstemon frémontii	Frémont Penstemon
Penstemon palmeri	Palmer Penstemon
Penstemon strictus	Rocky Mountain Penstemon
Penstemon utahensis	Utah Penstemon
Penstemon watsonii	Watson Penstemon
Verbascum thapsus	Woolly Mullein[1]
Solanaceae – Potato Family	
Datura stramonium	Jimsonweed
Datura wrightii	Sacred Datura; Moonflower; Angel's Trumpet
Lycium andersonii	Anderson Wolfberry
Lycium pallidum	Tomatillo; Pale Wolfberry
Lycium torreyi	Torrey Wolfberry
Nicotiana trigonophylla	Desert Tobacco
Physalis hederifolia var. *fendleri*	Fendler Groundcherry
Physalis longifolia	Common Groundcherry
Physalis virginiana	Virginia Groundcherry[5]
Solanum rostratum	Buffalobur[1]
Tamaricaceae – Tamarisk Family	
Tamarix chinensis	Tamarisk; Salt Cedar[1]
Typhaceae – Cattail Family	
Typha domingensis	Common Cattail
Typha latifolia	Broadleaf Cattail
Ulmaceae – Elm Family	
Celtis reticulata	Netleaf Hackberry
Ulmus pumila	Siberian Elm[1]

SCIENTIFIC NAME	COMMON NAME	Notes
Verbenaceae – Vervain Family		1. Exotic plant
Phyla cuneifolia	Wedgeleaf Frogfruit	2. Endemic plant
Verbena bracteata	Prostrate Vervain	3. Rare endemic plant
Viscaceae – Mistletoe Family		4. Rare plant
Arceuthobium cyanocarpum	Dwarf Mistletoe	5. Doubtful presence in Canyonlands
Phoradendron juniperinum ssp. *juniperinum*	Juniper Mistletoe	
Zygophyllaceae – Caltrop Family		
Kallstroemia californica	California Caltrop; Yellow Kallstroemia	
Tribulus terrestris	Goathead; Puncture Vine[1]	

Vertebrates of Canyonlands National Park

Adapted from species lists prepared by Canyonlands National Park and USGS Canyonlands Field Station staff, 2003.

FISH

Common Name	Scientific Name	Status
Suckers - Catostomidae		
bluehead sucker	*Catostomus discobolus*	NA
flannelmouth sucker	*Catostomus latipinnis*	EN
razorback sucker	*Xyrauchen texanus*	EN
white sucker	*Catostomus commersoni*	NN
flannelmouth X bluehead hybrid		
Sunfishes - Centrarchidae		
black crappie	*Pomoxis nigromaculatus*	NN
bluegill	*Lepomis macrochirus*	NN
green sunfish	*Lepomis cyanellus*	NN
largemouth bass	*Micropterus salmoides*	NN
smallmouth bass	*Micropterus dolomieui*	NN
Minnows - Cyprinidae		
brassey minnow	*Hybognathus hankensoni*	NN
bonytail	*Gila elegans*	EN
common carp	*Cyprinus carpio*	NN
Colorado pikeminnow	*Pitychocheilus lucius*	EN
fathead minnow	*Pimephales promelas*	NN
humpback chub	*Gila cypha*	EN
roundtail X humpback intergrade		
red shiner	*Notropis lutrensis*	NN
roundtail chub	*Gila robusta*	EN
speckled dace	*Rhinichthys osculus*	NA
shiner (red and sand)		
sand shiner	*Notropis stramineus*	NN
Utah chub	*Gila atraria*	NN
Killfishes - Cyprinodontidae		
plains killifish	*Fundulus zebrinus*	NN
Herrings - Clupeidae		
threadfin shad	*Dorosoma petense*	NN
Catfishes, Bullheads - Ictaluridae		
black bullhead	*Ictalurus melas*	NN
channel catfish	*Ictalurus punctatus*	NN
Perches - Percidae		
walleye	*Sitzostedion vitreum*	NN
Livebearers - Poecillidae		
Mosquitofish	*Gambusia affinis*	NN
Pikes - Esocidae		
northern pike	*Esox lucius*	NN

Trouts - Salmonidae

brown trout	*Salmo trutta*	NN
kokanee salmon	*Oncorhynchus nerka kennerlyi*	NN
rainbow trout	*Oncorhynchus mykis*	NN

Sea basses - Serranidae

striped bass	*Morone saxatilis*	NN

Status:

NA = Native to the drainage; EN = Endemic to the drainage; NN = Non-native, Introduced

---

AMPHIBIANS

Common Name	Scientific Name
Frogs - Ranidae	
bullfrog	*Rana catesbeiana*
northern leopard frog	*Rana pipiens pipiens*
canyon treefrog	*Hyla arenicolor*
Spadefoots - Pelobatidae	
Great Basin spadefoot	*Spea intermontana*
southern spadefoot	*Spea multiplicata*
True Toads - Bufonidae	
western Woodhouse toad	*Bufo woodhousii woodhousii*
red-spotted toad	*Bufo punctatus*
Salamanders - Ambystomatidae	
tiger salamander	*Ambystoma tigrinum nebulosum*

REPTILES

Common Name	Scientific Name
Lizards	
western collared lizard	*Crotaphytus collaris*
desert spiny lizard	*Sceloporus magister cephalaflavus*
eastern fence lizard	*Sceloporus undulatus elongatus*
sagebrush lizard	*Sceloporus graciosus graciosus*
leopard lizard	*Gambelia wislizenii punctatus*
plateau striped whiptail lizard	*Cnemidophorus velox*
western whiptail lizard	*Cnemidophorus tigris septentrionalis*
short-horned lizard	*Phrynosoma hernandesi*
side-blotched lizard	*Uta stansburiana*
tree lizard	*Urosaurus ornatus wrighti*
Snakes	
gopher snake	*Pituophis catenifer*
midget faded rattlesnake	*Crotalus viridis concolor*
Southwestern black-headed snake	*Tantilla hobartsmithi*
striped whipsnake	*Masticophis taeniatus*
wandering garter snake	*Thamnophis elegans vagrans*
western yellow-bellied racer	*Coluber constrictor mormon*
night snake	*Hypsiglena torquata*

MAMMALS

Common Name	Scientific Name	Status
Shrews - Soricidae		
Merriam's shrew	*Sorex merriami*	*
desert shrew	*Notiosorex crawfordii*	*
Common Bats - Vespertilionidae		
little brown bat	*Myotis lucifugus*	R

Common name	Scientific name	Status
Yuma myotis	*Myotis yumanensis*	*
long-eared myotis	*Myotis evotis*	R
fringed myotis	*Myotis thysanodes*	R
long-legged myotis	*Myotis volans*	*
California myotis	*Myotis californicus*	C
western pipistrelle	*Pipistrellus hesperus*	C
small-footed myotis	*Myotis ciliolabrum*	*
silver-haired bat	*Lasionycteris noctivagans*	O
big brown bat	*Eptesicus fuscus*	*
hoary bat	*Lasiurus cinereus*	U
Townsend's big-eared bat	*Corynorhinus townsendii*	O
Allen's big-eared bat	*Idionycteris phyllotis*	*
pallid bat	*Antrozous pallidus*	U
fringed myotis	*Myotis thysanodes*	U
spotted bat	*Euderma maculatum*	R
Free-tailed Bats - Molossidae		
big free-tailed bat	*Nyctinomops macrostis*	U
Mexican free-tailed bat	*Tadarida brasiliensis*	U
Rabbits and Hares - Leporidae		
desert cottontail	*Sylvilagus audubonii*	C
black-tailed jackrabbit	*Lepus californicus*	C
Squirrels - Sciuridae		
Colorado chipmunk	*Eutamias quadrivittatus*	C
white-tailed antelope squirrel	*Ammospermophilus leucurus*	C
rock squirrel	*Spermophilus variegatus*	U-C
white-tailed prairie dog	*Cynomys leucurus*	R
Pocket Gophers - Geomyidae		
Botta's pocket gopher	*Thomomys bottae*	R
Pocket Mice and Allies - Heteromyidae		
Apache pocket mouse	*Perognathus apache*	C
Ord's kangaroo rat	*Dipodomys ordii*	C
Beavers - Castoridae		
beaver	*Castor canadensis*	U
New World Mice and Rats - Cricetidae		
western harvest mouse	*Reithrodontomys megalotis*	U
deer mouse	*Peromyscus maniculatis*	C
canyon mouse	*Peromyscus crinitus*	C
brush mouse	*Peromyscus boylii*	U
pinyon mouse	*Peromyscus truei*	C
northern grasshopper mouse	*Onychomys leucogaster*	C
desert woodrat	*Neotoma lepida*	C
bushy-tailed woodrat (packrat)	*Neotoma cinerea*	U
muskrat	*Ondatra zibethicus*	R
Porcupines - Erethizontidae		
porcupine	*Erethizon dorsata*	U
Dogs and Allies - Canidae		
coyote	*Canis latrans*	C
kit fox	*Vulpes macrotis*	C
red fox	*Vulpes vulpes*	U
gray fox	*Urocyon cinereoargenteus*	C
Bears - Ursidae		
black bear	*Ursus americanus*	O

Raccoons and Allies - Procyonidae

raccoon	*Procyon lotor*	R
ringtail	*Bassariscus astutus*	U

Weasels and Allies - Mustelidae

badger	*Taxidea taxus*	U
long-tailed weasel	*Mustela frenata*	U
western spotted skunk	*Spilogale gracilis*	R
striped skunk	*Mephitis mephitis*	R
river otter	*Lutra canadensis*	R

Cats - Felidae

mountain lion	*Puma concolor*	R
bobcat	*Felis rufus*	R

Deer and Allies - Cervidae

mule deer	*Odocoileus hemionus*	C

Pronghorn - Antilocapridae

pronghorn	*Antilocapra americana*	O

Cows, Sheep, Goats, and Allies - Bovidae

desert bighorn sheep	*Ovis canadensis nelsoni*	R

Status/Occurrence:

C = common, seen regularly; U = uncommon, not likely to be seen by the casual observer; R = rare, unusual; O = occasional, 1 or 2 records; * = occurrence is strongly suspected

---

BIRDS

Common Name	Scientific Name	Status
Loons - Gaviidae		
Common Loon	*Gavia immer*	R/T
Grebes - Podicipedidae		
Eared Grebe	*Podiceps nigricollis*	R/W
Western Grebe	*Aechmophorus occidentalis*	O/T
Pied-billed Grebe	*Podilymbus podiceps*	R/W
Horned Grebe	*Podiceps auritus*	R/W
Clark's Grebe	*Aechmophorus clarkii*	O/S
Pelicans - Pelecanidae		
American White Pelican	*Pelecanus erythrorhynchos*	U/T
Herons and Egrets - Ardeidae		
Great Blue Heron	*Ardea herodias*	U/P (B)
Snowy Egret	*Egretta thula*	R/T
Black-crowned Night-Heron	*Nycticorax nycticora*	R/T
Green-backed Heron	*Butorides striatus*	R/T
Cattle Egret	*Bubulcus ibis*	R/T
Ibises - Threskiornithidae		
White-faced Ibis	*Plegadis chihi*	R/T
Swans, Geese, and Ducks - Anatidae		
Canada Goose	*Branta canadensis*	U/T
Green-winged Teal	*Anas crecca*	U/T
Mallard	*Anas platyrhynchos*	U/P (B?)
Northern Pintail	*Anas acuta*	*R/T
Blue-winged Teal	*Anas discors*	*O/T
Cinnamon Teal	*Anas cyanoptera*	O/T
Northern Shoveler	*Anas clypeata*	U/W
Gadwall	*Anas strepera*	O/T
American Wigeon	*Anas americana*	O/T
Ring-necked Duck	*Aythya collaris*	U/W

Lesser Scaup	*Aythya affinis*	R/T
Common Goldeneye	*Bucephala clangula*	O/T
Barrow's Goldeneye	*Bucephala islandica*	A/T
Bufflehead	*Bucephala albeola*	R/W
Common Merganser	*Mergus merganser*	R/T

New World Vultures - Cathartidae

Turkey Vulture	*Cathartes aura*	C/S

Osprey, Harriers, Hawks, and Eagles - Accipitridae

Osprey	*Pandion haliaetus*	R/T
Bald Eagle	*Haliaeetus leucocephalus*	U/W
Northern Harrier	*Circus cyaneus*	C/W
Sharp-shinned Hawk	*Accipiter striatus*	U/T
Cooper's Hawk	*Accipiter cooperii*	U/S (B)
Northern Goshawk	*Accipiter gentilis*	R/T (B)
Swainson's Hawk	*Buteo swainsoni*	O/T
Red-tailed Hawk	*Buteo jamaicensis*	C/P (B)
Ferruginous Hawk	*Buteo regalis*	O/T
Rough-legged Hawk	*Buteo lagopus*	R/W
Golden Eagle	*Aquila chrysaetos*	U/P (B)

Falcons - Falconidae

American Kestrel	*Falco sparverius*	C/S (B)
Merlin	*Falco columbaris*	O/T
Peregrine Falcon	*Falco peregrinus*	R/S (B)
Prairie Falcon	*Falco mexicanus*	U/P (B)

Quails and Pheasants - Phasianidae

Chukar	*Alextoris chukar*	U/P (B)
Ring-necked Pheasant	*Phasianus colchicus*	*U/P
Sage Grouse	*Centrocercus urophasianus*	R/P
Gambel's Quail	*Callipepla gambelii*	U/P (B)

Rails, Gallinules, and Coots - Rallidae

Virginia Rail	*Rallus limicola*	*O/T
Sora	*Porzana carolina*	R/S
American Coot	*Fulica americana*	*U/S
Sandhill Crane	*Grus canadensis*	R/T

Plovers - Charadriidae

Killdeer	*Charadrius vociferus*	U/S (B?)

Sandpipers - Scolopacidae

Greater Yellowlegs	*Tringa melanoleuca*	R/T
Solitary Sandpiper	*Tringa solitaria*	R/T
Spotted Sandpiper	*Actitis macularia*	U/S (B)
Willet	*Catoptrophorus semipalmatus*	U/T
Long-billed Dowitcher	*Limnodromus scolopaceus*	*O/T

Stilts and Avocets - Recurvirostridae

American Avocet	*Recurvirostra americana*	R/T
Black-necked Stilt	*Himantopus mexicanus*	R/T

Gulls, Terns, and Alcids - Laridae

Franklin's Gull	*Larus pipixcan*	R/T
Ring-billed Gull	*Larus delawarensis*	R/W
California Gull	*Larus californicus*	R/T
Forster's Tern	*Sterna forsteri*	R/T

Pigeons and Doves - Columbidae

Rock Dove	*Columba livia*	O/T
Mourning Dove	*Zenaida macroura*	C/S (B)

Cuckoos, Roadrunners, and Anis - Cuculidae

Yellow-billed Cuckoo	*Coccyzus americanus*	Acc.

Typical Owls - Strigidae

Flammulated Owl	*Otus flammeolus*	Acc.
Western Screech-Owl	*Otus kennicottii*	R/S (B?)
Great Horned Owl	*Bubo virginianus*	C/P (B)
Northern Pygmy-Owl	*Glaucidium gnoma*	R/T
Burrowing Owl	*Athene cunicularia*	O/T (B)
Spotted Owl	*Strix occidentalis*	U/P
Long-eared Owl	*Asio otus*	R/P (B)
Northern Saw-whet Owl	*Aegolius acadicus*	*O/T

Nighthawks and Poorwills - Caprimulgidae

Lesser Nighthawk	*Chordeiles acutipennis*	R/T
Common Nighthawk	*Chordeiles minor*	U/S
Common Poorwill	*Phalaenoptilus nuttallii*	U/T

Swifts - Apodidae

White-throated Swift	*Aeronautes saxatalis*	C/S (B)

Hummingbirds - Trochilidae

Black-chinned Hummingbird	*Archilochus alexandri*	C/S (B)
Broad-tailed Hummingbird	*Selasphorus platycercus*	U/T
Rufous Hummingbird	*Selasphorus rufus*	O/T

Kingfishers - Alcedinidae

Belted Kingfisher	*Ceryle alcyon*	R/P

Woodpeckers - Picidae

Lewis's Woodpecker	*Melanerpes lewis*	O/T
Williamson's Sapsucker	*Sphyrapicus thyroideus*	Acc.
Downy Woodpecker	*Picoides pubescens*	U/T
Hairy Woodpecker	*Picoides villosus*	U/P (B)
Northern Flicker	*Colaptes auratus*	U/P (B)
Red-naped Sapsucker	*Sphyrapicus nuchalis*	OT

Tyrant Flycatchers - Tyrannidae

Olive-sided Flycatcher	*Contopus borealis*	R/T
Western Wood-pewee	*Contopus sordidulus*	R/T
Willow Flycatcher	*Empidonax trailli*	R/S (B?)
Hammond's Flycatcher	*Empidonax hammondii*	R/T
Dusky Flycatcher	*Empidonax oberholser*	O/T (B?)
Gray Flycatcher	*Empidonax wrightii*	R/T (B?)
Cordilleran Flycatcher	*Empidonax occidentalis*	O/T
Black Phoebe	*Sayornis nigricans*	R/S
Say's Phoebe	*Sayornis saya*	C/S (B)
Ash-throated Flycatcher	*Myiarchus cinerascens*	C/S (B)
Cassin's Kingbird	*Tyrannus vociferans*	R/T (B)
Western Kingbird	*Tyrannus verticalis*	C/S (B)
Eastern Kingbird	*Tryannus tyrannus*	*O/T

Larks - Alaudidae

Horned Lark	*Eremophila alpestris*	C/P (B)

Swallows - Hirundinidae

Tree Swallow	*Tachycineta bicolor*	R/T
Violet-green Swallow	*Tachycineta thalassina*	C/S (B)
Northern Rough-winged Swallow	*Stelgidopteryx serripennis*	R/T
Bank Swallow	*Riparia riparia*	O/T
Cliff Swallow	*Hirundo pyrrhonota*	U/S (B)
Barn Swallow	*Hirundo rustica*	U/T (B?)

Jays, Magpies, and Crows - Corvidae

Gray Jay	*Perisoreus canadensis*	R/T
Steller's Jay	*Cyanocitta stelleri*	O
Western Scrub-Jay	*Aphelocoma coerulescens*	C/P (B)
Pinyon Jay	*Gymnorhinus cyanocephalus*	C/P
Clark's Nutcracker	*Nucifraga columbiana*	O/W
Black-billed Magpie	*Pica pica*	U/P (B)
American Crow	*Corvus brachyrhynchos*	O/T
Common Raven	*Corvus corax*	C/P (B)

Chickadees and Titmice - Paridae

Black-capped Chickadee	*Parus atricapillus*	C/W (B)
Mountain Chickadee	*Parus gambeli*	U/W
Plain Titmouse	*Parus inornatus*	C/P (B)

Bushtits - Aegithalidae

Bushtit	*Psaltriparus minimus*	C/P (B)

Nuthatches - Sittidae

Red-breasted Nuthatch	*Sitta canadensis*	R/T
White-breasted Nuthatch	*Sitta carolinensis*	O/T

Creepers - Cinclidae

Brown Creeper	*Certhia americana*	R/T

Wrens - Troglodytidae

Rock Wren	*Salpinctes obsoletus*	C/P (B)
Canyon Wren	*Catherpes mexicanus*	C/P (B)
Bewick's Wren	*Thryomanes bewickii*	C/P (B)
House Wren	*Troglodytes aedon*	U/T
Marsh Wren	*Cistothorus palustris*	R/W

Dippers - Cinclidae

American Dipper	*Cinclus mexicanus*	R/P

Kinglets and Gnatcatchers - Sylviidae

Golden-crowned Kinglet	*Regulus satrapa*	O/T
Ruby-crowned Kinglet	*Regulus calendula*	U/T
Blue-gray Gnatcatcher	*Polioptila caerulea*	C/S (B)
Black-tailed Gnatcatcher	*Polioptila melanura*	R/S

Bluebirds, Solitaires, and Thrushes - Turdidae

Western Bluebird	*Sialia mexicana*	O/T (B)
Mountain Bluebird	*Sialia currucoides*	C/P (B)
Townsend's Solitaire	*Myadestes townsendi*	R/T
Hermit Thrush	*Catharus guttatus*	R/T
American Robin	*Turdus migratorius*	U/P (B)
Swainson's Thrush	*Catharus ustulatus*	U

Mockingbirds and Thrashers - Mimidae

Northern Mockingbird	*Mimus polyglottos*	U/S (B)?
Sage Thrasher	*Oreoscoptes montanus*	R/T
Brown Thrasher	*Toxostoma rufum*	Acc./T
Gray Catbird	*Dumetella carolinensis*	R/S

Pipits - Motacillidae

American Pipit	*Anthus rubescens*	R/P

Waxwings - Bombycillidae

Cedar Waxwing	*Bombycilla cedrorum*	O/T
Phainopepla	*Phainopepla nitens*	O/T

Shrikes - Laniidae

Northern Shrike	*Lanius excubitor*	R/W
Loggerhead Shrike	*Lanius ludovicianus*	C/P (B)

Starlings - Sturnidae		
European Starling	*Sturnus vulgaris*	U/T
Vireos - Vireonidae		
Gray Vireo	*Vireo vicinior*	U/S (B)
Plumbeous Vireo	*Vireo plumbeus*	U/T (B)
Warbling Vireo	*Vireo gilvus*	C/T (B?)
Wood Warblers - Parulidae		
Orange-crowned Warbler	*Vermivora celata*	C/T
Nashville Warbler	*Vermivora ruficapilla*	R/T
Virginia's Warbler	*Vermivora virginiae*	C/T
Lucy's Warbler	*Vermivora luciae*	U/S
Yellow Warbler	*Dendroica petechia*	C/T
Yellow-rumped Warbler	*Dendroica coronata* – 2 races:	
"Myrtle Warbler"		O/T
"Audubon's Warbler"		C/T
Black-throated Gray Warbler	*Dendroica nigrescens*	C/T
Townsend's Warbler	*Dendroica townsendi*	O/T
Grace's Warbler	*Dendroica graciae*	R/T
MacGillivray's Warbler	*Oporonis tolmiei*	U/T
Northern Waterthrush	*Seiurus noveboracensis*	R/T
Common Yellowthroat	*Geothlypis trichas*	U/S (B?)
Wilson's Warbler	*Wilsonia pusilla*	C/T
Yellow-breasted Chat	*Icteria virens*	C/S (B?)
Tanagers - Thraupidae		
Western Tanager	*Piranga ludoviciana*	C/T
Grosbeaks and Buntings - Cardinalidae		
Black-headed Grosbeak	*Pheucticus melanocephalus*	C/T (B)
Blue Grosbeak	*Guiraca caerulea*	C/S (B)
Lazuli Bunting	*Passerina amoena*	C/S (B)
Indigo Bunting	*Passerina cyanea*	R/T
Towhees, Sparrows, and Juncos - Emberizidae		
Green-tailed Towhee	*Pipilo chlorurus*	C/T
Spotted Towhee	*Pipilo erythrophthalmus*	U/T (B)
Rufous-crowned Sparrow	*Aimophila carpalis*	R/T
Chipping Sparrow	*Spizella passerina*	C/T
Brewer's Sparrow	*Spizella breweri*	C/T
Vesper Sparrow	*Pooecetes gramineus*	C/T
Lark Sparrow	*Chondestes grammacus*	CT
Black-throated Sparrow	*Amphispiza bilineata*	C/S (B)
Sage Sparrow	*Amphispiza belli*	C/S (B)
Savannah Sparrow	*Passerculus sandwichensis*	O/T
Song Sparrow	*Melospiza melodia*	U/W
Lincoln's Sparrow	*Melospiza lincolnii*	U/W
White-crowned Sparrow	*Zonotrichia leucophrys*	C/W
Dark-eyed Junco	*Junco hyemalis* - 3 races:	
"Slate-colored Junco"		R/W
"Oregon Junco"		C/W
"Gray-headed Junco"		C/T
Meadowlarks, Blackbirds, and Orioles - Icteridae		
Red-winged Blackbird	*Agelaius phoeniceus*	U/S (B)
Western Meadowlark	*Sturnella neglecta*	U/S (B?)
Yellow-headed Blackbird	*Xanthocephalus xanthocephalus*	R/T

Brewer's Blackbird	*Euphagus cyanocephalus*	U/T
Brown-headed Cowbird	*Molothrus ater*	C/S (B)
Northern Oriole	*Icterus galbula*	U/S (B)
Scott's Oriole	*Icterus parisorum*	U/S (B)

Finches, Redpolls, Siskins, and Goldfinches - Fringillidae

Gray-crowned Rosy-Finch	*Leucosticte tephrocotis*	C/W
Black Rosy-Finch	*Leucosticte atrata*	C/W
Purple Finch	*Carpodacus purpureus*	R/T
Cassin's Finch	*Carpodacus cassinii*	O/T
House Finch	*Carpodacus mexicanus*	C/P (B)
Pine Siskin	*Carduelis pinus*	U/W
Lesser Goldfinch	*Carduelis psaltria*	U/T (B?)
American Goldfinch	*Carduelis tristis*	C/W

Weaver Finches - Passeridae

| House Sparrow | *Passer domesticus* | RT |

Names and the sequence of names, families, and subfamilies follow the Sixth Edition of the American Ornithologists' Union *Checklist of North American Birds*.

RELATIVE ABUNDANCE

C = Common: Occurs regularly, often in numbers; easily found in proper season and habitat.

U = Uncommon: Occurs more or less regularly, but generally in small numbers; usually found in proper season and habitat.

R = Rare: Three to six records total; unusual, but to be looked for each year; may be more common than the few records indicate.

O = Occasional: One or two records total; highly unusual, but not necessarily out of range; to be expected again.

Acc. = Accidental: One record only; out of range; not to be expected again.

SEASONAL STATUS

P = Permanent Resident: Present throughout the year. Generally implies nesting, but this not confirmed for all.

S = Summer Resident: Present only during the warmer months, and migrating elsewhere for the winter. Generally implies nesting, but this not confirmed for all.

W = Winter Visitant: Present only during the cooler months of the year, and migrating elsewhere for the summer.

T = Transient (through Migrant): Passes through the park in spring and fall migration, but does not remain to breed or to winter.

* = Recorded on lands or waters immediately adjacent to the park boundary, usually within 1/2-mile of the park, but as yet unrecorded within the park.

BREEDING

(B) = Known to breed in the park area; based on observation of nest building, nests with eggs, young in nests, or adults with dependent, very recently fledged young.

(B?) = Probably breeds; based on presence of adults throughout the usual nesting season, often singing and/or defending territories, but firm evidence of nesting is lacking.

AUTHORS

Dr. Jayne Belnap has lived and worked on the Colorado Plateau for the past 20 years. She has studied geology, marine biology, butterflies, birds, plants, and soil biota, giving her a broad background in the natural history of the area. She works for the U.S. Geological Survey and is based in Moab, Utah. She currently spends most of her time studying the effects of soil surface disturbance in desert ecosystems around the world.

John Weisheit is a senior river guide, specializing in the human and natural history of the Colorado Plateau, a subject on which he has published numerous articles. He is co-founder of the Colorado Plateau River Guides, which publishes the journal *The Confluence*.

Dr. Robert Webb is a hydrologist who has worked on long-term changes in arid and semiarid landscapes for more than 25 years in the southwestern United States. He has studied climatic change, vegetation dynamics, and various aspects of river systems. He also is a research advisor for geomorphology and sediment transport with the U.S. Geological Survey in Tucson, Arizona.

CONTRIBUTORS

Steve Anderson grew up on the banks of Salt Creek in northern Utah, which he credits with instilling in him a love of the natural world. He is currently a physician in Salt Lake City who spends much of his time admiring the natural world.

Eric Brunnemann holds two Master's degrees in archeological-anthropology. His work in archeology has taken him to Greece, Portugal, New Mexico, Texas, and Utah, where his responsibilities have included working closely with native tribes on the preservation, documentation, research, and interpretation of prehistoric and historic petroglyphs and habitation sites. Eric is currently the superintendent of War in the Pacific National Historical Park and American Memorial in Saipan.

Christopher Keener lives in Denver when he's not hiking and biking in the mountains and deserts of the West. Through his company, The Performance Works, he delivers corporate messages that bring humor and music to training initiatives and employee recognition events.

James Knipmeyer is a retired science teacher and avid western historian and the author of *Butch Cassidy Was Here: Historic Inscriptions of the Colorado Plateau* (University of Utah, 2002). He lives in Lee's Summit, Missouri.

Richard A. Valdez has a Ph.D. in Fisheries Ecology and more than twenty-five years of experience in aquatic ecosystems of western North America. He specializes in fisheries and aquatic ecology, and also has extensive experience in the area of environmental public policy. He is co-editor of the book *The 1996 Controlled Flood in Grand Canyon* and is contributing writer for the book *Water, Earth, and Sky: The Colorado River Basin* (Utah, 1999).

INDEX

debris fans, 164, 165

debris flows: in Big Drops, 199, 203, 206–7; defined, 55; frequency on Colorado Plateau of, 232–33; Halgaito Shale as source of, 165; at Mile Long Rapid, 162–63, 194, 195, 197; origin of rapids from, 59, 164–65, 191, 192, 233; at Rapid 5, 158, 164–65; at Tilted Park, 165–66

deer mice (*Peromyscus maniculatus*), 76, 77, 78, 80, 142, 178

Dellenbaugh, Frederick S., 17, 20, 128, 133, 209, 222

Denver, Colorado Cañon and Pacific Rail Road, 18, 20

Deseret system, 229–30n22

desert bighorn sheep (*Ovus canadensis nelsoni*), 65, 145, 221–23

desert cottontails (*Sylvilagus audubonii*), 144

desert olive (*Forestiera pumila*), 74, 76, 103, 108, 120–21, 163, 235

desert trumpet (*Eriogonum inflatum*), 77, 176

desert varnish, 80, 198

Desolation Canyon, 233

Dewey Bridge, 111, 115

dogbane (*Apocynum* sp.), 74

Doll House, 16, 17, 110, 131, 133

Doll House Trail, 133–34, 136

Domínguez-Escalante expedition, 126, 129

Dominy, Floyd, 215–16

driftwood: in Big Drops, 207; fish and, 207; floods and, 179–80; interest of, 210; jams, 219–20

Dubendorff, Seymour, 24, 25, 193

ducks, 220–21

Dunn, William, 15, 16, 208

Dutton, Clarence E., 63

dwarf lupine (*Lupinus pusillus*), 80

Eddy, Clyde, 30, 32, 155, 192, 208–9, 210

Edwards, William H., 21, 22–23

Eggloffstein, Frederick von, 37

Eisner, Thomas, 181

Ekker, A. C., 196–97

Elephant Canyon, 120

Elephant Canyon Formation, 46, 115, 132, 165

El Niño-Southern Oscillation (ENSO), 64

empress butterfly, 173

endolithic organisms, 223–24

Entrada Sandstone, 47

Escalante National Monument, 5

Faatz, Friend Grant, 22, 210

finches (*Carpodacus* sp.), 75

fire, 110; cottonwoods and, 178; ecology of, 131–32; in Lower Red Lake Canyon, 130, 131; tamarisk and, 128, 131

fish, 169–71; driftwood and, 207

fishhook cactus (*Sclerocactus whipplei*), 76

Flaming Gorge Dam, 101, 166, 171

flannelmouth sucker (*Catostomus latippinis*), 170

Flavell, George, 25, 217

flexible dropseed (*Sporobolus flexuosus*), 76

flies (Diptera), 181–82

floods: large, 52–54, 179–81, 237–38; sandbars and, 168–69

fluffgrass (*Erioneuron* sp.), 235

flycatchers (*Empidonax* sp.), 80

Fort Bottom, 110

four-wing saltbush (*Atriplex canescens*), 66, 76, 80, 163, 175, 235

Frémont, John C., 14, 37

Frémont barberry (*Mahonia fremontii*), 78, 157

Friendship Cruise, 127–28

galleta grass (*Hilaria jamesii*), 65, 80, 161, 235–36

Galloway, Nathaniel, 23–25, 33, 219

Galloway, Parley, 23

Galloway Cave, 24

Gambel's oak (*Quercus gambelii*), 66, 79, 108, 121, 139

garter snakes (*Thamnophis* sp.), 142

Gibson, George W., 18, 19

Gilbert, Grove Karl, 13, 14, 50

gilia (*Gilia* sp.), 78

Glen Canyon, 1, 51, 115

Glen Canyon Dam, 214

Glen Canyon Group, 47

globemallow (*Sphaeralcea* sp.), 66, 80

gnats, 137

golden corydalis (*Corydalis aurea*), 131

golden current (*Ribes aureum*), 74

Golden Eagles (*Aquila chrysaetos*), 190

goldenrod (*Solidago* sp.), 74

Goldwater, Barry M., 156, 200, 205, 206

Goodman, Frank, 15

goosefoot (*Chenopodium album*), 86

gopher snake (*Pituophis catenifer deserticola*), 141–42

grabens, 49, 58

Graham, G. M., 22

grama grass (*Bouteloua gracilis*), 74, 181

Grand Canyon: compared with Cataract canyon, 231–35; longitudinal profile of, 234

Grand Junction, Colorado, 111

grasshopper mice (*Onychomys leucogaster*), 80, 142

grassland communities, 80

Gray Canyon, 233

Gray-headed Juncos (*Junco hyemalis*), 75

grazing, 82, 128–31

greasewood (*Sarcobatus vermiculatus*), 68, 76, 77, 107

Great Blue Herons (*Ardea herodias*), 113

Green & Grand River and Moab Navigation Company, 25–26

razorback sucker (*Xyrauchen texanus*), 170
Red Lake Canyon, 130, 131, 148, 171
red-spotted toads (*Bufo punctatus*), 118
Red-tailed Hawks (*Buteo jamaicensis*), 190
Reeder, Bill, 28
Reid, Del, 205, 206
repeat photography, 29, 34, 37, 136
reptiles, 70–71, 75, 140–42
Reynolds, Ethan A., 18
Richards, Henry C., 18, 19, 20
Richmond, William C., 23
Rigney, Thomas P., 18
ringtails (*Bassariscus astutus*), 225–26
riparian communities, 74–76
river bottom communities, 76
river cobble/gravel terraces, 48, 103, 115
Robidoux, Francois, 13
rock art, 105
rockfalls, 129; at Big Drops, 203, 207; at Gypsum Canyon, 222, 223; insignificant effect upon river of, 164; at Rapid 18, 193; table of observed, 192
rock squirrels (*Spermophilus variegatus*), 77, 78
Rock Wrens (*Salpinctes obsoletus*), 77, 146
Ross, B. S., 20
roundleaf buffaloberry (*Shepardia rotundifolia*), 78
roundtail chub (*Gila robusta*), 170
Ruby Ranch, 103
Rufous Hummingbirds (*Selasphorus rufus*), 78, 80, 147
rusby milkweed (*Asclepias rusbyi*), 74
Russell, Charles Silver, 27–28, 155
Russian Knapweed (*Centaurea repens*), 86, 88, 237
Russian olive (*Elaeagnus angustifolia*), 92–93, 112
Russian thistle (tumbleweed; *Salsola kali*), 80, 128, 130, 131, 221
Rust, David Dexter, 33
Rutledge, Horace, 170

sagebrush (*Artemisia* sp.), 66, 68, 74, 76, 91, 107, 181, 182, 235
sagebrush lizards (*Sceloporus graciosus*), 69, 140
Sage Sparrows (*Amphispiza belli*), 80
saltbush (*Atriplex* sp.), 68, 77, 126, 182, 221. *See also* four-wing saltbush
Salt Creek, 7, 115, 120
salt grass (*Distichlis* sp.), 68
sandbars: changes in, 161, 168–69, 201; floods and, 168–69; terminology of, 169; types of 168
sand dropseed (*Sporobolus* sp.), 65, 66, 76, 80, 235
sand dunes, 80
sand sage (*Artemesia filifolia*), 66
San Juan River, 233: compared with Cataract Canyon, 234–35
sapping processes, 56–57

scarlet monkeyflower (*Mimulus eastwoodiae*), 80, 227
Schelz, C., 164
scorpions, 226–27
scrub oak (*Quercus* sp.), 66
sediment load, 99–100
seepwillow (*Baccharis* sp.), 74, 80, 121, 130, 149
Separation Rapid, 218
shadscale (*Atriplex confertifolia*), 66, 74, 76, 129, 149, 167, 175–76, 235
Sharp, Charles, 24
sheep, 131
shinnery oak (*Quercus harvardii*), 80
Shoemaker, Eugene, 34, 134, 222
side-blotched lizards (*Uta stansburiana*), 69, 140, 141
silt bars, 219, 221
singleleaf ash (*Fraxinus anomala*), 78, 139–40, 157, 235
sixweeks fescue (*Festuca octoflora*), 80
skunkbush/squawbush (*Rhus trilobata*), 78, 80, 135, 157, 176, 235
slickrock, 115, 139
Slide, the, 120
slump blocks, 191–92
Smith, Charles, 23, 29, 164
Smith, Jedediah S., 9
snakes, 141–42
snakeweed (*Gutierrezia sarothrae*), 66, 76, 80, 174–75, 235
soils, 82–83. *See also* biological soil crusts; gypsum soils
Somerville, William, 34
sound, 153–54
southwestern blackheaded snake (*Tantilla hobartsmithi*), 142
spadefoots (*Scaphiopus intermontanus*), 71, 72, 119
Spanish Bottom, 113, 130, 131, 132–33, 140, 148–49, 153
Spanish Valley, 2, 111–12
sparrows, 73, 76, 80
speckled dace (*Rhinichthys osculus*), 170
Stanton, Robert Brewster, 8, 18, 19–20, 24, 220
Steen, Charlie, 104
Stephens Hal G., 34; photographs by, 77, 79, 91, 102, 134, 201, 204, 222, 224
Stewart, Frogg, 205
Steward, John F., 17, 222
Stillwater Canyon, 1, 110
Stone, Julius F., 9, 23, 24–25, 29
stream capture, 50
stream orchid (*Epipactus gigantea*), 80
striped bass (*Morone saxatilis*), 237
Summeril, Frank H., 25
Sumner, John Colton, 14, 15, 16, 125, 155
Sundance Kid, 133
Sutherland, George A., 18
suturing, 209